THE ELEMENT
ENCYCLOPEDIA
OF
BIRTHDAYS

THE ELEMENT
ENCYCLOPEDIA
OF
BIRTHDAYS

Know your birthday
Discover your true personality
Reveal your destiny

Theresa Cheung

© 2007 by Theresa Cheung

This 2008 edition is published for Barnes & Noble, Inc.
by HarperCollins*Publishers*.

First published by Harper*Element* in 2006.

All rights reserved. No part of this publication may be reproduced, stored
in a retrieval system, or transmitted, in any form or by any means, electronic,
mechanical, photocopying, recording, or otherwise, without prior written
permission from the publisher.

Text illustrations by Andy Paciorek

ISBN: 978-1-4351-1083-0

Manufactured in China

4 6 8 10 9 7 5

Contents

Introduction   vii

The Birthday Profiles   1

    January   2

    February   46

    March   87

    April   131

    May   173

    June   217

    July   260

    August   303

    September   347

    October   390

    November   433

    December   475

Birthday Power Thoughts   518

Acknowledgments

This enormous project would not have been completed without the help of some unique and amazing people. Thank you to Katy Carrington for her extraordinary vision, insight, and encouragement; to Mark Bolland for his excellent editing and valued input; to Andy Paciorek for the wonderful illustrations; to Colin Hall for the fantastic page design; to Graham Holmes for his accomplished typesetting; and to Simon Gerratt for his skill, patience, and brilliance in making sure everything came together in one piece and on time. Last, but by no means least, special thanks to Ray, Robert, and Ruth for the love, inspiration, and support they give me every single day of each and every year.

Introduction

'As above, so below'

The Element Encyclopedia of Birthdays is a complete guide to personality and destiny for people born on each of the 366 days of the year. Simply by knowing the date of your birth you can gain insightful and astonishingly accurate luck-making information about yourself—your strengths, weaknesses, health, relationships, destiny, career, and life goals—as well as your friends, family, lovers, colleagues, and even people you have just met.

The power of your birthday is determined not just by your ruling planet but by a number of other invisible influences and patterns in place the day you were born. This book reaches far beyond basic Sun sign horoscopes, looking at these influences and patterns through the lens of psychological astrology, numerology, Tarot, and color theory or chromatherapy.

To help you understand how your birthday profile has been compiled you'll find the basic principles of these ancient arts and how they have put their stamp on you explained below; but if you want to dive straight into a specific birth sign or date, yours or one of some-body you know, you can always return here another time. However you decide to read this book, never forget that every person is born unique and full of potential.

The birthday profile

What exactly is a birthday profile? In short, it's the rebirth of four ancient arts—astrology, numerology, Tarot, and color theory or chromatherapy—joined together by a modern psychological interpretation. This combination results in a blend of cosmic and earthly influences that can significantly affect your personality and destiny, providing you with invaluable insight into yourself as well as the lives, feelings, hopes, and fears of family, friends and colleagues.

A brief introduction to astrology

Astrology sees humankind as being influenced not only by hereditary factors and the environment, but also by the state of our solar system at the moment of birth. The Sun, Moon and planets are regarded as basic life-forces, the tools we live by as well as the basis of our very substance. These planetary forces take on different forms, depending on their zodiacal position and on the way they relate to one another.

Astrology is one of the most ancient of the surviving occult sciences, and evidence of highly sophisticated systems in Babylonian, Egyptian and Aztec cultures has survived. For centuries in the West, astrology was a revered method of divination (fortune telling) supported by royal courts. With the development of science in the seventeenth century, astrology was relegated to the realm of superstition, but it never fell completely out of favor and today it is hugely popular, followed by people from all walks of life.

Popular astrology is concerned with the reading of a horoscope, a chart of the positions of the planets, Sun, Moon, and stars at the moment of one's birth and interpreting the influence of the planets on human affairs. The Sun travels through the twelve signs of the zodiac through the course of the year and so when someone is said to have been born under Pisces, they were born when the Sun was passing through the portion of the zodiac named after the constellation of Pisces.

Each of the 12 signs has its own personality traits (see individual zodiac sign profiles), with the daily position of the planets, and the element associated with the planet—fire, water, earth, and air— also affecting each Sun sign. In addition, for serious astrologers, as the Sun passes through the zodiac sign over the course of a month, it passes through three decanates, making each decanate approximately ten days long. Each of the decanates adds its own associated planet

and sign influences to the basic influences of the Sun sign. Therefore by considering the decanate as well as the Sun sign, the reading for an individual's birthday is fine-tuned. For example, an Aries born sometime in the third decanate (April 10 to 21) will also be under the influence of the third decanate sign of Sagittarius and the planet associated with Sagittarius, which is Jupiter. The ancient Egyptians considered the decanates as important as the Sun signs themselves.

Progressions are another widely used technique in the system of prediction. With this method the Sun takes about thirty years to journey (or progress) through each sign of the zodiac and in a person's lifetime it will typically progress through three to four zodiac signs, depending on the lifespan of the individual and their date of birth. Each time the Sun progresses from one sign to another, this indicates a significant birthday or time in your life when there is likely to be a dramatic change in either your circumstances or outlook. For example, the progressed Sun of a Scorpio born on November 9 will move into Sagittarius at the age of thirteen, into Capricorn at the age of forty-three and then Aquarius at the age of seventy-three.

Fixed stars associated with a particular day of the year also exert additional influences, but if decanates and progressions sound confusing, don't worry; to use this book you don't need to do any math or look anything up in complicated tables as the calculations and relevant interpretations have been taken into account when each birthday profile was compiled. All you need to do is read and enjoy.

Skeptics argue that astrology's suggested link between planetary position and human destiny is unproven, but recent scientific research about the seasons and even the month in which a person is born appears to suggest otherwise.

In the early 1970s, Professor Alan Smithers of Manchester University compiled data from the British population census showing clearly that architects tended to be born in the spring, secretaries in the summer, miners in the fall and electricians in the winter. He also asked members of the British Astrological Association (BAA) to indicate which signs were associated with the professions of nurse and labor union official. Without knowing what the BAA predicted, Smithers conducted a large survey of nurses and labor officials and discovered that, just as the astrologers had indicated, there was a statistical bias toward nurses being born under the signs of Taurus, Cancer, Virgo, Scorpio and Pisces, and labor union officials being born under one or other of the other signs.

Other research has focused on the influence of one star in particular, the Sun. This is because a type of radiation emitted by the Sun, ultraviolet (UVR), is believed to cause genetic changes in the developing baby that may have a shaping effect on their life and personality. This could explain why many of us believe that common characteristics and fates are shared by those born at the same time of the year. For example, researchers at the University of Rostock in Germany have analyzed data to see if the month in which you are born affects how long you will live. It does. Their research found that your chances of living beyond 100 were up to 16 percent higher than average if you were born in December, but if you were born in June, your chances were 23 per cent lower. Another study carried out by researchers at the University of Chicago and published in the *Journal of Anti-Aging Medicine* backed this up, finding that those born in December lived longer by about three years.

Experts believe that the reason people born in December might live longer could be that they were conceived in March, possibly avoiding the most harmful effects of radiation early on. They argue that solar radiation peaks at conception affect personality and health later in life and therefore where you are born is perhaps more important than the month you were born.

Here's a roundup of some findings by different researchers to date.

Happiness: Happy people are more likely to have been born in June, July and August, according to a University of Vienna study. Meanwhile a study at the University of Tokyo found that people born in December, January and February were likely to be more pessimistic than those born at other times of the year.

Personality: Psychiatrists at the University of Umea, in Sweden, looked at personality differences in 2,000 people and found that women born between February and April were more likely to be novelty seekers than those born in October and February. Men born in spring were more likely to be impulsive, while those born in winter were prone to introspection.

Intelligence: Winter-born children may end up being bigger and more academically inclined than those born in summer. Psychiatrists and anthropologists from Harvard and Queensland universities tracked the development of 21,000 boys and girls over seven years, finding seasonal variations in intelligence, weight, height, and head size. Another study from the University of Vienna, however, indicated that female students born in spring and summer achieved better exam marks than those born in fall and winter.

Health: Research from the University Hospital Clinic of Modena, Italy, showed that women born in the fall have the fewest symptoms at menopause and those born in spring have the most. Work at Bristol University has shown that those born in winter have a greater risk of developing heart disease, while another study from the University of Southampton indicated that being born in the winter months may increase the risk of obesity.

A brief introduction to numerology

Numerology assigns characteristics to the cosmic combinations of the digits 1 to 9, suggesting traits and weaknesses for every day of the year. It is based on the concept that the universe is mathematically constructed and the vibrational energy of people, places and things can be expressed through numbers. By reducing birth dates and names to numbers a person's personality and destiny can, allegedly, be determined.

Although numerology probably has its origins in ancient Babylonia and among the early Hebrews, and many different numerology systems have been used in different parts of the world, numerology is most often associated with the fifth-century BC Greek mathematician and philosopher, Pythagoras.

Pythagoras believed that there were mathematical connections between the gods, men and numbers that could be codified and if certain number patterns appeared they could be used to predict the fate of a person. According to Pythagoras, numbers were the source of energy in the world and the numbers 1 to 9 represent the nine stages of life. He is quoted as having said, "The world is built upon the power of numbers."

In numerology all numbers are reduced to a number between 1 and 9 and each number is also associated with a letter of the alphabet. Any larger number than 9 can be reduced to a single digit by adding all the digits together; for example, the number 123 becomes $1 + 2 + 3 = 6$. The qualities of 123 are therefore equivalent to the symbolic number 6. Using the single digits as a guide, the patterns of different dates and a person's name can be analyzed to define character and predict the future. Briefly, the numbers 1 to 9 represent:

1 Independent, creative, ambitious, extrovert
  Downside: can be selfish with tunnel vision

2 Sensitive, domestic, imaginative, musical
  Downside: can be timid and gullible

3 Scientific, powerful, knowledgeable, multi-talented
  Downside: can be superficial and hedonistic

4 Practical, stable, honest, trustworthy
  Downside: can be stubborn and overly serious

5 Energetic, sensual, daring, flirtatious

Downside: can find it hard to commit

6 Perfectionist, creative, artistic, compassionate
Downside: can be supersensitive and overemotional

7 Intellectual, philosophical, imaginative, intuitive
Downside: can be impractical and secretive

8 Practical, just, trustworthy, powerful
Downside: can be opinionated, impatient and intolerant

9 Spiritual, humanitarian, visionary and healer
Downside: can be self-serving, possessive and volatile

What astrology does through stars and Sun signs, numerology does through numbers. Like astrology, numerology is a symbolic system and one of the many tools we can use to understand ourselves and our life purpose better. Just as astrologers believe no one sign is better than another, numerologists believe no number is better or worse than any other. All the numbers have potential as well as a downside. The downside simply suggests challenges associated with this number; if these challenges can be faced and overcome, they can be a source of incredible strength.

In this book we will focus particularly on the qualitative interpretations of numbers in relation to a person's date of birth. In numerology, your date of birth is thought to have a permanent influence on your life. Although you grow older and may change your name, your birth date number (for example, if you

were born April 17 your birth date number is 1 + 7 = 8) always remains constant.

A brief introduction to Tarot

Your birth sign and your birth date number are also associated with specific Tarot cards.

Although the true origins of Tarot cards are unknown and may date back to ancient Egypt, the Tarot cards that we know today were created in Italy during the fifteenth century. The Tarot deck consists of seventy-eight cards in total, comprising the twenty-two major arcana cards which the nineteenth-century French occultist Eliphas Levi saw as having symbolic links to the twenty-two letters of the Hebrew alphabet, and the fifty-six minor arcana cards which are divided into four suits: wands, representing the element of fire; swords, the element of air; cups, the element of water; and pentacles, the element of earth. Many versions of the Tarot deck are in use today but most are based on the Rider–Waite deck designed by Arthur Edward Waite and Pamela Colman Smith in 1910.

Although each minor arcana card has a divinatory meaning, the major arcana cards are of greater significance in this book because they represent both archetypal symbols and the quest for self-knowledge. Their meanings are briefly summarized below:

The Fool: represents the divine child, one who is completely trusting of God. The Fool is beginning a journey and has no idea where it will lead, but is peaceful and content, and is living from his heart.

The Magician: represents creative power and having many options. Called the Magus in other Tarot decks, the Magician has access to all four elements of the Tarot to manifest the divine work he has come to earth to achieve.

The High Priestess: represents the psychic self, intuition, dreams and developing one's inner spiritual intuition.

The Empress: represents the ability to adapt and flow according to the needs of the moment.

The Emperor: is the balance to the Empress and represents work, money, grounding, and the ability to fully manifest on the material plane.

The Hierophant: a symbol of one's own inner spiritual authority, also known as your Higher Self. It's also a compilation of the previous four cards, synthesizing these initial stages of spiritual growth on a new level.

The Lovers: represent the awareness of opposites, the relationship between opposites, and the ability to balance what appear to be different aspects of the self.

The Chariot: represents an alignment of your personal will with the divine will, and the transformation of the personal self toward a more planetary consciousness.

Justice: represents a karmic rebalancing process, so what has been out of harmony within your consciousness will be brought into a proper relationship with God's love.

The Hermit: represents a time when the soul must learn to walk alone through darkness, guided by God and the inner light of spirit.

The Wheel of Fortune: represents a time of awakening to the awareness of one's own destiny and soul purpose.

Strength: represents the integration between the higher and lower self. This card is sometimes interpreted as the learning process of seeing yourself as capable of having what you want.

The Hanged Man: this card represents a deep spiritual surrender where all is given to God. The process of surrender turns the soul "upside down," so that life and God can be experienced from a new perspective.

Death: represents a letting-go process related to old emotional patterns, especially in relationships.

Temperance: a card of integration, transformation and alchemy, representing the transformation of opposites into a new element.

The Devil: represents the awareness of one's own negativity and darkness, and can also represent an encounter with negative energies.

The Tower: represents the shattering of illusion and the shattering of an old structure, which can be either a personality structure or a physical one.

The Star: represents divine spiritual healing and an opening to the higher dimension of light. This was made possible through the previous lessons which released the soul from illusion.

The Moon: symbolizes creativity, nurturing, family, and the emergence of subconscious negativity that has come to the surface to be healed and transformed.

The Sun: represents confidence and the emergence of one's true self, stepping out into visibility in its full spiritual and physical embodiment.

Judgment: represents resurrection and rebirth, and is a symbol of this time we are living in, the time of total transformation.

The World: represents a celebration of dance of life, and a time of completion of a major cycle. The World card includes all the previous cards, just as we are all a total of all the steps we have taken on our path. It is a time of fulfillment and joy.

Many astrologers and numerologists believe that the major arcana cards are related to astrological and numerological personality tendencies; for example, the Emperor card is ruled by the planet Mars, the astrological sign of Aries and the symbolic power of the number 9. As such these arcana cards present a powerful means of promoting self-awareness, especially when their implications are considered in conjunction with those indicated by astrology and numerology.

A brief introduction to color healing

According to color analysts or chromatherapists, every color is believed to vibrate with its own energy and to have specific effects on individuals. Seven colors in particular—red, orange, yellow, green, blue, indigo and violet, the colors of the rainbow—have carried religious, occult and mystical significance since ancient times (see box on page xiv). In the late nineteenth century color theory began to receive attention in the West; in 1878 Edwin Babbitt published *The Principles of Light and Colour*, highlighting ancient Pythagorean correspondences between music, color, numbers and sound.

Today modern science is able to provide evidence for some of the ancient claims about color. In the 1980s it was shown that colored light can trigger biochemical reactions in the body. Later research confirmed that blues and greens have a soothing effect, helping to lower stress, brain-wave activity and blood pressure. Warm colors such as orange and red have been shown to have a stimulating effect. Given the research, it is small wonder then that many psychologists use color to produce beneficial effects in the home, workplace and hospitals.

Putting it all together!

There was a star danced,
and under that was I born
William Shakespeare,
Much Ado About Nothing

As you can see, the basic principles of astrology, numerology, Tarot, and color analysis are interrelated, and this book uses a combination of them all to highlight the old axiom, "As above, so below." There is a world of possibility contained in each date of birth. You were born during a particular season, under a particular Sun sign, fixed star, and decanate. You have a ruling planet and belong to a particular element—air, earth, water, or fire. Each day also has a numerical vibration

Healing benefits of color

Each of the seven colors of the spectrum is associated with specific healing properties.

Violet

Violet promotes enlightenment, revelation, and spiritual awakening. Holistic healthcare providers use violet to soothe organs, relax muscles, and calm the nervous system.

Indigo

Indigo is also sedative and calming. It is said to promote intuition. Indigo may be useful in controlling bleeding and abscesses.

Blue

Blue promotes communication and knowledge. It eliminates toxins, and is used to treat liver disorders and jaundice.

Green

Because it is located in the middle of the color spectrum, green is associated with balance. Green is calming and is used by Ayurvedic practitioners to promote the healing of ulcers. It is said to have antiseptic, germicidal and anti-bacterial properties.

Yellow

Yellow is a sensory stimulant associated with wisdom and clarity. Yellow is thought to have decongestant and anti-bacterial properties, and is useful in stimulating both the digestive system and the lymphatic system.

Orange

Orange promotes pleasure, enthusiasm, and sexual stimulation. Ayurvedic practitioners believe it has anti-bacterial properties and may be useful in easing digestive system discomforts, such as flatulence or cramps.

Red

Red promotes energy, empowerment and stimulation. Physically, it is thought to improve circulation and stimulate red blood cell production.

In astrology and numerology, each astrological sign and number has an associated color or colors and, according to color therapists, these colors have a special significance in the birthday profile because our lives can be enhanced by surrounding ourselves with the colors that are most harmonious with our own personal vibrations for that day.

and color vibration that has a specific meaning and significance, and these vibrations can suggest numbers, dates and colors that are likely to be more beneficial than others. All these factors shape your personality and life experience; when combined with a modern psychological perspective, they can create a unique and in-depth personality profile for each day of the year.

The psychological approach used in this book involves you in becoming an expert on yourself and others. Think of your birthday profile as a modern tool to assist you on your voyage of self-discovery by translating and fine tuning the symbolic wisdom of your Sun sign, birth number, Tarot card, and personal colors into user-friendly advice. Use that advice to help you develop a deeper understanding of what makes you and other people tick. Use it to help you discover what your strengths are and to find ways to compensate for your weaknesses. Use it to work towards positive growth and change in all aspects of your life. Use it to help you attract luck and success into your life.

Ultimately this book is a celebration of growth and change—the process of growth and change that can be seen each year as the seasons melt into one another; the process of growth and change that can be seen in all human development and transformation.

Only by finding ways to change and work towards your true potential today can you transform your tomorrows and start discovering all the wonderful gifts the universe has bestowed upon you. Your birthday profile is a defining factor that distinguishes you from other people. But never forget that your profile merely highlights potential strengths and weaknesses, and that you always have a choice. You can refuse to budge or you can seize the day. You can wait for luck or you can make your own luck. You can sleep or you can dance under the stars!

Birthday quotes

And in the end, it's not the years in your life that count. It's the life in your years.

Abraham Lincoln

The more you praise and celebrate your life, the more there is in life to celebrate.

Oprah Winfrey

The best birthdays of all are those that haven't arrived yet.

Robert Orben

The bad news is time flies. The good news is you're the pilot.

Michael Althsuler

Our birthdays are feathers in the broad wing of time.

Jean Paul Richter

Let us celebrate the occasion with wine and sweet words.

Plautus

Birthdays? Yes, in a general way;
For the most if not for the best of men:
You were born (I suppose) on a
certain day: So was I: or perhaps in
the night: what then?

James Kenneth Stephen

All the world is birthday cake, so take a piece, but not too much.

    George Harrison

No wise man ever wished to be younger.

    Jonathan Swift

Mere color, unspoiled by meaning, and unallied with definite form, can speak to the soul in a thousand different ways.

    Oscar Wilde

One of the signs of passing youth is the birth of a sense of fellowship with other human beings as we take our place among them.

    Virginia Woolf

Astrology is assured of recognition from psychology, without further restrictions, because astrology represents the summation of all the psychological knowledge of antiquity.

    C. G. Jung

The greatest comfort of my old age, and that which gives me the highest satisfaction, is the pleasing remembrance of the many benefits and friendly offices I have done to others.

    Marcus Cato

A note on Sun sign dates

You may notice variations in the dates given for your Sun sign, depending upon which source you read or astrologer you consult. This is because the zodiac only has 360 degrees whereas a year can have 365 days (normal year) or 366 days (leap year). Moreover, the speed of the Sun's movement is irregular and does not always enter the various sections of the zodiac at exactly the same dates each year. The dates given in this book are ones that take into account variations that occur from one year to another. If you were born within two or three days of the dates given for each astrological sign, your birthday lies on what astrologers call the "cusp" and you should read the Sun sign information for both signs on either side of your birthday. For example, if you were born on February 17, you will have both Piscean and Aquarian characteristics.

THE ELEMENT
ENCYCLOPEDIA
OF
BIRTHDAYS

1 January

the birthday of
self-improvement

Your greatest challenge is

to stop beating yourself up about making mistakes

The way forward is ...

to learn from your mistakes, turning regret into positive resolve. Let the powerful energy of positivity sweep into your life and raise your game.

Full of energy and enthusiasm, those born on January 1 like to show others the way forward. Once they settle on a goal, their drive, integrity and originality attract good fortune and assure success. However, the very qualities that draw success to them can also hold them back.

It is extremely important for people born on January 1 to realize that "mistakes" are going to happen in life. If they go through life expecting that things will always turn out the way they wanted and that people will always do what they said they would do, they will feel perpetually frustrated when life does not go according to plan. They need to deviate from the familiar, learn from mistakes and accept the unexpected. And when they are finally able to turn rejection into resolve they will discover an emotional resilience that will drive them forward and break through their fear.

Above all, January 1 people value dedication, discipline and anything to do with education, psychology and study. They truly are born to lead and inspire, both at home and at work. There is always a voice inside them urging them to work harder, faster and longer. This quality can make them charismatic achievers who set an example to others. They are the bosses who burn the midnight oil, the teachers who give up their spare time to help struggling pupils or the politicians who take a pay cut. The only disadvantage is that they can get so caught up in the process of self-improvement that they forget their goal, their sense of humor and the bigger picture.

January 1 people, especially those under the age of thirty, do run the risk of becoming too focused on work and responsibility, and pushing themselves and others hard in the process. But once they figure out that optimism, resilience and listening to the opinions of others are just as important ingredients for success and happiness as hard work and dedication they possess tremendous potential for creativity, insight and inspired leadership.

On the dark side

Oversensitive, impatient, manipulative

At your best

Drive, dedication, honesty

2 January

the birthday of the intuitive leader

Your greatest challenge is

overcoming feelings of isolation and loneliness

The way forward is ...

to go beyond your dark moods, recreate yourself and achieve a goal that involves the help and healing of others.

Those born on January 2 have a remarkable ability to tune into their surroundings, and this sensitivity toward others, combined with their unusual insight into what makes other people tick, can put them head and shoulders above less observant people.

The intuitive power of these people can, however, work against them, making them at times feel alone and different, rather than unique and natural. But once they are able to recognize and celebrate their uniqueness, January 2 people can unlock incredible energy, creativity, endurance, flexibility and commitment. And when their confidence is high, their intuition works at its best with an extremely powerful shift toward this inner life around the age of forty-nine. Unfortunately their acute sensitivity also makes them prone to unpredictability and extreme mood swings. These can create problems for them and for those who care about them. However, once they become aware that they are masters of their own thoughts, a more stable self-confidence will emerge.

Although by nature reserved, January 2 people possess an uncanny knack of being in the right place at the right time; this gives them excellent opportunities for success. If they believe in themselves they can go all the way to the top. If they cannot believe in themselves they may find that they are working in positions beneath their abilities. The same applies to their relationships; if they lower their expectations and don't set clear boundaries they could find that their gentle nature is taken advantage of by others.

Extremely hard working and committed, those born on this day make highly dependable team leaders and negotiators. The danger is that they can overburden themselves with huge responsibilities and this, coupled with their belief that they are different in some way, can set them up to experience frustration and alienation from others. Even though they are often more than capable of fulfilling their responsibilities it is extremely important for them to keep both their feet on the ground with hobbies, social activities and time spent relaxing with family and friends.

On the dark side

Moody, antisocial, indecisive

At your best

Sensitive, spiritual, intuitive

3 January

the birthday of
determination

Your greatest challenge is

resisting boredom

The way forward is ...

to experiment with different concepts, make your own decisions and, instead of waiting for others to catch up, to strike out alone.

Failure is never an option for people born on January 3. They often have a wild, impulsive energy but they are not quitters. It is not in their nature to pass along responsibilities, and their persistence and sense of duty mean that they can overcome incredible odds. Sometimes, however, their stubbornness to see things through to the bitter end, combined with their inability to admit defeat, can make them appear inflexible and intolerant.

Stubborn by nature, January 3 people can impose unbearable pressure not just on themselves but also on others, and when pushed into a corner they can resort to using their charm to help them get what they want. This isn't to say they are dishonest—dishonesty isn't in their nature—but they are capable of using their seductive powers if they think it will help them achieve their goals.

The rock-solid determination of people born on January 3 can stretch the patience of those around them; in fact opposition and barriers just tend to strengthen their resolve even further and they are at their most inventive when challenged or confronted. It really is hard to throw them off course, and even if it looks like they have lost or need to reconsider they will secretly be planning their comeback or, in some cases, their revenge. The only chink in their armor is that appearance matters a bit too much too them. Nothing pleases them more than a compliment. They have a strong eye for beauty and style but their intolerance for imperfection can, if left unchecked, exasperate and occasionally alienate others.

With their survival instinct and natural understanding that determination is power, people born on January 3 possess the potential for outstanding success, and they can and do overcome impossible odds. Typically, in their forties, sometimes sooner, they tend to realize that they are at their happiest and best when they connect with their intuition; this enables them to find ways to develop their unique talents and leave their personal stamp on the world.

On the dark side

Stubborn, erratic, controlling

At your best

Charming, controlled, determined

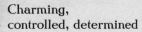

4 January

the birthday of
the eclectic

Your greatest challenge is

coping with not feeling understood

The way forward is ...

to put yourself in the other person's shoes; slow down and explain your perspective.

Those born on January 4 like everything eclectic. In other words, they like to collect, sort and then select only the best, and they use this quick-witted, creative approach in all aspects of their lives. A list of their friends looks like a media mogul's address book, and their work résumé—with numerous stints in different lines of work—reflects their curious personality and unlimited powers of imagination. To others this may look like an undisciplined and erratic approach, but there is always method in the madness of those born on this day. By learning all that can be learned from a variety of sources, they eventually emerge triumphant with an encyclopedic knowledge of life that appears to serve them well in almost any situation.

Because of their eclectic nature and interest in so many aspects of life, January 4 people tend to be the catalyst that stirs up issues in others and makes them face things that they might rather not face. They are very direct people and any interaction with them has to have meaning and purpose, otherwise they quickly lose interest. Their directness and inability to indulge in chit-chat can work against them—as idle conversation is often a means of establishing rapport and common ground with others—but more often than not their ability to sum up a situation and to come straight to the point is welcomed as a breath of fresh air.

Although these people do know how to have fun—especially when they are young—they don't tend to be diverted by the trivial for long. In their thirties and beyond they prefer to exert their considerable energies and talents on a variety of projects to give them fulfillment; these are the years when their potential for professional success comes to the fore. Those born on this day really do need to concentrate their energies on finding a line of work that indulges their need for change but also allows them to be the creative, spontaneous and innovative person they were born to be.

On the dark side

Cold, controlling, intolerant

At your best

Independent, imaginative, methodical

5

5 January

the birthday of

resilience

Those born on January 5 have a great deal of emotional resilience, possessing the ability to recover quickly from setbacks and difficult situations. They can do this because, unlike other less resilient souls, they have the remarkable ability to leave the past where it belongs—in the past. They also have an understanding that loss and disappointment are part of life's journey, and this understanding means they are often wise beyond their years.

Their leadership qualities are strong and they are capable of great dedication and personal sacrifice. They are the resourceful, centered person to whom people turn in a crisis and they thrive on this kind of dynamic. The only danger is that January 5 people can get easily bored when there is no crisis.

Although people born on this day can bounce back from disaster, this doesn't mean to say they are thick skinned. They can appear emotionally aloof at times but more often than not this hides a deeply sensitive and empathetic nature that is simply afraid to reveal or give of itself unconditionally. If they do open up it is only to the most trusted and valued of friends and loved ones.

Their resilient approach to life wins people born on this day many admirers but taken to extremes it can also make them unrealistically optimistic. They need to avoid becoming so upbeat in their approach that they ignore the motives and minimize the concerns of people around them.

Although they should keep their options open and stay flexible, people born on this day are at their best when they have a plan of action. They have a tendency to avoid responsibility and commitment in their teens and twenties but, until they choose a path, they will never feel truly fulfilled. By their early forties, often somewhat sooner, they have usually learned to rein in their curiosity and their love of adventure and travel, choosing a path or a purpose that allows them to concentrate on and express their extraordinary potential for bringing out the best in other people.

On the dark side

Over-confident, superficial, unreliable

At your best

Powerful, expressive, spiritual

6 January

the birthday of
the philosopher

Your greatest challenge is

to avoid feeling burdened down with responsibilities at work

The way forward is ...

to devote as much time to your personal life as to achieving your ideological objectives.

People born on January 6 are forever looking beneath the surface for meaning and significance in events. They always try to see the spark of goodness in others but this spiritual, philosophical approach to life can mean that other people often dismiss them as childlike or naïve, in the process underestimating their tremendous energy and intelligence.

Although philosophical in their thinking, January 6 people are extremely ambitious and goal orientated, tending eventually to get what they want in life. Willing to work hard and dedicate themselves to their goals, those born on this day can overcome their natural shyness, introspection and gentleness when they are called to defend their convictions and their ideals. However, because they trust their instincts so much and believe that everything that happens to them has significance, there is a danger of them always rejecting alternative viewpoints and being labeled unrealistic, unreasonable and stubborn at times. The tendency to expect others to think like them can prove too challenging for those who are not as philosophically minded.

Despite their stubborn streak and outspokenness, January 6 people also have a tender side to them that can be easily hurt when their input isn't valued or people don't take them seriously. They may deal with their hurt by rebelling against authority or indulging in irresponsible behavior, but later in life, around the age of forty-five, they learn that, although cathartic, constant rebellion can never be the whole answer. It is important for them to find a place to express their wild side, but sport or work or study is often their savior because it provides the boundaries and calls upon the discipline they need to help them handle their emotions and channel their energies.

At the end of the day, even when criticized or rejected, the idealism and honesty of people born on January 6 never fails to shine through. Once they find what they should devote their life to, their determination and ability to impart their ideals in an inspirational way will attract both admirers and considerable success their way.

On the dark side

Naïve, unrealistic, unreasonable

At your best

Idealistic, philosophical, understanding

7 January

the birthday of
the practical dreamer

Your greatest challenge is

to stop worrying about what people might think

The way forward is ...

to realize that what others think is their concern, not yours.

Although those born on January 7 give the impression of being serious and intense, they are irresistibly drawn to anything different, strange and unfamiliar. They have a strong sense of duty and responsibility but secretly dream of living an unconventional life in which they can follow their own rules.

Mentally those born on this day are both logical and intuitive, which makes them unique. They are artists with a scientific mind or scientists with an intuitive flair. They have the instinctive gift of being able to sense the moods of other people and, despite their apparent distance from a situation, they can often understand more about what is going on around them than anyone else. Their nature is also highly sensitive. They find it hard to switch off from the suffering and injustices of the world; as a result, they may frequently become involved in charity work or generously give their time for the benefit of others. Because they can tune in so quickly to what is going on around them, they are always in danger of absorbing negativity from others. Seeking out situations and people that are positive and steady, and avoiding the negative, are therefore important.

January 7 people are dreamers but they rarely let themselves get carried away. As a result, their occasional tendency to drift off into a world of their own can make them feel lonely and cut off from everything and everyone around them. They often have a real sense of connection with the natural world and an extraordinary imagination. Fascination with the mystical, with unexplained phenomena and the afterlife is common, especially after the age of forty-four, sometimes sooner, although fear of being criticized or thought "weird" may prevent them from pursuing their interests.

It is extremely important for those born on this day to develop their self-confidence and to accept that the opinions of others, although valuable, are not final. In this way they will be able to let their frustration go and find the freedom of expression that is so crucial for their happiness and fulfillment.

On the dark side

Isolated, intense, dreamy

At your best

Unusual, intuitive, generous

8 January

the birthday of
dynamic strength

Your greatest challenge is

handling the feeling that others aren't giving you enough respect

The way forward is ...

to understand that respect is a two-way street; if you want respect, treat others with respect first.

People born on January 8 always make their presence felt. They are born with stunning potential to rise and shine above all obstacles and make an impact on the world around them.

Those born on this day expect to be acknowledged by others; as a result, others always come away impressed. Single-minded, hard-working, courageous and forceful, they have the potential within them to achieve almost everything they want. Because of their determined nature there can sometimes be a tendency to overdo things, so they need to make sure they do not become too obsessive by spending time with friends and loved ones, and having plenty of interests.

The belief, enthusiasm and dedication that people born on this day have for projects they love is not the only thing that makes them stand out from the crowd. They also possess great charm and sensitivity, and the ability to put people at ease. Although naturally intuitive, it is important that they do not let practicality and worldly ambition obscure this talent as it will serve them well in all areas of life, in particular their close personal relationships. After the age of forty-three their intuition and emotional sensitivity often increase.

The irony is that despite their almost superhuman confidence and self-possessed exterior, underneath they do from time to time feel anxious and insecure, with a tendency to wallow in dark moods and become despondent and demanding. Their hidden insecurities can also manifest in an impatience and intolerance of others or an egotistical desire to put others down. Every now and again they need to step off the pedestal they have made for themselves so that they can devote both their time and their considerable energy to nurturing friendships based on mutual love, understanding and respect.

If they can stay positive and develop tolerance and humility in their relationships with others, there is nothing to hold back people born on this day. They are meant to shine and, with their inspired awareness, inner strength and self-discipline, shine they well.

On the dark side

Egotistical, impatient, intolerant

At your best

Courageous, forceful, authoritative

9 January

the birthday of the striver

Your greatest challenge is

learning not to lose your temper

The way forward is ...

to take a break. Go for a walk. A nap can clear things out; so can chatting with friends or putting yourself in someone else's shoes. If you're going to lose it, keep your cool until you can blow off some steam somewhere safe.

People born on January 9 tend to be fast-acting, thinking and feeling. They want to rise to the top and will do what it takes to get them there. In both their work and their home life they strive for nothing but the best. They demand high standards from both themselves and others, and they detest mediocrity with a passion. Yet because January 9 people place a high value on initiative and their personal freedom, they often prefer to work or forge ahead alone rather than in a group.

So focused are January 9 people on striving that they rarely take time to savor their achievements or even the present moment; they find it particularly hard to relax or switch off. It is of great importance for them to have a partner, friend or even a pet to help them unwind and take themselves and their goals a little less seriously. Typically around the age of forty-two, sometimes sooner, their sensitivity toward others and their inner life becomes more prominent.

January 9 people are amazingly good at overcoming obstacles and difficulties, and can bounce back from almost anything. However in the process of recovery they can also manifest a ruthless side. If knocked down they will claw their way back by whatever means are available, even if that means upsetting trusted friends along the way and making enemies. They need to learn that one of the secrets of success is not to have enemies. Anger, sometimes violent anger, is often their first response, but if they can remain a little more detached and learn some objectivity they will discover that there are always other ways of dealing with a frustrating situation.

Totally fearless, those born on this day have an abundance of admirable qualities. If they can learn to listen to their conscience and strive to maintain balance as hard as they strive to attain success, there is nothing to stop them enjoying the liberating benefits of a purposeful life that sparkles with happiness and excitement.

On the dark side

Ruthless, mistrustful, reckless

At your best

Ambitious, forceful, resilient

10 January

the birthday of
the realist

Your greatest challenge is

showing your true feelings

The way forward is ...

to tell yourself that vulnerability is not a sign of weakness but a sign of strength.

People born on January 10 are a force to be reckoned with. They feel an irresistible urge to speak their mind at all times. As a result they are highly valued by others for their honesty and for their realistic assessment of a situation. They are never afraid to support an unconventional viewpoint and to champion the underdog.

Those born on this day tell it like it is, and this quality can bring them success and admiration, taking them to the very top. On the downside, their inability to sugarcoat or dress up the truth can on occasion upset people around them, stopping them advancing as fast in life as their more diplomatic peers. The trouble with the straight-shooting approach is that it doesn't take into account the possibility of hope, and so January 10 people can sometimes come across as grumpy. This isn't, however, a fair reflection of their personality. They are neither negative people nor are they unhappy; they just see things the way they are, warts and all. Typically around the age of forty-one, often sooner, they become more emotionally sensitive to the needs of others.

Although the no-nonsense approach of people born on this day can shock others on first contact, in the long term people often find their clear-sighted approach very refreshing; in times of crisis or uncertainty people will seek advice from people born on this day. Although more than happy to take on this role—as the respect of others is important for them—the very same qualities that earned them respect from others can also create distance as they may find it hard to empathize with people less able to cope with change and the ups and downs of life. Once they begin to understand that not everyone is as clear-sighted as they are, and that a gentle approach can help them achieve their objectives more effectively, people born on this day discover that not only can they earn the lasting loyalty of others, they also have the ability to make a powerful impact on the world around them.

On the dark side

Tactless, jealous, distant

At your best

Honest, direct, accepting

11 January

the birthday of

the expert assessor

Your greatest challenge is

coping with feeling powerless to change things

The way forward is ...

to understand that you can only change the things that you can. When a situation can't be changed, you need to have faith and learn to let go.

Those born on January 11 have a natural talent for assessing every situation and measuring everyone they meet. They find little difficulty in discarding what isn't needed and see to the heart of people and situations, judging them according to their own very high standards. When the formidable powers of perception of people born on this day are combined with their great intelligence, this results in individuals who are outstanding decision makers.

Underlying this talent for assessment is a strong sense of justice that always strives to be fair. They feel compelled to do the right thing in life and to pass judgment but sometimes they can have problems distinguishing what the right thing or judgment is for them and what the right thing is for others. As a result they can easily convince themselves into thinking that they need to take responsibility for everyone and everything; this is when problems can start, as it can lead to domineering or controlling behavior and the belief that their word really is the law.

It is important for people born on this day to learn to pronounce their opinions less forcibly so that they do not offend those who do not share their point of view. This won't always be easy, but alongside their inflexibility there is also a very caring and compassionate nature. If they can tap more into that, they will begin to understand that it is not just their right, but everybody's right, to have a difference of opinion. Typically around the age of forty, often sooner, their emotional sensitivity becomes stronger and they develop a more powerful inner life.

Those born on this day place high standards on others but they place even higher standards upon themselves. Because they have the courage and determination to live up to these standards, they often do find themselves in the very position they crave: that of the judgment maker. Others will seek them out for advice, judgment and, when they learn to be a little less inflexible, inspiration.

On the dark side

Dominating, stubborn, superior

At your best

Balanced, objective, fair

12 January

the birthday of

single-mindedness

Your greatest challenge is

handling feelings of being ignored

The way forward is ...

to stop thinking you need to prove yourself to others. If you back off for a while and spend time listening and connecting, you'll naturally attract enough respect and attention.

People born on January 12 don't do things by half measures and once they have settled on a goal they pursue it with intense and single-minded dedication. Whatever their calling in life, whether it be raising a family, teaching a class or running for president, it becomes their single purpose in life. They are forever on the look-out for opportunities, ideas and people that can help them achieve their goals. Because work is so important to them and they run the risk of sacrificing their personal identity to it, it is vital that they choose their careers wisely.

The need to be the center of attention that characterizes people born on this day is more often than not a result of putting their emotional life on hold in pursuit of their goals in life. Sometimes they can be so driven that they lose touch not only with their friends and family but also with themselves. It is extremely important therefore for people born on this day to remember to respect not only their own feelings but also the feelings of others. They need to carve out a personal life separate from work and a spiritual life that gives them regular time out. Typically around the age of thirty-nine, hopefully sooner, they place more emphasis on their emotional life; this is reflected in their dreams and their visions, as well as the way in which they interact with others.

The single-minded approach of people born on this day, combined with their sharp wit and strong level of commitment, can promise great potential for success. And if all that wasn't enough, they also appear to be blessed with uncanny good fortune. Just as they can swing between high and low moods, their lives can also swing between disaster and sudden good fortune. Out of the blue they may receive a gift, a promotion or the break that they need. Finding balance by placing more emphasis on emotional and spiritual ideals is the key to their survival and their ability to attract all that they need to rise to the very top.

On the dark side

Restricted, extreme, arrogant

At your best

Tolerant, dedicated, insightful

13 January

progression

Your greatest challenge is

knowing how to cope with anger or disappointment

The way forward is ...

to understand that painful feelings are only released when they are faced. Remember the only way out is through.

Progression is the key word for those born on January 13. They never stand still, always moving forward in their lives, whatever their circumstances or start in life. Their ability to overcome obstacles and make even the most difficult of transitions or tasks seem easy gives them a natural charisma.

Those who make life seem easy are universally favored, and people born on this day not only have the ability to succeed; they also have the ability to keep their cool when all around are losing theirs. When setbacks occur they pick themselves up, learn from their mistakes and do all it takes to reach their goals; and reach them they will.

People born on this day have no problems leaving their past behind them. They understand the importance of letting go in order to progress and move beyond limitations. They particularly enjoy initiating new projects and ideas, and they work steadily and in a disciplined way until they have attained what they desire. Although their imagination and intelligence give them the potential to succeed in many areas, the arena of social and humanitarian reform has particular appeal for them. Of course they feel disappointment and disillusion at times—they are human like everyone else—but typically after the age of thirty-eight, more often than not sooner, they discover the importance of making their mind work for rather than against themselves.

It's impossible for people born on January 13 to hold back in any way and they cannot see the point of doing anything unless one hundred per cent of one's attention and energy is given. If others are not committed or are lazy or not paying attention, they will let them know. They will progress faster if they can understand that not everyone has the same drive or need for achievement as they have, and that sometimes the price for having high ideals means that they have to stand alone. By taking time out to relax they can discover whether they have been pushing themselves too hard or have become too detached from the world they are so committed to improving.

On the dark side

Stubborn, rebellious, bossy

At your best

High achiever, expert, revolutionary

14 January

the birthday of

conviction

Your greatest challenge is

finding direction and purpose for your life

The way forward is ...

to understand that you succeed best when you find an activity you truly love and believe in.

One of the greatest strengths of those born on January 14 is their ability to take in vast amounts of information and still see the bigger picture. They are shrewd judges of people and situations, and their inquisitive mind is forever hungry for new ideas, new information and new challenges. Because they have this panoramic view, they are particularly good at decision making. Their strong sense of right and wrong, combined with their highly developed sense of conviction and certainty, makes them excellent and much-sought-after peacemakers, both at home and at work.

Unfortunately the conviction and certainty possessed by those born on this day also have their attendant dangers. Once they have settled on a course of action, it is almost impossible for them to change course and they may go to extreme lengths to see things through to the bitter end. Ironically for people who are so uncompromising and committed in their work life, they aren't always able to make that same level of commitment to their personal life. In fact their personal life definitely takes second place. This may be because they believe that emotions and connections with other people are a distraction from their primary purpose in life, but it may also be the result of a fear of being disappointed. The way forward for them is to apply the same level of commitment to potential friends and partners, and to learn to respect and appreciate the emotional support of others.

Although they appear to be extremely confident and have the ability to implement radical change, they are inwardly far more complex than they appear. Behind the solid, strong image and the apparent love of risk-taking and innovation lies a person who often feels misunderstood; these feelings are heightened if they haven't found a direction in life to which to devote their considerable energies. Once they understand that it is not leadership, material wealth or high rank that they crave but personal freedom and the ability to bring about positive change in the world, they can leave their insecurities behind and achieve miracles.

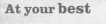

On the dark side

Stubborn, obsessed, insecure

At your best

Peacemaker, inquisitive, risk-taker

15 January

the birthday of the protagonist

Your greatest challenge is

coping with lack of recognition for your efforts

The way forward is ...

to learn patience. If you keep working for the best possible outcome for yourself and for others, your time will come.

Idealistic, ambitious and determined, those born on January 15 have a strong desire to lead and inspire. For them, nothing occurs which does not have some deep ethical significance, and this, coupled with their uncanny sense of the motivations of others, gives them a talent for seeing life as an exciting drama, pregnant with possibilities for both good and evil.

Motivated perhaps by inspirational role models in their childhood or student years, those born on this day are full of innovative ideas and dynamic energy, combined with a passionate desire to make the world a better place. They are especially sensitive to the feelings of others, giving them great interpersonal skills. They have the ability to win others over to their position, and although others may find them uncompromising at times, they will also admire their seductive and fascinating power and are more than happy to follow their lead.

The Achilles heel for people born on this day is their desire for recognition or credit. They are unlikely to feel fulfilled toiling anonymously for their cause as they feel it is their purpose to lead and raise awareness. Since they are most likely to devote themselves to idealistic and ethical concerns, this is not generally a problem; but if they are drawn toward matters less worthy of them, there is a danger that this need for praise and recognition can become obsessive and ego-driven.

People born on this day do like the world to see them as the invincible conqueror and, with their dramatic flair, people tend to see them in exactly that way. This can create problems for them, however, because they possess a sensitive, generous and vulnerable side that needs to be allowed to express itself. Typically at around the age of thirty-six, sometimes sooner, their emotional sensitivity becomes more enhanced. This shift toward the inner life is an extremely positive thing for people born on this day, because when they are able to manage rather than suppress their hidden vulnerabilities they will discover what it really is like to be the protagonist and wear a hero's crown.

On the dark side

Obsessive, self-centered, indulgent

At your best

Idealistic, dedicated, inspirational

16 January

the birthday of

satisfaction

Your greatest challenge is

learning to feel that you are good enough

The way forward is ...

to be grateful for what you have achieved so far and to focus on what is good about your life right now.

Those born on January 16 love the idea of successfully completing projects to the best of their ability. They have great organizational skills and it gives them enormous satisfaction and fulfillment to see a job well done. Although satisfactory completion is their goal, it is important for them not to become overly critical or negative about themselves or others when results are not as good as expected.

January 16 people prefer structure, routine and certainty to variation and uncertainty, as they believe it will increase their chances of accomplishing tasks or projects. Paradoxically, though, when their lives become too structured they can become restless and prone to risk-taking or attempting impossible challenges or goals.

Even though they are often highly valued and admired, when things don't go according to plan they can become over-anxious about their future direction, or prone to the belief that they can never live up to their own expectations. It's possible that in childhood great things were expected of them by their parents and this created a tendency toward introspection and living in the future; if allowed to develop to its extreme, this can lead to feelings of inferiority and despair. They need to understand that they are destined for success, but driving themselves and others into the ground in the process is not necessarily the right approach. Once they have learned to value what they do have, they will discover that the satisfaction they crave comes not just from a job well done but from within and from close personal relationships.

Typically around the age of thirty-five, often sooner, they reach a turning-point that emphasizes the importance of being more in touch with their emotions and the present moment. Above all, they must not settle for fear and uncertainty about what may happen in the future because within them is the strength they need to deal with setbacks; once they can view their mistakes not as failures but as opportunities to learn and grow, they have the potential for an extraordinary life.

On the dark side

Irresponsible, dissatisfied, anxious

At your best

Responsible, insightful, thorough

17 January

the birthday of

the leader

Your greatest challenge is

coping with feeling helpless or reaching boiling point

The way forward is ...

to understand that once you discover the power of positive thought you need never feel helpless or furious again.

People born on January 17 prefer to take the lead, not because they are highly ambitious, egotistical or driven to succeed, but because having assessed the situation and weighed up the pros and cons, it is clear to them that they really are the best person for the job. Despite being cautious and respectful of tradition, people born on this day can also hold some progressive ideas with respect to social reform. They like not only to lead but also to help others.

A defining characteristic of people born on this day is their firm self-belief and strong will. Often their tough-minded approach to life has developed as a result of early hardships, and these difficulties may have taught them that the only person upon whom they can really rely at the end of the day is themselves. This gives them an almost superhuman degree of self-control that is simultaneously inspirational and alarming to others. They really do know the meaning of the word "struggle," and are a model of success achieved through one's own efforts.

Leading and defending their position as leader come naturally to people born on this day. Their uncompromising attitude to life and to work can alienate others, and they would do well to learn that there are alternative ways to get people on their side, such as cooperation and good will. Perhaps because of the struggles they have been through, or the past hurts they have experienced, they can find it hard to trust others.

Although those born on this day realize how important it is to feel in control of their lives, there is a danger for some of them in focusing their energy on changing their outside circumstances instead of the way they think and feel about themselves. Fortunately, in their early thirties, often earlier, there is a shift toward this inner life. Once they begin to understand that self-control starts from within not without—and that negative thoughts and feelings can be challenged—their originality and directness aren't just admired by others, they are considered inspirational.

On the dark side

Argumentative, narrow-minded, reckless

At your best

Purposeful, tough, committed

18

18 January

the birthday of

fantasy

Your greatest challenge is

learning to concentrate for long periods of time

The way forward is ...

to never stop day-dreaming, as this is the secret to your creativity; but if you persistently notice that your mind wanders away from what you are supposed to be focusing on right now, simply say to yourself: Be here now.

The imaginative and creative powers of people born on January 18 can lead them to extraordinary heights. They have a quick wit that can delight others, and their company and irreverent opinions are always in demand. In fact they often attract other people like a magnet.

Optimistic, trusting and childlike in nature, the only things that can bring down these friendly souls are rules, regulations and authority. Although they have boundless energy and drive, and love interacting with people, they don't tend to thrive in a team or in a mundane job, unless they are one hundred per cent committed. They place an extremely high value on independence of thought and action; this can lead to reckless behavior and a stubborn refusal to conform. This trait is evident in both childhood and adulthood, and all the normal procedures for dealing with their rebellion don't tend to work; they will simply withdraw even more as a result. They need to find an environment in which their need for freedom is respected, and once they do find that their gratitude, loyalty and devotion to it will be immense. They also need to make sure that they find ways to express their playful and friendly side, and their original sense of humor, as this will help them keep bitterness at bay.

People born on this day can become bored quickly, losing their concentration and retreating into a world of fantasy or fits of temper if their needs aren't being met or becoming restless and impatient if they feel too confined by responsibilities. They need to learn to find ways to deal more appropriately with a situation; this kind of emotional maturity tends to emerge in their early thirties, sometimes sooner, sometimes later. Asking them to be more realistic simply isn't an option—the way forward is for them not to deny their fantasies but to find ways to positively integrate their innovative ideas and extraordinary insights into their lives. By so doing they will be able to make not just their own lives—but those of all they touch—truly magical.

On the dark side

Childish, impractical, undisciplined

At your best

Visionary, creative, stimulating

19 January

the birthday of

originality

Your greatest challenge is

to stop getting bored and bogged down with detail

The way forward is ...

to keep your ego in check. Paying attention to the little things helps you get the big things done, whether you like it or not.

Those born on January 19 are honest and direct people with a great sense of the beauty in life. They have the ability to look at the world as if through the eyes of a child, seeing everything in a joyous light. Above all they are people of energy and wonder. This is the birthday of true originality.

The originality that defines people born on this day goes hand in hand with a personality that is independent and free-spirited. They really don't care too much what people think and can from time to time indulge in flamboyant or outrageous behavior. Even if they appear respectable on the outside, anyone who gets to know them will soon appreciate what a truly unique individual they are.

January 19 people often surprise others with their reactions because they are able to sense what others miss. Occasionally they will fight against their intuitive side but it is important for them to find ways to balance and incorporate it into their lives. Typically around the age of thirty-two, frequently sooner, there is an emphasis toward their inner life. They learn the importance of working with, not against, their intuition.

These people are destined to shine brightly and to attract others to them like magnets; those born on this day who try to fit in or repress their creativity and originality are on the road to unhappiness. It may take a while before others understand their undoubted gifts but the power of these people is so great that they have the ability to win almost anyone over to their side. The only danger is that the dynamism and unconventionality of these people can lead to attention-seeking and sometimes immature behavior in an attempt to impress. They may also find it hard to lead to stable lives, constantly changing focus and unable to balance their imaginative powers with normal working life.

Blessed with natural drive, curiosity and originality of thought, when they have finally learned to be true to themselves and others, not only can they lead and inspire others, there is the potential for real greatness.

On the dark side

Attention-seeking, immature, pretentious

At your best

Curious, free-spirited, independent

AQUARIUS

THE WATER CARRIER
(JANUARY 2o – FEBRUARY 18)

* **Element:** Air
* **Ruling planets:** Saturn, the teacher and Uranus, the visionary
* **Symbol:** The Water Carrier
* **Tarot card:** The Star (hope)
* **Number:** 4
* **Favorable colors:** Blue, turquoise, yellow
* **Key phrase:** I express my original ideas

Although they are often known for their friendliness, Aquarians are fiercely independent and often quite private people. They like to do things their own way but can also be swayed by a logical argument. They find it difficult to conform to the expectations of others, but their genuine desire to help people and make the world a better place often marks them out as the compassionate visionaries of the zodiac.

Personality potential

Aquarians care deeply about the world in which they live and the people that inhabit it, and so nothing makes them feel more fulfilled than when they are able to use their knowledge, skills and intelligence to help others. Given these personality traits, it's hardly surprising that many people born under this sign are connected in some way with human rights, the environment and people management. Aquarians are friendly, intuitive, broadminded, inventive and original, and their strong need for independence can often earn them a reputation for being eccentric—a reputation in which they clearly take pride.

Although Aquarians have little notion of time, little respect for rules and regulations and a liking for doing things their own way, they will not use their original and inventive ideas in a destructive fashion. Their aim is always to use their intelligence to bring benefit and insight not just to themselves or a select group of people but to everyone.

As well as being ruled by the planet of discipline, Saturn, this sign is also ruled by Uranus, the planet of originality, idealism, unpredictability and constant change. This explains why Aquarians don't just cope well with change, they thrive on it. There can be no greater delight in the world for them than finding out or trying something new. They are friendly by nature and can adapt themselves to any group of people, but despite being highly sociable, reliable and engaging they have the ability to detach themselves from situations and remain objective. This objectivity gives them incredibly clarity and ensures that their choices are usually the soundest ones that everyone respects—and ultimately follows. This isn't to say, however, that Aquarians aren't capable of deep friendships; they give a lot of themselves to their friends and will literally do anything to help and support those close to them.

Above all, these people are ahead of their times and when inspired they are capable of flashes of intuition and insight that can be breathtaking in their scope and originality. Blessed with a temperament that allows them to enjoy what they achieve in life, they are also extremely upbeat and optimistic, even when things are going badly for them.

"Aquarians don't just cope well with change, they thrive on it..."

On the dark side

The personality of Aquarians can be unpredictable and quirky, depending on which planetary ruler—Saturn, the teacher or Uranus, the visionary—is strongest at the time of their birth. When Saturn dominates, negative personality traits include bouts of crankiness and stubbornness; when Uranus dominates, they may be prone to chaotic, wayward and rebellious behavior. In addition, Aquarians often possess a streak of perfectionism that can destroy their chances of fulfillment and happiness. Fanaticism and bigotry can sometimes find expression in this sign's desire to make the world a better place. With their strong desire for change, they may rebel simply for the sake of rebelling or follow a set of ideals blindly, without pausing to consider alternative approaches.

The objectivity and detachment of people born under this sign can sometimes come across as coldness. They are idealistic people but not necessarily warmhearted; revolutionaries but not necessarily understanding; altruists but not necessarily sensitive. In fact they can be downright tactless and perverse at times. They are also prone to investing so much of themselves in a cause or set of ideals that they have very little left over for their family or people close to them. And when the pressure of responsibility or expectation is put on Aquarians, it's in their nature to do exactly the opposite of what is needed or requested—for the simple reason that they like to be perverse. And although they often have large numbers of friends, many of these are in fact merely acquaintances; because of this, Aquarians would do well in exercising more discrimination regarding their friendships. Real friendships require that a person opens up and shares their feelings; this is something with which Aquarians struggle and is the reason they have more acquaintances than friends in their lives.

Symbol

The symbol for Aquarius is the water carrier, because water represents emotion and Aquarians are often noted for their compassion. The symbol is also frequently thought to represent the joining together of intuition and reason for the greater good or the cause of humanity.

Darkest secret

It may come as a surprise—given that many Aquarians present a distinct, rather eccentric face to the world—that they are often quite unsure of who they actually are. This uncertainty can also drive them toward non-conformist behavior in the misguided belief that rebellion will give them the identity and the sense of purpose they crave.

Love

Appealing, cheerful and magnetic, Aquarians tend to be popular people. They enjoy both being in a group and interacting with individuals. They pride themselves on being able to get along with just about anybody.

They need a partner who can share their spirit of adventure and zest for life, because someone who is too timid will simply frustrate them.

When it comes to close, intimate relationships Aquarians may struggle because their perfectionist nature finds the complications that emotion brings difficult to process. With their powerful desire for independence, of all the signs they may find it the hardest to settle into and stay in a relationship in the conventional sense. Letting another person into their lives is interpreted as an invasion of their freedom—both physically and psychologically—and they may prefer to stay as they are rather than change. The danger here is that they become so set in their ways that it's impossible for them to share and they end up permanently alone. Having said this, Aquarians do enjoy the excitement of romance and when they find a quick-witted individual who has as much common sense, sense of adventure and versatility as they do, they can make loyal and loving companions.

Love matches: Gemini, Leo and Aquarius

The Aquarian man

You can expect the unexpected from the Aquarian man. He won't behave the way people expect him to and rarely reveals his true feelings. Everybody is his friend—even his enemies—but there are few, if any, people who are really close to him. In fact if he says he doesn't like someone this is perhaps the clearest indication that he does in fact like that person. Sounds confusing? Welcome to the Age of Aquarius!

An Aquarian man likes to keep his real motives, feelings and intentions hidden. Not because he necessarily has anything to hide, but because he takes great pleasure in surprising others. He also obtains considerable satisfaction in discovering what makes others tick. When he can't understand someone, he won't rest until he has unraveled their mystery—then, when he feels he knows enough, he is off to the next challenge. The person who wants to have a relationship with an Aquarian man must therefore first intrigue him. The "what you see is what you get" kind of person won't attract him at all. He's interested in someone who has many complex layers to their personality, and perhaps the best way to attract his attention is to ignore him.

When he does meet someone who continues to intrigue him enough to make him want to move the relationship onto the next stage, the Aquarian male may struggle. He isn't against marriage or commitment but he doesn't take to it as easily as the other water signs, Cancer and Scorpio. In fact, even when he's head over heels in love he may try to hold off marriage for as long as possible. He may come up with all sorts of plausible reasons why it would be best to delay, which is a shame because once the Aquarian male finally decides to take the plunge—which he will eventually do even if it happens later than with most of his peers—he really comes into his own. He finally starts to relax and open up, bringing endless surprises and excitement to the relationship.

The Aquarian woman

If you want to understand an Aquarian woman, you may as well forget it. She's a paradox. She's faithful and yet detached. She's committed and yet relaxed. She loves everyone, and yet no one. She's sociable but also a loner. She's gentle and yet tough. She's passionate but she can also be platonic. In short, she's predictable in her unpredictability.

Conversations with Aquarian women can be incredible. She seems to be well informed about everyone and everything, possessing the ability to meet people on their level, rather than impose her own opinions on them. She's so charming and fascinating that it's easy to see why she's often surrounded by admirers; but when the question of marriage is raised, she won't rush into anything. She will want to weigh up all the pros and cons and take her time, because the line between friendship and love is very thin for Aquarian women. Talk of marriage may come as a surprise to her. She's not really the romantic type and too much togetherness can make her feel smothered.

If you want to win the heart of this independent, fascinating butterfly you must not be jealous, possessive, critical or conservative in any way. However, once in a relationship the Aquarian woman can be fiercely loyal, tolerant and understanding of their partner's eccentricities—in fact the more eccentricities their partner has the better, because the Aquarian woman can't stand the conventional and the conservative. She will need space in which to breathe and may even suggest a live-apart arrangement or separate bedrooms instead of co-habiting; but whether you live together or apart, a relationship with an Aquarian woman will always seem like a first-time love affair—unpredictable on the one hand, but exciting, spontaneous and magical on the other.

Family

Aquarian children often seem to be very self-sufficient, happy and positive, and from an early age they will show a strong desire to do their own thing. They respect those in authority over them but they won't necessarily agree with them. Their love of surprising others will show itself fairly early in life, and perhaps the best strategy for parents to get an Aquarian child to do something is to tell them to do the opposite. As far as school is concerned, they don't tend to thrive in schools that are heavily academic, traditional and disciplinarian; as soon as they start school their teachers had better watch out, because these children will almost certainly challenge the blind following of rules. They will want to know the logic and reason behind them first. Fortunately, if the logic and reason is clearly explained to them they are sensible and level headed enough to give the appearance at least of toeing the line.

Aquarian children need to be given plenty of opportunities to experiment with their ideas and to make discoveries of their own, because many of them have the talent to be budding inventors. Naturally friendly and willing to chat with just about anyone, young Aquarians need reminding more often than other children about stranger danger. Encouraging them to get involved in community or charity work will be very beneficial, because humanitarianism is strongly associated with this sign. At school they may also excel in art and drama, as well as science.

The Aquarian parent is typically lively and eager to bring the best out of their child or children. They will approach parenthood as a big adventure and their children can often be sure of an unconventional approach to their education and upbringing. This is fine if their children enjoy the unusual but not so fine if they are the kind of children who prefer the more conventional. Aquarian parents need to acknowledge that some children have a greater need for security and structure than others. Learning to really listen to their children's needs and viewing the world from their point of view is therefore of great importance for Aquarian parents.

Career

Whatever career Aquarians choose they will never feel fulfilled unless it allows them to be inventive, in either a scientific or a creative way. They may even become inventors in some capacity. Others do well in careers involving communication, such as people management, public relations, journalism, the media, television, radio and the internet. Another field in which they may excel is humanitarianism and they make excellent social workers, charity workers and international campaigners. Above all, their intention is to help human beings progress in some way, so they may be attracted to science, physics, technology, research, anthropology, archaeology, sociology, ecology, forensics, space research and astronomy.

> **"Above all, their intention is to help human beings progress in some way..."**

Aquarians have such inquisitive minds and love variety so much that they may change jobs quite frequently during their working life and even make a complete change of career later in life.

Health and leisure

The average Aquarian—if there is such a person—will thrive best on a diet that is simple, light and nourishing. They should steer clear of fatty and fried foods that will just slow them down mentally and physically, and aim for foods that are as natural as possible. This is because the more natural their food, the more metabolism-boosting nutrients they are likely to get. A mainly vegetarian diet rich in fruits, vegetables, oily fish, legumes, nuts and seeds is therefore preferable to a diet rich in animal products and refined, processed food.

Aquarians may suffer when the weather is very hot and, like Capricorns, may feel fitter and more mentally alert when the weather is cooler. They may sometimes suffer from circulation problems so they should ensure they wear plenty of layers to keep warm. Regular exercise will also help boost their circulation and they should aim for at least 30 minutes every day. Exercise with a creative element, such as dancing or some forms of sport, will suit them better than repetitive exercise. Jogging or brisk walking is highly beneficial, but they should

avoid the dullness of the treadmill and head outside to the countryside or to parks. Regular stretching before and after exercise is important because their ankles are vulnerable to injury and they should also make sure they wear supportive footwear.

When it comes to hobbies, Aquarians will often have several unusual or eccentric ones, from train- and UFO-spotting to garden-gnome collecting, and from astronomy to science fiction conventions. They also enjoy team sports, socializing and campaigning for a cause they believe in, and are very knowledgeable about computers. Mind–body therapies such as yoga and tai chi, physical therapies such as massage, and even simply thumping a punch bag can help them unwind when the going gets tough. Wearing, meditating on and surrounding themselves with the color orange will encourage them to feel less detached and more passionate toward others and warmer inside.

Born between January 20 and January 31

Aquarians born between these dates like surprises, and the unexpected is something on which they thrive. Even if they have a stable home or work situation they like to shake things up from time to time to keep everyone on their toes. Still, they are very loyal when it comes to most personal relationships.

Born between February 1 and 10

It's difficult for people born between these dates to maintain relationships with people who aren't prepared to evolve and experiment in the same way as they are. These people are constantly re-inventing themselves, trying to stimulate themselves and everyone around them to be better.

Born between February 11 and 18

There's a universal quality about these Aquarians. Although they often appear aloof and detached, inwardly they are sensitive and romantic. They prefer to associate with people who share the same diverse views on life as they do. Their life will be many things, but it will never be dull.

Life lessons

Aquarius is perhaps the most progressive and rebellious sign of the zodiac. Forward thinking and willing to challenge the status quo, these people can bring positive and enlightening change to the world and fiercely champion the cause of the underprivileged. Problems, however, may arise for them on a personal and intimate level. Although they can hold their own in any room, crowd or party, intimate contact frightens them because underneath their exuberant exterior is someone who is shy and lacking in self-confidence.

Lacking in personal identity, Aquarians can sometimes project a detached and even androgynous energy onto the world. With uncertainty masking their true identity, they may find a sense of security in being different or eccentric. The problem with this is that eccentricity should never be an identity but rather should only be an expression of someone's true identity. What drives Aquarians to rebel and seek progress? Only when they can understand this can they begin to establish a real identity for themselves.

Another challenge for Aquarians is to learn to live more in the present and not always look ahead to the next challenge. If they can learn to enjoy the present moment and recognize that their only reality is what they have right now, they will find the inner peace to replace their restlessness.

Other signs of the zodiac can offer Aquarians help with their life lessons. Taureans can help them learn to respect, value and understand rules and traditions. Arians can help them separate rebellion for its own sake from rebellion for a cause. Cancerians can show them the joy of compassion and empathy. Leos can encourage them to be more spontaneous and fun loving, while Scorpios can teach them not to be afraid to get to know themselves, and others, intimately.

20 January

Your greatest challenge is

overcoming your lack of self-confidence

The way forward is ...

to stop comparing yourself to others. You are a special and unique person and you are totally irreplaceable.

People born on January 20 are life's ad-libbers. They may not always be sure where they are going but they also have no doubt that they will get somewhere. They are liberal, sensitive and charming individuals with a remarkable skill for cooperation and improvisation. They are constantly learning, adapting and perfecting their skills, and these qualities helps them climb the ladder of success, sometimes to the very top.

Others may sometimes mistake people born on this day as dreamy, disorganized and scatter-brained. Although they give the appearance of confusion, every detail is stored in their methodical and analytical mind and they simply have an original way of approaching life. They are capable of remarkable endurance, their flexible style ensuring that they overcome the toughest of setbacks with their sense of humor intact.

People born on this day have a genuine compassion and love for people, and will go to extraordinary lengths to help them. They are typically supportive of the underdog but when they are thrown into the role of leader they can come across as dictatorial. It is important for them to carefully consider their approach to leadership, given that their attitude toward the authority of others tends to be light-hearted rather than respectful.

Although they appear tough, the respect of others is extremely important, sometimes too important to them. They need to learn to trust their own judgments more as they are usually right. Fortunately, around the age of thirty there is often a turning point which heightens their sense of self-worth and emphasizes the need for working with their gut instinct.

The considerable personal charm and flexibility that characterizes people born on this day suggests that they have the potential to become well-rounded personalities. Once they can build a sense of self-worth and find a direction and sense of balance, people born on January 20 can display surprisingly intense powers of concentration and commitment that not only assure success but also win them the lasting admiration and respect of others.

On the dark side

Insecure, suspicious, dreamy

At your best

Agreeable, intuitive, focused

21 January

the birthday of the trendsetter

Your greatest challenge is

learning to distinguish between your fear and your intuition

The way forward is ...

to understand that intuition is a lot quieter than fear; you just know something without a lot of words to explain it.

Those born on January 21 are life's trendsetters. It doesn't matter what they are doing or what they are saying, people tend to want to follow them and listen to their opinions. They also have tremendous charm and the ability to get along with just about anyone; when all this is combined with their soaring ambition, they have all they need to get to the top.

Freedom of expression is particularly important for people born on this day. They will never find happiness if they are forced to follow the rules or expectations of others, needing to be allowed to follow their own instincts. If they make mistakes it will still be beneficial as they have the ability to learn from their mistakes.

Leadership is something that those born on this day would seem ideally suited to and they often find it thrust upon them, but in the long term they are not natural leaders. This is because they simply aren't ruthless enough to impose discipline and routine. They are the people with the ideas and the energy to start something new, but it is up to others to see it through to the end.

Alongside their undoubted star quality, people born on this day have a tendency to speak quickly, sometimes spilling out their ideas in a confused way. They also have a tremendous need to be liked, and this can lead to debilitating nervousness and indecision. It is important for them to acknowledge the importance of thinking before they speak and to be less swayed by others' criticism. Fortunately, a turning point occurs around their thirtieth birthday, sometimes sooner, when their sense of self matures and they begin to rely more on their own instincts.

Their unusual charm and personality enable them to forge ahead in life and to go places very few people are able to go. They don't like to be tied down but if they can learn that a little staying power sometimes goes a long way, these boldly original people really can break boundaries and set new limits for others to aspire to.

On the dark side

Needy, chaotic, nervous

At your best

Inventive, optimistic, likable

22 January

the birthday of
the visionary

Your greatest challenge is

avoiding feeling unable to commit to a person or a project

The way forward is ...

to find out what's holding you back. If it is fear, be the bold, adventurous person you really are and take a risk.

People born on January 22 have an electrifying energy about them. Their imaginative powers are often so advanced that the world isn't always ready for them. This can create a sense of frustration, but if they believe in themselves, hold onto their vision and direct their energy constructively, the world will eventually sit up and notice. Their greatest enemy is not responsibility or even authority but tedium and bureaucracy.

The restless, explosive energy of people born on this day gives them the ability to be extraordinarily successful in whatever goal they choose but they do need to learn the importance of patience and discipline if they are to find stability and satisfaction in their lives. If people born on this day don't understand or they can't see their way ahead they are also likely to lose their temper, with explosive results. They would make their lives considerably easier if they learned to appreciate the opinions of others more, even if they differ from their own. This will fuel their creativity further and encourage others to work cooperatively with them instead of against them. Fortunately, by the age of twenty-nine they typically begin to develop a sense of self-restraint and discipline, and this will mark an important turning point in their life.

Above all, people born on this day have the ability to reach out to the world and to explain or present it with something totally unique. Being an unconventional visionary is their special gift. They don't just break the rules, they destroy them and make new ones.

Not surprisingly their uncompromising approach to life will earn them a number of critics along the way, but opposition neither surprises nor disturbs them. Honor and being true to themselves are important, and they will always do what they know to be right, regardless of what others think. This is a high-risk approach to life that has its dangers, but they should never be scared to be themselves—others will respect, admire and ultimately benefit from them for it.

On the dark side

Headstrong, hasty, explosive

At your best

Passionate, imaginative, ground-breaking

23 January

the birthday of
the dissenter

Your greatest challenge is

to stop feeling insecure about yourself

The way forward is ...

to try to make sure that every thought or action of the day is one that supports and encourages you. Nurture yourself for a day and the habit will grow.

People born on January 23 are dissenters. They dislike and often refuse to take orders or even advice from other people and prefer to live according to their own rules, devoting themselves to their own ideals. Although this approach has its risks, more often than not their courageous and buoyant character sees them making, rather than obeying, the rules.

Rarely motivated by financial reward alone, January 23 people are idealistic and desire to live a richly rewarding life. This quality, along with their original thinking and natural sense of style, makes them stand out from the crowd in a positive way. They truly are inspirational figures.

Despite their can-do attitude and charisma, people born on this day never feel quite worthy of the admiration they attract. Although this adds further to their charm, it can sometimes hold them back. However, once they are able to believe in themselves, there is nothing to stop them achieving their own dreams.

With their splendid disregard for convention and highly intellectual and original approach to life, January 23 people find that they can get along with almost everyone they meet, although people with more materialistic motivations present a challenge; people who throw their money about, or who are trying to impress others and climb socially, particularly repulse them. This is because integrity and moral strength are the ideals by which they live their lives.

Understanding the limitations of the human body, those born on this day prefer to live an intellectual life. This can make those close to them occasionally feel excluded and it is important for them to understand that they need a fully integrated personality able to offer others a sensitive depth of understanding. Typically around the age of twenty-eight they become more emotionally receptive and sensitive toward the needs of others.

If those born on this day can make sure that their fascination with the abstract does not take precedence over their personal relationships, they have the potential to become rebels not just with a cause but with ideals that will have an influence on the world around them.

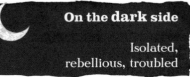

On the dark side

Isolated, rebellious, troubled

At your best

Principled, independent, courageous

24 January

the birthday of the idol

Your greatest challenge is

learning not to fear criticism

The way forward is ...

to use criticism as a powerful incentive to learn and improve. As flattering as praise is, it teaches us nothing, so instead of seeking praise seek criticism.

People born on January 24 are blessed with the ability to stun all those who come into contact with them with their larger-than-life glamor. Everybody wants a piece of them and they are never short of admirers.

Although people are drawn to them sometimes to the point of infatuation, those born on this day have an aloof quality about them. Few know them really well and even fewer get close enough to know their hearts. This may be because behind their natural ability to excite others there is a deep-seated fear of experiencing a negative reaction. To protect themselves from this they prefer to keep everyone at arm's length and to keep quiet about what really excites them. In the short term this approach seems to only increase their popularity, but in the long run this suppression of their true feelings can lead to emotional damage. It is important for them to move away from suspicion of others to the belief that true friends will appreciate them just as they are. Typically around the age of twenty-seven there is a turning point, which suggests a movement away from total independence to greater emotional sensitivity.

Despite feeling insecure at times and misunderstood most of the time, the unique qualities and spark of genius people born on this day possess mean that they are never short of original ideas. They are capable of making great breakthroughs in their careers while at the same time being a delight to have around. They do enjoy being in this position but the danger is that it can lead to vanity. It really is better for their psychological growth to come down to earth with everybody else from time to time.

If those born on this day can find the courage to break down the barriers they have put up and become the person they really are, they may lose some of their idol status but they will gain something far greater in return: self-knowledge. And when they are finally able to understand themselves better, the potential for true greatness lies within them.

On the dark side

Vain, insecure, aloof

At your best

Energetic, exciting, stunning

25 January

the birthday of
purpose

Your greatest challenge is

finding direction
or a purpose
in life

*The way
forward is ...*

to let feelings of
envy point you in
the direction of
what you need.

People born on January 25 come into this world with a powerful sense of destiny or purpose. They feel as if they have been sent with a mission, and until they are able to find and then achieve that mission they will feel unfulfilled. If those born on this day are able to find a sense of purpose, their hardworking and disciplined approach to life will assure their success. They have the ability to focus their energies on their goals; these goals tend to be for the good of others rather than for themselves alone. They are at their happiest when they are totally immersed in a project, but their over-involvement is never at the expense of their individuality. People born on this day refuse to conform, and personal freedom is extremely important to them. Friendship is also important for them, and with their sharp wit they are never boring.

People born on this day are trendsetters, and you will often see them working one step ahead of the rest, using their intuition to push forward in a new direction. Occasionally they run the risk of pushing themselves too far forward and their off-the-wall experimentation with their appearance and their ideas can leave others feeling bewildered. This willingness to experiment is all part of the powerful sense of destiny that marks them out. Although they do see themselves as uniquely talented, they can also see themselves as uniquely flawed, and when there is tendency to dwell too much on their supposed deficiencies this can result in self-defeating behavior. It is important for them to come to terms with who they are and to feel comfortable with their personality. Typically around the age of twenty-six, sometimes later, they develop a greater sense of emotional identity and honesty.

Once people born on this day recognize that there really is nothing wrong with them and that emotions are not fixed but constantly changing, they have the potential to become bold and effective leaders in their work and dynamic and fascinating people in their personal life.

On the dark side

Nervous, self-
defeating, impatient

At your best

Profound, altruistic,
individual

26 January

the birthday of the last word

Your greatest challenge is

inability to cope when your authority or your ideas are questioned

The way forward is ...

Always listen to differing viewpoints from your own as sometimes other people can see what you might have missed.

People born on January 26 are strong-willed, enterprising individuals with a commanding presence. They like to be spearheading new trends and ideas, and their determination and success-orientated approach to life give them the potential to turn their dreams into reality.

The commanding air of authority, and insistence on having the last word, that people born on this day are blessed with make them excellent leaders and they excel at motivating and organizing other people. They firmly believe that for things to move forward the only way is for somebody—preferably themselves—to take control. They are pioneers of new ventures who generally earn the respect of others, in particular those who are subordinate to them.

While they have an honest approach and an air of authority, people born on this day are not known for their patience. They are prone to making snap decisions about people and to taking decisions without consulting others. This can lead to trouble and antagonism from others; the one thing people born on this day don't like is having their authority questioned. It is important for them to keep an open mind about others and to carefully weigh up the pros and cons before making decisions. Once they are able to recognize the importance of compromise, their down-to-earth approach and dynamic energy will guarantee their success and the loyalty of others.

Those born on this day are usually to be found where the action is. They are extremely success orientated, but to lead a fully balanced life and to achieve greater happiness they do need to pay more attention to their inner life and their relationships with others. Fortunately, after the age of approximately twenty-five, sometimes later, they begin to become more sensitive and inner-focused and less externally orientated.

Part of the secret of the success that people born on this day attract is their ability to recover from setbacks. During troubled times in childhood and adolescence they learned that they have the ability to surprise all who doubt them and, once they know what they want, nothing can stand in their way.

On the dark side

Inflexible, opinionated, dictatorial

At your best

Dynamic, enterprising, determined

27 January

Your greatest challenge is

learning to control your emotions

The way forward is ...

to understand that your emotions are not in charge of you; you are in charge of your emotions. You are the one who decides how you feel.

The unique spirit and outstanding creative talents of people born on January 27 are often evident early in their lives, typically before they reach the age of thirty, and much of the rest of their lives is spent developing these gifts to their full potential.

Financial reward is not likely to be the motivating force of people born on this day; their motivation is more a personal desire to prove themselves and push themselves to their limits. They love the journey more than the arrival and the thrill of the chase rather than the prize. Unusually creative and intelligent, they often pick things up very quickly, an ability they demonstrated in their childhood or their teens. Sometimes their talent for adapting so quickly to the new can distance them from others with a more slow-moving approach, but it can also turn them into trendsetters. Their original perspective can also inspire them to make improvements to systems that are long past their sell-by date. Rarely will these people be on the sidelines; they are decision makers and life's movers and shakers.

The biggest challenge for those born on this day is to learn to slow down and discriminate. Because they are capable of moving so fast ahead of others, their ideas may take off prematurely. They need to develop a disciplined work ethic that matches their versatility and helps them achieve the success they deserve. This doesn't mean they should repress their exuberance; it just means they need to be more realistic in their approach to life. If they are unable to do this they may find themselves unable to hold down a job or a relationship. Fortunately, from the age of twenty-four there is a turning point which offers them opportunities to become more emotionally mature and show the world that their early promise can be fulfilled.

Above all, those born on this day have the ability to astonish everyone around them. Their energetic and sometimes childlike approach to life can mean that they are wrongly dismissed as lightweights, but once they learn concentration they are capable of great accomplishments.

On the dark side

Immature, restless, undisciplined

At your best

Gifted, enthusiastic, intelligent

28 January

the birthday of
the star performer

Your greatest challenge is

managing your constant need to be admired

The way forward is ...

to understand that seeking reassurance from others will never give you real fulfillment; the happiness, joy, and inspiration you are looking for lie within you.

Charming and attractive, those born on January 28 know how to project a confident image to others. They are star performers who don't really care what other people think and their creative potential is as strong as their desire to impress others. Impressing others means as much to them as their achievements, and more often than not their achievements are so special that others have every reason to be impressed.

People born on this day will be themselves and follow their own path no matter what. They prefer to think independently, and when their rebellious streak is properly channeled it can help them forge ahead of the rest. Although they do love to be the center of attention and to be admired, they also have great depth and a shrewd insight into the motivations and feelings of others. This can help them achieve their goals, earning them friends along the way.

Sometimes those born on this day may find themselves sitting on the sidelines watching others, perhaps because they are too outrageous to be included; but sooner or later their creativity and individuality pull them back into the action where they belong. Despite their star quality, those born on this day do understand the importance of hard work and their desire to achieve something great never obscures for them the need to put in the hard work. And this combination of courage and individuality with practicality and discipline makes them the pioneer they were born to be.

Those born on January 28 run the risk of needing to be told over and over again how special they are. They may also make foolish, unrealistic decisions in their attempt to be noticed. Fortunately, around the age of twenty-three and again around the age of fifty-three there is a powerful shift toward greater emotional maturity; this emphasis on intuition will serve them well. Once people born on this day learn to listen to their intuition, not only will they attract amazing opportunities to show the world just how brilliant they really are, but their life will feel more complete.

On the dark side

Attention-seeking, unrealistic, foolish

At your best

Curious, progressive, hardworking

29 January

the birthday of
the mystic warrior

Your greatest challenge is

dealing with confrontation

The way forward is ...

not to withdraw but to calmly state your opinion and be true to yourself. Whenever you start compromising your identity and beliefs you reduce your chances of both success and happiness.

People born on January 29 are highly intuitive but also very persuasive in their approach to others. They always say what they think, being direct and forceful without being offensive. Their generous nature and strong belief that there is good in everyone earn them not just the respect but the love of all who cross their path.

People born on this day may use their creative, quietly rebellious streak to support the rights of others. Their excellent communication skills serve them well in both their work and social life. The keys to their success as a negotiator and as a person are their intuitive power and their desire to work cooperatively rather than independently. They have the ability to sense what others are thinking and feeling, and when the moment is right to make a move. They also understand the power of synergy and how a group of people working toward a common goal is the greatest force of all.

Although they are open-minded and generally tolerant of the viewpoints of others, they may occasionally withdraw into unassertive behavior and—in extreme cases—into inertia; once they are able to trust their ability to make the right decision they can, however, reach for the stars. Fortunately, around the ages of twenty-two and fifty-two there are powerful turning points in their lives when they develop a greater degree of self-awareness. Life generally becomes much easier for them in their early thirties and beyond, as they start to realize that within them is the power to achieve almost anything.

Once people born on this day have developed their self-belief, their formidable determination to right wrongs can evoke extreme reactions from others; when the reaction is positive they grow in courage, but when negative they may feel hurt. It is important for them to understand that it is impossible to please everyone; sometimes there is a need to be cruel to be kind. And when they learn this they can fulfill their role as the mystic warrior: strong-willed and with the ability to inspire others and gather support for their chosen cause.

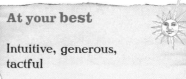

On the dark side

Withdrawn, unassertive, indecisive

At your best

Intuitive, generous, tactful

30 January

Your greatest challenge is

coping with being left alone while others enjoy the companionship you long for

The way forward is ...

to learn to accept people the way they are, and not find too much fault in them or expect them always to agree with you.

People born on January 30 are confident in their convictions and beliefs and like to put their personal mark on things. They live their life according to their own moral code and are always on the side of the underdog or those less privileged. Their strong social conscience, combined with their determination, charm and intelligence, means they are born to take control.

Everybody who knows people born on this day will be in no doubt of where they stand on the important issues. They have a talent for bringing like-minded people together; living in a commune on the edge of society would not be unacceptable to them if it meant they could live according to their all-important ideals. Although they arrive at their position of certainty through reasoned judgment, they do also rely heavily on their instincts. This ability to combine intuition with logic will mark them out as exceptionally gifted leaders.

Although self-assured and with strong convictions, people born on this day are prone to worry and to acting impulsively just like everyone else. A need to win the approval of others can lead them to fudge the truth if they feel it will get others on their side. It is important for them to find some sort of balance between their convictions and reality, and to know when to stick to a plan regardless of opposition or difficulties. Once they understand that their determination to succeed, if channeled positively, will always help them win, they will be less prone to anxiety and mood swings. Fortunately, around the age of twenty-one and then again at the age of fifty-one there are significant turning points which make them more confident and assertive.

Highly ambitious and strong-willed people born on this day like to give rather than take orders, and although they give orders extremely well they should learn to value the viewpoints of others. Once they have learned to discover their humility and to listen for and trust their inner guidance, they can move mountains with both their convictions and their generosity of spirit.

On the dark side

Driven, temperamental, untruthful

At your best

Generous, outspoken, creative

31 January

Your greatest challenge is

to stop losing interest quickly if others don't give you their heartfelt support

The way forward is ...

not to try something else but to trust your instincts and make your own decision about what is or is not right for you.

People born on January 31 have an overwhelming need to be noticed, heard and taken seriously. And because more often than not these bright, appealing people achieve this goal with ease, they are admired by others for their creativity, vision and originality.

Strong will-power, steadfastness and an emphasis on self-expression define people who are born on this day. They may also be quite progressive, with a touch of the genius about them. Although they can appear absent-minded and chaotic at times, this is only because their thoughts are always on fast-forward, their mind being filled with original and ingenious ideas and concepts.

When they feel they have made some kind of breakthrough they run the risk of getting over-excited, but others tend to find this endearing rather than annoying. In fact people born on this day are generally well liked for being so inventive and entertaining in their never-ending quest for knowledge. They are magnetic personalities but harbor a tendency to be occasionally oversensitive, reading hidden meanings into the actions and words of others. When they feel upstaged, put upon or let down they may overreact and either withdraw completely and become depressed, or startle others with their sharp tongue. They need to learn to be a little less intense in their relationships and to accept that sometimes other people want to share the limelight.

Occasionally people born on this day may feel pressured to conform to others' expectations of them in order to be liked; by so doing they run the risk of losing their unique charm. Fortunately, around the age of twenty there is a turning point which suggests they are able to develop greater self-reliance; at the age of fifty there is another turning point which highlights their fighting spirit and emotional resilience.

Above all, people born on January 31 are bright spirits who have the ability to light up the world with their bubbly personalities and brilliance. Once they learn to truly value themselves they have the potential not only to bring great happiness to the world but also to influence and inspire.

On the dark side

Uncertain, suspicious, groveling

At your best

Appealing, original, strong

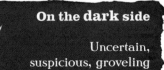

1 February

the birthday of
the spectacular turnaround

Your greatest challenge is

coping with feeling unsure about what to do with your life

The way forward is ...

to analyze your emotions like a scientist. Once you can identify what gives you joy, you are closer to finding your answer.

Those born on February 1 tend to be multi-talented individuals who refuse to conform to traditional ways of thinking or doing things. Despite the fact that others are often swayed by their conviction, it is not uncommon for them to make a spectacular turnaround a month or so later.

This unique combination of originality, intuition and flexibility means that people born on this day have an ability to attract and keep success. They can assess a situation quickly and formulate an appropriate course of action but they are also capable of dramatically changing direction as long as it takes them in the direction they want to go. They can do this with ease because they have the maturity to understand that there will always be different viewpoints. They have values and beliefs to guide them but they never shut out options that could potentially bring good fortune their way.

The willingness to learn and adapt that people born on this day favor means that they are a unique mixture of seriousness and fun, easily able to relate to and influence everyone they meet. The only danger is that by accommodating themselves to others they can lose touch with who they are. It is especially important for them to shift their focus more toward greater self-understanding and to become more aware of the effect others can have on them. Fortunately, from around the age of nineteen there is a turning point which places the emphasis firmly on developing and understanding their goals in life; at around the age of forty-nine there is a shift toward even deeper self-awareness.

With their ability to adapt and strike out in any new direction, people born on this day are often trail-blazers. Although it can sometimes be tough for them to decide what to do, once they know where they are heading and, more importantly, who they want to be, their powers of communication, combined with their versatility and charisma, have the potential to attract more success than they could ever have dreamed of.

On the dark side

Stubborn, fickle, self-absorbed

At your best

Inspiring, original, mentally quick

2 February

the birthday of

elegance

Your greatest challenge is

learning how to let down your guard

The way forward is ...

to develop your self-awareness and to understand that trust and intimacy are not weaknesses but strengths.

Those born on February 2 tend to be sophisticated people with their own elegant style, dress code and mode of behavior. They often resist any attempt to impose rules and regulations on them but, despite their fierce need to do things their own way, they are also extremely open-minded. This makes them very easy to get along with and their presence is soothing and reassuring for others when they are troubled. They also possess the ability to stick to something to the bitter end; this determination and conviction give them a formidable energy and power.

Although people born on this day are often surrounded by admirers, they tend to keep close emotional relationships at arm's length. This could be because they can get so absorbed in their work, their ideas or their projects that they place close human contact at the bottom of the list. Their focus is often the universal, the social, the bigger picture or the group, and they are in many respects the wounded healers of this world. They are the politicians, doctors and social reformers who make great changes for the good of others but have little time for the welfare of their own family. They are the counselors and psychologists who can help others work through their emotional traumas but are unable to identify their own. They are the mystics and psychics who can see the bigger picture but can't see their own loneliness. It is crucial for their own psychological growth that they become more self-aware and respect themselves enough to let others get close to them. Fortunately, around the age of eighteen and then again around the age of forty-eight there are opportunities for them to develop stronger emotional bonds with others.

Above all, people born on this day are perceptive and unique individuals. If they can learn to apply the same level of intuitive understanding to themselves as they apply to others and the world around them, they have the potential to be not just rare and elegant, but truly inspirational individuals.

On the dark side

Uncompassionate, aloof, stubborn

At your best

Elegant, stylish, dynamic

47

3 February

the birthday of new frontiers

Your
greatest
challenge is

dealing with
boredom

*The way
forward is ...*

to think of
boredom as an
opportunity to
relax, unwind
and spend time
thinking about
what you really
want from life.

People born on February 3 have a probing and inquisitive mind that thrives on variety and constant change. They are boundary breakers and nothing excites them more than a challenge or a new experience. What makes them unique, however, is that when they are actively involved in a task they can give it their undivided attention.

Once people born on this day have broken things down and learned all they think they can, they will immediately move on to something else. There is a danger that this approach to life can lead to flitting from one subject to another without acquiring any real depth. However, when they do find something that really challenges them they will probe into every minute aspect of it with an incomparable eye for detail.

These people don't just enjoy challenges, however, they need them to feel alive; if there are none to engage their active mind they may attempt to make their life more difficult. For example, they may set themselves impossible deadlines at work or push themselves to the limits physically. It is therefore important for them to learn to find ways to deal with their boredom.

Their greatest fear is to have their personal freedom to explore new frontiers taken away. This could result in a fear of commitment to partners and family, and unreliable or erratic behavior. This isn't to say they are incapable of closeness; they simply need to feel that their personal freedom has not been sacrificed. Between the ages of seventeen and forty-six there are opportunities for them to develop greater emotional closeness; after the age of forty-seven there is a turning point that gives them the emotional confidence to handle commitment.

People born on this day will achieve greater happiness when they understand that when others try to seek to be close to them they are not necessarily trying to trap them. In fact, once they have learned to resist the tendency to back off when things get intense, there are very few problems or situations that the adaptable nature of these strong individuals cannot resolve.

On the dark side

Aloof,
restless, unreliable

At your best

Inventive,
original, detailed

4 February

the birthday of
the bedazzler

Your greatest challenge is

understanding the feeling that you are different

The way forward is ...

to understand that everyone is unique and gifted in their own way; you just happen to be a little more unique than others.

People born on February 4 often try to fit in but, however hard they try, they will always stand out. They have the ability to bedazzle others with their original thoughts and flashes of brilliance. Their methods may not always be orthodox but their thought-processes are always original and their problem-solving techniques always effective.

Although people born on this day are often admired for their sincerity, discipline and ability to work extremely hard, the logic behind their thoughts and actions is often incomprehensible not just to others but sometimes to themselves. Their speed of thought and energy may also exhaust those around them and they may find that people respond to them with bewilderment rather than bedazzlement. Feeling that they are a square peg in a round hole can make them feel insecure and confused; they may try to ward off feelings of difference and aloneness by attempting to fit in. This is a mistake because they shouldn't try to win the admiration of others by limiting their greatest strength: their originality.

People born on this day do often feel as if they are different from other people but they are at their happiest and most bedazzling when they are able to be themselves. Because there is often so much going on in their heads they may pay little attention to their emotions; analyzing their feelings is not easy for them. As a result they can be incredibly harsh on themselves, expecting more from themselves than anyone else. They can also be impatient and impulsive without thinking through the impact of their actions on themselves and others. Fortunately, between the ages of sixteen and forty-five there are opportunities to become more emotionally self-aware; after the age of forty-five a significant turning point comes when they become bolder, more self-accepting and assertive.

If people born on this day can understand that others will respect and admire them far more if they are themselves, they have the potential to bring about real innovations in both their personal and their professional lives.

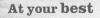

On the dark side

Uncommunicative, confused, unstable

At your best

Imaginative, unconventional, sincere

5 February

the birthday of
the smooth operator

Your greatest challenge is

to open up about what you really feel

The way forward is ...

to understand that emotions should never be repressed or ignored. If you aren't in touch with your feelings you can never be truly happy.

People born on February 5 are often admired by others for their quiet confidence, razor-sharp wit and ability to undertake almost any task with ease. They are smooth operators with the gift of the gab and an ability to deliver the goods.

Although people born on this day may seem to be extremely capable, sometimes to the point of over-confidence, underneath they are no less insecure than anyone else. They have simply learned to mask their insecurities with a smooth, articulate and daring façade. The admiration of others means a lot more to them than they would admit, which is why they relish the role of caretaker or educator of others.

Incredibly bright, these people express themselves with ease and are at their happiest when surrounded by equally witty and intelligent people. If they are starved of intellectual stimulation there is a danger of their alienating others with a lofty and intimidating manner. Fortunately, between the ages of fifteen and forty-four their emotional sensitivity toward others becomes more emphasized; after the age of forty-four there comes a turning point which suggests they feel even greater empathy for others.

People born on this day can be exceptional thinkers as well as speakers, and nothing thrills them more than philosophy, psychology, mystery and intrigue. With an ever-curious mind, if they are able to develop their unique ideas they have remarkable potential to excel in their chosen field. They need to be careful, however, not to become too detached in the process. It is important for them sometimes to think a little less and feel a little more, as they have the tendency to over-analyze rather than acknowledge feelings.

February 5 people work particularly well in a team or for a cause where their need for intellectual stimulation and flair for management can be fully utilized. When they learn to hold back less, trust a little more and allow others to catch up with their frenetic pace, the compelling charm of these smooth operators can take them all the way to the top.

On the dark side

Condescending, inconsistent, cocky

At your best

Articulate, versatile, daring

6 February

the birthday of
the charmer

Your greatest challenge is

to moderate your desire to be needed by everyone

The way forward is ...

to understand that people will like you for who you are and not because you are accommodating.

People born on February 6 are generous, accommodating individuals who are generally liked by everyone they meet. It's almost impossible not to like them because they have such a winning manner and enthusiastic personality. As a result they are often extremely popular and respected.

Positive feedback and approval from others really matters to people born on this day, but this need for affection isn't a one-way street; in many ways life is one big love affair for them. The only downside to this approach to life is that when things don't go their own way, or when love and generosity are met with contempt and selfishness, they can get hurt and emotional. Sometimes disappointment and disillusionment can make them behave in dramatic or insecure ways which can irritate rather than endear them to others.

Although they are insecure at times, the generous and positive nature of people born on this day attracts plenty of love, admiration and success their way. They do need to be careful, however, that in their role as people pleaser they don't become too accommodating and lose touch with their own emotional needs or act inappropriately. They need to understand that friendship is not just about accommodation but also about trust, respect, generosity and boundaries. There is a turning point around the age of forty-four when they become more assertive and aware of their own character.

The flexible nature of these people also applies to their thought processes. They are never wrong-footed by the unexpected, always being willing to explore new territory. They can sometimes be guilty of courting popularity for popularity's sake, but more often than not the unpretentious nature of these people earns them respect and praise in good and bad times alike. As long as they don't take the respect of others for granted, remembering that their self-worth needs to be based on more than popularity, these charming and thoughtful people pleasers want life to be good to them, and more often than not it is.

On the dark side

Needy, uncertain, insecure

At your best

Loving, generous, likable

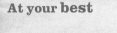

7 February

the birthday of the prophet

Your greatest challenge is

to get others to take you seriously

The way forward is ...

to prove you mean business by acting out rather than talking about your ideals.

People born on February 7 are progressive individuals with a keen intellect and an inherent sense of justice. It is impossible for them to witness injustice or cruelty without speaking out. Above all, they are prophets with a vision and a burning desire to change social attitudes and right wrongs.

They have a wonderful imagination and a youthful approach to life, but also have a tendency to exaggerate or embellish things. This, together with their openness and spontaneity, can sometimes make them appear naïve or childlike. Others may dismiss them or take them for granted but this is a mistake. Although they like to share their dreams with others, the difference between them and other dreamers lies in their ability to turn dreams into reality.

Quick to identify solutions to problems, these people often pursue their goals with zest and enthusiasm, sometimes with fanatical zeal. This approach makes others sit up and take notice, but occasionally they haven't thought through their plans. Although their great communication skills easily win them supporters, when things don't run smoothly and others start to find fault, February 7 people can hide their disillusionment behind a wall of cynicism. They must understand that life is too complex to be seen in terms of right or wrong or quick-fix solutions. They need to learn to accept that there will always be viewpoints differing from their own and that there are many paths—not one—to the greater good. Around the age of forty-three there is a significant turning point which helps them fine-tune their relationship skills and become more open minded.

People born on this day like nothing better than to help others; one thing they will not accommodate, however, is authority. They have little patience for enforced conformity and if forced into a corner they may resort to subversive or disruptive behavior. As well as a rebellious streak they also have great determination; once they can find an outlet for their self-expression and fully commit to it, these modern-day prophets really can make the world a better and fairer place.

On the dark side

Critical, unrealistic, dissatisfied

At your best

Visionary, fair, spontaneous

8 February

the birthday of
the hypnotist

Your greatest challenge is

avoiding the seedier, self-destructive side of life

The way forward is ...

to come to terms with your shadow side first, so you will have less need to explore it in the outside world.

People born on February 8 may not necessarily be able to see into the future but they have the ability to shape it with their thoughts and words. They have an intuitive understanding of people and situations, and are often able to spot future trends and then point everybody in that direction.

The hypnotic power that they possess gives them tremendous influence over the people and situations in which they find themselves. This influence often astounds those who may have made more obvious efforts to move things forward and who may have dismissed them as dreamers.

Perhaps because they are aware of their influence over and responsibility toward others, those born on this day can come across as grave or serious. They can tolerate but don't really enjoy chit-chat and much prefer to get their teeth into life's problems. As a result they often find themselves the treasured confidant of friends and loved ones. On the downside, in personal relationships there is both a passive side to them, as well as a shadow side that draws them toward people who aren't good for them. Fortunately, although there are opportunities earlier, in their early forties there is a significant turning point which can help them become more self-aware and assertive.

The profound sensitivity and intuitive powers of these people mean that they can effortlessly tune into the moods of others. They also run the risk of over-identifying with another person's problems and can easily fall into the worry trap, although few people will notice as they tend to conceal their true feelings to avoid being hurt. It is important for them to learn where other people end and they begin.

When people born on this day find a project that captures their interest they have all the drive and determination they need to succeed; procrastination will become a thing of the past. They can think on a grand scale, and once they learn how to project success they may well find that their bright ideas lead to great progress and reform.

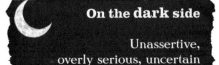

On the dark side

Unassertive, overly serious, uncertain

At your best

Driven, charming, sensitive

9 February

the birthday of the winning attitude

Your greatest challenge is

learning not to beat yourself up for some perceived weakness

The way forward is ...

when you do mess up to talk to yourself as though you were a small child; be positive, supportive and gentle.

People born on February 9 are independent and generous individuals with their own unique and at times non-conformist perspective on life. They are shrewd observers of human nature and capable of enormous understanding of others' problems. Above all, though, they are fighters; life may have given them a few knocks but they have managed to bounce back with resilience, and this winning attitude can lead them to great achievements.

The remarkable ability of people born on this day to understand people and situations, even those they have not met themselves, makes them much sought after for advice and support. They make great teachers and leaders, and they influence and inspire not so much by technique but by example, showing others through their own actions how to rise above challenges with a winning attitude.

Yet when it comes to applying that same penetrating insight to their own lives and relationships they tend to be overly critical, measuring themselves by an impossibly high ideal. It is important for them to learn to be as tolerant and supportive of themselves as they are of others. Before the age of forty the needs and approval of others tend to be dominant but at the age of forty there is a turning point which places a greater emphasis on self-awareness and acceptance, as well as a need to take the initiative in all areas of their lives, possibly with a new relationship or venture.

The strong presence of people born on this day can sometimes make people think of them as aggressive, but behind this they possess a soft side that takes rejection and criticism to heart. They also have a tendency to act rashly; they need to remain calm under pressure and not allow their good will to be exploited. Once they are able to regard themselves more positively—and to be less harsh in their self-criticism— they will be able to achieve the high goals they set themselves, in the process becoming an inspirational model to everyone lucky enough to wander across their path.

On the dark side

Inconsistent, long-suffering, anxious

At your best

Powerful, generous, resilient

10 February

the birthday of

achievement

Your greatest challenge is

to learn to give others a chance

The way forward is ...

to understand that giving others a chance to prove themselves is an important part of their psychological development.

People born on February 10 have a clear picture of what they want to achieve and how they want to get there. The pursuit of their goals is likely to take precedence over anything else. Achievement matters greatly to them, as do the approval and recognition of others. Their clear-sighted recognition of their aspirations, along with their ability to concentrate, means that they are more than likely to surpass their professional goals.

Once they settle on a chosen course, the drive these people are blessed with can take them right to the top. They do need, however, to be careful that they don't thereby become obsessive. It is important for them to look deep within to identify and hold onto the real motivation for their determination. They may well find that it is not material success but rather making their mark on the world and winning the approval of others.

Although the ambition and drive of people born on this day is explosive, it never leads them to stab others in the back. Intuitive, honest and decent, their ideal is to achieve success in the right way without harming or hurting others in the process. Unfortunately, though, there are people they are capable of hurting without realizing it; these are the people closest to them whom they tend to neglect when their goals take precedence over everything and everyone else. If they aren't careful, this can leave them emotionally isolated and, in extreme cases, alone. Fortunately, between the ages of twenty and thirty-nine there are many opportunities for them to open their hearts and turn the spotlight from themselves onto others. At forty there is a turning point where they feel the need to be more assertive but at the same time more passionate in their relationships with other people.

As long as people born on this day remember that admiration is no substitute for affection, and can learn from any setbacks they experience, their considerable achievements will earn them both personal fulfillment and a large number of fans.

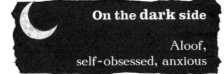

On the dark side

Aloof, self-obsessed, anxious

At your best

Positive, creative, bold

11 February

the birthday of
the upgrader

Your greatest challenge is

to allow others
to do things
their way

*The way
forward is ...*

to understand
that sometimes
the only way
for other people
to learn is
through making
mistakes and
finding their
own solutions.

People born on February 11 feel they were sent to this world for one purpose only; to improve the lives of those around them. In their minds, both people and things are always in need of improvement or an upgrade. They often have an earnest quality about them, and an energy and drive that makes others want to learn from them. They also have a talent for invention and enjoy finding new ways to make life easier for others around them. They do this not for material benefit or even recognition but because they believe that the less stress and discomfort people have, the more they can devote themselves to more meaningful and spiritual pursuits.

Although they prefer to motivate by example rather than words, people born on this day have a knack for making others feel good about themselves. Their curious and inventive mind means they have a great need for intellectual stimulation; their current absorption in a project or social group should not, however, make them neglect close personal relationships. Thinking of themselves as improvers and educators, they should understand that not everyone appreciates or wants their help. Some people like to work out for themselves what will make their life easier and they may get resentful if another person tries to point things out, especially if they do so in a blunt manner. It is important for people born on this day to develop their intuition and sensitivity toward others. Fortunately, between the ages of nineteen and thirty-eight there is an emphasis on emotional sensitivity; but after the age of thirty-nine directness toward others takes center stage and it is more important than ever that they learn to channel this directness positively and sensitively.

With their inventive mind and sharp insight into what a situation or a person needs, there is little doubt that people born on this day (as long as they can master the art of diplomacy) will make a mark on the world by helping and educating others.

On the dark side

Tactless,
self indulgent, excessive

At your best

Progressive,
inventive, knowing

12 February

Your greatest challenge is

to focus your energy on one project alone

The way forward is ...

to understand that developing concentration is essential to anyone who aspires to take charge of their lives. An essential skill for success, its absence means our efforts get scattered.

Those born on February 12 have a talent for integration; they have the ability to marshal all the available information, evaluate opposing viewpoints and then bring everything and everyone together in a united front. Nothing matters more to them than the status quo and if need be they will boldly and courageously defend it. This makes them highly valued in both their professional and their personal lives.

People born on this day like to see themselves in the role of peacekeeper, pointing others in the right direction; that direction is, of course, the one they believe to be correct. This isn't to say that they are stubborn and inflexible, but they possess the tendency to ignore what others think and to believe that the best course of action is always their own. It is important for them to recognize the importance of consensus and to understand that although their ability to see and evaluate the bigger picture more than qualifies them to take the lead, great leadership is not about dictatorship but about motivating others in the direction you want them to go.

As well as being able to unite others and see the way forward with single-minded tenacity, people born on this day have a host of other talents, including confidence, originality and creativity. They do need to be careful that their talents don't cause them to squander their energies in many different directions. Until their late thirties there are opportunities for them to develop greater self-awareness, but in their forties and beyond there is a focus on personal integration and purpose; in many ways, this is when these people really come into their own.

People with a February 12 birthday have strong convictions and a progressive instinct, both of which have been developed through their powers of original thought, and high moral and ethical standards. They have the courage and charisma to lead and inspire others, and more often than not others will find them living out their mission to make the world a better and more peaceful place.

On the dark side

Inflexible, moody, intolerant

At your best

Patience, purpose, originality

13 February

the birthday of
the enigmatic extrovert

Your greatest challenge is

to avoid rushing into things

The way forward is ...

to learn to take a deep breath, ask others for their opinion and to list the pros and cons before making a decision.

Those born on February 13 are difficult to ignore. They are open and uninhibited in almost all that they undertake and bursting with energy, originality and fun. Often regarded as trendsetters, they are at their best when performing to an audience.

People born on this day have a unique approach to life, and their ideas and plans have the potential to make them a fortune. Because they are rebellious and more than a little wild, they will almost certainly encounter criticism and rejection in their life, in particular their teens and early twenties. It is important for them to hold fast to their individuality and to resist the urge to fit in. They just need to find the right path and the right goals to devote their considerable energy to—and the right people to encourage them to be themselves—and their success is assured.

Exuberant, original and daring, these people see a world of possibilities and potential around them. Sometimes in their enthusiasm to move forward they can come across as bossy or eccentric; they do need to learn to slow down and look before they leap. They are often guilty of following their hearts before their heads and this can also get them into trouble, leading them to hurt other people in the process. After the age of thirty-seven there is a turning point, suggesting that they will become more aggressive and focused in pursuit of their goals. It is more important than ever for them to learn to center themselves and find a sense of inner security.

February 13 people have a flair for the dramatic and although their uninhibited nature relishes being the center of attention, there are certain aspects of themselves that they keep strictly private. This gives them a fascinating enigmatic quality and complexity that only serves to intrigue and delight their audience even more. Once they are able to control rather than repress their exuberant spontaneity, these elusive but extrovert individuals can often be found entertaining, educating and intriguing their adoring fans.

On the dark side

Wacky, reckless, bossy

At your best

Uninhibited, unique, fun

14 February

the birthday of
the vulnerable wit

Your greatest challenge is

to keep confidential information to yourself

The way forward is ...

to understand that the trust and respect of others are far more rewarding than the short-lived thrill of being the center of attention.

Charming, intelligent and warm-hearted, people born on February 14 are shrewd observers of human foibles. They think quickly and analytically, tending to express themselves succinctly in great one-liners.

The incisive wit of these people can work both for and against them. Their biting sense of humor can make them wonderful and entertaining company, and formidable allies in the workplace, but they can also be blunt to the point of sarcasm, driving others away with deeply wounding comments. Their sarcasm tends to surface most when they feel impatient or frustrated because others aren't attending to their demands. And because other people tend to reveal personal information to them, they need to be careful that they don't become gossips.

Jovial banter can be a way for people born on this day to camouflage their true emotions. They are typically the first to cry when a sad song is being played or to feel heartbreaking empathy with those in the world who are suffering misfortune. This vulnerability can often surprise those around them as they often expect someone with such a cool and incisive wit to be emotionally stronger.

Those born on this day should apply some of their penetrating insight to themselves as well as others, and understand that their emotions bubble quickly to the surface because they have an important message to deliver. They should listen to that message because the strong reactions they have to the misfortunes of others are often a sign of their own repressed emotion searching for an outlet. Fortunately, around the age of thirty-six there is a turning point, emphasizing that they should become more self-aware and assertive regarding their own emotions.

A lamb in wolf's clothing, people born on February 14 may appear tough but they don't take themselves too seriously. This isn't to say they are superficial; there is great emotional depth behind their banter. It simply means they are great company to keep because, whenever they are around, life always seems easier, lighter and much, much happier.

On the dark side

Insensitive, cutting, demanding

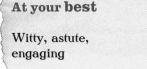

At your best

Witty, astute, engaging

15 February

the birthday of
the enterprising adventurer

Your greatest challenge is

to pay attention to the details

The way forward is ...

to understand that details and the routine that often accompanies them are unavoidable in human existence; to ignore them is often to ignore something truly special.

People born on February 15 are full of vitality, adventure and fun. They like to walk on the wild side of life, and have great enthusiasm and ingenuity, especially when it comes to exploring novel things. When faced with a challenge, it is impossible for them to sit on the sidelines; they have to jump in and offer a solution—their solution.

The charming, energetic people born on this day have the ability to master skills quickly, using their enterprise and ingenuity to raise a skill, craft or project to undreamed-of heights. They like to live life in the fast lane and have no intention of slowing or calming down. Although this approach means they are often a powerful force to be reckoned with, it can also mean that they sometimes find it hard to know when to stop.

Those born on February 15 value their intellectual freedom above all else and they like to experience or investigate just about anything. This can lead, however, to burnout or information overload; when this happens, they may come across as chaotic or irresponsible rebels without a cause. Their moods may also swing from high to low for no reason; this is a result of living in too heightened a state. It is important for these people to understand that sometimes discipline and limits have great value. Fortunately, they tend to grow more self-disciplined when they are older; around the age of thirty-five they can become extremely assertive, so they should channel that dynamic energy positively rather than negatively.

As long as they learn the importance of self-discipline and goal setting—and others allow them to explore the wonders of the world—these multi-talented individuals have the potential to realize their original and intelligent dreams. They may have an alarming wild streak that often lands them in trouble but they are genuinely motivated by a desire to make the world a happier and more exciting place. With them around, life can be many things but it is never dull.

On the dark side

Critical, wild, moody

At your best

Self-starter, curious, bold

16 February

the birthday of
the alchemist

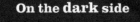

Your greatest challenge is

to resist being a know-all

The way forward is ...

to understand that just as you have learned from your mistakes, sometimes other people need to learn from theirs.

People born on February 16 have the ability to transform even the most difficult of experiences into something positive. There is a touch of the alchemist about them in their ability to see the bigger picture, bring together all the relevant information and cut right to the essence or truth of a situation.

It is likely that people born on this day have at some point in their lives experienced some form of upheaval, trauma or setback. Whatever the nature of this was, they have taken it in their stride, learned from it and grown stronger. The positive side is that it has given them great confidence; even if they sometimes appear quiet on the outside, underneath one can sense an inner strength and brightness. They also have an astute understanding of others and how the world works; rarely, if ever, do they miss a trick. The downside is that they can sometimes appear cold and detached, and their bluntness or impatience with the weaknesses of others may come across as arrogance. Others may at times resent the imperious manner that these people possess, but more often than not people end up admiring their cleverness and ability to know exactly what to say, what to do and how to do it.

If they can learn to control their bossiness, their tremendous capacity to be realistic and intuitive, both in their assessment of others and their own abilities, makes them potentially great leaders. Around the age of thirty-four there is a turning point when their ambition and focus take center stage. It is particularly important at this point in their life that they become more conscious of their emotions, rather than masking them with a bossy or imperious manner or, in some cases, with emotional reserve and detachment.

When people born on this day are able to strike a balance between their inner and outer life, they really are capable of striking gold both personally and professionally, which is after all every true alchemist's dream.

On the dark side

Arrogance, blunt, detached

At your best

Realistic, intuitive, confidence

17 February

the birthday of
self discipline

Your greatest challenge is

to learn to let others in

The way forward is ...

to understand that success may earn the admiration of others but it will not necessarily win their love.

People born on February 17 often figure out early in their life that the key to success in life is discipline. They are determined, ambitious people with a clear idea of where they want to go and what they need to do to get there. These qualities, combined with their remarkable self-discipline, can give them the appearance of invincibility.

Although they may appear superhuman and extraordinary, others generally warm instantly to them, respecting their honesty and ability to be true to themselves and their beliefs. Underneath their tough exterior they really are sensitive souls who can be profoundly hurt by the careless words or actions of others. In fact, neglect or criticism may have been a feature of their early life, leading them to the realization that if they are to survive in the world they need to develop a tough exterior. Occasionally, they can make their defenses so strong that others find it impossible to break through. When this happens, they run the risk of becoming emotionally detached and inflexible in their approach to others.

People born on this day have a tunnel-vision approach to their goals and objectives, giving them the potential to rise to the top. They are the athletes who train relentlessly, the entrepreneurs who sacrifice everything for their shot at success, the artists or scientists who devote their lives to their art or research. The downside, however, is that anything that hinders their quest for fulfillment will be ignored; all too often this is personal relationships. They should make sure that their emotional happiness does not take a backseat to their professional, especially after the age of thirty-three when they often become even more determined and aggressive in their approach to life.

The incredible endurance, intelligence and stamina of people born on this day mean they are able to achieve a level of self-mastery and resulting satisfaction to which others can only aspire. Once they figure out what they are best at, there is nothing that can stop them achieving remarkable things with their life.

On the dark side

Isolated, inflexible, suspicious

At your best

Disciplined, determined, appealing

18 February

Your greatest challenge is

knowing when to stop

The way forward is ...

to understand that with all things there is a tipping point and, more often than not, less is more.

Whatever their age, people born on February 18 never grow old in their minds and hearts. With a charismatic energy about them, they never fail to brighten up their surroundings with their infectious optimism and enthusiasm for new ideas and projects, however far-fetched and impossible.

Those who are born on this day are also courageous risk-takers. They will always be the first to volunteer or put themselves forward, loving nothing better than to live life on the edge. There is of course a danger with this reckless approach to life; it can lead them into serious trouble and on more than one occasion it will do just that. They are never happier than when they are pushing things one degree harder, higher or faster, but they do need to ask themselves why they feel the need to live like this. More often than not deep-seated fears and insecurities are hidden behind their mask of indestructibility.

With their youthful spirit and the endearing vulnerabilities that go with it, these people don't really understand that other people will be drawn to their sunny optimism. They may even find that others look to them for leadership but they aren't always happy in that role as it hinders their freedom to experience and explore the wonders of the world. Although their life does sparkle with variety and adventure, there is a price to pay. One day they may find themselves looking at their life and wondering why they haven't got a sense of real achievement. It is important for them to learn to focus their energies rather than scattering them; fortunately, after the age of thirty-two they become more assertive and self-disciplined in their daily affairs.

As long as people born on this day avoid looking in the wrong direction for a sense of risk and adventure, and understand that showing off isn't the most fulfilling or grown-up way to gain supporters, they have the potential to win the admiration and respect of others, and most important of all a sense of pride in themselves and their achievements.

On the dark side

Reckless, immature, impatient

At your best

Youthful, dynamic, charismatic

PISCES

THE FISHES (FEBRUARY 19 – MARCH 20)

✳ **Element:** Water

✳ **Ruling planets:** Jupiter, the philosopher and
Neptune, the speculator

✳ **Symbol:** Two Fishes

✳ **Tarot card:** The Moon (intuition)

✳ **Number:** 7

✳ **Favorable colors:** Green, silver, violet

✳ **Key phrase:** I uncover hidden depths

People born under the sun sign Pisces are deeply concerned with the world of emotions, creativity, imagination and intuition. Their nature is to be dreamy, spiritual and romantic, and they can easily adjust to different environments. They can also, however, be over-emotional and too easily influenced by the feelings and moods of those around them.

Personality potential

The last sun sign and the last water sign, it's often the case that people born under the sun sign Pisces are the everyman and everywoman of the zodiac. There is a little bit of everyone in their personality and this is why they can so easily relate to and understand others. It also explains why they care so deeply about others and why they can often be found working in hospitals, day care centers, counseling services, prisons or anywhere where lost or hurt people, or the underdogs of society, can be found. Their compassion and unwillingness to judge marks them out as truly caring and sensitive individuals.

Pisceans are often generous to a fault with others, not just with those close to them but anyone who is genuinely in need. They rarely miss an opportunity to do some good. The logic underpinning their generosity is that—just as a school of fish is a community in which every member relies on every other member for survival—for Pisceans doing good for others is a mark of mutual respect and civilized interaction. And it's often the case that the greatest good fortune occurs for a Piscean when someone remembers and returns their help.

As well as being caring and generous, people born under this sun sign are also romantic dreamers with a vast imagination and highly intuitive resources. They are not unrealistic, however, in their approach to life. In fact, they have broad vision and the ability to see the bigger picture, while others struggle with the details. It's just that Pisceans don't want only to dream; they want to make life as beautiful as it is in their

dreams. Their ideas and plans are original and idealistic, and they will never hesitate to put themselves on the line to reach a new and wonderful experience.

Multitalented and able to adapt to a wide variety of different situations, these people have the intelligence and discipline to succeed in whatever they decide to put their energies. Part of the reason for their success is that they trust their feelings—and their feelings are almost always right. For Pisceans, feelings underpin everything in their life and the more they listen to their powerful intuition, the more harmonious and enriched their lives become.

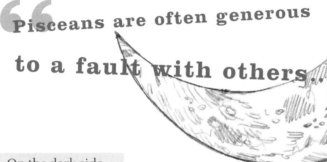

"Pisceans are often generous to a fault with others..."

On the dark side

Being so sensitive and open, it's relatively easy for Pisceans to lose themselves in someone else's problems or personality. Lacking confidence in themselves, they may take the softer option of living through and for someone else, rather than tackling their own issues and finding out who they are and what they want. Fading into someone else's life means that they put their own lives on hold, so it's vital for Pisceans to believe in themselves and discover their true potential.

Another negative personality trait for Pisceans is the ease with which they slip into self-pity or wronged-victim mode. Their sensitivity can make them incredibly vulnerable to rejection, criticism and personal slights. Their confidence is easily knocked off course and, instead of learning to get a handle on their insecurity, they may escape into a world of drugs, drink or dependency on anything that can numb their feelings. They can also be irritatingly indecisive. They have such a panoramic view of life and such awareness of all the different choices out there that they find it impossible to decide what they want to do and end up doing nothing instead. This can make them appear weak willed.

With their moods constantly shifting and changing, sometimes from one extreme to the other, people often have a hard time figuring out where they stand and may walk on egg shells around them for fear of upsetting them. In addition, because Pisceans hate upsetting others or making mistakes, they may resort to lying or manipulation to avoid having the finger of guilt pointed at them. Perhaps the most impressionable, and in some cases the most naïve and gullible sign of the zodiac, these people should also guard against attracting people into their life who don't have their best interests at heart. They can believe in almost anyone and anything but themselves—this lack of self-belief is something that can stop them from progressing in life and achieving the success and recognition they deserve.

Symbol

The symbol of Pisces is two fish pulling away from each other and it's a perfect expression of the broad vision—but also the tension—that often underpins the Piscean character. Swimming in opposite directions but tied together, Pisceans have a 360-degree view of the world around them but their nature is also vacillating, confusing and fluid.

Darkest secret

Pisceans may give the appearance of being gentle and easygoing but in reality they are people of extremes; they can either rise to the very top in life, or sink deep and drown. They may not fully realize or accept it, but work that improves the lot of humanity is an essential ingredient to help them rise to the top. This is because more than with any other sign, Pisceans have underused talents, so the key to their success is to recognize these talents and turn their dreams of a world of compassion and beauty into reality.

Love

Although Pisceans can at first be fairly hard to pin down, once a relationship is well established it's likely to be deep and lifelong.

Piscean love is so readily poured into a relationship that it can be overwhelming at times, but if they are able to take charge of their emotions they can bring something very special, romantic and magical to a relationship. They have a tendency to wear rose-colored spectacles and to put their partner on a pedestal, but fortunately they do have a clear view of reality that eventually helps them accept both the good and the not-so-good in a relationship. When it comes to the bedroom, people born under this sun sign tend to be more romantic and tender rather than passionate and earthy.

Sensitive and temperamental, Pisceans need a partner who is tolerant, calm, cheerful and stable to offset their whims, inconsistencies or outbursts. It also helps if their partner is creative and romantic like them, because someone with artistic leanings is likely to understand the constantly shifting moods of the Piscean.

Love matches:
Cancer, Scorpio and Capricorn

The Piscean man

Imagine your perfect man. The Piscean man can be that man. In fact, he can be anything you want him to be. This man is a romantic dreamer at heart and when he falls in love, he falls in deep—so deep that it can be hard to tell where you begin and he ends. The problem comes when you want a bit of independence and freedom in your relationship. The Piscean man struggles to take a step back. This isn't to say he is clingy, needy or the jealous type; it's just that he has the ability to identify with his partner's moods and emotions so much that any form of distance will trigger insecurities. He is also sensitive and easily hurt, and once he has merged with another person he will quite literally feel their pain and dream their dreams.

As well as encouraging the dreams of others, the Piscean man has plenty of dreams of his own; it's important that these dreams are never forgotten or trodden on. If he gets the chance to turn them into reality, his potential for success—not just emotionally and personally but financially and materially—is outstanding. He doesn't need many material possessions to feel fulfilled, but through making good use of his intuition and lucky opportunities he often ends up wealthy. He will need an incredible amount of encouragement along the way, however, and some people may find the sensitivity of the Piscean male alarming. That said, a relationship with him can not only be deeply rewarding; it can be creative, enchanting and mesmerizing. Even if he's prone to bouts of uncertainty and low self-esteem, his potential to succeed in life and love should never be underestimated. Sensitive he may be, but he's also a survivor with an uncanny ability to plunge into the unknown, somehow coming up with hidden treasures and a blueprint for a better tomorrow.

The Piscean woman

Charming, sensitive, compassionate, dreamy and with little desire to dominate in a relationship, women born under the sign of Pisces are never short of ardent admirers. Deliciously feminine and sophisticated, she can be soft and womanly. She has the ability to adapt to different situations and social settings effortlessly. Devoted to the well-being of others, her drive is to belong to a group or to a partner.

Although her fragility and vulnerability can be very appealing, this isn't to say that this woman is a soft touch. She is far stronger than she appears to be, and much more capable than

she knows; she will subtly get things organized exactly the way she wants them. When her feelings are hurt she can lash out with bitterness and disappointment just like anyone else. However, being critical or judgmental simply isn't in her nature. This woman is deeply compassionate and understanding. To help and to heal are her first instincts, but for all her understanding and compassion she can be frustratingly elusive. She hates giving direct answers and opinions and, even to those she knows really well, what she really feels and thinks remains as unfathomable as the depths of the sea.

There's always something untouchable and lonely about the Piscean woman, however many friends and loved ones she has in her life. It's almost as if she lives in lonely understanding of a truth that is simply too deep to express to others in words. Those who want to love or get close to this beautiful creature will have to get used to their elusive, otherworldly air, and her need to be constantly shifting, constantly moving.

Family

Piscean children often have a wisdom way beyond their years. It's important for parents to teach them the value of honesty because there may be a tendency to embellish or manipulate the truth to serve their own ends or to keep the peace. Extraordinarily imaginative, these children often excel in the arts or in anything where they can be creative. They should be encouraged to have interests that fire their imagination and make them put themselves forward in a positive way at as early an age as possible. Lack of self-confidence may be an issue, and they can easily lose their motivation when other children get better results or run faster than them. Parents need to help them understand that there will always be people who do things better, but that this should be regarded as an incentive to improve or do better next time, not as a sign of failure. Piscean children can become quite clingy and passive—and bullying by others may be an issue—so again nurturing self-confidence is vital.

The Piscean tendency to be dreamy and disorganized often manifests in their attitude toward schoolwork, and parents can help by encouraging their child to develop their powers of concentration. They also need help becoming more practical and tidy so that they don't grow up always being late for things. Too much television watching isn't advised as Piscean children are highly suggestible, and when they are growing up they need to discover their identity from their own interests not from what they see on the television or internet. If they show an interest in science it should be encouraged as they can excel in this field.

Piscean parents are devoted and loving, and will always put their children first and encourage them to develop to their full potential. They can, however, also make the mistake of being too easygoing. Vagueness about what is or is not acceptable can be frustrating for children who need firm guidelines to feel secure.

Career

Careers that are creative and artistic tend to suit Pisceans best, and they may be drawn toward the worlds of art, music, acting, dancing, photography, writing and designing clothes. Being so aware of the suffering of others, their drive to help others is strong so they may excel as counselors, therapists, teachers, nurses, psychiatrists, social workers, prison officers and doctors. Attracted to the mystical side of life, Pisceans might consider alternative therapies or the work of a priest, healer, astrologer or tarot card reader. Strong links to the sea might also suggest careers related to ships and fishing.

"Careers that are creative and artistic tend to suit pisceans best..."

Pisceans aren't typically very good in careers that require organizational skills and aren't natural choices for managerial roles because they prefer to work selflessly in the background. Having said that, they can step out from behind the scenes to successfully take the reigns of power if they feel the cause is worthy enough. Their dual nature may also mean that they are very good at holding down two jobs at the same time.

Health

Pisceans are excellent at caring for others but not so great when it comes to caring for themselves. Therefore it's important for them to pay due care and attention to their diet, health and lifestyle. They are also very sensitive to the atmosphere surrounding them, and can be easily affected by almost anything from personal criticism and bad weather to distressing stories on the evening news. This sensitivity can affect their appetite and their constitution, triggering headaches, weight loss or weight gain. If they can become more aware of just how much outside events affect their health, it will help them understand that many of the health problems they experience are in fact related to their emotional state.

Taking comfort in food and drink when they feel low is destructive and unhealthy, and Pisceans need to learn to distinguish between real hunger and emotional hunger. Keeping a mood and food diary will help them recognize what triggers their unhealthy eating habits and, once they know the trigger, they can take steps to avoid it. They should also try to eat in a peaceful, calm environment and really concentrate on their food.

Pisceans are particularly susceptible to nicotine so quitting smoking is advised because smoking will age their skin, give them bad breath and increase their risk of heart disease. Recreational drugs should also be avoided at all costs, for obvious reasons. Many Pisceans have a medicine cabinet full of

medications for almost every ailment under the sun, but unless medication has been prescribed by their doctor they should try to limit their use of over-the-counter medications unless absolutely necessary, and experiment with natural medicine instead.

Leisure time is extremely important for Pisceans because it's time when they can live their dreams, whether in practice or through books, classes and in their imagination. Hobbies and pastimes that might interest them include dance, creative writing, poetry and painting, and figure skating classes. Waterskiing and hang gliding, as well as visiting museums and historical sights, may also appeal.

Pisceans can get extremely wound up and tense about the injustices of the world, so regular relaxation is essential in the form of meditation, gentle, rhythmical exercise such as yoga and, if they are religious, prayer. Wearing, meditating on and surrounding themselves with the color purple will encourage them to look within, instead of without for a sense of purpose, identity and fulfillment.

Born between February 19 and February 29

Those born between these dates will often be highly idealistic but also at times inconsistent and impractical. Success and fulfillment tend to come later in life when there will be sudden gains in personal power and exciting opportunities to express their vision of life.

Born between March 1 and March 10

These Pisceans have exceptional artistic gifts and creative potential. They should avoid drugs and dependent behavior at all costs. The security of a loving home is important to them.

Born between March 11 and March 20

Compassionate service to the world is the destiny for people born between these dates. They must be free to live their lives on their own terms; if they are able to do so, not only will they be more secure within themselves, they will also bring great happiness to those lucky enough to come into contact with them.

Life lessons

Perhaps the biggest challenge for those born under the sign of Pisces is to learn to empathize with others without taking on their pain. It's vital that they learn to be more objective.

Pisceans tend to have a highly subjective view of the world around them. They do have tremendous sympathy and compassion for others, but they often end up giving too much of themselves. Not only does this make them vulnerable to hangers-on or co-dependents who take advantage of them, but all their personal energy is drained listening to and serving the needs of others. Being so malleable a sign, Pisceans can also be too dependent on the guidance of others; learning to set boundaries and to trust their own judgment is therefore crucial.

Pisceans are prone to escapism when the world around them becomes overwhelming. This is fine if they channel their sensitivity into creative or artistic endeavors, but disastrous if they seek refuge in drugs and addictive, dependent behavior. Creativity is their greatest strength but they do need to find ways to direct and ground this creativity in practical ways so that they don't waste their magnificent potential in daydreams that never materialize.

Another reason why Pisceans have a desire to escape is that they often find the routine and mundanity of daily life deadening. Paying bills, having a job, being on time and keeping a house tidy can be soul destroying for Pisceans, who prefer their lives to be spontaneous and free flowing. Their impracticality can, however, get them into a lot of trouble and result in missed opportunities. If they want to succeed they must learn to balance their ethereal nature with the necessities of daily life.

Since they have a bit of every sign of the zodiac in them, Pisceans can get help and inspiration with the task of grounding themselves from all the other signs of the zodiac. Virgos can encourage Pisceans to be more organized, tidy and efficient. Aquarians can encourage them to speak out and push the boundaries. Geminis and Librans can help them to be more intellectual and less emotional in their approach to life. Cancerians can encourage them to ask for help when they need it, and Taureans and Capricorns can help them become more grounded in and appreciative of the beauty of the material world. Scorpios can help them distinguish between genuine pleas for help and people who are using them, and Sagittarians, Arians and Leos can help them be more optimistic, fun loving and adventurous in their approach to life.

19 February

the birthday of

wonderlust

Your greatest challenge is

to finish what you started

The way forward is ...

to understand that your ability to share the load and finish what you started determines whether you will be labeled a leader or a loser.

There is only one way for people born February 19 to do things and that is their way. They value their independence above all else and don't like to be ordered around, particularly by their parents. They want to find their own way in life, even if that means making mistakes along the way. As a result, they often have a lust for travel, thriving on new situations and new people.

With their independent spirit and need to stamp their individuality on everything they undertake, these people can often be found at the cutting edge of their chosen field. Although they perform best alone, they can also make inspirational leaders or enthusiastic team players; those who work alongside them will find themselves surprised by the strength of their wholehearted commitment to success.

People born on this day quickly make a name for themselves wherever they go—and they tend to go to a lot of places. Their appetite for life and new situations is huge, and even when they appear to be settling down in a career or a relationship, their eye is always on the horizon, wondering what else might be out there for them. The danger with this inquisitive approach to life is that they might appear reckless at times or, at worst, selfish. They should learn that their go-it-alone approach to life can prevent them connecting with the needs of others. At around the age of thirty-one their ambition becomes more apparent and they may start new projects or pioneer new ideas. It is particularly important for them at this stage in life and beyond not to scatter their energies selfishly.

The life path of people born on this day will always be littered with opportunities because they have a knack of knowing where to find them. Along the way their fiercely individual approach to life may encounter setbacks or rejections; but they never let these disillusion them. In their mind and their life, the only way is their way and that way is always up.

On the dark side

Indecisive, rash, selfish

At your best

Inspiring, wholehearted, independent

20 February

Your greatest challenge is

learning to say no

The way forward is ...

to understand that only after you give to yourself can you give to others. If you neglect yourself, you can't be a real help to others.

People born on February 20 are often thoughtful and receptive personalities, with the ability to immediately tune into the moods of those around them, adjusting their reactions instantly. Highly ambitious, they are sure to stand out in their career, at home, or on the social scene. They have an appealing personality and an easy charm, but it's impossible to dismiss them as superficial because behind their looks and charm there is always great intelligence.

People with a February 20 birthday have a great deal of compassion, instinctively dealing with anyone—whatever their background or social status—with great understanding and warmth. In some cases they can become over-sensitive and impressionable, unable to separate their own emotions from the emotions of other people. This is because they identify so much with the viewpoint of others that they risk losing their own perspective in the process. It is vitally important for them to learn to protect themselves from over-identification. Before the age of thirty, this tendency to merge completely with other people is emphasized, but after the age of thirty they become more assertive, confident and self-protective.

There is a danger when people born on this day do become more aware and confident of their ability to instinctively relate to others that they can misuse it. It is important therefore for them to learn not to compromise themselves or take advantage of others in the single-minded pursuit of their goals.

Those people born on this day who remain true to their principles and who learn to make their receptivity work for and not against them have remarkable potential to make a difference and to be highly valued by others. They are rarely happy to sit on the sidelines and desperately want to make their mark; although they have all the drive, intelligence and charisma they need to climb right to the top, what they don't often realize is that simply being themselves already makes a huge difference; this is because when they are around, people just feel better about themselves.

On the dark side

Indecisive, hyper-sensitive, impressionable

At your best

Intelligent, appealing, intuitive

21 February

the dominating presence

Your greatest challenge is

to take on board the advice of others

The way forward is ...

to understand that although your strength is to take your place at the helm, great leaders seek the advice of others.

People born on February 21 have a creative, individual mind and a dominating presence. They feel most comfortable when taking the lead and least comfortable when required to follow. Their fierce independence may be a result of a tough childhood where rules, regulations or expectations often took precedence over real intimacy.

People born on this day may spend many years trying out various occupations or roles, often feeling that they don't quite fit in and occasionally reacting childishly as a form of rebellion. It is only when they understand that the key to their success is to be themselves and to lead and inspire others with their forceful presence that they truly come into their own. Fortunately, around the age of twenty-nine they tend to become more assertive and adventurous, and begin to enjoy greater self-awareness.

Although they may have developed a tough outer shell to protect them from the outside world, those who know them well will know that they can also be extremely sensitive, even shy. This sensitivity can in part explain their need to push themselves forward, as they may have suffered disappointments at the hands of others. It is important that they learn to be true to themselves—it is also important that they do not become too aggressive or cynical in the process, for their emotions lie at the center of their being and it is their sensitivity that can give them sudden flashes of inspiration.

People born on this day have great dreams, and once they learn to listen to their hearts as well as their heads and to respect the ideas of others there is little that can prevent them getting exactly what they want out of life. Wherever they go, others tend to regard them as a tower of strength and will often look to them for motivation and inspiration. This is because when they have settled on a chosen course they are a shining example of how it is possible to rise above challenges and criticism by respecting your own judgment.

On the dark side

Immature, detached, inflexible

At your best

Creative, influential, honest

22 February

the birthday of
the investigator

Your
greatest
challenge is

to be less self-
critical

*The way
forward is ...*

to understand
that perfection
is an impossible
ideal; our failures
sometimes
propel us toward
success and our
vulnerabilities
bring others
closer to us.

People born on February 22 love nothing better than a good mystery. They are born problem solvers with an inquisitive, intuitive mind and a natural talent for unearthing the truth.

The chances are people born on this day don't have a conventional career or if they do their hobbies or interests reflect their eclectic tastes. They may have many different ideas about their life path, trying to do opposing things at once; this can confuse and frustrate others while also fascinating them. There is always method in the "madness" of these dynamic people. They believe that people are defined not by what they do but by how they do it. Whatever activity they pursue, one thing remains paramount: they can indulge their passion for investigation and problem solving.

Although these people are particularly good at uncovering information and proposing a solution, one area of their life is often neglected—their own inner life. Because they tend to be self-reliant individuals, they often expect others to be the same. They deny themselves emotional security by not sharing their anxieties with those closest to them. They also have rather high standards; when others don't live up to these they can become overly critical and pessimistic. They should learn to open up to others, and be more understanding of those who can't meet their high standards, including themselves. They can be extremely self-critical if they don't find an answer immediately, and will benefit from a more compassionate approach to themselves and others.

The tendency of these people to experiment with lots of different directions is highlighted between the ages of twenty-eight and fifty-seven. After the age of fifty-seven they may focus their energies in one direction. But whatever age they are and whatever goal they are currently choosing to focus on, one thing is sure. It will always be a fascinating one that may take them a step closer to their ultimate goal of making their own life—and the lives of others—a little less complicated and a whole lot more truthful.

On the dark side

Detached,
over-critical, pessimistic

At your best

Dynamic, problem
solving, articulate

23 February

the birthday of
the capable front runner

Your greatest challenge is

to overcome any shyness

The way forward is ...

simply to pretend you are confident. The more you pretend, the easier it will be to slip into that role naturally.

People born on February 23 have an optimistic, positive, can-do approach to life, and this is the key to their success. They are quietly rather than openly confident, believing that their accomplishments will speak for themselves. Because they aren't flashy, pretentious or showy in any way, other people tend to be drawn to them.

February 23 people take great care in every aspect of their lives and have an analytical approach to problems, but they most certainly aren't ponderous in their approach. They can be incredibly efficient, capable of delivering quality results for any task that they undertake. They often find great joy in the work itself rather than the reward. They believe that, having weighed up the alternatives, they are the best person for the job, with the best approach to it. The confident certainty they project can appear uncompromising but it is also infectious. More often than not, others believe exactly what they say and put enormous trust in them.

Another strength of people born on this day is their power of self-expression. Not only are they extremely articulate, they are also excellent listeners, an unusual combination that distinguishes them from other great speakers. They often find themselves in the position of confidant, this can sometimes give them an unfair advantage; they should beware of becoming manipulative when things aren't going their way. They should use their verbal skills and their empathy for others positively, especially between the ages of twenty-seven and fifty-six, when they become more confident and ambitious, and are likely to start many new ventures.

Above all, these people pride themselves on being the best person for the job. They will devote much effort to making everything in their lives, including themselves, the very best that it can be, and as a result it often is. As long as they are able to accept that life isn't—and wasn't meant to be—perfect, these capable front runners have the potential to earn great respect and affection from all those who cross their path.

On the dark side

Manipulative, cautious, uncompromising

At your best

Capable, self-starting, articulate

24 February

the birthday of
the romantic bard

Your greatest challenge is

learning to assert yourself

The way forward is ...

to take charge of your life, say no when you need to, express your true feelings and don't let others treat you like a doormat.

People born on February 24 have an intuitive, generous and loving spirit that makes them a much-sought-after friend, acquaintance or partner. Highly romantic, they sometimes see the world through the eyes of a poet blinded by the power of love. Intimacy is extremely important to them—without it they can wither and pine away like the hero or heroine in a romantic novel.

Those born on this day are highly sensitive to their environment and they are constantly tuning into the moods of others and the situations going on around them. This makes them good peacemakers and valuable members of a team or family, as they can often spot trouble or find ways to resolve a situation without offending anyone. The danger lies when they concentrate on the emotional needs of others rather than on their own. It is vital for them to set boundaries in their interpersonal relationships. This won't be easy for them, and they may even bend the truth if they think it will avoid an argument. In the long run, this kind of evasive and dishonest behavior can make them feel anxious and uncertain. Fortunately, between the ages of twenty-six and fifty-six there are opportunities for them to develop their assertiveness and to be more straightforward in their relationships. Then, after the age of fifty-six, they become even steadier and more mature.

The longing for intimacy or emotional connection possessed by these people always rules their life in some way. They may have tried to suppress emotional traumas in the past, but, whatever their background or experience, these will somehow manifest themselves, perhaps in a quest for the perfect partner or in a passionate devotion to a cause.

People born on this day have a desire to use their energies selflessly on behalf of others. Once they have learned that love isn't just about pain, but also about joy, and that intimacy is not just about sacrificing and giving, but also about receiving and gaining, they will discover within themselves the tenacity and vision to achieve just about anything.

On the dark side

Needy, moody, passive

At your best

Loving, generous, altruistic

25 February

the birthday of the guru

Your
greatest
challenge is

to think less and
do more

*The way
forward is ...*

to understand
that although
there is a place for
planning and
strategy, to make a
real impact you
have to put
your money where
your mouth is.

Although people born on February 25 have a high degree of self-confidence and are fiercely individualistic, they often believe that the collective is more important than the personal. They can be radical in their desire to right social wrongs, being selfless in the pursuit of their goals. There is a touch of the guru about them, in that they desire not only to master their own destiny but to help others master theirs.

People born on this day never try to be anything by themselves. They have a simple, unaffected style that can cross boundaries, helping them relate to people from all walks of life. Everyone they meet is impressed by their honesty, optimism and desire to make a difference. As a result, they are good team players, preferring to take the role of advisor or guru rather than leader. They are the consultants with the winning formula, the brilliant teachers guiding and inspiring the next generation, the coaches who dedicate themselves to the welfare of the team, the directors with their eye on what the camera and the world see.

These people are often found working their magic on the sidelines; nothing gives them more satisfaction than engineering success for others. They can come across as silent and detached, but to those who know them well they are capable of making the most profound and helpful observations. They should beware, however, that they do not turn their greatest strengths into weaknesses by becoming so lost in the world of thought that they become secretive, negative and out of touch with reality. Fortunately, between the ages of twenty-five and fifty-four they become more self-assertive, experiencing an occasional need to step from the shadows onto center stage. Then, after the age of fifty-four, they seek more calm and steadiness in their lives.

Above all, February 25 individuals have a team-player mentality, a profound sense of justice and a desire to help the worthy win. This is a powerful combination that can inspire others to transform difficult circumstances into something better.

On the dark side

Obsessed,
unrealistic, secretive

At your best

Intense, spiritual,
ambitious

26 February

the birthday of
the wise soul

Your greatest challenge is

to take yourself a little less seriously

The way forward is ...

to understand that humor, when used positively, can be a powerful force for good.

People born on February 26 may often be described by others as old souls because they seem comfortable in their own skin. They often have great insight into how the world works and what the motivations of other people are.

When the great insight of these people is combined with their somewhat impersonal and detached persona, this can make others stand back in awe. In fact, they have quite a hypnotic power over others; people tend to do what they say or follow their example. It is important for them that they don't abuse this power—fortunately they rarely do as they also have a powerful sense of integrity and social justice. They like to find something to like in everybody and in every situation, and their unfailing optimism is truly enlightening.

One danger for people born on this day is a tendency to preach and rant, or be rigid or harsh in their opinions. They will often be unaware when they are showing this side of their personality, which is emphasized between the ages of twenty-four to fifty-four. During these years they should surround themselves with close friends or loved ones who can warn them when they are heading off track. Fortunately, they respond extremely well to constructive criticism, possessing the ability to change their ways. If someone reaches out to them emotionally and opens their heart, they will more often than not transform themselves into a more fully rounded human being.

Often blessed with great wisdom, their ability to arouse and inspire others will help them achieve worldly success. Although they do enjoy social recognition, part of them feels more comfortable as an outsider looking in. They will sometimes feel an urge to be alone with their thoughts or to sacrifice themselves to a higher cause. Being wise souls, however, they will have also learned the importance of emotional connection with others, so when they do feel the need to withdraw it will not be to isolate themselves but simply to recharge before they take the next step forward.

On the dark side

Dogmatic, moody, harsh

At your best

Insightful, hypnotic, honest

27 February

the birthday of

hypnotic allure

Your greatest challenge is

to learn to take charge of your emotions in your personal life

The way forward is ...

to understand that you are in charge of your emotions; they will not take you over unless you allow them to.

People born on February 27 have the ability to turn heads and win hearts wherever they go. There is a magnetic and striking intensity about them that can hold others spellbound.

These people like to be in the limelight, and sooner or later they will be. Others admire them, not just for their hypnotic personality but because they stride confidently and with purpose through life, achieving their goals with ease and grace. They have a mind forever open to the new but they are also able to analyze in depth. By devoting a great deal of their energy to understanding how things work, their knowledge base increases steadily until it becomes so solid that it can see them through from one ambitious project to the next, taking them to the very top. There is one area of their lives, however, unlikely to be envied by others: their personal lives.

Although this may appear contradictory—given their cool and charismatic image—February 27 people often have a chaotic emotional life, with broken relationships littered around them. The reason is that they have a deeply emotional nature; although they have learned to control it when it comes to impersonal relationships, their own personal relationships are threatened by their impulse to follow their heart. It is extremely important for people born on this day to apply discipline to personal relationships and to stop making unreasonable, childish demands on others, especially between the ages of twenty-three and fifty-two when they will become even more active and adventurous. If self-discipline isn't learned during this period, the result could be emotional and personal chaos.

At their worst, people born on this day can be social-climbing attention seekers. At their best, however, they are lovable and spontaneous creatures who can both intoxicate and inspire others with their presence. They may often be described as a little crazy by those who know them, but once they invest their energy into a worthwhile cause they can achieve great things and enjoy the limelight they seem destined for.

On the dark side

Confused, highly strung, social climber

At your best

Magnetic, creative, versatile

84

28 February

Your greatest challenge is

learning to rein in your impulses

The way forward is ...

to understand that you can replace addictions with preferences.

People born on February 28 have a warm glow about them and can light up their lives of others with their energy and originality. They love to be center stage and are often in just that spot at social gatherings. Natural performers, they are never short of admirers and are blessed with the ability to charm just about anyone they meet.

Articulate and entertaining, people born on this day will go out of their way to get a laugh or reaction from others, even if this involves exaggerating the truth. They thrive on being noticed, but attention seeking isn't what drives them. Their motivation is a thirst for adventure and they will enthusiastically follow wherever their impulses direct them. Underlying their restlessness, however, is a deep-seated fear of standing still; the fear of it will drive them toward sensation-seeking and sometimes self-destructive behavior.

They won't ever lose the glint in their eye, but underneath their bravado they do secretly long to find a real purpose and achieve lasting success in the eyes of the world. This won't be possible until they discover that self-esteem is not created by thrill-seeking but by being the person they are. It is important for these people to learn to be more comfortable with being rather than doing, because until they can reach this level of awareness their life may hurtle chaotically from one situation to another and one person to another. They should learn to cultivate an inner calmness between the ages of twenty-two and fifty-one, when there is an emphasis in their life on new directions and ventures.

Because people born on this day live in such a vibrant and wholehearted way, they will experience life more intensely than others. They do, however, need to rein in their compulsion to indulge their every whim and learn greater self-control. They should never suppress their optimism and curiosity, but if they can just try to look before they leap, they can become far more than original charmers; they can become life's pioneers, boldly going where none have gone before.

On the dark side

Thoughtless, melodramatic, reckless

At your best

Charming, original, vibrant

29 February

the birthday of
wistful vivacity

Your greatest challenge is

to believe in yourself

The way forward is ...

to stop comparing yourself with other people and to remind yourself that you are a special and unique person.

In their early years people born on this day may find it hard to be taken seriously. They may also sense something different about themselves, since they only celebrate a real birthday every four years.

Those born on this unusual day are likable and diplomatic, the latter skill perhaps learned early in life when they had to compromise over the date of their birthday. They have great social skills and the ability to relate to just about anyone. In addition, they have an ethereal quality that makes them appear less resilient than they really are. Although others may dismiss them as dreamers or social butterflies, they are in fact surprisingly tough and ambitious.

They may feel driven to aggressively validate their self-perceived differences by working harder to achieve their goals—a strategy that they may take to self-destructive extremes, especially between the ages of twenty-one and fifty-one, during which there is an emphasis on being assertive and ambitious. They should understand that over-promoting themselves is more likely to alienate than impress others.

People born on this day often have great insight into what makes people tick but others are unlikely to understand what motivates them, although their motivation is simple. They simply want to fit in, to feel needed and—above all—to feel no different from everyone else. Thus they tend to be very caring and nurturing toward the problems of others and sincere in their desire to help in times of crisis. However, being rather sensitive, if their efforts do not receive the response or gratitude they expect, they can withdraw into immature or indulgent behavior.

They do have a tendency to over-compensate for their feelings of difference and they should try to avoid extremes of behavior. Once they realize their powerful intuition and youthful vivacity are strengths not weaknesses, these special individuals will find that others not only accept but highly value their unique qualities.

On the dark side

Immature, unfocused, moody

At your best

Youthful, intuitive, offbeat

1 March

the birthday of
the practical visionary

Your greatest challenge is

learning to cope with feelings of worry and anxiety

The way forward is ...

to imagine yourself being calm and to bring that image to mind every time you feel anxious or fearful.

People born on March 1 have a talent for lifting the moods of others and for transforming concepts or thoughts into solid achievements. They tend to have an eye for beauty, seeing the world with the vision of an artist. However, they can also be extremely practical and level-headed; anyone who dismisses them as lightweights will be making a big mistake.

When the strong will-power of people born on this day is focused, they can accomplish miracles through their determination and conviction. Unfortunately, despite this incredible potential to succeed, they are also prone to panic, negative thinking and lack of confidence. When in a state of anxiety, they are easily influenced and likely to attract people who will take advantage of their talents. It is important for them to build up their self-esteem so they can steer their life in the right direction instead of others jumping into the driving seat.

Until the age of nineteen it is likely that their plans for the future will be fairly vague or constantly shifting; this is the period when they are at their most vulnerable to negative influences or causes that aren't worthy of them. Fortunately, between the ages of twenty and forty-nine they enter a phase when they became more assertive and self-assured, if a little controlling, selfish or impatient when things aren't going their way. After the age of fifty they will feel a need to establish themselves and to devote themselves either to their loved ones or to a variety of humanitarian causes. In fact, throughout their lives they often feel a deep concern for the well-being of others, although it may not be until later in life that they inject practicality into those concerns and get going with them.

Despite their tendency to self-doubt, these people have great intelligence, charisma and originality. Once they learn to take responsibility for their decisions, they often find themselves in the position of a leader making a difference and paving the way for others less fortunate through the power of their personality.

On the dark side

Controlling, selfish, impatient

At your best

Refined, artistic, ambitious

87

2 March

the birthday of personal vision

Your greatest challenge is

dealing with confrontation

The way forward is...

to be more relaxed and pragmatic in your approach and not to shy away from conflict; conflict is inevitable, but it can encourage creativity, change and progress.

People born on March 2 have strong convictions and their own personal vision which they will pursue with undying loyalty, regardless of the opinions of others or the changing climate around them. They are truly independent thinkers with the ability to inspire and occasionally alarm others with their intensity.

Once those born on this day have committed to an ideal or decided on a course of action, they will hold fast to it. They can occasionally take this to an extreme, blocking out everything and everyone else. Although others have much to learn from their dedication, they can have a one-track mind and a tendency to deny themselves opportunities that could potentially enrich their work. It is important for these people to make sure that their personal convictions neither exclude the possibility of change nor alienate them from the closeness and security of personal relationships. They need to be especially careful of this tendency between the ages of eighteen and forty-eight, during which period there is an emphasis on assertiveness and activity, and their personal vision is most likely to dominate their lives.

The personal vision March 2 people dedicate themselves to so passionately is often one that tries to make positive changes to their world or environment. This is challenge enough, but by far the greatest test for these devoted souls is that of balancing their personal needs with the needs of the world. If they are unable to find that sense of balance, the people most likely to suffer are those closest to them. They are the politicians or the campaigners devoted to their party who are never there for their loved ones; the artists or writers absorbed in their work but neglectful of their family, especially their children. If, however, people born on this day find a way to bring harmony both to their own personal lives and to the wider world, their unwavering dedication to their personal vision gives them the potential to be powerful and potent forces for positive change and progress.

On the dark side

Inflexible, escapist, needy

At your best

Loyal, trusting, purposeful

3 March

the birthday of
proposal

Your greatest challenge is

building your self-esteem

The way forward is ...

to write a success list that includes everything that is meaningful to you personally. Keep adding to the list every day.

People born on March 3 may feel from an early age that they were destined for something great. Intelligent, determined and versatile, there is no question that they have great potential. The question is more about where to begin; they may find themselves taken up with plans and proposals for the best step forward.

Extremely pragmatic without being pessimistic, people born on this day feel the need to prepare carefully. They are quick to recognize any defects and potential problems in their preparation, and although they are aware of the bigger picture they have an eye for detail and nothing escapes their attention. In fact, they love the preparation stage, often enjoying it more than the actual presentation or execution of a project. This approach has both its upsides and downsides. The upside is that they are fully focused on the present. The downside is that they can get bogged down in details and planning and lose momentum, direction and spontaneity.

It is important for them to work on their decision-making skills and to stop holding themselves and others back with an endless succession of "what ifs." Fortunately, between the ages eighteen and forty-seven there is an emphasis on assertiveness, activity and courage. After the age of forty-eight they may feel an increased need for calm and stability.

It is probably better for these people to make a decision about which course they want to pursue in life and stick to it. If they remain uncommitted or in the planning stage for much of their life, they need to examine why they fear commitment or execution. If fear of failure holds them back, they need to learn that it is who they are and not what they do that is a mark of success. And those March 3 individuals who do settle on a course need to be careful that they don't get so lost in their activities that they lose touch with who they are because who they are is a remarkable person with the ability to achieve great things.

On the dark side

Moody, compulsive, lazy

At your best

Generous, intelligent, determined

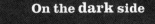

4 March

the birthday of
inspired aloneness

Your greatest challenge is

learning to express your feelings

The way forward is ...

to understand that if you don't say what you mean or ask for what you want, people won't understand you or be able to help you.

People born on March 4 tend to come across as self-contained individuals with an ingenuity that does not require outside stimulation and a creativity that is self-generated. They are able to work and, if need be, live alone. It's not that they are antisocial or seek to cut themselves off from the outside world; it's just that striking out alone is a dominant trend in their lives, often leading to success.

For people born on this day, being alone isn't scary; it's a liberating experience and an opportunity for them to concentrate and be productive. Extremely comfortable with themselves, they often feel confined or trapped by social pressure and conformity. When they are alone they feel free rather than isolated; even when given the option to interact more, they will often choose to go it alone. This can come across as shyness or fear of involvement, but this misses the point about these gentle people.

Although they hate confrontation and will withdraw at signs of conflict, they aren't shy or passive but aware that they are most productive when living and working within guidelines set by themselves. They have an innovative and ingenious mind that works best when left alone and an ability to explore concepts with tenacity. Between the ages of seventeen and forty-six there is an emphasis on daring new ventures and, along with this, many opportunities for them to develop their assertiveness; these people need to ensure that others don't take all the credit.

The big danger for these people is that they indulge their natural tendency for self-involvement so much that they cut themselves off from reality, and from the joys and rewards of close personal relationships. It's unfortunate if this happens, as they do love to share the results or benefits of their work with others, despite their natural reserve. They also have a great empathy for others, and when they choose to reveal or share their talents to the outside world they have the potential to influence, intrigue and inspire others with their vision.

On the dark side

Impersonal,
self-involved, shy

At your best

Tenacious, independent,
ingenious

5 March

the birthday of
agony and ecstasy

Your greatest challenge is

staying calm and in control when things don't go your way

The way forward is ...

to put yourself and not your emotions in the driving seat of your life.

On the surface people born on March 5 are smooth and charming individuals with the gift of the gab, but troubled waters lie below. Their easy style conceals a complex personality that is as fascinating as it is frustrating.

The emotional current that flows beneath the light-hearted exterior of people born on this day is extraordinarily powerful. One moment they're entertaining and empathetic companions who can put everyone about them at their ease with their sharp wit and incisive mind. The next moment, however, when their emotional equilibrium is unbalanced, they can dissolve into insecurity, negativity and fits of temper. Given the instability of their emotional life, it is very important for these people to learn to manage their emotions, especially between the ages of sixteen and forty-five when they become more aggressive, assertive and determined to make their mark. After the age of forty-seven there is another turning point which sees them slow down a little, searching for stability in all areas of their lives.

Underneath the sociable and confident façade of people born on this day is a highly sensitive soul that desperately needs regular time out in quiet and solitary reflection. Inside they may have many hidden fears and insecurities to deal with; if they don't allow themselves time to acknowledge these demons, they are the mercy of their impulses and there is no telling in what direction they will go. People born on this day may worry that becoming more balanced and stable will result in a loss of intensity or edge, but they need to understand that cultivating personal will-power and self-control will not lessen but strengthen their creativity and the impact they have on others.

With their emotional honesty, March 5 people have the ability to bring out both the best and the worst in themselves and others. If they can learn to find balance and use their power over others responsibly, the world will always be a brighter place with these impulsive individuals around.

On the dark side

Insecure, unreliable, negative

At your best

Entertaining, intelligent, witty

6 March

the birthday of

refinement

Your greatest challenge is

to avoid searching for perfection

The way forward is ...

to understand that in life there are no exact measurements for what is right because we are not statistics and geometry.

People born on March 6 are at their happiest when they are searching for or surrounded by beauty. They find themselves pulled irresistibly toward ideals of loveliness, perfection and refinement that appeal to their senses and, although they are unlikely to realize it, they also have a strange beauty of their own.

They have the gift of being able to open the eyes of others to the beauty of the world around them and to teach them to appreciate every nuance of nature. They really can see eternity in a grain of sand, and the childlike wonder that they project is one of their most endearing qualities. There is a danger, however, that in their idealization of everything and everyone around them they can lose touch with what or who is actually there. Others may feel that they are more in love with the idea of romance and beauty than with the reality. And when reality does finally bite and their initial intensity fades, disenchantment may be the cruel result.

It is important for people born on this day to learn to be a little more objective in their assessment of situations and people, especially between the ages of fifteen and forty-four, during which they are likely to become more active and assertive but also more vulnerable to disillusionment. Fortunately, after the age of forty-five they often become more emotionally steady and practical.

Above all, these people are motivated by a desire to experience and be uplifted by the ideal of true beauty. Much of their lives will be devoted to a never-ending quest to translate this perfect ideal into reality. Others may see this as pleasure seeking or superficiality, but there is real depth and originality under their often charming and sensuous exterior. They do need to learn to develop a more realistic and less demanding attitude, accepting that their lofty standards may not always be attained. In their search for true excellence, however, they are a constant source of energy, inspiration and beauty for all those who cross their path.

On the dark side

Naïve, lazy, confused

At your best

Youthful, refined, sensual

7 March

the birthday of

extraordinary vision

Your greatest challenge is

learning to assert yourself

The way forward is ...

to be as encouraging and as positive as you can be when trying to get a point across. Be critical of people's ideas, not people themselves.

Despite their ability to instantly establish rapport with anyone they meet, people born on March 7 often have an otherworldly quality about them. This is because they have a tendency to live in an abstract world of thoughts and ideals produced by their own vivid imagination.

People born on this day possess the gift of extraordinary vision and their minds love to roam far and wide. Typically, they can manifest these ideas in practical form by analyzing situations, experiences and people. Along the way, they will do their best to ensure that they get the support of colleagues, friends and loved ones, taking great care to make sure everyone feels involved. At work they never forget a name or a personal detail about their colleagues; at home they will ensure everyone can voice their opinions.

Even though they are often surrounded by friends and admirers, there is a haunting loneliness about these people; because they dislike conflict, they tend to withdraw when there is heated discussion or criticism of their methods. In their self-imposed isolation, they may also become insecure about themselves and their abilities, and secretive and suspicious of others. People born on this day should find other ways to cope when they feel under pressure; although they are unlikely to become close to large numbers of people, they should make sure they have the love and support of their family and/or a few good friends. Up to the age of forty-three they are active and assertive, a positive sign for them with their natural tendency to withdraw. After the age of forty-four there is an emphasis on greater emotional and financial stability.

Because they are so receptive to all kinds of intellectual pursuits, these people may take a while to settle on their chosen aim. However, once they are able to focus their vision and energy in a worthwhile direction, their intelligent and sensitive approach assures success. A part of them will always remain untouchable but this doesn't make them appear or feel lonely—it just adds to their magic.

On the dark side

Detached, isolated, secretive

At your best

Thoughtful, generous, intelligent

8 March

the uncompromising rebel

**Your
greatest
challenge is**

to retain your
independence
without alienating
others in the
process

*The way
forward is ...*

to understand that
compromise is the
glue that holds
society together
and sometimes
the greater good
outweighs
individual need.

People born on March 8 are fiercely uncompromising spirits. They may sometimes hide their non-conformity behind an agreeable exterior but anyone who knows them well will know that deep down they are independent thinkers filled with the courage of their convictions.

These people resent being told what to do, probably demonstrating their feisty nature from an early age, much to the frustration of their parents. They often have an innate distrust and in some cases a complete lack of respect for authority; they passionately believe that everybody deserves the right to think for themselves. Their somewhat subversive approach to life can wear others out but it is not usually prompted by a need to be difficult for the sake of it. More often than not their rebellion is prompted by an ability to easily spot the flaws or weaknesses in a situation that has been previously unchallenged and to identify a better approach. In fact, these people are outstanding lateral thinkers with great empathy toward others, and this marks them out as potentially great reformers in whatever field they choose to specialize.

March 8 people have a great zest for life and a need for challenge and variety. They often feel the need to strike out or break away, not just from their background, but from the current situation they are in. They are capable of commitment and loyalty, however, and may even stay in the same field for many years, but sooner or later the aggressive and uncompromising aspect of their personality demands change and progress. Their uncompromising tendencies tend to be emphasized before the age of forty-two and in this period their lives are likely to be stormy. Then, after the age of forty-three, there is a turning point which suggests a need for more emotional and financial stability.

Although these people have a knack of alienating people with their forceful opinions, they are also blessed with considerable charm; they should understand the hypnotic, addictive power they can have over people and use it wisely.

On the dark side

Disrespectful,
irresponsible, demanding

At your best

Independent,
honest, magnetic

9 March

the birthday of

the bold explorer

Your greatest challenge is

coping with the needs of others

The way forward is ...

to understand that some people need more help than others to stand on their own two feet.

People born on March 9 are innovative explorers who are always willing to take risks and venture boldly into the unknown or to experiment with new ideas and concepts. Their courageous style is often admired by others and, because they are so independent, their lives are often packed with excitement and suspense.

Despite their colorful and independent approach to life these people can be over-sensitive to the opinions of others, easily getting hurt when criticized. With a tendency to take things personally, it is important for them to learn to calm down between the ages of fourteen and forty-one, a period when their lives are full of aggression, assertiveness and new ventures. After the age of forty-two they often have a need for greater calm and emotional steadiness.

People born on this day are often bursting with energy and enthusiasm, moving so fast it can wear themselves and others out. They can quite easily flit from one job or relationship to another, as they love variety and challenge. Although others may regard them as reckless, they are in fact far less impulsive than they appear. From an early age they have learned to trust themselves because their intuition frequently leads them in the right direction. They have an ability to see the world from an unusual viewpoint and for this reason they make great advisors and friends, upon whom people can become dependent. The dependency of others, however, can cause feelings of frustration in them when others can't or won't stand on their own two feet.

A part of people born on this day always longs to fly away but, once they have found a way to balance their need for responsibility with their need to rush headlong into uncharted lands, they have the perception, charisma and enthusiasm to push forward social reforms. Although capable of great commitment once they have found a cause they believe in, they should make sure that they never lose touch of the key to their personality and success—their adventurous and curious spirit.

On the dark side

Reckless, subjective, nervous

At your best

Bold, innovative, intuitive

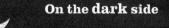

10 March

the birthday of

sensitivity

Your greatest challenge is

building your self-esteem

The way forward is ...

to understand that just because you think something about yourself does not mean it is true.

People born on March 10 have a fragile, vulnerable quality about them however successful they may appear on the world's stage. This is because a part of them is always searching for greater self-understanding or knowledge. Although they can be highly driven and energetic individuals, it is the inner world of ideals that defines and occupies people born on March 10. They are also extremely empathetic toward others, particularly the underdog or those less fortunate.

Because they are constantly aware of their own feelings and tuned into the feelings of those around them, these highly sensitive people tend to experience life intensely and deeply. They have the capacity to show tremendous kindness and love toward others, but they do need to be careful that they don't become self-sacrificing, overprotective and jealous in the process.

Although they are highly perceptive and insightful in their relationships, they can also get deeply hurt by the words or actions of others. Instead of facing their pain when they are wounded, they are more likely to withdraw into their own private world of torment. It's important for these people to find ways to balance their sensitivity with their need to make a difference in the world. Fortunately, before the age of forty there is an emphasis in their life on assertiveness and a desire to be more active in the world. This can help them express themselves more outwardly. After the age of forty-one they often gravitate toward greater material and emotional stability, and this will help them stave off uncertainty and vulnerability.

Preoccupied with their inner conflicts, there is always a danger for these people to become self-involved; but, if they can learn not to use their sensitivity as a way of escaping responsibility and confrontation, the emphasis they place on internal rather than external fulfillment marks them out as very special people. Caring, contemplative and visionary, they will direct their intelligent and original thoughts toward the common good and, by so doing, positively influence and inspire all those who encounter them.

On the dark side

Vulnerable, over-protective, jealous

At your best

Kind, empathetic, energetic

11 March

the birthday of
the magician

Your greatest challenge is

to learn to relax the need to control everyone and everything

The way forward is ...

to understand that however important you are, no one, including yourself, is indispensable.

Individuals born on March 11 are progressive individuals with one foot lightly placed in the present and another firmly placed in the future. The key to their success is their intuition. They use this not in a dreamy but in a highly productive way to increase their chances of success. Magician-like, they have learned to harness its power to achieve their goals.

The keen mind and visionary ability of these people gives them an uncanny knack of seeking out opportunities and people that will help them progress. They always seem to be one step ahead and, if they are not the source of a trend, they will use their imagination and energy to work with that trend or, better still, move beyond it. The upside of all this is that they are often right at the cutting edge; the downside is that they can lapse into selfish or manipulative behavior if it will help them get what they want.

Although they do possess strong ambition and a powerful influence over others, their goals are generally personal rather than global. Once they set out to achieve a goal, they will work tirelessly until it is theirs. Their emphasis on looking ahead is highlighted in their lives from childhood until the age of thirty-nine; these are the years in which they develop their self-confidence. After the age of forty, however, they become more relaxed about their goals, less focused on change and more on recognition and stability.

The key to their success lies in an ability to get their powerful intuition to work for, rather than against, them. It is their intuition that values objects, situations or people and their intuition which eventually teaches them to value their own judgment over everything else. Once they have settled on a course that is worthy of them, understanding that there are some things they can never control, they often use their intuition and strong will-power not only to successfully predict the future but also to play a part in creating it.

On the dark side

Domineering, gossipy, selfish

At your best

Progressive, intuitive, powerful

12 March

the birthday of
the untamed spirit

Your greatest challenge is

to avoid extreme attention-seeking behavior

The way forward is ...

to understand that you are unique and special; you do not have to do something crazy to prove it.

People born on March 12 have tremendous spirit and a desire to explore as many aspects of life as they can in order to gain knowledge and test themselves in increasingly demanding challenges and adventures. Others may fear for their safety or warn them to be more responsible but it's impossible for these untamed spirits to listen, let alone heed this advice.

Although they thrive on competition, these people are not generally motivated by a need to score points over others. The motivation is to challenge themselves and see how far they can go with their own natural abilities. In their work life they think nothing of leaving a secure job to start a new venture; in their personal lives they are attracted to people with an air of danger about them. Sometimes their exploits will land them in big trouble, but they will usually have considered the risks beforehand so that they know what they are letting themselves in for. Because they are so courageous, they tend to be resilient enough to withstand any setbacks, learn from their mistakes and bounce back even stronger.

The danger for these people is a lack of direction; they need to settle on a course that is worthy of their courage and resilience. Since they are often multi-talented it can be hard for them to find focus but it is important for them to specialize in a particular field if they are to come into their own. Up until the age of thirty-eight there is an emphasis on change and new ventures. Then, after the age of thirty-nine, there is a turning point when they tend to slow down, feeling a greater need for stability and financial security.

Strong believers in an afterlife and fate, these people have a profoundly intuitive and reflective side which they would do well to cultivate. Whatever they end up doing, one thing is sure: wherever these creative and courageous spirits are to be found, there will always be an element of danger, controversy and excitement swirling about them.

On the dark side

Impulsive, irresponsible, insecure

At your best

Spontaneous, creative, courageous

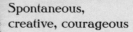

13 March

the birthday of
otherworldly possibilities

Your greatest challenge is

steering clear of cynicism

The way forward is ...

to understand the power of your thoughts. If you think of something often enough, there is an increased likelihood of it becoming a self-fulfilling prophecy.

People born on March 13 seem to have come into this world with an unshakable belief in their own fatalistic view. They are multitalented, curious and intelligent individuals instinctively drawn to what is unconventional and unexplained. Whether they are religious or not, they often believe in fate and otherworldly possibilities.

These people like to study the world and the people around them, often making predictions and judgments with wise finality. They have a talent for public discourse, and others tend to value their insights and come to them for advice. From an early age they probably challenged conventional thought and exhausted their parents and teachers with endless hows and whys. This insatiable curiosity seems to grow stronger as they grow older.

While it is important for these people to carry on exploring and understanding the unknown, they need to have a more pragmatic approach to the world. If they don't, they can get lost in esoteric or metaphysical worlds, never realizing their potential and not being taken seriously by others. There is also a risk that because they believe so strongly in predestination, they unwittingly steer events a certain way so that they become self-fulfilling prophecies. This is especially dangerous as they are prone to cynicism or negative expectation when life disappoints them. This tendency tends to be highlighted after the age of thirty-seven when there is greater inflexibility in their life. It is therefore important for people born on this day, especially when they grow older, to keep the spirit of optimism alive.

However tough things get for them, these people will always have an unshakable belief that there is more to life than has yet been discovered. This belief can help them overcome challenges and criticism that others would find overwhelming. They are often greatly admired for their resilience and incredible insight and as long as they aren't side-tracked by self-importance or negative expectation these people are capable of truly unique thoughts and achievements.

On the dark side

Cynical, passive, self-important

At your best

Farsighted, wise, courageous

14 March

Your greatest challenge is

making a decision

The way forward is ...

to weigh up the pros and cons and follow your instincts. Making a decision keeps you moving forward because you can learn from your experience.

The potential for success for people born on March 14 lies in their intelligence, versatility and open-mindedness. They have the mental dexterity to jump from one idea to another without losing track of the bigger picture.

The universal attitude that people born on this day possess encourages a humanitarian outlook. Abhorring intolerance and bigotry, they are extremely sensitive to the feelings of others; this makes them extremely popular at home and at work. They have the ability to take what is familiar and transform it into something new by presenting it in an unexpected way.

Although there is a dash of brilliance about them, these people can have problems making decisions. This is not the result of a lack of direction; quite the opposite, as these people often have a very clear vision. Because they have such a universal outlook—visualizing countless future scenarios—they can sometimes find it hard to decide on a single course of action that takes into account all viewpoints.

The only danger with this approach is that it can lead to information overload, so they should find a stance they can champion or a direction they remain faithful to, even if it means disagreeing with other viewpoints. If they can't do that, the risks they run are confusion and lack of direction. Until the age of thirty-six the emphasis tends to be on swift changes of mind and direction. Fortunately, after the age of thirty-seven these people are able to make a stand; by the age of forty most of them find their focus and really come into their own.

As well as indecisiveness, people born on March 14 also need to overcome their tendency to be self-effacing. To fulfill their potential they need to trust what they feel, allowing their minds to take them to unfrequented places. Once they have learned to be bold, making decisions if life demands it, the uncommon intellectual gifts and daring inventiveness they are blessed with ensure that there will be no end to the wonders they can create.

On the dark side

Indecisive, preoccupied, passive

At your best

Inventive, curious, affectionate

15 March

the birthday of
the mountain climber

Your greatest challenge is

to stop regarding everyone else as competition

The way forward is ...

to understand that another person's success will not limit your own; success is something that everyone deserves.

People born on March 15 are adventurous and determined individuals with the potential to become leaders in whatever area they choose to focus on. They have great personal magnetism and others tend to follow where they lead. They might, however, be arrogant and competitive in their race to get ahead, but once they reach the summit they can keep this in check, making intelligent and benevolent leaders. They should be careful not to alienate friends and loved ones, as they depend on the support of those they really care about.

Progress in their chosen line of work tends to be rapid for people born on this day. Although they are adventurous they aren't reckless, and have the ability to weigh up positives and negatives, form a plan of action and concentrate on achieving their aims. This is a winning combination, especially when allied to their enthusiasm and lovable personality. Before the age of thirty-five they may experiment with various different directions; during this time they are most likely to place greater emphasis on getting ahead than the goal itself. This can impact their personal happiness but fortunately after the age of thirty-six they seek a meaningful direction for their ambition. This is when they really come into their own, although they should watch out for a streak of obstinacy during these years.

Given their desire to scale the heights in their chosen field, people born on this day are often attracted to activities that can, quite literally, take them higher, such as mountain climbing, skiing and flying. Those who are more timid may well find that it is failure in their chosen field that terrifies them more than high places.

Potential leaders of others, these people need to learn not to overwhelm themselves and others with their restless drive to succeed. Once they have learned to ground themselves with the support of others and a goal worthy of their intelligence and courage, they have all the originality and dynamic power they need to reach their place of destiny—the very top.

On the dark side

Driven, competitive, obstinate

At your best

Charismatic, ambitious, enthusiastic

16 March

the birthday of
equilibrium

Your greatest challenge is

to show your passion for what you believe in

The way forward is ...

to understand that being passionate about what you want or believe in does not mean you have lost your cool.

People born on March 16 generally appear to others as well-balanced personalities who manage to combine their imaginative potential with a practical, grounded approach. Their talent for maintaining equilibrium or seeking the middle way is the secret of their success.

People born on this day are at their best when they can find a sense of balance; they have a great talent for negotiation and for making people pull together as a team. Their love of balance also displays itself in their personal life. At work they are paragons of ambition and discipline but at home they know how to unwind and reflect. They have a dreamy, intuitive side that is sensitive to the needs of others but they are not impractical and can use their common sense to make sure everyone feels important. Their homes and workplaces are tidy and elegant but not obsessively so; as a result, people often feel instantly comfortable when visiting.

Because of the high value they place on balance, there is often a kind of wholesomeness about these people. There is a danger, however, that their balanced outlook sometimes overlooks the possibility of unexpected setbacks; they need to learn to pay attention to warning signs before trouble actually hits. They also need to be careful that their own views or values don't become so muted that they disappear altogether, especially after the age of thirty-four when they can express a need for less change and conflict, and more stability and security in their lives. They need to be careful during this time not to let their practical, hedonistic side overshadow their idealistic and intuitive side.

Above all, these people are multi-talented individuals who can channel their imagination and originality into schemes that are both visionary and practical. Once they are able to accept rather than deny their own changeable nature and take on responsibilities with excitement rather than apprehension, they will not only find a true sense of balance and equilibrium, but also the exhilarating sense of achievement and fulfillment that goes with it.

On the dark side

Inconsistent, dreamy, foolish

At your best

Practical, imaginative, insightful

17 March

Your greatest challenge is

to make a commitment and stick to it

The way forward is ...

to understand that commitments can only drag you down if you fear them. If you face them, they can bring great satisfaction.

People born on March 17 have an ethereal quality about them and often appear to others to be floating through life. This isn't to say that they are lazy or never experience setbacks and difficulties; quite the contrary, as they are incredibly hardworking with their fair share of frustrations. Yet however tough life gets, they always seem able to transcend the mundane, endowing all their actions with a lightness and sparkle.

Often charismatic with creative talents, people born on this day are also imaginative, optimistic and receptive, making enchanting company both at home and at work. Their difficulty lies in their drifting from one interest to another; rather than facing a challenge, they prefer to avoid or flow around it. There are many possible reasons for this: lack of self-confidence, dislike of confrontation and, above all, a fear of commitment and responsibility.

When properly channeled, their curiosity and sense of optimism can bring great rewards, and the admiration and support of others. However, the more they evade conflict and difficult situations when a project or relationship encounters setbacks, the more they might be considered irresponsible, flighty and unreliable. It is important for these people to learn to face up to tedious or difficult situations; this will provide them with greater satisfaction than drifting lightly but aimlessly through life. Before the age of thirty-three there is an emphasis on change and new ventures, but thereafter they often become more secure, responsible and less flighty.

Blessed with a caring nature, these people are often in a position to help others. The responsibility of this may be a struggle for these sparkling souls, but the ability to be patient and reliable in their relationships with others and in their professional life forms a vital part of their self-confidence. Once their butterfly nature has learned that touching the ground doesn't mean the death of their creativity and optimism but rather the making of it, they have the potential to lead not just exciting and creative lives but truly magical ones.

On the dark side

Self-effacing, irresponsible, flighty

At your best

Inspired, hardworking, adaptable

18 March

the birthday of spiritual strength

Your greatest challenge is

spending enough time with loved ones

The way forward is ...

to understand that as satisfying as personal ambition is, it can never replace the rewards and fulfillment of close personal relationships.

People born on March 18 are blessed with great courage, resilience and the ability to recover from adverse circumstances not once but time after time. They have remarkable physical, emotional and spiritual strength and, if they can learn the lessons from each setback, they've the potential to become inspirational motivators and leaders.

People born on this day are intelligent, multi-talented and resourceful. They will use their considerable energy and willpower to overcome all obstacles. Their life may have been particularly challenging during their youth and these early knocks have given them the resilience they need to succeed. They have a knack of being in the right place at the right time, a great sense of humor and an optimistic outlook; as a result, people find them appealing but also exhausting, as they tend to live at a fast pace.

The danger for these people is that their preoccupation with moving forward or bouncing back can cause them to neglect not just important details but also the feelings of others. It is important for them to pay greater attention to details so these don't create problems later and to make sure the demands of those close to them are met. Before the age of thirty-two they are likely to be more confident and assertive but also more obsessive and chaotic in their approach to their goals. After the age of thirty-three they are likely to slow down a little and become more thorough, secure and settled.

The recuperative powers of people born on this day are remarkable. This is partly due to their spiritual strength and patience; they have an unshakable belief that however tough things are now they will be better tomorrow. More often than not, life rewards this positive attitude and things improve significantly. Once these generous, courageous and resourceful people learn to avoid a tendency toward ruthlessness, they can earn the admiration and support of others. Whatever field they choose to work in, the lives of those they touch will be changed forever by their intensity and bravery.

On the dark side

Obsessive, needy, ruthless

At your best

Powerful, resilient, courageous

19 March

the birthday of
true grit

Your greatest challenge is

learning to listen to the viewpoints of others

The way forward is ...

to understand that by listening to others you will learn far more than by clinging to your beliefs.

People born on March 19 are blessed with considerable motivation and vitality. Others are often drawn to them because they possess a childlike energy and openness. Although they may give the appearance of being dreamy at times, they are extremely practical and determined.

Once they have settled on a goal, these people will work tirelessly to achieve it. They are a brilliant combination of imagination and action, creating a mental image of what they want and then taking assertive, methodical and practical steps to achieve it. In fact, they are virtually unstoppable when they have put their action plan in place, and however difficult, mundane or repetitious things are, they will see it through.

This determined approach is a recipe for success and—if directed toward a worthy goal—can take them not just to the top but to new ground. It can, however, also backfire. When their goals can't be realized, it can leave them feeling disappointed and depressed. Part of the problem is that many of their goals and dreams are based on material success and the recognition of others. They need to learn that fulfillment does not just come from outward things but also from inner contentment. Only when they are able to look within and understand the importance of both personal and professional satisfaction will they achieve lasting happiness and success.

Until the age of thirty-one there is a tendency for these people to be active in the pursuit of their goals. From the age of thirty-two to sixty-two they may be more relaxed but may also show signs of stubbornness. These are the years in which they should not neglect the importance of their inner life or stop sharing their feelings with their numerous friends.

The blend of vision and action that people born on this day possess is a powerful and seductive combination. As long as they remember to keep their ego in check and acquire a degree of self-knowledge, they have both the fantasy and the fire to make their dreams come true.

On the dark side

Inflexible, depressed, materialistic

At your best

Determined, charming, thorough

20 March

the birthday of
the insightful wanderer

Your greatest challenge is

putting your needs first

The way forward is ...

to understand that only after you know how to give to yourself can you give to others.

People born on March 20 were born on the last day of the Zodiac wheel, and in many ways they are the most insightful and fully evolved individuals of the year. They possess such a wealth of gifts that it is hard to pinpoint one, but underneath their versatility lies their great compassion for others, a gift that can bring them great rewards, but at a price.

Those born on this day can feel overwhelmed by their feelings for others and therefore prone to depression and feelings of helplessness. They are also natural optimists, believing in the basic goodness of people, with a talent for boosting morale and getting people to work together. The danger for these people is that they can become confused to the point of indecision when they empathize too strongly with others' emotions.

Although they should never repress their sensitivity—it is one of the greatest assets—they should strive to become emotionally stronger. Until the age of thirty, if they don't learn to protect themselves, others will sometimes try to take advantage of their vulnerability and generosity. After thirty-one they have the potential for greater emotional stability; this is when they become more effective instruments for good. After the age of sixty-one they are more interested in communication and the exchange of ideas.

There is a deep longing within these people to make the world a better place. There may be many changes of direction as they experiment with different roles, and their experiences will help them discover who they really are and what they really want from their lives. Once they do settle on a goal, often to improve the lives of others in some way, they will achieve their dreams because they are both practical and idealistic. They will also find that the older they get, the more confident they become. In their later years they will draw on their rich experience of life to become a wise elder with a wealth of invaluable advice to offer the next generation.

On the dark side

Indecisive, unsure, oversensitive

At your best

Optimistic, compassionate, versatile

ARIES

THE RAM (MARCH 21 – APRIL 19)

* **Element:** Fire
* **Ruling planet:** Mars, the warrior
* **Symbol:** The Ram
* **Tarot card:** The Emperor (authority)
* **Number:** 9
* **Favorable colors:** Red and white
* **Key phrase:** I am born to lead

forge their way through life's ups and downs with daring, initiative and enterprise. Straightforward and assertive, they are never afraid to stand out from the crowd. Routine and predictability frustrate them, and their appetite for challenge and adventure is insatiable. No matter their age, they have endless reserves of energy and will propel themselves headfirst into the world every day without fear or reservation.

Personality potential

Some Arians come across as loud while others are subtler in their approach, but either way they are impossible to ignore. They lead from the front, and make dynamic bosses and motivators. As the first sign of the zodiac, they are like a spark that can ignite the enthusiasm of others. Because they are highly individualistic, compromise does not come easily to them; their rock-solid self-confidence that obstacles can—and will—be overcome inspires and energizes all those with whom they come into contact.

Initiative, courage, assertiveness, independence, passion and leadership are all key words for Arians. This isn't surprising given that Mars, planet of the Roman god of war, is their ruling planet and that their element is fire, which sparkles, crackles, burns and molds. There is something refreshingly straightforward and honest about people born under this sign. Anything that is not strictly necessary to their end goal is stripped away. This ability to see clearly to the heart of the matter and let go of negative emotions and grudges can be off-putting and mystifying to some, but to others it can encourage respect, trust, admiration and sometimes awe.

Aries people are movers and shakers; they make things happen. Nothing excites an Arian more than challenge and—when combined with their impulsive nature—this makes them natural risk takers. Details aren't important to them. Their concern is always and only for the bigger picture; once a challenge has been met, their restless nature likes to forge ahead quickly to bigger and better tests. Achievement matters a great deal to Arians, and nothing or no one can stand in the way of their goals. Headstrong and determined, their aim is to win no matter what setbacks or competition stands in their way. They are extremely independent and, if they can't lead a team, they prefer to work alone. If things don't work out—which is always likely to occur if you take the risks to which Arians are prone—you won't find them wallowing in self-pity. They will simply dust themselves off, and move onwards and upwards until they reach the very top, the place they have always believed themselves destined to be.

> **They are extremely independent and if they can't lead a team they prefer to work alone.**

On the dark side

Although the impulsiveness and childlike eagerness of Arians can be endearing, it can also make them vulnerable to those who are less honest and truthful. They may have to learn the hard way that in life honesty is sometimes not the best policy. More subtlety and less bluntness are required to take them where they want to go or to enable them to get their point of view across. They also need to be aware that although their natural leadership potential can make them invaluable during times of crisis, when there isn't a battle to be fought their love of combat can make them prone to hot-headedness and impatience with those more cautious souls who are less willing to rush headlong into things. When fired up, the Arian temper can burst explosively and without warning.

Arians do tend toward self-centeredness, not because they are selfish but simply because they are so wrapped up in themselves they don't notice what is going on around them.

Fortunately, as soon as they are made aware of what they have missed they will fight unselfishly and wholeheartedly for those less privileged or capable than themselves. It's also fairly common for Arians to rush into projects or relationships firing on all cylinders; but if things aren't going their way, or they suddenly lose interest, they tend to drop that project or person through boredom. Prone to be bossy, reckless and bad tempered, these personality pitfalls can be exorcized by lots of physical exercise. Patience and endurance are qualities that would greatly improve the lives of Arians.

Symbol

The symbol of Aries is the ram, and they certainly possess a tendency to ram their ideas down people's throats or crash headlong into things without looking where they are going. There is, however, a softer and more subdued side to them that is more lamb than ram; but in general these people are true to their symbol—blunt, forceful and to the point, just like a battering ram.

Darkest secret

Without doubt Arians like to win, but their desire to lead and stand out is not because they think they are necessarily more gifted than others but because they long to be noticed, appreciated and respected by others. What other people think matters far more to them than they would be willing to admit to themselves.

Love

A world without love is a world in which an Arian could not survive. Love is a necessity of life for them, and they demand it from their partners and lovers. If they sense that the love and devotion of a partner is being withdrawn, panic will set in. This can only be calmed by repeated assurances, if not from their partner then from other people. Arians are passionate by nature and sex matters more to them than to most others. In love they expect absolute devotion and fidelity but not necessarily from themselves. They adore the excitement of a new relationship and make wonderfully spontaneous, passionate and experimental lovers; but, just as in other matters, they can get restless if their relationships become too comfortable or routine. For relationships to be long term there need to be plenty of challenges and mutual interests to keep them engaged.

Love matches: Leo, Libra and Sagittarius

The Arian man

Typically, an Arian man will be a whirlwind of activity. Mobile phone glued to his ear or dressed for action he is often fiercely competitive and self-assured, and there may even be a hint of arrogance. He takes the initiative and likes others to follow his lead. Above all, the Arian man likes to win in love and life; even if he doesn't appear to be a winner at first glance, there is always the possibility that one day he will discover his natural leadership potential and find some way to rise head and shoulders above the rest.

Deeply affectionate and prone to grand and generous gestures, an Arian man doesn't expect people who love him to hold back, physically or emotionally. If he falls in love he will put his partner on a pedestal and shower them with gifts; but if his partner can't cope or keep up with his constant need for enthusiasm and romance, he may try to look somewhere else. This doesn't always mean, however, that he will start an affair. Although he is passionate and impulsive, he is also honest and in most instances he will not launch himself into an affair without first ending his current relationship.

If you are trying to get the interest of an Arian man, play it cool and don't make the first move. He loves challenges and likes to take the lead in love; but if you do eventually end up in a relationship with him, forget about flirting with other men. He is extremely possessive and exceedingly jealous, and needs to know that he—and only he—comes first in your life.

The Arian woman

The Arian woman, like the Arian man, is typically energetic and active, with attractive, strong features. Her life will be busy and she can solve almost any problem. She doesn't appear to need any man to hold a door open for her but that notwithstanding, she can also be extremely feminine. Rather like Scarlet O'Hara in the classic film *Gone with the Wind*, while she is flirtatious and headstrong she is also resilient and endlessly optimistic. If things don't work out today she knows that "tomorrow is another day." Arian women have total confidence in their abilities and like to be the first one to do anything. At times, her independence and supreme confidence can batter a male ego but an Arian woman does not want a partner who is fragile or who is like a puppy. She wants a partner but not one who is totally devoted to her. The best way, therefore, to grab the attention of an Arian woman is to be detached and to leave her guessing. Let her think that you can easily resist her charms and she will then try to prove that she is the one for you.

In short, an Arian woman will never lack admirers but she will always secretly be yearning after the one she can't get. She is tough, strong and an equal to any man but she can also play the role of the vulnerable female to perfection. The person

who can win her heart will find that beneath her confidence and assertive exterior there is a gentle and loving soul full of optimism, hope, faith and magical dreams for the future.

Family

The Arian child thrives on attention and affection. They need constant stimulation and have an enormous supply of energy for a wide number of interests but their enthusiasm can dwindle quickly. Parents are therefore advised to hold back a while before spending money on equipment or lessons to see if their current interest is more than just a passing phase. As far as schoolwork is concerned, they will show flashes of brilliance but their progress will be marred by their boredom with the attention to detail that studying requires. Fortunately, they come to life again around examination time as examinations appeal to their desire to score points and forge ahead of the rest. Because they often have very little fear they are injury prone and parents need to get used to the inevitable bumps, bruises and even broken bones. They also should try to get used to their desire to challenge authority. Clear boundaries have to be firmly set in place so that the Arian child doesn't end up running the show. The best way to parent an Arian child, however, is not to set down endless rules but to give them plenty of opportunities to show you what a natural winner they are. Tell them that you don't expect they will be able to do or achieve something in a set period of time and this challenge will bring out the best in them.

As parents Arians indulge their own childlike nature and have no difficulty at all understanding and relating to children. They will be warm and affectionate, and will encourage their children to be as active as possible. This works fine if they have a child who loves movement and activity as much as they do, but if they have a child who is far happier doing quieter activities such as reading and who doesn't take naturally to risk taking, it's important for them not to be selfish and force a child to do things they don't want to. Although it can get chaotic and noisy at times, Arian parents will ensure that their children have plenty of love, laughter and magic in their lives. They will also encourage their children to see the wonder and potential in everyone and everything.

Career

At work, Arians are highly competitive and driven; they are quick to create plans and initiate products. Routine 9 to 5 office jobs are not for them; but if they have to be tolerated it's essential that outside interests or hobbies are well established. In choosing careers Arians need to look for jobs that give them plenty of freedom of expression and challenge. Above all, their career should give them a chance to innovate and lead from the front.

> "Above all their career should give them a chance to innovate and lead from the front."

Arians are strong willed and can excel in almost any field but the following jobs may be particularly suited to their energetic, pioneering spirit: the armed services, the electronics industry, fire fighting, police work, psychiatry, surgery, travel writing, politics, public relations, athletics, journalism and any business career that offers management opportunities. World leaders are often drawn from Arian ranks because they are such forceful agents for change. They do extremely well at presentation and therefore make great sales people; this is especially true within a single market because Arians work better when they narrow down their focus. The world of art and music may also appeal to them because they can be emotional as well as highly communicative and they could flourish in the performing arts or the world of entertainment.

Health and leisure

Arians need to make sure they give themselves plenty of time in which to relax and unwind as they do suffer from a tendency to burn the candle at both ends and to push themselves way too hard mentally, emotionally and physically. They would benefit enormously from walks in the countryside where they can observe the magical workings of the natural world. Getting at least 7 hours' sleep a night is important but long lie-ins should be avoided as Arians are at their best in the early morning. As far as diet is concerned, they are unlikely to have any weight problems—even if their lifestyle is sedentary they are so active that they are likely to be fidgets—but if they do put on a bit of weight they should cut back on refined and processed foods that are rich in sugar, salt and additives, and eat more nutritious foods rich in whole grains, fruits and vegetables. Spicy foods don't tend to agree with them so they should try to eat foods that are as simple and natural as possible

Regular exercise is a must, not just because it helps burn off some of that excess energy but also because it can encourage them to take time out. They are at their happiest and their best when active, and leisure pursuits that suit them best include cycling, running and activities such as mountain climbing that test their stamina. Martial arts and extreme sports may also appeal and, although they are not natural team players, they may nevertheless enjoy competitive team sports like hockey, soccer, boxing, rugby, baseball and basketball.

Arians may suffer more than most from headaches. They are also prone to cuts, bruises and even minor burns; they should therefore adopt the motto "more haste, less speed." Wearing, meditating or surrounding themselves with the color green will help restore calm, natural balance and healing into their lives.

Born between March 21 and March 30

The planet Mars will be a particularly strong influence here. March Arians tend to be quite demanding and intolerant of different viewpoints to their own, but this Martian energy boost will also give them incredible mental and physical stamina. They are never afraid to rush in headfirst where angels fear to tread, but they need to make sure that they are not so focused on their goals that they walk over others while achieving them.

Born between March 31 and April 10

People born between these dates have traces of one of the other fire signs, Leo, in their psychological make-up. They are humorous, honest, bright spirits who attract people very easily, but their power to impose their will on others, often without opposition, is one that needs to be used responsibly.

Born between April 11 and April 19

Arians born toward the end of their sun sign are often endowed with greater humanitarian tendencies. This means that although they have great courage and optimism and like to get things done their way, they also tend to be gentler in their approach to life and are more willing to champion the underdog or the underprivileged.

Life lessons

People born under the sign of Aries are energetic and have a true zest for living, but if there is one thing the Arian would benefit from learning it's the value of patience. There are exceptions, of course, but in general Arians are the most impatient people on the planet and this can cause a lot of trouble for them.

If an Arian wants something they want it right now. They hate waiting for anything and anyone, but they need to learn that some things in life require time and patience before results can be achieved. Arians are also great at starting up new projects, relationships or enterprises; but when things require discipline or dedication, or start to become tedious, they start looking at other options. This can cost them dearly and they would do well do stop and think carefully about what they might lose before they drop out of college, change jobs or end a relationship.

Being overly competitive is another challenge for Arians and they make especially bad losers. Although they won't lose often, it's important for them to learn how to lose graciously and to allow others to step into the limelight now and again. If they are worried that this will make people forget about them, they shouldn't be; Arians are born leaders and, in some cases, born stars. The same goes for their relationships. Arians are very good at taking and directing but not so good at giving and accepting. They need to learn the pure joy of giving pleasure to others.

As Arians journey through life they do need to work on their impatience, impulsiveness and naivety, as well as their lack of attention both to details and to the feelings of others around them. Above all, they need to learn to see something through to completion. Arians can look to other signs in the zodiac to learn these life lessons. Those born under Cancer can teach them to be more sensitive to the needs of others, and to develop empathy and understanding for the people they care about. Those born under Libra can teach them the joys of team work and the importance of thinking before they speak or looking before they leap. And finally, Arians can learn all about the value of hard work, dedication and commitment from Virgos and Capricorns who can help them persevere even when things have become boring and tedious.

> "Aries is very good at taking and directing but not so good at giving and accepting."

21 March

the birthday of clear sightedness

Your greatest challenge is

learning to be more tactful

The way forward is ...

to understand that compromise or softening your focus or your words to accommodate others does not mean you have sold out on your values.

People born on March 21 have their own set of values and refuse to compromise in any way. In keeping with the pivotal significance of their birthday—the beginning of Spring and the Zodiac year—they are powerful, free-thinking individuals with an iron will to succeed whose single-mindedness almost always works.

People born on this day do not care much for convention. They are honest and direct in all their dealings and opinions; their thoughts are often so transparent that they don't need to say much to make their feelings known. They are clear-sighted in their beliefs and other people know exactly where they stand with them. This isn't to say they are aggressive and overbearing; quite the opposite, as they are often quiet in their confidence. They simply live according to their own values and if other people don't understand these, they aren't prepared to explain themselves, much preferring to go it alone.

Although remarkably clear-sighted and independent, these people can come across as inflexible, passive and antisocial when they choose to withdraw and live in splendid isolation. They also have an inclination to be stubborn and can become argumentative and blunt to get their own way. They should learn not to alienate others when pursuing their goals, accepting that success does not always result from following a direct path. Between the ages of thirty and sixty their stubborn tendencies are likely to be highlighted. During these years they need to make sure they work on transforming their way of thinking so that it takes into account the viewpoints of others.

Once they learn to moderate their impatience and their tendency to isolate themselves when things aren't going their way, they have the potential to become exceptional leaders, utilizing their powers of perception, intuition and considerable energy to great effect. When these people find themselves in a position to impress others with their talents and free-thinking action, all who come into contact with them will be more spontaneous and clear-sighted about who they are and what they want.

On the dark side

Passive, inflexible, unsociable

At your best

Perceptive, honest, powerful

22 March

the birthday of
frankness

Your greatest challenge is

learning to show tact

The way forward is ...

to understand that sometimes directness comes across as self-importance. Being tactful is presenting the truth in a way that considers the feelings of others.

People born on March 22 tend to be frank, confident individuals without a hidden agenda. They really are an open book, soon gaining the respect, protection and support of almost everyone they meet. Their honorable nature and reliability may even earn them a well-deserved following or, at the very least, a small group of ardent admirers.

Although they possess a powerful desire to achieve their goals, it is never at the expense of their personal values. They are the sort of people who always speak their minds because they value truth above all else. Although this can sometimes offend and wound others, more often than not others find themselves assimilating what these people say. The power and influence they have over others is an awesome responsibility for them and, if they can learn to channel it sensitively, they really can help others search for the truth or see the facts of a situation.

People born on this day may be uncompromising, and occasionally overbearing and proud, but they are not stubborn or inflexible when it comes to learning something new. They are often full of a curiosity that can draw them toward diverse experiences, and nothing fascinates them more than new technology and scientific discoveries. Their wondering mind may also be responsible for the many changes of direction in their lives, especially in their twenties. After the age of twenty-nine, however, there may be less emphasis on change and new ventures and more on stability and security, and this is when they really come into their own.

These people can get carried away by heroic images of themselves and by their enthusiasm for their current project or ideal; but generally, when they find a goal that is worthy of them, their refusal to be diverted from their chosen course of action gives them enormous potential for success. And when that success is achieved—which it inevitably is—there will be few who begrudge them it or feel that these honest, reliable and honorable individuals do not deserve every second of it.

On the dark side

Overbearing, unaware, proud

At your best

Reliable, confident, curious

23 March

the birthday of
the eternal student

Your greatest challenge is

to pay attention to your emotional needs.

The way forward is ...

to understand that if you aren't in touch with your feelings, your self-knowledge and self-esteem will be poor.

People born on March 23 are fascinated by everyone and everything. They are driven by a desire to learn not just how and why things work, but also what makes people tick. To this end they tend to draw toward them as many people as will feed their insatiable curiosity.

When these people learn that a good mind and education are the keys to success, their intelligence and versatility can take them to the top of their chosen field. They have great insight into the strengths and weaknesses of others, yet can sometimes be lacking in empathy. Often too emotionally detached to be fired up by compassion for others, they tend to rely on encyclopedic knowledge, rather than personal experience. Even though they have the ability to make friends easily and are often surrounded by fellow debaters, they do run the risk of becoming observers rather than participators.

Eternal students of human nature, the issues that most interest them—the meaning of life, the hows and whys of human emotion and behavior—are those that they could most benefit from applying to themselves. Their information-gathering approach has both its strengths and its weaknesses; it does not take into account the importance of a person's inner life and how that can provide meaning and comfort. Their tendency to observe and over-analyze is most pronounced between the ages of twenty-eight and fifty-eight, when it is important that they learn to recognize their own and other people's emotional and spiritual needs. If they aren't able to, they may be prone to sudden and, to their frustration, unexplained bouts of insecurity and sadness.

These perceptive, inquisitive and eager-to-learn people are wonderfully entertaining and stimulating to have around and they never fail to surprise and delight others with their insights. Once they have learned to look within as well as outside of themselves for stimulation, they have all the enthusiasm and determination they need not only to make startling observations but also to act upon them with dramatic and often life-enhancing benefits.

On the dark side

Skeptical, uninvolved, insecure

At your best

Progressive, insightful, flexible

24 March

the birthday of
stormy tranquility

Your greatest challenge is

dealing with your anger

The way forward is ...

to deal promptly with minor threats so anger doesn't build up. Think about what is worth getting angry about and what isn't.

Externally, people born on March 24 appear tranquil and uncomplicated, even to the point of childlike innocence. They take great pleasure in the simple things of life, but there is often a dark cloud of stormy malcontent underneath their calm exterior.

These captivating individuals do prefer simple solutions to complicated alternatives and their nature is strictly no fuss, no frills. With the ability to take swift and decisive action, they will rarely be found dithering with indecision. They are at their happiest and best when their achievements are recognized and when their private life is simple and steady. Despite their child-like charms, their lives are often far removed from the tranquility they dream of. In fact, difficult situations and challenges seem to be attracted to them; these will continue to test them until they come to terms with their own inner conflicts.

These people should neither ignore nor suppress the dark feelings they have about themselves and life, learning to face them head-on. When they are able to do this, they will find there is far less to fear than they thought. Negative emotions, such as fear, anger, jealousy and insecurity, exist to alert them to areas of discomfort in their lives, signaling a need for change. It is important for them to listen to the messages their emotions convey, especially between the ages of twenty-seven and fifty-seven, during which there is an emphasis on material or outward success, stability and security.

Other people may find it hard to understand why these lovely people with an army of admirers so often get themselves into trouble or occasionally explode with rage. As such, they present an enigma. Their optimistic approach to life and willingness to believe the best in others can make them vulnerable and easily exploited. As well as learning to face their inner demons, they need to take a more realistic approach to life. This should not, however, be at the expense of their simplicity and sweetness, since their most powerful strength is to light up the lives of others.

On the dark side

Dreamy, vulnerable, unrealistic

At your best

Warm, trusting, direct

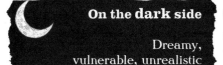

25 March

the birthday of
electric energy

Your greatest challenge is

learning to keep a lid on your temper

The way forward is ...

to understand that when you lash out in frustration or uncontrolled rage, it's often because your inner equilibrium is disturbed.

People born on March 25 like to be where the action is, and that is where they are often found. They have bags of enthusiasm and an endless supply of energy, never being afraid of taking an independent position when convinced it is necessary. Their dynamism marks them out as natural leaders as others tend to follow when they show the way; but their natural preference is often to go it alone.

These people are resilient individuals but are also compassionate and imaginative. They may have developed a tough skin to protect themselves from life's knocks but they have a sense of natural justice and strong protective instincts toward the vulnerable. Quirky and original with a rich imaginative life, what really distinguishes them is their boundless energy.

They are daring, independent and direct with an active mind and body and bright ideas. Making hasty decisions without proper plans, sometimes their spontaneity gets them into trouble. Adopting a more mature, reflective attitude will help them make smoother progress. Until the age of twenty-five they tend to be daring and carefree but after the age of twenty-six there is greater emphasis on the need for direction, consistency, security and stability. In their thirties, forties and beyond they really come into their own.

Although much of their electric energy is externally directed, these people also have a profound need for periods of solitude and reflection; these help them avoid mood swings and temper tantrums. This need for a private life where they can be allowed to daydream can confuse those who regard them as whirlwinds of constant energy; but others need to understand that it is vital for them. It is important for them to have supportive and caring friends but these friends have to give them the freedom to be alone and recharge. If they keep a lid on their temper and give themselves those regular times out, the electric and highly creative energy and imagination of people born on this day will help them surge right to the front of their chosen field.

On the dark side

Moody, critical, childish

At your best

Dynamic, individual, compassionate

26 March

the birthday of
honesty

Your greatest challenge is

to speak your mind when the situation demands it

The way forward is ...

to understand that holding back isn't always the right approach. It can make people feel that you aren't sufficiently committed.

People born on March 26 are astute, determined and courageous, with the intensity and power to achieve much in life. They can appear easygoing and unassuming; to a certain extent this is true. But they are not lazy or unmotivated; rather, they like to cut straight to the heart of the matter, not wishing to make things more complicated than they are. They don't have much time for small talk or window dressing; directness, both intellectual and emotional, is their goal.

A desire for honesty dominates the personality of these people, encouraging them to confront and explore situations others might avoid. It also helps them get things done quickly and efficiently; because they are so bold, clear-sighted and practical, they have a knack of making even the hardest of tasks seem easy. The only problem with their straightforward approach is that they can sometimes become too relaxed or detached, putting them behind those who are more aggressive and passionate.

They also have a tendency to make judgments based on their insight and then to close their mind to alternative viewpoints. It is important for them to keep their minds open and to understand that the less-is-more approach to life isn't always appropriate. Until the age of twenty-four they are likely to be active and adventurous but from the age of twenty-five to fifty-five there is an emphasis on stability and security. It is important during these years that they discover ways to express their creativity and passion.

True satisfaction for people born on this day often comes through achievements based on their own efforts. They like to work at their own pace, trusting their own impeccable judgment. Easily bored and dissatisfied when relying on the efforts and opinions of others, they are usually the best judge of what does or does not work for them. As long as they don't lose touch of their spontaneity and wry sense of humor, they are capable of producing work of great quality and, surprisingly for someone with such a laid-back exterior, incredible depth.

On the dark side

Inflexible, passive, insecure

At your best

Bold, mature, effortless

27 March

the birthday of the individual

Your greatest challenge is

not letting work rule your life

The way forward is ...

to strike a balance between your inner and outer needs; losing your identity to work will lead to lack of fulfillment.

There is something about people born on March 27 that is wholly endearing. They are true individuals with their own inimitable style of dress and behavior, attracting attention wherever they go. They don't just have star quality; they have something far more special: the likability factor.

Despite always being in demand, these strongly independent and individualistic people are more concerned with following their own unique path than gaining the approval of others. Their work is important to them; any success they achieve is earned because they understand the importance of discipline and will push themselves single-mindedly to achieve their goals. This determination and refusal to fit in often results from youthful struggles and setbacks; although this gives them resilience and a unique persona, it can also make them unsympathetic to the feelings of others. Other people may be attracted to them but deep down March 27 people aren't that interested in other people at all; it is their work that fascinates them.

Occasionally the driven personality and tendency to lack empathy for others can make these people appear tense, aloof or self-absorbed. As wonderful and as fascinating as they are, it's important for them to learn to step outside themselves every now and again, and they should realize there is a whole world out there. This tendency toward self-absorption is especially highlighted between their mid twenties and mid fifties; during these years they need to make sure they get in touch with the feelings and concerns of others.

These people often have great courage and strength, and in times of crisis they are the ones who instinctively take control, typically saving or helping others before themselves. Ironically, it is during periods of stability and security that they struggle most to find meaning and purpose, and may lapse into bouts of inaction. It is important for these multi-talented, charismatic individuals to understand that they don't actually need to wait for a crisis to make their mark. They can start to make a contribution that is wonderfully and uniquely their own right now.

On the dark side

Aloof, tense, difficult

At your best

Dynamic, stylish, imaginative

28 March

the birthday of
magnificent remoteness

Your greatest challenge is

to stop doubting yourself

The way forward is ...

to change the way you talk to yourself. Most of your negative beliefs aren't founded in reality, so train yourself to believe positive things.

Although people born on March 28 tend to be independent loners at heart, they often find themselves at the center of others' attention. This is because of their sunny and common-sense approach to life, as well as their morality, compassion and generosity toward others. They also have the ability to respond brilliantly in a crisis and, whether they like it or not, a recurring theme in their life will be offering their advice and support to others.

These people often have a burning desire to create something special in their chosen field. Their work is very important to them and a source of great fulfillment. With an incredible ability to focus, they remain calm and emotionally detached during the most difficult of situations. Despite their serenity and obvious intellectual talents, they may find that they don't advance as fast or as high as they deserve. There is a reason for this: their lack of self-confidence and self-belief.

Although their modest, self-effacing nature is endearing, they should find ways to build their self-esteem. Until they do so, they will doubt their abilities and will move forward with difficulty. From their early twenties to their early fifties it is important for them to work on building their self-confidence, as they need to establish security and stability. They also need to make sure that they don't settle for second best, sacrificing their personal fulfillment in the process. After the age of fifty-three there is a turning point in their life that highlights communication skills and the need for greater self-expression.

Charming, inspirational and popular, these people need privacy, and others should not try to impose restrictions or limitations on them as their remoteness is in many ways the key to their success. They need regular downtime and a degree of solitude to gather their strength and protect themselves from feeling vulnerable. Then, when they feel ready, they can rejoin the world, bringing to it their unique brand of humor, optimism, courage and magnificent calm in the face of adversity.

On the dark side

Unaware, vacillating, unrealistic

At your best

Independent, optimistic, focused

29 March

the birthday of
the discerning presence

Your greatest challenge is

asserting yourself

The way forward is ...

to understand that being assertive is not the same as being aggressive or rude. You are simply making sure your valuable contribution is recognized.

Undoubtedly intuitive, people born on March 29 like to observe everything that is going on around them, carefully considering all aspects of a situation before making a decision. This slow and steady approach to life often proves highly successful. Others may criticize them for being overly cautious or for lacking focus, passion and commitment, but they are the ones with the knack of winning in the end.

These people are often polite and genuine in every aspect of their life. Not to be so would imply rudeness or insincerity; their intellect, sensitivity and honesty would not stand for this. They are not driven by personal ambition but by a desire to make a positive difference in the world through their intellect and perception. In fact, they are perhaps a little too wise at times, which can lead them to being disillusioned if they are not careful, especially when it comes to close personal relationships.

The danger for people born on this day is that their caution can lead to negativity or pessimism; it is important for them not to spiral into depression if people do let them down. They need to understand that human beings are complex creatures with both strengths and weaknesses and that it is far better to believe the best of people than the worst. People have a tendency to live up to the expectations we have of them. Between the ages of twenty-one and fifty-one they need to be especially careful not to sink into cynicism and inflexibility, as there is an emphasis in their life on security and stability and establishing themselves.

Although they do like to keep themselves to themselves, when in public their discerning presence has a calming and soothing influence on those around them. Their self-containment can also—much to their surprise—thrust them into the limelight. These authentic, loyal and coolly intelligent individuals, with their own enigmatic purity and beauty, when put into positions of authority and leadership, are more than qualified to assume the reins of power.

On the dark side

Lacking in focus, aloof, cautious

At your best

Creative, genuine, perceptive

30 March

Your greatest challenge is

learning how bide your time

The way forward is ...

to understand that the very impulsiveness that drives you can also sabotage your efforts. You need to consider the effects of your words and deeds.

People born on March 30 are an irresistible combination of dynamic confidence and courage, and touching earnestness and vulnerability. Although their conviction is strong enough to help them bounce back from setbacks and criticism, it's impossible for them to hide their pain, bewilderment and disappointment. For this reason they can both antagonize and endear themselves to people, more often than not at the same time.

These people are at their happiest and best when allowed the freedom to work alone and set their own agenda. They may appear selfish to friends and colleagues, but they are not. They simply love to absorb themselves in their personal goals, fearing that if they allow others to distract them from their vision they might never attain it. It is important for them, however, to take the time to unwind; otherwise they run the risk of becoming driven at work and isolated in their personal life. They should not neglect their emotional and social needs between the ages of twenty and fifty, during which there is an emphasis on acquiring wealth, status and material security. After the age of fifty they may feel a need to communicate and exchange ideas; this is when their talents are most likely to mature and gain recognition.

With a hint of the dramatic and the irresistible in their make-up, these people have an attractive, energetic but mild manner which masks a hidden sensuality and complexity. Because they are so upbeat, passionate and focused about their goals in life, they may find that they have more than their fair share of good luck. If, however, they surrender their natural optimism the opposite may be true, so it is important for them to keep as positive as possible.

As long as these people don't allow themselves to become buried by their ambitions or their tendency toward perfectionism—and others allow them the freedom to pursue their highly creative vision—they have the potential not just to achieve outstanding success but to provoke feelings of adoration in others.

On the dark side

Antisocial, impatient, selfish

At your best

Dynamic, innovative, driven

31 March

the birthday of
the commanding presence

Your greatest challenge is

learning to control your temper

The way forward is ...

to find an activity that helps release pent-up tension, such as sport, gardening, studying, or starting a new hobby.

People born on March 31 are often stable individuals with a profound sense of who they are. Their presence is commanding and the force of their authority unquestioned. They have little time for small talk but plenty of time and energy for action and common sense.

There's a calmness and steadiness about these people, making them highly valued in both professional and personal environments. With a pragmatic and determined approach, they are also capable of compromise if life demands it, because they value making progress in an orderly and direct manner. If, however, they feel that others are standing in the way or complicating matters, they can be extremely argumentative and demanding.

The air of authority of these people marks them out as potential leaders but they tend to feel comfortable when they are contributing ideas or working within a team where their contagious energy motivates others to go along with them. They aren't great risk-takers as they prefer security to gambling, but it's important for them not to let opportunities to express their talents pass them by. They are most likely to favor a steady and pragmatic approach to life between the ages of twenty and fifty; during this time they should get out of their comfort zone every now and again, taking the odd calculated risk. After the age of fifty there is a greater emphasis on experimentation and new ventures.

These people do tend to be led by their head rather than their heart. Emotional control is important to them. When they feel threatened by their emotions, cynicism or sudden outbursts of temper are often their ways of avoiding dealing with them. Recognizing their need for greater emotional expression, life has a way of forcing them to get in touch with their feelings, through either the people they meet or the situations they experience. Once they learn to listen to their emotions as much as their common sense, these resourceful, realistic, energetic and remarkably influential people are destined for a rare combination of success in every aspect of their lives.

On the dark side

Unambitious, repressed, argumentative

At your best

Commanding, energetic, tenacious

1 April

the birthday of

quiet confidence

Your greatest challenge is

coping with work and the requests of others

The way forward is ...

to learn to delegate your responsibilities and to stop expecting so much from yourself.

Despite the reputation of their birthday, people born on April 1 are far from being April Fools. They often display wisdom and a quiet confidence way in advance of their years. They were the children on whom parents and teachers knew they could rely and in their adult life they continue to be dependable, the ones who show up punctually, always giving one hundred per cent.

Although they have a reputation for being reliable and responsible, these people are rarely plodding or dull as they have a youthful and wholesome appeal that draws others to them. Incapable of hiding their emotions, their emotional spontaneity earns them many admirers; their natural shyness and reserve may, however, make it hard for them to respond and appreciate this attention. They also have a great need for privacy and personal space, loving to sit thinking for long hours and coming up with highly original plans and projects.

The aura of quiet confidence and honesty with which these people are blessed is capable of inspiring enormous faith and trust in others. They make excellent leaders but their motive is never a desire for self-aggrandizement as it is the work itself rather than being the center of attention that inspires them. All they really want is to be allowed to get on with their work, as a job well done gives them enormous satisfaction. Although their outstanding ability to focus on their work assures their success in virtually any field, they do need to be careful that in the process they don't become isolated workaholics, especially between the ages of nineteen and forty-nine, during which they seek stability, security and routine. After the age of fifty, however, they move toward new interests, learning and communication.

The one similarity between the archetypal jester and these mature souls may be the sense of affection they inspire in others. Their responsible and quietly confident approach to life and lack of desire to promote themselves—unless thought necessary for the task in hand—is a true joy to behold.

On the dark side

Shy, workaholic, isolated

At your best

Focused, responsible, genuine

2 April

the birthday of

utopia

Your greatest challenge is

listening to different viewpoints

The way forward is ...

to understand that one of the best ways to win the respect and support of others is to listen and make them feel included.

People born on April 2 have a fresh, youthful outlook and a utopian view of the world. The purity of their intentions and genuine belief in their dreams of a better world can earn them great respect. They are also extremely compassionate and never fail to be moved by the suffering of others.

These people love to talk about their dreams and vision of a better future. These dreams, however, often don't take into account the possibility of obstacles or complications, so this idealism can test the patience of those with a more realistic approach to life. They may also become so passionate in their convictions that they are unable or unwilling to see differing viewpoints, which may alarm others.

When they have problems inspiring a similar level of zeal in others, these people may alienate themselves from a group with their inability to compromise. It's important for them to have a more objective view of the impact their ideals have on others and to try to find less aggressive ways of enlisting others' support. Between the ages of eighteen and forty-eight their tendency to express their convictions too forcefully is heightened, so they should learn to accept differences of opinion, tempering their idealism with realism; this will increase their chances of success and protect them from disappointment. After the age of forty-nine they become more flexible and more willing to entertain different viewpoints.

These people with a strong sense of justice do possess a subtle power and once they have learned to discipline and direct it positively, they have enormous potential to overcome almost any obstacle. Their motives may be misunderstood and criticized as naïve and futile, but this is unlikely to deter them. What matters to them isn't what others think but their personal vision and being true to themselves and their beliefs. As long as they direct their passion to goals that are worthy of them, their honesty, single-mindedness and determination to see the best in everybody can help even the most cynical believe in undreamed-of possibilities.

On the dark side

Naïve, insecure, vulnerable

At your best

Idealistic, generous, pure

132

3 April

the birthday of
the keynote

Your greatest challenge is

to learn to work independently

The way forward is ...

to understand that working in a team gives tremendous rewards but the greatest adventures often occur when you strike out on your own.

People born on April 3 are at their happiest and best when they can occupy the key position at home or at work. It gives them enormous satisfaction to feel indispensable; and with their remarkable creativity and energy, they often are.

Because they like to be at the center of things, life is seldom dull for these people. They have strong motivation and excellent communication skills; these, plus their outgoing and generous nature, give them great powers of persuasion. They thrive on challenges, but if they feel left out on the action they can become moody. Fortunately, this doesn't happen often since people value their contribution and love having them around.

These people don't dislike being on their own but they often flourish in a group. With the ability to gather a diverse collection of people together and transform them into a team, they like to occupy the key position. The only danger with this approach is that team members and friends tend to become too dependent on them, which can also create frustrations when they want to change direction.

Change is a theme for people born on this day. Their childhood and early teens may have been quite restless and reckless; their adult life will continue to see changes, some positive, some negative, because although they are highly intuitive they can sometimes be naïve. Despite these changes, however, their enthusiasm and motivation will ensure that some, if not all, of their dreams are fulfilled. In fact, the challenge and variety offered by change is essential for them because staying in one role limits the discovery and development of their vision and enthusiasm.

They make great leaders because they like to feel needed and because their natural charisma is so strong it tends to attract less energetic people. As long as they learn to respect the viewpoints of others and not to become oversensitive when they encounter criticism, their ability to energize and orchestrate others toward a common goal is second to none.

On the dark side

Naïve, moody, spoiled

At your best

Outgoing, generous, warm

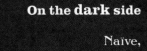

4 April

the birthday of
the catalyst

Your greatest challenge is

learning to persevere

The way forward is ...

to understand that seeing things through to the conclusion is more satisfying and rewarding than initiating them.

Those born on April 4 are catalysts—people who affect the lives of others in a profound way. Their creative energy is explosive, and both at home and at work they have little trouble initiating projects and inspiring others to join their cause.

When they are inspired, these people will typically throw their considerable energy, tenacity and organizational skills into a project, giving them huge potential for outstanding success. Above all, they like to initiate; they also have tremendous courage, happy to strike out in a completely new direction. Too often, however, they move on to the next crusade before the previous one has been completed, leaving those who are less impulsive to reap the rewards. To find true fulfillment, they should settle on a goal and see it through to the end. If they cannot slow down their shocking pace they may eventually wear themselves out, losing their unique and unusual energy.

From their late teens unto the age of forty-six there is an emphasis on security and stability; during these years their dedication and enthusiasm are likely to have a positive influence on everyone they meet or work with. After the age of forty-seven, they become interested in new learning and communication; it is important during these years that they establish their financial security before exploring any new interests.

Catalysts that they are, these people are attracted to challenges and opportunities. They are driven and inspired, and others admire them but may have trouble keeping up with their constant shifts of direction. If they aren't careful, they may end up alone because others regard them as unreliable. They should surround themselves with friends or loved ones who can gently warn them when they are heading off course. They also need to learn that perseverance and self-discipline are the keys to success. However, once they have learned to ground themselves in reality, they should always be allowed to generate and express their ideas. The world would be a less colorful place without them.

On the dark side

Changeable, impulsive, unreliable

At your best

Original, creative, energetic

5 April

the birthday of
the athlete

Your greatest challenge is

learning to relax and unwind

The way forward is ...

to understand that time out isn't time wasted but time gained. Returning to the task in hand you will feel refreshed and more productive.

People born on April 5 have star quality, but they don't tend to seek out fame or even fortune. For them, the satisfaction and reward always lies in the work itself. Like true athletes totally dedicated to their sport, their goal is to constantly learn, improve and strive for their personal best.

These people tend to focus on work and career, valuing solid achievement but, because they are highly principled, their success will never be at the expense of others. They need to feel that they deserve their success and, given the fact that they are blessed with both creativity to inspire others and tenacity to see things through, they have great potential to succeed in life. Their manner tends to be quiet and unassuming, and they like to avoid conflict if they can. This doesn't mean they are pushovers. When their plans are threatened or their beliefs criticized, others may be surprised at their bluntness and drive to succeed. Once they have settled on a chosen course, they will stick to it and defend it passionately. Although this dedicated approach will attract success, it is important for them to understand that some change is essential for progress and development.

Their tendency toward stubbornness is highlighted between the ages of fifteen and forty-five, during which there is an emphasis in their life on security and stability. After the age of forty-six, however, they become more interested in travel, communication, learning new skills, and change. If they can take advantage of the opportunities offered to them, this can be an extremely positive period in their life.

The strong and consistent personality of these people makes them natural candidates for leadership; but because they set extremely high standards, they should be careful that they don't become too demanding of themselves and others in the process. They also have the determination to overcome the most frustrating of obstacles and, even though they don't seek or even realize it, their energy, dedication and will-power will earn them the applause of all their contemporaries.

On the dark side

Stubborn, inflexible, repetitive

At your best

Hardworking, dedicated, energetic

6 April

the birthday of
irresistible curiosity

Your greatest challenge is

learning to trust yourself

The way forward is ...

to understand that although others can offer their insight, nobody knows you better than you.

People born on April 6 have charisma, with lots to spare. There is a kind of wild-eyed excitement about them, ruled as they are by desire, the love of beautiful things and a restless quest for knowledge. They have an irresistible urge to discover everything about the world and the people around them, their minds always being open to new and better ways of doing things.

These people are great fun to have around. They are willing to try almost anything, with the refreshing ability to laugh at themselves. Others are often happy to help them achieve their goals because their ego never gets in the way. They are multi-talented, with a knack for finding innovative solutions in all aspects of life. This makes them the home improvement experts, the planners and organizers at work, and the life and soul of the party.

With so much going for them it's easy to see why they seem destined for great success but also why some fail to realize their full potential. Lack of discrimination is their problem both professionally and at home, and this can lead to low self-esteem. Their naïvety and openness may lead them down many wrong paths, attracting controlling individuals to them and those who haven't got their best interests at heart.

It is important for them to learn to trust their intuition more and to beware of giving too much too soon. Between the ages of fourteen and forty-four they may search for security and stability; they should use this time to develop their self-confidence and sense of direction so that they are not so easily led. After the age of forty-five they may concentrate on learning new skills and expanding their interests.

People born on this day seem to have limitless energy and the ability to visualize undreamed-of possibilities. As long as they can get in touch with their feelings and become more discriminating, they have the potential to be great innovators and to lead others to previously uncharted areas.

On the dark side

Unrealistic, gullible, superficial

At your best

Curious, original, energetic

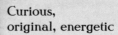

7 April

the birthday of
intensity

Your greatest challenge is

to learn not to alienate others who disagree with you

The way forward is ...

to understand that listening objectively to the views of others doesn't weaken your position, it strengthens it.

People born on April 7 are bold and forthright individuals with deep beliefs they will fight to the death to defend. When they commit themselves to an idea, a project or a person they burn with a passion and an intensity that can drive them to extremes of thought and behaviour.

There are often two sides to the personality of these people: the vibrant, positive side that inspires them to devote themselves passionately to progress; and a more negative, impatient side that can manifest in wild-eyed fury or rebellious behavior when their expectations are not met. There is no middle ground between these two extremes of behavior and they will often swing between them, alienating others when they feel disgruntled.

Although they are blessed with unlimited zeal, determination and optimism, possessing the ability and drive to get where they want to in life, it is important for these people—and to their benefit—to learn to adopt a more considered approach. Rebellion will almost certainly be a feature of their childhood, but between the ages of fifteen and forty-three they may have opportunities to adopt a more considered approach to life. After the age of forty-four they may find new areas of interest, as well as a greater desire for communication and learning new skills. If by this age they have learned the importance of finding the middle way, they are likely to come into their own.

Although they are forthright and courageous people, they also have the hearts of dreamers. They often see different futures unfolding, and this proves invaluable to their planning. They may also feel there is a meaning to their lives but as they search for it there may be setbacks; they may rush into what they believe is their destiny only to find that they lose interest or that it wasn't really for them. Their positive expectations of happiness are, however, often rewarded. This means that although they may not find their meaning and purpose until later in life, when they do find it they discover that waiting was worthwhile.

On the dark side

Unrealistic, negative, rebellious

At your best

Deep, imaginative, vibrant

8 April

the birthday of
noble intention

Your greatest challenge is

learning to give to yourself

The way forward is ...

to understand that until you have met your own physical and emotional needs, you can't muster sufficient resources for helping others.

People born on April 8 have a passionate sense of right and wrong, with a strong focus on humanitarian concerns. Their intentions are extremely noble, being motivated by a deep passion for the underdog or those who haven't been given a chance to develop their potential. The admiration or respect of others is not their main concern; what matters to them is the well-being of others.

Despite their compassion, there is a tendency for these people to see things in black and white; as a result they run the risk of becoming intolerant or dismissive. They passionately believe that everyone is equal, and if they see any form of injustice they can become extremely critical. In the process, they can gain more enemies than friends. It is therefore important for them to learn to control their impulses and find more effective ways of getting their point across.

Since they often find it hard to express their emotions freely they can appear somewhat detached or reserved. When there is a crisis, however, they are a tower of strength. Despite their apparent steadiness they may also alternate between being warm and responsible, and cold and indifferent.

Beneath their self-confidence lie fears of inadequacy that can manifest in self-sacrificing behavior; but if they can overcome these fears, their enormous determination, combined with their incisive and methodical mind, can help them achieve almost anything. Before the age of forty-two there is an emphasis on establishing security and stability, but after that age their focus is on new interests and on communication. These are the years when their self-confidence tends to flower and they really come into their own.

As well as being noble in their intentions, they are independent and daring, keen to express themselves with originality. Their drive to succeed is great but not usually selfish, as they prefer to express their uniqueness through humanitarian deeds that benefit many people. This is what gives these enigmatic but lovely people the potential to bring harmony to the world.

On the dark side

Self-doubting, detached, intolerant

At your best

Compassionate, intense, responsible

9 April

the birthday of

the whirlwind

Your greatest challenge is

knowing when to stop

The way forward is ...

to understand that stopping yourself when you still want more is the way to keep desire and motivation alive; over-indulgence simply kills it.

People born on April 9 have fantastic stamina. They live and love like a whirlwind, possessing an insatiable appetite for all the pleasures of life. Although they love to have a good time, they can also work very hard. Blessed with prodigious energy, originality and single-mindedness, they have great potential to achieve their ambitions.

These people have a strong personality and don't like to be in a subservient position. In their professional life, their understanding of what people need can make them accurate predictors of social trends. They have the ability to turn their ideas into reality, and by so doing they not only enrich the lives of others, they can also profit themselves.

Others are often seduced by their charm, although some find their outspokenness somewhat excessive. They have to win every argument, often somewhat bluntly, and they also don't take kindly to criticism, regarding any such comment as a form of betrayal. Their fondness for pushing the limits by indulging in physical pleasures can alarm others, especially when their lavish lifestyle attracts those who do not have their best interests at heart.

Until the age of forty-one they may concentrate on material stability; it is important during this time that they base their life around positive rather than negative values. After the age of forty-two they may broaden their horizons, becoming more interested in furthering their own spiritual and psychological growth. It is during these years that their generosity, openness and warmth are most likely to be offset by their lack of reliability.

Although people born on this day can be erratic and extreme, their drive and strength of purpose can sweep others off their feet, carrying them along in a whirlwind of enthusiasm. There's little time for quiet reflection along the way but there will be plenty of excitement. This is because life rarely stands still for these people; it's an action-packed adventure with many surprises and opportunities. If they can put these opportunities to good use, they can become energetic campaigners for greater self-expression and for progress.

On the dark side

Excessive, reckless, unreliable

At your best

Energetic, bold, progressive

139

10 April

the birthday of
the shrewd hero/heroine

Your greatest challenge is

to come out of your shell

The way forward is ...

to understand that without the emotional fulfillment of close personal relationships, achievements in the outside world lose some of their magic.

People born on April 10 have a dazzling personality that likes to do courageous and daring things. Their life tends to be a roller-coaster but, although they do take considerable risks both professionally and personally, they are neither foolish nor reckless. Without a doubt they are action heroes and heroines, but shrewd ones.

While those who do not know them well may be taken aback by their daring or radical approach, these people are in fact confident of success, secure in the knowledge that they have carefully evaluated the risks. They may appear impulsive but behind the scenes there is always a soundly considered plan of action to realize their ambitions. This combination of pragmatism and adventure, combined with their undoubted intelligence and enormous energy, augurs well for success.

It can sometimes be difficult for them to slow down, even with their closest friends. Restless and action orientated, they have a tendency to race through life as if they are afraid of missing out on something. It is important for them to learn to relax. Until the age of forty they may concentrate on security and stability, but after this age they will want to learn new skills; it is important that they learn to slow down and reflect on their progress.

Curiously the private lives of these bold people may be marked by a certain degree of detachment from others, as well as by attacks of anxiety or even phobias. These private fears might indicate a fear of failure or rejection; these can be resolved once they learn to connect with their feelings, experiencing the joys of sharing and intimacy with others.

Since people born on this day find it easier to compete than to cooperate, they are excellent self-starters with real leadership potential. Naturally charming, their nonconformist perspective often attracts many admirers. Once they are able to balance their restlessness with sensitivity and patience, there is no doubt that these warriors, with their ability to plan and complete a project, will go far.

On the dark side

Workaholic, detached, unstable

At your best

Daring, competitive, dedicated

11 April

the birthday of
the mediator

Your greatest challenge is

responding to the needs of loved ones

The way forward is ...

to understand that shirking your domestic responsibilities for more stimulating pursuits will not bring you the fulfillment you crave.

The assertive but warm-hearted individuals born on April 11 have the ability to see problems in both an emotional and a practical way, making them excellent problem solvers and mediators. They are capable of bringing even the most divergent of opinions into harmony with great charm and tact.

If there is a good cause to promote, these people are often the first to volunteer to help. They are eternally optimistic, with the ability to devote their energy and interpersonal skills to a plan of action, then promoting it with tenacity. They are also realistic enough to know that the support of others will benefit them; so they set out to charm and convert any opposition to their cause by means of skilled diplomacy.

Although they often find themselves the center of attention, these people do not purposely seek the limelight, preferring to be a part rather than a focus of the action. In their professional life, they are more concerned with ideas than image, working tirelessly to find common ground for agreement.

Unfortunately, they aren't always as diplomatic in their private lives and at times they can be unresponsive to the needs of those closest to them. They often have plenty of admirers, loving nothing better than planning get-togethers where large numbers of people can mingle; but to their nearest and dearest they can be cool. Fortunately, around the age of forty they are likely to focus their energies less on financial security and popularity, and more on close friends and loved ones.

They also are great communicators, working particularly well when given charge of a team with the opportunity to inspire and encourage others. They run the risk that in knowing what is best for the common good they refuse to consider alternative viewpoints, so it is important for their psychological growth to keep their minds open to other, perhaps better, ways of doing things. Once they have learned greater flexibility, they can use their powers of persuasion, tenacity and clear-sightedness to champion justice, creating a more nurturing and peaceful world.

On the dark side

Impersonal, unenthusiastic, selfish

At your best

Diplomatic, intelligent, intuitive

12 April

the birthday of
the enigmatic interviewer

Your greatest challenge is

to get to know your depths

The way forward is ...

to stand back every now and again from the fast pace of life and examine objectively your thoughts and feelings.

People born on April 12 are often surrounded by a fascinated group of listeners. They are well liked for their ability to get others to open up to them, possessing the knack of making people laugh at their own insecurities, offering others an opportunity thereby to rise above themselves.

Stimulating, witty and fun, they are interested in everyone and everything. Their inquisitive minds are forever on the alert, looking out for the latest news or research to inform or entertain. Curiously, they find it hard to share their feelings, being more comfortable in the role of interviewer, entertainer or informer than of confidant. This elusiveness can cause tension both at home and at work; it is important for them to learn to open up about their own feelings.

These people don't like to miss a thing and they may therefore spend a great deal of their twenties and thirties wandering from job to job or even country to country in search of a satisfying profession. While this would prove disastrous for most, for them it can work because every experience they have, even the ones that disappoint and frustrate, is regarded as a learning opportunity. Then, some time in their forties, through this process of trial and error, they find a goal or purpose which can make use of the vast store of knowledge and experience they have thus far accumulated.

Keen observers of the human condition, people born on this day prize knowledge above all else and love to share what they have learned with others. There is a danger that they can become judgmental in the process or heavily influenced by the opinions of others; it is important for them to stay curious and open-minded, and not become dogmatic. Getting to know who they are and what they, not others, think about things is central to their success. This is because when they get in touch with their own feelings, as well as those of others, they can not only entertain and inform, but inspire as well.

On the dark side

Elusive, opinionated, frustrated

At your best

Interested, articulate, perceptive

13 April

the birthday of
the reformer

Your greatest challenge is

learning not to lose faith in yourself

The way forward is ...

to draw on the strength and support of those closest to you and to remind yourself that there is only one you with your unique contribution.

People born on April 13 are born reformers, willing to work tirelessly to make changes they consider crucial. They are an endless source of new ideas and, although some of these might be considered eccentric, people appreciate their unusual approach to problem solving.

These highly intelligent people can often handle tasks that most others find exacting. They excel at resolving problems and coming up with a better way of doing things. Mental stimulation is essential to them and if they don't feel challenged they can get easily bored and restless, with a tendency to fidget. They don't like sitting still and try to inject as much activity as they can into every moment. Their propensity to seek out new challenges is particularly highlighted after the age of thirty-seven, when their focus changes from that of material stability to intellectual curiosity.

These people don't actively seek out the company of others because they are essentially private, preferring to connect with the world and make their mark through their work. Their greatest satisfaction comes from moving humanity forward or from employing their considerable talents in projects that benefit others. They derive great satisfaction from the comfort and support of a few close friends and family, preferably those who validate their vision and provide them with support when their ideas are criticized. Although skeptical of convention and compelled to seek out alternative solutions, they are nonetheless deeply sensitive to the opinions of others; even if these opinions hurt, they are rarely deflected from their chosen course.

Because people born on this day value their solitude, often feeling the need to withdraw from scrutiny, especially when working on a project, they can often be criticized for being remote, distant or in extreme cases weird. But the truth is that they are highly sensitive individuals with a need for privacy. But when the time feels right they can overcome any fear or hesitation they might have and, like the true pioneers they are, can step out with boldness, often breaking new ground in the process.

On the dark side

Reclusive, misunderstood, anxious

At your best

Innovative, bold, eclectic

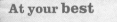

14 April

the birthday of

respect

Your greatest challenge is

not getting
bogged down
in details

*The way
forward is ...*

to understand that
as important as
the details are,
they should never
make you lose
sight of your
ultimate goal.

People born on April 14 often have outstanding communication skills and a wonderful way with people. Their obvious leadership skills earn them the admiration of others. Whatever situation or line of work they find themselves in, others tend to listen to and respect them.

The respect of others matters greatly to these people, as they themselves have great respect for the past and a strong desire to follow in the footsteps of others. Creating new systems or methods doesn't interest them as much as reaching the heights others have already scaled. This doesn't mean they're stuck in the past; quite the opposite, as they will always put a unique stamp on their work. It just means they have a powerful sense of tradition and great respect for the work of others. As a result, conservative methods will often be preferred to more radical ones.

These people are at their happiest and best when their home and work lives are stable, giving them the feeling of security they need to excel in their chosen field. It is therefore important for them not to take the love and support of those closest to them for granted. Until the age of thirty-six they concentrate on material security, building a solid foundation. After the age of thirty-seven they enter a period of new ideas and increased productivity during which they may use their excellent communication skills to become a mouthpiece for an organization or group.

These people like to be in control, both at work and at home, but despite this autocratic tendency they are also intuitive, often quick to realize when they have crossed the line, adjusting their behavior accordingly. Their respectful attitude toward others serves them well, their success rarely being resented. Even though they do suffer from bouts of anxiety and uncertainty—manifested in their obsession with details—it is important that they put their talents to good use because all forms of communication invigorate their lives, so they not only follow in the footsteps of the great, but become great themselves.

On the dark side

Fussy,
anxious, autocratic

At your best

Respectful,
ambitious, disciplined

15 April

intellectual incisiveness

Your greatest challenge is

explaining your vision to others

The way forward is ...

to put yourself into someone else's shoes; try to see things from their point of view.

The charismatic individuals born on April 15 are sensitive and charming, yet ambitious and powerful. The key to their complex and seemingly contradictory personality is their intellectual incisiveness which enables them to formulate well-structured strategies in response to almost any challenge.

The powerful intellect they are blessed with can make them extraordinarily sensitive to what is going on around them. Sometimes they can take their skills of observation to the extreme; this can become a source of friction with loved ones, who want to be seen for who they actually are, not for what they could be. It can also contribute to feelings of anxiety and insecurity, as people born on this day may hear or observe something out of context and draw the incorrect conclusions. Their passion for detailed observation and analysis may make them take themselves and everyone else a little too seriously, so they forget the importance of relaxing and simply having fun. On the plus side, and it's a big plus, their acute intellect and powers of observation enable them to detect a vital piece of information or the missing link needed to remedy or explain a situation. The compassionate, wise side of their nature also means that others often turn to them for support, encouragement and advice.

Their ability to see life in broad rather than specific terms may be regarded by others as unrealistic or impossible and it may be that the world is not yet ready for their sweeping and imaginative ideas. Until the age of thirty-five the emphasis in their life is on practical considerations, but after the age of thirty-six they are likely to place more significance on knowledge, communication and mental exploration, and these are the years when people born on this day really come into their own.

These people long to make their mark on the world and, if they can learn to channel their rare combination of great imagination, brilliant organization and tenacity into a direction that others find acceptable, they have the potential to be truly inspirational.

On the dark side

Judgmental, frantic, overly serious

At your best

Observant, intelligent, powerful

16 April

the birthday of
the truth seeker

Your greatest challenge is

not being exploited

The way forward is ...

to think carefully about who you want to help or be with. You should make sure you don't give to people who are lazy or self-destructive.

People born on April 16 love to talk about the meaning of life, being fascinated by life's mysteries. At the same time they are seductive, charming and very amusing. They know how to make other people smile, and friends, loved ones and colleagues will often regard these humorous and dreamy individuals with great affection.

Although they have the ability to see the humor in almost any situation, they are not superficial individuals. Quite the opposite; they have a deep awareness of life's tragedies, which gives them the insight to understand that humor is one of the best and most cathartic responses. Despite being wise and insightful, they can be generous to the point of stupidity; others often take advantage of their willingness to share. They also tend to over-indulge in everything they enjoy, easily slipping into irresponsible behavior.

In general, strong emotions make these people feel uncomfortable and they like to lighten intense moments with humor. This can make their contribution invaluable during times of stress, as it teaches others how to deal effectively with setbacks. It can, however, also work against them; instead of facing situations that need to be resolved, they avoid them. It is important for them to resist the temptation to sidestep conflict, as this can lead to hidden resentments in the future.

These people can appear as if they are living in a world of dreams. While it is true that they are visionaries, they are able to translate their dreams into reality. Until the age of thirty-four they focus on building a secure foundation for their dreams. Then, after the age of thirty-five, they have a greater interest in interpersonal relationships and communication skills. This is a positive development for them, as becoming more aware of the dreams and ideals of others—and not just their own—aids their psychological growth. Once they strike a healthy balance between their inner and outer selves, others will admire them not only for their humor and gentle presence, but also for their inspirational strength of purpose.

On the dark side

Dreamy, extreme, permissive

At your best

Entertaining, kind, generous

17 April

the birthday of
will-power

Your greatest challenge is

telling others how you really feel

The way forward is ...

to understand that everyone, even those with incredible self-control, has times when they feel low or vulnerable.

People born on April 17 are confident, ambitious and opportunistic individuals. When knocked down, they have the will-power and resilience to bounce right back. They know their own mind, having a clear idea of where they are going and how to get there. Determined to succeed, they also have a talent for spotting opportunities, not just for themselves, but for others.

Despite often being quietly spoken, the impression these people make on others is often strong because they promote their ideals with absolute conviction. They expect others to agree with them and, because of their intense will-power, others often do. They also have the ability to translate their ideals into action and may find themselves leading those who are less determined. Although it can seem as if they were born to be successful, they do have to work hard to get to the top. This isn't a problem for them, though, as they do whatever it takes to make their mark. They thrive on challenge and love a good battle and, in the process, make either loyal friends or resentful enemies.

These people are prone to mood swings and like to spend time alone when dark moments are upon them. Although this can be beneficial in their professional relationships, in their personal relationships it can be detrimental; refusing to share their ups and downs limits the depth of close bonds. Their tendency is to divide everything into positive and negative; just as it's important for them to appreciate the complexity of their emotional life, they also need to acknowledge the complexities in the world around them. Until the age of thirty-three they strive for security and certainty, but after the age of thirty-four they may move toward a more flexible world view.

It is important for them to ensure that their amazing will-power does not make them too judgmental or serious. Once they inject a little light-heartedness into their lives, they will discover that their authority isn't weakened but strengthened, and that wherever their dreams take them, others will gladly follow.

On the dark side

Moody, judgmental, harsh

At your best

Purposeful, opportunistic, resilient

18 April

the birthday of dignity

Your greatest challenge is

learning to let down your guard

The way forward is ...

to understand that being yourself is the best and only way to earn the respect of others, even if that means appearing ungainly or vulnerable.

People born on April 18 are powerful, strong, dependable and influential. They stand firm in their beliefs, possessing boundless energy and conviction. Often taking the lead in conversations or projects, they like to think of themselves as confident and dignified; this is exactly how they come across to others.

In some ways similar to a comic-book superhero, they are bold, hardworking and dignified, and also like to defend the underdog. Sometimes, though, their views are so lofty and their standards so high that they set themselves up for frustration and disappointment. This can manifest itself in sudden and unexpected outbursts of temper or, even worse, disdain.

The respect of others is extremely important for them and they take great care how they present themselves to others. They are particularly vulnerable to attacks on their dignity or performance but, because they are so well prepared, these rarely occur. Generally, they have an extremely positive effect on others, their main problem being recognition of their own and others' limits. They need to be careful that they don't become extreme or fanatical, especially before the age of thirty-two. During this period, the influence of either their mother or father over their choice of career may be strong. After the age of thirty-three they may develop a desire to become more knowledgeable and communicative, and therefore more flexible and independent. Around the age of sixty-two there is another important shift, which accentuates their emotional needs, home and friends.

Despite the seriousness of their ideals, most people born on this day understand the importance of relaxation, and this can help them avoid becoming obsessive. They may even have a slightly mischievous streak and they should never seek to repress that positive energy. This is because when they are able to become more spontaneous in their words and deeds, they have the potential to earn both the respect of others, and their loyalty, admiration and affection.

On the dark side

Proud, unrealistic, uncontrolled

At your best

Loyal, dignified, influential

19 April

the birthday of
magnetic self-sufficiency

Your greatest challenge is

discovering where your talents lie

The way forward is ...

to gather information and listen to the advice of people who know you well or who have worked with you in the past.

Liberally endowed with originality, stamina, intelligence and ambition, people born on April 19 possess unlimited faith in their own knowledge. This means they will also take some knocks but much of their confidence is gained through their experience of victory and defeat.

Possessing a strong competitive streak, if something isn't difficult or nearly impossible, these people are not interested. With the ability to turn weaknesses into strengths, they are often the unqualified workers who soar up through the ranks. Although career focused, they are rarely materialistic, often being generous with both their time and their money. Their goal is not necessarily to be rich but to be self-sufficient, as in their eyes dependency on another is a sign of weakness. Learning to accept financial support—or any type of support for that matter—from family and friends may be difficult, given the high value they place on self-sufficiency, but reaching out will take them a step forward in personal development.

It is important for them to learn to step back now and again, and let others take the lead. Until the age of thirty-one there is an emphasis on security and routine in their life and they need to be careful not to be over-controlling or to ignore the feelings of others. After the age of thirty-two, however, they may widen their interests, placing more emphasis on learning, knowledge and new skills. If they can teach themselves and others to experiment with new and untested approaches to situations this period in their lives can be extremely productive.

Nothing gives them more satisfaction than knowing that the success they have achieved has been of their own making. They instinctively take control, providing vision and direction in cooperative ventures; others tend to look to them for leadership because their confidence and poise under fire make their advice difficult to ignore. Once they have learned to delegate, to listen more and talk just a little less, their stamina, mental acuity and personal magnetism can help them succeed in virtually anything.

On the dark side

Over-bearing, dismissive, self-centered

At your best

Committed, skillful, charismatic

149

TAURUS

THE BULL (APRIL 20 – MAY 20)

* **Element:** Earth
* **Ruling planet:** Venus, the lover
* **Symbol:** The Bull
* **Tarot card:** The Heirophant (determination)
* **Number:** 6
* **Favorable colors:** Green, pink, pale blue
* **Key phrase:** I have what I need

Taureans tend to be reliable, hardworking and determined characters, but if they are to function at their peak they must feel emotionally and financially secure. Although they have terrific common sense and stacks of creativity, these can sometimes be coupled with a lack of flexibility and an unwillingness to make changes or take risks in life. They often like to surround themselves with beautiful things, not only to remind themselves and others that they are progressing in society but also to draw attention to their softer, gentler, more artistic and sensual side.

Personality potential

People born under the sun sign Taurus are strong, resilient and determined. At first glance these appear to be masculine traits but Taurus is ruled by Venus, the planet of harmony, love and beauty. This means that Taureans are a delightful combination of strength and softness, dynamism and compassion, who work long and hard but who also enjoy the fruits of their success. A Taurean will give his or her all to a project but when it's completed they really know how to switch off, unwind and take pleasure in what they have achieved.

The Taurean mind is methodical, careful and decisive and as people they will quietly and carefully build themselves both a fulfilling career and a fulfilling life. For a Taurean, if something is worth doing it's worth doing properly. Shortcuts are not their style. They like to think things through carefully and pay close attention to the details; as a result the solutions they come up with are always practical and creative. Their most irresistible characteristic is perhaps their natural charm, which they can express in a variety of ways. They usually have enchanting speaking voices and will always find time to listen

to and encourage those in need of support. They will work hard to make sure their living and working environment is harmonious, and they enjoy being surrounded by good friends and good food. They are especially good at offering practical advice. There is also a lighter, sociable side to their character that appreciates the arts and the good things in life.

Personal integrity matters a great deal to the resilient people born under this sun sign. They can be relied upon to do the right thing and to carry things through to the end, no matter what obstacles or setbacks they encounter along the way. Taureans simply don't know how to quit. Although they are without doubt loyal, trustworthy and reliable people, this does not mean they are dull. Once you get to know them you will find that complementing their tenacity and determination is an endearing, earthy charm and a surprising creativity; these qualities can win them countless friends and admirers.

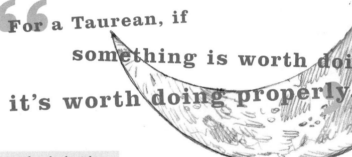

For a Taurean, if something is worth doing it's worth doing properly.

On the dark side

Taurus is the first earth sign of the zodiac and, like the earth herself, they can be unforgiving, stubborn and harsh. A more flexible approach to life would certainly benefit them. They possess a distinct reluctance to take risks or try anything new, and they can also be guilty of self-indulgence and shallowness in their relentless pursuit of earthly pleasures.

Although Taureans often have an air of authority about them, they sometimes lack confidence in themselves; this can make them appear undisciplined and lazy. Perhaps the most unattractive aspect of the Taurean character, however, is their possessiveness. Their friends and loved ones are cherished, respected and admired, but they are often regarded as possessions or property without freewill of their own. Add to this a stubborn streak that makes it hard for them to forget and virtually impossible for them to forgive, and you have a person with selfish, at times bullish tendencies.

Their bouts of low self-esteem, possessiveness, stubbornness and jealousy often stem from their overwhelming need to feel secure. If their sense of ownership—whether this be of a person, friend, lover, possession or project—is threatened, their fury may explode in a blind rage. Just as this fury has taken a long time to build up, it will also take a long time to subside and, like an erupting volcano, it will leave a trail of devastation in its wake.

Symbol

The symbol of Taurus is the bull and, if you can conjure an image in your mind of a bull in a rage, you'll know this is a distressing sight. The bull can put up with a lot of goading and tormenting—perhaps more than any other sign can stand—but there will come a time when it stops, turns around and wreaks indiscriminate devastation and destruction on anyone or anything in its path.

Darkest secret

Nothing terrifies a Taurean more than having no money in the bank or not being able to "keep up with the Joneses." This isn't necessarily because money is their main motivation in life, but because so much of their personal identity is tied up with being able to surround themselves with material possessions. Outwards signs of success count for a great deal to Taureans.

Love

Those born under the warm Taurean sun are the most sensual lovers of the zodiac; they delight in cuddling and lovemaking, and are wonderfully passionate, dedicated and romantic partners in love.

However, when it comes to the choice of a long-term partner, they tend to be methodical in their approach. There may be a lengthy engagement period, for example, during which they test the waters; this is because a successful partnership matters a great deal to them and they don't want to make any mistakes. To thrive they need to have peace and harmony in their relationships. Emotional security is vital and, if that is threatened in any way, their possessiveness and jealously will kick in and gradually build up until they explode in sudden flashes of temper that can shake the foundations of any relationship.

Taureans will do everything in their power, however, to avoid getting to this point and in the great majority of circumstances they are loving, kind, respectful and generous with their affections and their finances. Once they have committed themselves to a relationship there can be no doubt of their loyalty and devotion, but they do need to be careful that this devotion does not turn into complacency and that routine and their extreme desire to possess their partner—body, mind and soul—does not stifle their relationship.

Love matches:
Cancer, Virgo and Capricorn

The Taurean man

As the image of a bull suggests, the Taurean man tends to be strong, determined and hardworking. At first glance he may appear conservative in his appearance, but if you take a closer look you'll notice how well tailored and expensive his clothes are. He may be the quiet, unassuming one working hard and untiringly in the corner, but check back in a couple of years and you'll probably find that this sensible, practical and determined guy is now running the place. In other words, never underestimate the power and potential of the male Taurean. Once he has set his mind on something or someone he almost always gets what he wants and he can wear people down with his dogged persistence.

When it comes to choosing a partner, the Taurean male prefers one with grace and intelligence who can balance his own maturity. He likes his freedom and doesn't want a clinging vine, but he also wants someone he feels needs his support. It may be true that the bull isn't a wild dreamer and he won't sweep his potential partner off their feet, but you can be sure that when he says he will ring back or do something he will do it. There are no mind games here. This man means business and you should be in no doubt about his intentions. Once he has captured your heart he'll work untiringly to build a secure future for the both of you—a future that includes a secure and beautiful home, regular holidays, plenty of luxuries, and strong but gentle arms protecting you from life's storms.

The Taurean woman

The Taurean woman is typically fiercely protective and supportive of those she loves. She's also one of the most courageous women of the zodiac, both morally and emotionally. And because she appreciates people for who they are, she also has the remarkable ability to get on with just about everyone from scientist to street sweeper.

It's a rare Taurean woman who doesn't try to make her home look clean—even beautiful—and she is very intolerant of untidiness and sloppy habits. Many have a marked talent or appreciation for the arts, in particular music. Although she is often very sensual and passionate in the bedroom, in everyday life she likes to take her time and do things her own way. If you try to rush her or hurry her along, she may become irritable. It isn't wise to get her angry because if she is goaded too much she can burst into a violent temper that will take a long time for you and her to forget.

When it comes to choosing a partner she despises weakness and will look for someone who is willing to contribute as much as she does to the relationship. Once she is in a

relationship she will be fiercely loyal and will stand by those she loves, even when all others have deserted them. She will also never fail to inspire her partner with her brave, determined example. Those lucky enough to have a Taurus woman fall in love with them will find that her dependable strength and practicality can quite literally move mountains.

Family

As children, Taureans tend to be fairly content and passive. Mealtimes are unlikely to be a problem and their happy, smiling faces earn them the label of a well-behaved child early in life. It may take a while, however, for them to learn to walk. The transition from crawling to walking takes a great deal of effort and the Taurean child gets a lot of enjoyment from crawling. Parents need not worry, however, that this child is going to suffer from delayed development. When they are ready they will take their first steps with confidence, and their strong, steady legs and feet will keep them balanced where others may fall. They are also quick to learn, and when they learn something they are unlikely to forget it. Discipline is extremely important for them because if they don't get enough they will feel insecure and will start testing their boundaries. Once they know what those boundaries are and what is expected of them they will stop feeling anxious and are far more likely to excel. They do have a stubborn side and the only way to get through to them when they are being obstinate is to appeal to their morality by asking them to consider what the right thing to do is.

Taurean parents will provide their children with secure and loving homes. Discipline will be strong, which is fine for children who respond to this kind of approach; but to children who are dreamier and more artistic it can be stifling and might lead to rebellion, so a more flexible approach is encouraged. Providing their children with security is important to Taurean parents, but ironically they may work so long and hard to achieve this goal that they end up missing out on quality time with their children while they are growing up. The danger then is that their children grow up with their material needs met but their emotional needs neglected. Striking a balance is crucial.

Career

The ideal job for a Taurean is one in which there aren't too many distractions or changes from routine, meaning that they can work steadily toward a goal. They don't tend to do well in jobs that require on-the-spot decisions, as they prefer to take their time contemplating the alternatives. Their ideal workplace would be calm, low key and well ordered. Jobs that may suit them best include banking, insurance, building, investment, architecture, interior design, farming or caring for the land, music, singing or voice coaching, jewelry, antiques and art dealing or any job that requires hard work, stability and reliability. Work that gives respectability in established institutions will also appeal, and their love of good food and wine makes them excellent restaurateurs.

" The ideal job for a Taurean is one in which there aren't too many distractions or changes from routine... "

Health and leisure

Taureans have a tendency to weight gain because they enjoy their food so much. It's therefore important for them to make sure they eat a healthy, balanced diet rich in whole grains, fruits, vegetables, legumes, nuts, seeds and oily fish; but this can sometimes be difficult to achieve because they tend to work long hours. Avoiding large meals in the evening is recommended, as is making sure they eat breakfast and take a proper break at lunchtime to eat a healthy meal. Regular exercise is also essential, and most Taureans enjoy team games and exercise classes. Because they have a propensity to move fairly slowly they would benefit from aerobics, brisk walking, jogging, wrestling, judo and dancing to help speed them up. Colds, sore throats and bronchial problems may plague Taureans from time to time, but good posture and regular exercise will help sort out any shoulder and neck tension.

Most Taureans have no problem enjoying their leisure time and they like nothing better than entertaining or spending

time with friends. In fact they can be extremely generous with their time and their money. Comfort of any kind—including good food, good company, sex, luxury and retail therapy—is high on their list of priorities. They run the risk, however, of laziness and time wasting. To avoid lethargy, especially during retirement, they are advised to take up new and interesting hobbies; working for charity and travel are especially appropriate. Patience and attention to detail are their strengths, so hobbies they may particularly enjoy include gardening, painting, golf and embroidery. Their love of their home manifests itself in collecting art, interior decoration and upholstery. Reading, meditating on or wearing the color orange will encourage them to be more flexible and creative in their approach to life.

Born between April 20 and April 29

The influence of the plant Venus is particularly strong here, and people born between these dates are likely to be incredibly sensual and loving. They do possess, however, a tendency to crave the biggest and best of everything, and learning the art of simple contentment may be one of their biggest life challenges.

Born between April 30 and May 10

People born between these dates tend to have very active and creative minds, but there is a danger that they can be highly critical of themselves. Their path to happiness lies in their ability to trust their intuition as much as their ability to analyze every detail.

Born between May 11 and May 20

These people have a very strong financial sense and are also highly practical and success orientated. That said, they should be careful to ensure they don't become workaholics in their pursuit of financial security. To feel truly fulfilled they need to get in touch with their Taurean sensuality, and to constantly remind themselves that they need a balance of giving and receiving, of work and play.

Life lessons

Taureans may be delightfully sensual and tactile, but along with this pleasure-orientated approach to life they often have a large dose of laziness and self-indulgence to go with it. Taureans see absolutely no reason why they can't have everything they want in life and this reasoning can sometimes lead them into materialistic greed. They need to learn how to distinguish between what they need and what they want, because underneath their love of luxury and pleasures lies the misleading idea that others will respect them for what they have, not for who they are.

The major life lesson for Taureans is therefore to learn that their self-worth is not tied up with their job, their house or what they own, but with who they are. Self-worth is an internal state that can't be bought by money or material things, or obtained from other people. Taureans also need to work on their possessive nature and learn that if you truly love someone you set them free.

Being quite stubborn and aggressive—even combative—when they get angry, Taureans need to understand that no one can control the way they feel but themselves. Their intense desire to stick to the status quo and prevent change can also hold them back, so they need to recognize that not all change is bad; in fact sometimes it can be very positive. Change means growth because it opens the door to new choices and points of view that can lead to great improvement. The secret for success is for Taureans to learn to have more belief in themselves and their ability to handle uncertainty and change. For steady, predictable Taurus, uncertainty can be terrifying but what they need to understand is that it's only terrifying because they *think* it is. If Taureans can change their mind about change and uncertainty, they will almost certainly change their life for the better.

Other signs of the zodiac can help Taureans to learn some of these crucial life lessons. Scorpios can teach Taureans to be subtle rather than stubborn in their approach when things aren't going to plan. Leos can teach them self-confidence and the ability to thrive on the challenges change offers. Arians can encourage them to step out of their comfort zone and Sagittarians can encourage them to be more adventurous. Taureans can draw inspiration from Pisceans and Aquarians and their ability to place ideals above material gain. And, along with the other two air signs, Gemini and Libra, Taureans may even be encouraged to value and perhaps even enjoy change.

2O April

the birthday of
the hypnotic personality

Your greatest challenge is

dealing with negative feedback

The way forward is ...

to understand that any kind of feedback, positive or negative, is helpful. The secret is to learn from it.

People born on April 20 often have a hypnotic personality; others willingly follow their lead, sometimes even blindly. They are hungry for success and the admiration of others, with a burning desire to see their goals realized. Fortunately, they also have a highly developed sense of fair play; only rarely will they use their hypnotic powers for personal gain or unworthy causes.

Once they find a cause or a goal to inspire them, these people will often identify with it. Despite identifying strongly with group values there is, however, a side to them that remains deeply private, sensual and sensitive. In tune with all their senses, physical touch is their sustenance; to break down barriers, they will often be the first to kiss, hug or hold hands. This combination of ambition and sensitivity can occasionally make them moody and needy, but it also gives them an enigmatic and compelling quality.

When these determined and charismatic people set their minds on something, they will allow nothing and no one to stand in their way. Such ambition and tenacity suggest that they have the potential for outstanding success in all areas of their lives. The danger with their clarity of vision and purpose is that it can inspire strong opposition. Since they find it hard to accept criticism of any sort, they have a tendency to block out alternative opinions and viewpoints, often dominating others. They also have a tendency, if thwarted, to retreat into a fantasy world far removed from the reality of others.

It is important for people born on this day to recognize the importance of maintaining an open mind and to accept that, despite their personal magnetism and ability to inspire others, they may not always be right. This tendency to be inflexible is highlighted in their first thirty years, but after the age of thirty they become more interested in learning and communication. If they can take advantage of this opportunity to become more open-minded, there is nothing to stop them achieving the ambitions that inspire them.

On the dark side

Egotistical, isolated, stubborn

At your best

Sensual, charismatic, inspirational

21 April

Your greatest challenge is

learning how to accept help from others

The way forward is ...

to understand that other people have just as great a need for help and support as you have; don't deny them that opportunity.

The majestic people born on April 21 often inspire others with their graciousness and hard-working approach. Willing to push themselves hard, they often end up way ahead of others. Financial reward and getting ahead of others are not their motivation, however; what motivates them is a desire to push themselves as far as they can go.

They like to set themselves high standards, and so strong is their self-knowledge that only the most unforeseen of circumstances will prevent them from achieving their goals. They are dignified and self-assured people whose reliability, tenacity and sensitivity to alternative viewpoints earn them the respect of others, who tend to regard them as noble, gracious, loyal individuals. Never afraid to voice their opinions, they will only do so in a positive, constructive way.

Although they are highly driven, they know how to relax and make themselves and others laugh. They also have a love for the good things in life and, although this is in keeping with the regal or privileged inclinations of their personality, it can provoke addictions to sex, food, drink, and other "pleasurable" pastimes. They are especially vulnerable when their reputation at work is criticized. Fortunately, after the age of thirty, when they put greater emphasis on clear communication and new interests than on material things, they become more resilient and less at risk from losing themselves in these ways.

These people love nothing better than to help others reach their full potential, and can be generous with their time and love. They should be careful not to become too controlling and to give those in their charge the chance to make their own mistakes. There may be some chopping and changing in their professional life, particularly in their thirties and early forties, but when they do find their feet their single-mindedness and endearing desire to see others progress will help them realize their ambitions and, like the gracious nobles they are, earn them the respect and loyalty of others.

On the dark side

Pleasure-seeking, controlling, obsessive

At your best

Honest, regal, energetic

22 April

the birthday of quality

Your greatest challenge is

to avoid becoming materialistic

The way forward is ...

to understand that the old cliché is true: as pleasurable as physical or material things are, true happiness can only be found within.

The charismatic people born on April 22 tend to devote their considerable skills to the pursuit of quality; they want the best job, best car and best home. They often exude power but in a quiet, understated way, and friends and family rarely resent their ambitions because they are likely to lavish praise and recognition on others. They also have a hypnotic charm and the ability to make others change their minds about almost anything.

They believe that they are born to create something of quality with their lives. Their talents and imposing physical presence express themselves best in their organizational skills and ability to motivate others to work toward a common goal. Those who work alongside them respect their down-to-earth approach and ability to offer positive encouragement. These people are altogether confident and charming, so life really should be easy for them, but their stumbling block is their intense desire for power. There is a real danger that they can be controlling, opinionated, overbearing and, in extreme cases, unkind and critical of others.

To avoid alienating themselves from the goodwill of others, these people need to make sure that they use their imposing presence wisely and don't become enslaved by materialistic concerns. Up to the age of twenty-eight they are most likely to be concerned with power and establishing themselves financially, but after the age of twenty-nine they develop an interest in education and learning new skills. This will continue until their fifties, when there is a shift toward their feelings, and the growing importance of friends and family.

It is extremely important for these people to reject values, goals and people that are inconsistent with moral and social justice. Developing their spiritual side will help them to become more aware of their own power without the need for external validation. Once they find a goal, and a technique for attaining that goal, their clear-sighted vision, pragmatic outlook, excellent communication skills, and fierce resilience will help them make their own very special mark on the world.

On the dark side

Pleasure-seeking, controlling, opinionated

At your best

Ambitious, imposing, charismatic

23 April

the birthday of
the elusive guide

Your greatest challenge is

not getting stuck in your ways

The way forward is ...

to understand that change is essential to your psychological growth. Without it, you won't learn, grow or reach your full potential.

There's an elusive quality about people born on April 23 and they tend to be known only to their most intimate friends. This is because, although they are non-conformist, they like to make others feel comfortable and so others can form a false image of them. Being misread, however, is unlikely to bother them, as they have enough self-awareness to allow others to think of them what they will.

Although they have the confidence to be accommodating, this doesn't mean they are always compliant. Quite the opposite; from an early age they are likely to have had a strong desire to establish their individuality and make their mark on the world. They would prefer to act as a guide to others rather than follow in someone else's footsteps. As innovators, they are often able to sense future trends, but their visionary talents never cut them off from practical reality.

Their progressive outlook puts them ahead of their contemporaries but they do have an odd tendency to become set in their ways, favoring routine and control over spontaneity. There is also a possessive and anxious streak to their nature. They should try to overcome reservations, especially regarding close relationships, because they tend to be at their happiest and best in the security of one loving union. Until the age of twenty-seven they may cling to the safety of routine and be set in their ways; after the age of twenty-eight they are more receptive to new ideas, ways of thinking and doing things. This process continues until the end of their fifties, when there is a positive shift toward their emotional needs, especially those concerning home and family.

Compassionate and popular on the one hand, blessed with great insight, originality and tenacity on the other, they can achieve great things. Once they can free themselves from routine and allow themselves to become the innovators that they really are, they can not only make their mark on the world but also act as a guide and source of hope to others.

On the dark side

Detached, misleading, anxious

At your best

Insightful, innovative, popular

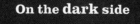

24 April

the birthday of
devotion

Your greatest challenge is

resisting the need to respond to every request

The way forward is ...

to understand that there is a difference between generosity and stupidity. Don't give to people who are capable of helping themselves.

Nothing gives people born on April 24 greater satisfaction that knowing they have inspired or guided the lives of others. They have enormous hearts, and devoted and protective friends who believe the world should be a place of universal love and equality.

They can have a strong protective instinct toward those they love, but the parental role they like to assume can be alternately endearing and exasperating. Others are grateful for their attentions but may also find them draining and restrictive. They can be the nurturing parent who finds it hard to let go when a child wants to spread their wings or the lover who cannot think of a world outside their relationship. They can also feel let down when those they love fall from the lofty pedestal by somehow failing to obey their directions. They should learn to allow others the chance to follow their own hearts and, if need be, make their own mistakes.

As well as being devoted to close relationships, they can also become completely dedicated to their career, often fully identifying with it. It can be enormously painful for them if there is a conflict between commitment to work or family, and they may agonize over maintaining a balance. This is because they find it hard to separate their heart and their lives; but if they learn to give a little less and sometimes put themselves first, they may find that it is possible to be more accommodating.

Until the age of twenty-six their lives are often centered on a need for affection and material security; after the age of twenty-seven there are opportunities for them to develop more interests. There is another turning point after the age of fifty-seven, placing more emphasis on fulfilling their emotional needs. Throughout their lives, learning to confidently use the word "no" will help them feel less torn between career and family. It will also allow them to make their unique mark on the world and to put their organizational capabilities, creative energies and single-mindedness to their best possible use.

On the dark side

Indecisive, moody, smothering

At your best

Devoted, nurturing, creative

25 April

the birthday of
imposing vigor

Your greatest challenge is

learning to value life beyond the material

The way forward is ...

to understand that when you forget to take care of your soul you become nervous, stressed and afraid.

People born on April 25 are hard to ignore. Whatever their physical size, their presence and energy are dynamic and imposing. Strong-minded, they are more interested in action than reflection, and their drive to succeed inspires awe in those who are less self-assured.

When they employ their remarkable energy, intellectual focus and steadfast determination, they have enormous potential to achieve all their aims. Despite their unwavering sense of purpose they can, however, unwittingly sabotage their own efforts by making snap decisions and putting themselves unnecessarily at risk. They don't seek danger but they are courageous and, if presented with a demanding challenge, they are unlikely to avoid it but rather face it head on.

They tend to concentrate their energies on the practical; the subtle aspects of life are often lost on them. This can-do approach with little time for ideas, theories or small talk means that there is nothing vague or undefined about them; indeed they often establish themselves fairly early in life. The danger, however, is their lack of interest in the spiritual or abstract side of life. When things are going well they are unlikely to notice this area of their life is limited, but when things are going badly or they feel in need of comfort, they will feel a sense of loss, confusion and bewilderment.

Fortunately, after the age of twenty-six there are opportunities for them to communicate and exchange ideas, stretching themselves mentally with new kinds of study. They should ensure that the emphasis is not just on the practical but also on the theoretical or spiritual. After the age of fifty-six they are likely to feel the need to be closer to those they love and care for. This again is significant, as until then the focus of their energies is likely to have been their career.

Above all, they have the ability to effortlessly command respect and, as long as they remember to check their impulsiveness and nurture their spiritual self, there is little that they cannot accomplish.

On the dark side

Overbearing, mundane, hasty

At your best

Energetic, imposing, steadfast

26 April

the birthday of
beautiful logic

Your greatest challenge is

learning there are no exact moral measurements

The way forward is ...

to understand that people, yourself included, are not statistics or geometry. In human terms, perfection is about being imperfect.

Although those born on April 26 can be bold and visionary in their plans, one of their defining characteristics is a meticulous attention to detail. Making sure everything is cut to the right size and shape matters greatly to them. They instinctively understand that, for a project to be successful, logical planning and careful preparation is essential. They are pillars of logic and common sense.

Having considered and worked through all the possibilities and contingencies without losing focus on their ultimate objective, it's no surprise that they are often found presiding over smooth-running projects. They are often greatly admired for their dependability, efficiency and, as great self-starters, their independence. They are highly confident in their abilities; there is a risk, however, that they become rigid in their beliefs and dismiss any other way but their way. This controlling tendency can have a damaging effect on personal and professional relationships; they need to learn to respect diversity of opinion and the individuality of others.

Until the age of twenty-five, their stubbornness is likely to dominate; but after the age of twenty-six they may become more flexible in their thinking and in their approach to life by studying and communicating. After the age of fifty-six they feel the need to be close to those they love and care for.

Throughout their lives they need to make sure that their love of logic, order and detail does not estrange them from their heart. They need to understand that perfecting themselves is not the way to a fulfilling life. The sooner they can start getting in touch with their feelings and the feelings of others, the sooner they can enjoy a more balanced and healthy life. In their dedication to perfection they can become isolated from others. Learning to embrace and enjoy the inconsistencies of others will help them feel less lonely.

Once they understand that human beings aren't perfect or logical there is no reason why their inspired and productive strategies can't help them achieve and even exceed their goals.

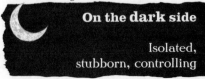

On the dark side

Isolated, stubborn, controlling

At your best

Rational, dependable, independent

27 April

the birthday of
charming self-reliance

Your greatest challenge is

not to isolate yourself

The way forward is ...

to understand that although you can be highly productive when you are alone, it is important for your psychological growth and personal happiness to share your ideas.

People born on April 27 tend to direct a lot of their energies inward, often preferring the inner world of ideas over the distractions of social activity. They like to spend time alone but they are hardly ever lonely. This is because they are self-reliant individuals who don't feel the need to seek the approval or validation of others. Despite their natural reserve and inward focus, when they do find themselves part of a social group others often find them both charming and fascinating.

More outgoing people may regard them as shy or antisocial but they are highly intuitive and compassionate individuals who will willingly offer their help and support to others if needed. In fact, they really come into their own in a group setting; they will often amaze others who have only previously interacted with them on a one-to-one basis with their gregariousness, willingness to give almost anything a go and highly developed sense of humor. They can get frustrated at times when others don't offer as much support as they do, but it is important that they don't take their bitterness to extremes and cut themselves off from the benefits of being with others.

There will always be a tendency for these reflective people to favor the world of concepts and knowledge over everything else. They may also be tempted by some form of fundamentalism or extremism; this will impede their psychological growth. Fortunately, between the ages of twenty-four and fifty-four they experience an increased need to communicate and exchange ideas. This can be an extremely positive and productive time during which they expand their ideas, learn new skills or take up new areas of study.

Their tendency to withdraw into their private world, coupled with their sensitivity and strong sense of realism, gives them great potential for creativity and innovation. As long as they make sure they remain emotionally open and live in the present and not some distant future, they can achieve considerable success, at the same time inspiring and improving the lives of others.

On the dark side

Withdrawn, serious, shy

At your best

Independent, charming, dedicated

28 April

Your greatest challenge is

learning to let go

The way forward is ...

to understand that great leadership is about empowering others to take charge of their own destinies.

When people born on April 28 have decided on a chosen course of action, nothing can divert them from it. Energetic and radiant people, they can motivate others with their imposing emotional, physical and psychological presence. Life is a dance or an orchestra and they are the choreographer or conductor.

Among the most focused individuals of the entire year, they never give up until they see the light at the end of the tunnel. Others instinctively recognize their strength and dependability, and they are often the first to be called on for help during a crisis. They immediately take charge of situations, encouraging others to take positive action and coming up with workable solutions. They try to be as honest as they can be with everyone they meet. Some people may find them too blunt, but they would rather risk offending someone than be involved in any kind of deception.

They take great care to always look the part, and you will rarely find them looking anything less than their best. They are also able to stay in tune with what others are thinking and feeling; this helps them guide and direct others with sensitivity and respect, rather than with overbearing authority. Occasionally they can lapse into stubbornness, but this is often a manifestation of their fear of not being needed. They should learn that the greatest leaders, parents and guides are those who can give their charges or children the confidence and skills they need to survive without their support.

Cultivating a wide range of interests outside the home and learning to take themselves less seriously will help them develop the psychological strength to let others take control of their own lives. Fortunately, from the ages of twenty-three to fifty-three the pace of their life increases; they find new interests, skills and forms of communication. If they can take advantage of these opportunities for growth and diversification, they can use their powers of pragmatism, resourcefulness and creativity to single-mindedly work toward the fulfillment of their goals and their dreams.

On the dark side

Inflexible, over protective, blunt

At your best

Radiant, focused, dependable

29 April

the birthday of
impeccable manners

Your greatest challenge is

learning to let your hair down

The way forward is ...

to understand that those with the ability to laugh at themselves are more likely to get others on their side and lead a satisfying life.

The dignified but warm individuals born on April 29 devote a considerable amount of their energy to the image they present to the world. With their impeccable manners and appreciation of the finer things in life they prefer the company of equally poised people, but they have the flexibility to alter their behavior according to the company they keep. This doesn't mean they are insecure. Quite the contrary; they have a clear self-image. It's just that the positive opinion of others, from whatever walk of life, matters greatly to them.

Friends and co-workers are unlikely to find them unprepared for any situation they are in. They will do their utmost to present themselves as positively as possible and to perform to the best of their ability. And because they are so reliable, they often find themselves in positions of responsibility. The downside of this is that constantly presenting a perfect, self-assured image can be exhausting, especially as they love nothing better than to occasionally relax and let their hair down.

It is vital for them to make sure they do find time to enjoy the lighter side of life as always being counted on by others may give them an exaggerated sense of self-importance. Fortunately, between the ages of twenty-two and fifty-two there are many opportunities for them to increase the tempo of their lives with new interests and new skills. Around the age of fifty-two they may concentrate on emotional security.

They tend to be givers rather than takers, always having an interest in and a kind word for others. There are times, however, when they might feel deeply insecure for no apparent reason; this is usually because they aren't paying sufficient attention to their feelings. If they can learn to tap into their hidden creativity and get their sensitivity to the moods and feelings of others to work for, not against them, they will discover an unlimited resource for guidance, transformation and self-empowerment, and the key to unlocking outstanding potential for success in all aspects of their lives.

On the dark side

Self-involved, proud, moody

At your best

Dignified, meticulous, dependable

30 April

the birthday of commitment

not feeling
burdened by
responsibility

*The way
forward is ...*

to understand the
need to remove
yourself
temporarily from
the demands of
others, to recharge
your batteries and
to concentrate on
your own needs.

People born on April 30 often give the impression of being calm and collected. They love the good things in life, approaching others with affection. They can be extremely funny, as long as the joke is not on them, and their natural good cheer ensures they are the center of attention. However, contrary to their relaxed exterior, such is their intelligence and drive that they will feel unfulfilled unless they can devote themselves to their work or another person.

They tend to value commitment, responsibility and duty above all else; this is why they present a hardworking, cheerful and reliable front to the world. They are extremely capable practically and intellectually, trying their hands at almost any task. As pillars of the community, they may feel inclined to take up a charitable cause or generally do good deeds in the neighborhood.

There is a danger that their commitment to their boss, family or friends is so powerful it can become unquestioning and they end up performing tasks or running errands unworthy of them. They should not to be blind in their devotion or let the rank of a person intimidate them into compliance. They should also be careful that their dedication to a method, cause or project does not turn into stubbornness and obstinacy when alternatives are presented. Any form of aggression or criticism is likely to be met with anger or veiled threats; they need to learn to take criticism for what it is: someone else's opinion. Fortunately, between the ages of twenty-one and fifty-one they may concentrate on new interests and acquiring knowledge; during this period they should try to treat criticism as a learning experience.

These charming, multi-talented and reliable people have the potential to make their mark on whatever project or goal interests them. They should be careful, however, that in their need to feel committed they don't relinquish their objectivity. But when they do commit themselves to a worthwhile cause, they can surprise everyone with their spontaneity and ability to bring about progress.

On the dark side

Rank-conscious,
obstinate, blinkered

At your best

Reliable,
committed, upbeat

1 May

the birthday of

perspicacity

Your greatest challenge is

seizing opportunities

The way forward is ...

to understand that excessive caution can be as dangerous to your psychological growth as excessive risk.

There is little that escapes the attention of people born on May 1. Blessed with remarkable powers of intellectual perception, they are calm and insightful but often aren't talkative. When they do speak, their few but well-chosen words have considerable impact because they are based on close observation.

Perspicacity is the greatest strength and driving force of these people. Because they are highly intuitive they notice what is going on around them and also what is being implied; this enables them to rely on their instincts, and then apply logic and reason to establish an effective plan of action. Their calm and considered approach to life can, however, become a handicap as others tend to rely on them to maintain a sense of perspective; this can keep them from pushing themselves forward. They should use their emotional intelligence to their own advantage as well as others.

These people need to have more faith in their own abilities. In most cases they are capable of achieving far more than they realize. They are highly imaginative, with natural leadership abilities, even though some may not appreciate their bluntness or their satirical and cleverly observed humor. They tend to like the familiar; change or new situations may alarm them, even if they don't show that fear on the surface. It is important for them, however, to embrace change as this offers them opportunities for psychological growth. Between the ages of twenty and fifty they have an increased desire to relate more with their immediate environment; this is extremely positive as it will encourage them to diversify, experiment and step out of their comfort zone. After the age of fifty there is an emphasis on emotional stability.

The deceptively calm people born on this day have a lot going for them; they just don't always realize it. However, once they wake up to their huge potential they will surprise themselves and others with their creativity and the passion through which that creative spirit can manifest.

On the dark side

Cautious, tactless, passive

At your best

Witty, insightful, calm

2 May

Your greatest challenge is

learning to be more sensitive to the feelings of others

The way forward is ...

to understand that people can find it hard to cope with the truth; a gentler way of introducing them to it is needed.

People born on May 2 have a no-nonsense approach to life, believing in results not theories. Although others admire them for their intellectual gifts and ability to organize their original thoughts with logical coherence, they do have a tendency to express themselves bluntly. Fiercely honest, they don't ever set out to wound others as they are naturally inclined toward cooperation and harmony; they simply believe that the best way to effect improvement is to tell others exactly how it is.

These people are blessed with inquisitiveness and great insight into the workings of the human mind. It's not easy to fool them and they don't believe in pulling the wool over anyone's eyes. They will be respected for their intelligence and honesty but their bluntness may sometimes come across as insensitivity, earning them unnecessary enemies. They should use their intelligence and insight into human nature to avoid this. They also should avoid gossiping; even though this is not fueled by malice but more by their natural curiosity, it can upset others. Respecting the privacy of others is important between the ages of nineteen and forty-nine, during which there is an emphasis on communication and exchanging ideas. After the age of forty-nine they may feel the growing importance of getting in touch with their own feelings as well as those of others.

As perfectionists, they often shine in whatever task is set them and motivate others to emulate their fantastic organizational skills. Although they can work well in a team, they are at their most productive when they are making an individual contribution. This desire to work alone can cross over to their personal life; and their private life is exactly that—private. Despite their reticence, they are at their happiest when they feel supported by friends and family.

These people are, above all, intelligent and caring; if they can listen to the honest advice they give others and apply it to themselves, they have the potential to achieve outstanding success, whatever path in life they choose.

On the dark side

Tactless, demanding, workaholic

At your best

Generous, ambitious, realistic

3 May

the birthday of
spectacular efficiency

Your greatest challenge is

learning to trust

The way forward is ...

to understand that if you expect to be let down, the chances are you will be. Change your expectations to more positive ones.

People born on May 3 are not just well-organized; they are spectacularly efficient. Their houses and offices are often tidy, and their natural charm and politeness earn them many friends and admirers.

The lives of these people reflect their efficient approach; they are often the ones others count on to keep things running smoothly, both at home and at work. Slow but steady improvements are a feature of their lives rather than sudden changes of fortune. In their teenage years they may feel restricted in some way but any setbacks they experience pave the way for two good things: determination and patience. As long as they keep pushing steadily forward, life will reward them with success and happiness.

Between the ages of eighteen and forty-eight there will be a big need to communicate; this can be an extremely positive time for them if they allow their natural potential to blossom and don't smother it with routine or fear of change. After the age of forty-nine they will feel an increased need for emotional security. Again this can be extremely positive if they accept the fact that feelings can't be categorized and controlled.

Stubborn and strong willed, these people may find themselves in conflict with less systematic individuals. They may judge people and situations harshly and they need to avoid becoming rigid, negative or demanding in their objectivity. They also have a tendency to worry too much and work too hard to prove themselves or their ability. Fortunately, they are perceptive individuals and their lives will improve if they can occasionally take an honest look at themselves, their behavior and the effect they have on others.

Above all, people born on this day are valued by others for their rare gift of objective insight and their ability to organize and lead with spectacular efficiency. They have much to teach others and as long as they remember to curb their tendency to detach emotionally—especially when it comes to those closest to them—and to listen to their heart as well as their head, they have the potential to make their big dreams of reform and progress a reality.

On the dark side

Negative, demanding, workaholic

At your best

Analytical, insightful, popular

4 May

the birthday of
sparkling goodness

Your greatest challenge is

not becoming worn down serving others

The way forward is ...

to understand that the best way to help others become self-sufficient is to be an example of someone who can support themselves.

Even though their manners are often gentle and reserved, those born on May 4 often have an easy charm and hypnotic sparkle that draws those to them who are seeking guidance, direction or support. Whatever situation they are in, they frequently end up in the position of teacher and guide, and rightly so; others have much to learn from them.

These people are acutely perceptive but not judgmental. Though they are affectionate and quick to perceive goodness in everyone, they possess a strong will-power and inner strength. These can sometimes translate into stubbornness, especially when their opinions or ideals are called into question. Because they appear calm and stable, people who need practical and emotional guidance will seek them out. It is therefore important for them not to become too self-denying.

Many of these people do find themselves giving a lot of themselves to others, particularly friends and family. This should not stop them following their own dreams, which could leave them resentful of their responsibility toward others. Their home life is likely to be very important to them but again they need to make sure that they don't allow those closest to them to take over their lives completely.

They prefer to encourage or help others through deeds, and the example of dependability and compassion they set, rather than through words or theories. Their calm and common-sense approach to life earns them many fans but surprisingly there is a deep need within them to take more risks. They should not repress this need but confront it; when the time comes for them to make big changes—typically between the ages of seventeen and forty-seven, during which there is an emphasis on new directions—they need to make them. This will not damage their sense of responsibility or their sparkling reputation, it will enhance it, because to feel truly fulfilled, these perceptive, nurturing and inspiring individuals need to do more than dream about their hopes and ideals; they need to live them.

On the dark side

Unfulfilled, stubborn, self-sacrificing

At your best

Giving, supportive, warm

5 May

the birthday of
motivating energy

Your greatest challenge is

to avoid becoming controlling in your dealings with others

The way forward is ...

to understand that others should learn life's lessons by themselves; the best guidance is to encourage others to be more independent.

People born on May 5 are often full of original and innovative solutions, and know the best way to implement them. Others rely on them to offer ideas when things have ground to a halt or to inject their special brand of motivating energy. They have enough energy for everyone and, unless they feel undermined or threatened, they never seem to tire.

They have excellent communication skills and the ability to impart knowledge or insight to others. This isn't to say they are know-alls; it is just that they love nothing better than to motivate and inspire others toward action. They do this by getting to the heart of the matter; in some cases this may involve pointing out some uncomfortable home truths. Their aim is not to wound but to help others progress, although their interpersonal skills might improve if they learned the importance of listening a bit more.

They may find it hard to sit back when they witness a lack of awareness in others, and will quickly assume the role of parent or mentor. They do take this role extremely seriously and, if it is threatened in any way, they can become jealous, manipulative and aggressive. They should learn to be less possessive and more accepting of the need of others to make their own mistakes, especially between the ages of sixteen to forty-six during which there is an emphasis in their lives on communication in all forms. After the age of forty-six they may become more sensitive toward their own feelings and the feelings of others.

Hidden beneath the knowledgeable but practical exterior of these people there is a highly idealistic individual. To stop them becoming overly serious, they need to learn to use their unusual sense of humor; to feel more fulfilled they need to trust more in their instincts. This sense of their own power will give them the self-confidence and spontaneity they need to focus their energy not just on guiding others but on motivating themselves to express and develop their own highly creative potential.

On the dark side

Didactic, smothering, jealous

At your best

Knowledgeable, energetic, generous

6 May

the birthday of
the sensitive star

Your greatest challenge is

coping with your extreme sensitivity

The way forward is ...

to understand that there are ways to survive and thrive when the world threatens to overwhelm you. Take regular time out, and pace yourself.

The highly imaginative and intuitive people born on May 6 are often acutely sensitive to the feelings, dreams and hopes of others, especially those less fortunate. Fascinated by the human psyche and keen to learn what it is that motivates and inspires others, they often feel compelled to pass their wisdom on to others. If they aren't guiding and directing others, they will be inspiring them by living out dreams and fantasies that most of us repress.

As well as being finely tuned to the feelings of others, they are highly sensitive themselves; this can lead to misunderstandings and hurts that really aren't necessary. They should learn to be objective in their dealings with others; otherwise they will experience insecurity, uncertainty and disappointment. Between the ages of fifteen and forty-five there is an emphasis on communication and the exchange of ideas, so they should not take everything so personally. After the age of forty-five these people focus more on emotional closeness, family and security.

Their interest in human nature can take them beyond social interaction and business to a deep desire to do something meaningful in the world. This may involve fighting for a cause in the world and will stop them feeling unfulfilled. The most common block to their progress is a lack of faith in their own abilities; this can trigger sudden changes of mood and bouts of indecision. Being prone to excessive highs and lows, they need to turn the understanding they have of unpredictable behavior in others upon themselves. If they can do this, they will see that much of their emotional instability stems from their lack of self-belief.

Their self-doubt may also result in their taking a secondary role rather than making full use of their creative potential. They do, however, respond extremely well to advice and encouragement; reading self-help books or biographies about people they admire will help them gain control of their lives. They should remember that every step they take toward fulfilling their ambitions and dreams works to inspire and motivate others.

On the dark side

Insecure, indecisive, moody

At your best

Sensitive, artistic, astute

7 May

the birthday of absolute perfection

Your greatest challenge is

living up to your high standards

The way forward is ...

to understand that there is nothing wrong with high standards but we all have room for improvement.

People born on May 7 are a curious mixture of inward-looking spirituality and outward-orientated concern with personal image. Although they are able to recognize that the most important values are non-materialistic, they also have a great desire to make an impression on others. This combination of inner and outer expectation is, however, in keeping with their quest for absolute perfection in all areas of their lives.

As well as being deeply sensitive and compassionate, they are also elegant and gifted communicators who can inspire others with their ideals. Often devoted to these ideals, they are willing to give them every ounce of their mental, physical and spiritual energy. This can develop into a tendency to give too much of themselves, but most of them are self-aware enough to know where and when to draw the line. They should ensure they retain a sense of perspective in their twenties, thirties and early forties, when there is an emphasis on change, communication and learning new skills. After the age of forty it is vital for them not to lose a sense of self, because this is a turning point when they are likely to focus more on emotional relationships, family and their instinctual understanding of others' needs.

It is their search for perfection, however, that best defines these people. There is always a danger that this will manifest in unrealistic fantasies and expectations, and they need to focus on making some of their high ideals a workable reality. Materially, their intelligence and drive will help them succeed; making money is not a problem for them, although—because they like enjoying and sharing the good things in life—keeping it sometimes is.

As far as spiritual or inner goals are concerned, they have to come to terms with the fact that finding their spirituality or inner meaning will be a lifelong mission. They should use their natural intuition to get in touch with their wisdom and creativity which, if allowed to express themselves freely, will be able to satisfy their deepest yearnings for fulfillment.

On the dark side

Unrealistic, frustrated, superficial

At your best

Refined, discerning, dedicated

8 May

the birthday of
the irresistible messenger

Your greatest challenge is

listening to alternative viewpoints

The way forward is ...

to understand that by listening to what people have to say, you earn their trust and respect.

People born on May 8 are strong-willed individuals who rarely back down. They are totally dedicated to their ideals, often stepping forward as spokesperson for a group. Their extraordinary self-belief is so irresistible that others find it impossible not to be moved or inspired by their message.

They will typically possess powerful convictions, striving to promote these as persuasively as possible. When they are particularly impassioned, they may sometimes come across as too forceful, judgmental and harsh. Diplomacy isn't one of their strengths but they have the potential to be excellent communicators. Once they have learned the art of getting their message over using gentle persuasion, they instinctively understand and successfully exploit the value of converting rather than alienating others.

Although their conviction earns them the admiration of others, it can also make people slightly afraid of them. But underneath their tough exterior lies a gentle, caring and generous side which—as they tend to regard any kind of vulnerability as a weakness—they will only reveal to their nearest and dearest. It is important for them to understand that strength and power can be found in gentleness. They can sometimes be too strong willed and serious, and often need to be more flexible and take a lighter approach. Between the ages of thirteen and forty-three there will be many opportunities for them to discover their playful side as there is an emphasis on communication and diversification. After the age of forty-three they will focus on emotional connections with others, and again, if they can learn to lighten up, happiness and fulfillment are within easy reach.

With an innate appreciation of beauty, they will often feel a strong connection with the natural world or their immediate man-made surroundings. They may therefore devote themselves to environmental concerns, to preserving historical buildings or simply to improving their homes or local neighborhood. Wherever they decide to devote their energies, the art of diplomacy will make it easier for them to realize their ambitions.

On the dark side

Judgmental, harsh, tough

At your best

Outspoken, caring, persuasive

9 May

the birthday of the activist

Your greatest challenge is

dealing with your anger

The way forward is ...

to understand what triggers your anger and have a plan ready to counteract it.

People born on May 9 may appear calm and steady on the surface, but to those who know them well they radiate energy and drive. They possess a clear-cut sense of morality and fair play, and are compelled to place themselves in the role of reformer, protester or activist if they witness any kind of injustice or abuse.

Above all, their desire is to be a support to those who are less fortunate or to play a part in highlighting their cause or reversing their fortunes. Occasionally, they have such a strong sense of honor that they seem to belong to a more civilized age. When responding to a humanitarian cause or championing the rights of the oppressed, they draw on their powers of compassion, steadfastness and courage which may have developed as a result of hardships or difficulties they have struggled to overcome in their past, perhaps in their childhood or teenage years. Until the age of forty-two there is an emphasis on sudden changes of direction and this may involve learning through struggle and setback; but after the age of forty-three life tends to get easier for them and they can concentrate on security, both emotional and financial.

Because people born on this day are so committed to their progressive visions, they can find it hard to forgive the failings of others, expecting them to live up to their own lofty standards. When they do experience disappointment or disillusionment at home or at work, they can astonish with their sudden flashes of temper. It is important for them to learn to manage their anger, because all the support and respect their charisma, focus and persuasive power may have gathered can vanish in an instant when their temperamental tendencies surge to the fore.

Once they learn to be more flexible and to respond in more constructive ways when they see something that upsets them, their success, and more important to them the success of the ideals they believe in, are virtually guaranteed.

On the dark side

Temperamental, unforgiving, naïve

At your best

Ethical, honorable, fair

1O May

the birthday of
natural rhythm

Your greatest challenge is

finding time or energy for others

The way forward is ...

to understand that relationships with other people are not incompatible with single-minded dedication to a project; all that's needed is to find balance.

People born on May 10 follow their own natural rhythm. They often glide rather than struggle through life. They intuitively seem to know when to make a move, when to step back, when to quicken their pace and when to slow it down; their intuitive approach is more often right than wrong.

These people like to go their own way and, although their suggestions are often innovative, they tend to work best as an individual rather than as part of a team. They can become wholly absorbed in projects that fuel their imagination and are willing to take a lone stand when necessary. Although they have the communication skills and tenacity to enlist the support of others, they have an impulsive, thoughtless and occasionally self-indulgent side that can make them enemies or lead them into trouble.

They should always learn to look before they leap, making sure that they devote their great tenacity and energy to a worthy cause. Before the age of forty-two they risk getting involved in questionable pursuits; during this period they may need to be guided by those close to them or by a mentor who has their best interests at heart. After the age of forty-three they may concentrate on emotional security and they need to take advantage of this opportunity to connect more deeply with their own and others' feelings. If they don't open up and ignore the seemingly trivial obligations of close relationships, they are likely to become alienated from the joys of interaction.

Movement and activity are extremely important to these people and they may even get depressed if they don't take enough exercise. They have enhanced sensual qualities and these make them fine lovers; they do, however, need to beware of over-indulgence in any form. With a highly developed imagination, sensibility and intelligence, they enjoy looking at the world with a perspective that is often way ahead of their time. All these qualities endow people born on this day with the potential to make their mark on the world as far-sighted innovators.

On the dark side

Thoughtless, selfish, uncertain

At your best

Agile, intuitive, courageous

11 May

Your greatest challenge is

working well in a team

The way forward is ...

to understand that isolating yourself from other people removes you from potentially beneficial and diverse influences.

People born on May 11 are blessed with a highly developed and independent aesthetic sense that refuses to be constrained by the rules, regulations and ideals of others. They live in a world of their own creation and enjoy adding their colorful, light-hearted but extremely distinctive flair to any situation they are in.

These highly creative people excel at making what is seemingly mundane or routine appear entertaining or new. They are the people who can turn household chores into games or study assignments into exciting challenges. With a burning desire to learn the truth for themselves, their approach causes them to challenge, side-step or walk all over conventional thinking. Their questing and imaginative powers are supplemented by their powers of perception, originality and stubborn tenacity.

Among the many gifts with which people born on this day are blessed is their ability to make life more colorful and exciting, and for that they earn the gratitude of others, but unfortunately not always their respect. This is because, although they are brilliant at inspiring and entertaining, they can get so immersed in their dream world that they lose touch with reality. Although some have a talent for making a profit from their unusual thoughts, others with less self-mastery often struggle to make their dreams and imaginations work. They should never lose touch of their audience when expressing their unique creativity. If they don't stick to the facts and what is realistically workable, they may be branded highly intelligent but ineffective.

Until the age of forty they will focus on change and new interests. This is often a period of study and experimentation, and they need to be careful not to lose themselves in exaggeration or fantasy. After the age of forty-one their sensitivity increases and they place more emphasis on home and family life. They need to understand that they have the potential to achieve something better than the admiration of others; that is, the respect and undying loyalty of all those lucky enough to wander across their path.

On the dark side

Unrealistic, eccentric, detached

At your best

Creative, distinctive, fun-loving

12 May

the birthday of

lucidity

Your greatest challenge is

to be tactful when expressing your opinions

The way forward is ...

to understand that people generally respond better to you when you make them feel good about themselves.

People born on May 12 may appear steady and sensible on first acquaintance but past the small-talk stage a witty and engaging person emerges. In fact, their wealth of intelligent perspectives often takes other people by surprise.

They have tremendous energy and will-power and although they do not necessarily seek leadership, they often find themselves promoted to that position because of their hard work and dedication. Independent and self-assured but also easy to approach, they inspire confidence in the people they live and work with. They are also extremely observant and their well-honed critical faculties can work to their advantage. Although they use humor and the element of surprise to question and challenge conventional thinking, this can degenerate into criticism and sarcasm. They do need to learn to curb their biting observations and avoid alienating those close to them.

Until the age of thirty-nine there is an emphasis on study and developing their communication skills; during this time they should learn to soften their sharp tongue with humor. After the age of forty they perceive the importance of home and the need to care emotionally for themselves, as well as others. During these years they need to show their generous side by highlighting the strengths of others as well as their weaknesses, and by praising as much as they criticize. Once they understand that the more they give, the more they get back, there is nothing to stop them reaching for their dreams.

When it comes to their own ideas and dreams, however, there is a tendency for these people to be reticent. As a result, others may sense something in them that always remains distant and a mystery. There is nothing wrong with keeping a part of themselves private; the only danger is that by not revealing what they think and criticizing what others think, others may accuse them of only finding problems and not solutions. This, however, is unjust as they have a unique perspective on the world that has tremendous potential to motivate and inspire others with its expansive optimism.

On the dark side

Sarcastic, difficult, distant

At your best

Observant, ironic, analytical

13 May

the birthday of
the wild child

Your greatest challenge is

learning to control your impulses

The way forward is ...

to understand that self-control is the key to success in your life; without it you are like a reed blown about by the wind.

Other people find themselves instantly drawn to the natural charisma and playful charm of people born on May 13. These untamed spirits follow their instincts and, although they often clash with the conventions and restrictions placed upon them by society, their wild-child presence always has an electrifying effect on others.

These people are often self-taught in some way and their approach to situations and people is easy and natural. They have the ability to win friends quickly and easily and, as a result, to attract good fortune. Unfortunately, this can sometimes make them the object of envy or resentment. They should be aware of the effect their success and popularity have on others; if necessary they should tone down their lighthearted approach or find the appropriate level of intensity for their audience.

In keeping with their wild-child personality, they find practical concerns and routine boring and unfulfilling. With a love of movement, change and variety, if they do find themselves stuck or restricted in any way, they may get depressed or behave recklessly. Although this butterfly approach makes them fascinating individuals with a wealth of knowledge and experience, if those born on this day delved more deeply into subjects or situations they would discover how enriching and enlightening a more intense knowledge or commitment can be. Before the age of thirty-seven they should deepen their approach and outlook; after the age of thirty-eight they may be more concerned with emotional commitment.

Although they appear to breeze through life, it's highly likely that at some point a significant event, generally one with unpleasant or painful consequences, will have given them the impetus to focus on their more serious side and have concern for the welfare of others. When this newfound earnestness and sense of purpose is combined with the enthusiastic enjoyment of life that is their defining feature, the possibilities for them to achieve success in all areas of their lives are limitless.

On the dark side

Wild, flighty, superficial

At your best

Impulsive, natural, energetic

14 May

Your greatest challenge is

being kind to yourself

The way forward is ...

to understand that driving yourself too hard won't improve your chances of success but decrease them. To achieve success you need to feel energetic and alert.

The articulate individuals born on May 14 are progressive in their outlook and are intellectually far in advance of other members of their generation. Their forward-thinking, progressive outlook allows them to see potential and opportunities that those who are less imaginative may miss.

They are extremely energetic, being propelled forward by their nervous energy and unlimited curiosity. Proud and independent self-starters, they are unlikely to seek help from others but such is the power of their vision that influential people are often standing by to offer assistance if they ask. With the ability to lift whatever enterprise they undertake to the next level, the only way for them to feel more fulfilled is to take on the mantle of progress in some way.

As indefatigable workers who strive for excellence in all areas of their lives, they usually achieve this excellence but there's a price to pay. Physical and emotional burnout and a high degree of stress and nervous tension are very real dangers for them. It is important that they recognize their limits and, as fascinating as the future is, all they really have is the present moment. This tendency to drive themselves too hard or be extremely critical of their performance is a theme throughout their lives but is especially strong before the age of thirty-six. At the age of thirty-seven they may concentrate on the growing importance of home, family and emotional needs. Then, after the age of sixty-six, they become far more confident and self-assured.

Because people born on this day always have their eye on the future, there may be times when their opinions or visions are misinterpreted or, worse still for them, ridiculed. This can cause them great distress, but if they learn to back down and bide their time, more often than not others will eventually come around to their way of thinking. And once they learn to be less critical of themselves and more patient with others, these progressive souls may well be the ones who come up with groundbreaking ideas capable of changing the world.

On the dark side

Perfectionist, difficult, stressed

At your best

Innovative, articulate, energetic

15 May

the birthday of
delightful introspection

Your greatest challenge is

overcoming a tendency toward shyness

The way forward is ...

to concentrate more on others than on yourself when you enter a room or a new situation.

People born on May 15 are blessed with intelligence, charm and a rich and powerful imagination. Young at heart, they have the ability to touch the hearts and minds of all those lucky enough to wander across their path.

What makes people born on this day so special is their creativity. They are the ones with the brightest solutions or magical ideas and when they are around the world always seems a fresher and more colorful place. They often live in their dreams, so their plans frequently come to nothing while they are sitting back expecting others to come forward or to seek their advice. At work they may see a way forward but they are unlikely to volunteer this information to their boss unless asked for it; in their personal life they may expect others to make the first move. It is important for them to put themselves forward and take responsibility for their creativity and talent, because this is the only way they will be able to reach their potential and fulfill their dreams.

From about the age of six to the age of thirty-six, there is an emphasis on education, communication and new interests; this is one of the reasons why their imaginative faculties are so advanced and why they may opt to stay in school longer or train longer than others. Around the age of thirty-six, however, home and family life present opportunities for them to shake off their passivity and become more confident of themselves and their abilities.

They are often seen by others as being rather otherworldly or living in a world of their own; in many respects this assumption is correct as they do have an irresistible urge to acquire knowledge, oftentimes mystical knowledge. Despite the dreamy image they present, once they learn to take responsibility for their talents they are rarely isolated from others. This is because others will always be drawn to their capacity to present the inspirational fruits of their mental adventures and, by so doing, bring great happiness and illumination to the world.

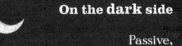

On the dark side

Passive, unfulfilled, detached

At your best

Imaginative, intelligent, charming

16 May

the birthday of
bright color

Your greatest challenge is

adopting a more considered approach to yourself and others

The way forward is ...

to spend more quiet time alone, as this will give you greater insight into the best way of achieving your ambitions.

People born on May 16 are blessed with a wild energy that manifests itself in diverse, hidden or outrageous ways. Early in life they may have recognized in themselves a need to fly in the face of convention or rebel in their own distinctive and often flamboyant way. They are colorful and expressive, and life may be unpredictable when they are around but it is never boring.

Some of these people are less extrovert and perhaps quieter in their approach to life, but this tendency toward flamboyance will still express itself when their passions are aroused or their interests are threatened. In fact, whether introvert or extrovert, they can be extremely volatile and others soon learn to tread carefully around them. If they can't learn to control their wildness, they run the risk of wasting their energy and their potential on dramatic but ultimately futile displays of temper. If, however, they learn to harness their energy and passion, their potential, especially for creative ventures, is limitless.

Life for these people is often one of extremes. It is important for them to take charge of their emotions, learning to be less reactive so that when the bad times come they have better coping mechanisms to rise above them. Until the age of thirty-five there is an emphasis in their lives on learning and education; this would be the ideal time for them to learn to manage their emotions better as they are then at their most receptive to new ways of thinking and doing things. After the age of thirty-six they will focus on emotional security, home and family life; for their professional and personal lives to be a success during this time, self-discipline again must be a priority.

Although self-mastery is the key to their success, this should never be at the expense of their colorful and expressive personality. It is through their dynamic style of expression and passionately held convictions that they are able to impress others. By so doing, they add a touch of the colorful or exotic to the world around them.

On the dark side

Moody, unstable, volatile

At your best

Expressive, colorful, sensual

17 May

Your greatest challenge is

asking for help

The way forward is ...

to understand that if you want to make something happen, you must dare to ask for what you want.

People born on May 17 have a clear-cut code of personal behavior which guides them through every decision they make. Straightforward and to the point, they have a talent for making simple but profound comments on situations.

With little time for small talk, they say what they mean and mean what they say. They are an inspiring example to others but don't have much patience with those who try to shirk their responsibilities; if they notice someone slacking or not pulling their weight, they are likely to tell them straight out. This clear-cut approach can, unfortunately, win them as many enemies as supporters and so they might benefit from learning more tact. Their insightful and original approach, combined with their refusal to be diverted from their chosen course, would appear to be a recipe for success. Where this is not the case it is because they have a tendency to overestimate the power of what they can achieve through determination and will-power alone. They often prefer to go it alone, but if this works against them they should recognize the power of a group of people working together to achieve a goal.

Until their mid thirties there is an emphasis in their lives on learning in all its forms and they need to take advantage of these opportunities to communicate and exchange ideas with others. After the age of thirty-four they may focus more on emotional intimacy and security. If they can learn to get in touch with their own feelings and the feelings of others during this period, it promises great fulfillment and happiness.

There is no denying that these people often have fixed views on things. This can hold them back as life is not as black and white as they think it is. However, if they learn to develop a more tolerant approach it will not only help them achieve their aims and attract a following, it will also open up within them the compassion and determination to improve the lives of others and a creativity that might otherwise have remained dormant.

On the dark side

Tactless, judgmental, stressed

At your best

Dedicated, honorable, insightful

18 May

the birthday of
the brave stance

Your greatest challenge is

knowing when to back down

The way forward is ...

to understand that backing down from your position if life gives you a reason to do so is a sign of strength not weakness.

People born on May 18 care deeply about the world they live in. Their greatest desire is often to alleviate the suffering of others and improve social systems. When convinced of their moral position, they will not flinch from taking a brave stance until their views have been heard or the challenge has been overcome.

As well as being progressive in their thought, compassionate in their desire to right wrongs and unwavering in their defense of what they believe to be right, they are also extremely practical. Presenting a logical, rational approach to situations, they are much-sought-after business allies or co-workers, although their black-and-white approach to life and inability to back down can at times make them seem stern and insensitive. They are the bosses who forget that trainees have a lot to learn or the parents who unintentionally stifle their child's creativity with relentless rationalism. They should learn that not everyone is as practical or capable as they are and that humility, mystery and wonder have their special place in life.

These people often have a passion of some kind; this can take any form, from charity work to archeology. They also tend to mix with people who share their passion and would benefit from meeting people from other walks of life, as they may give too much of themselves to their passion. Until the age of thirty-three they may focus on learning, communication and study but are still unsure of themselves and the direction in which they want to head. Typically, by the age of thirty-four they have settled on their chosen course as they see a need for more security and stability. At this stage they need to be on their guard against their tendency to become overzealous or fanatical when promoting their chosen cause.

Above all, whatever path in life they choose, these people are energetic campaigners for human progress. They have tremendous courage, vigor and steadfastness, and these, combined with their considerable compassion, sets them apart as the true movers and shakers of this world.

On the dark side

Driven, stern, self-sacrificing

At your best

Progressive, energetic, principled

190

19 May

the birthday of
the convincing candidate

Your greatest challenge is

becoming less materialistic in your values

The way forward is ...

to understand that the size of your house or wallet is no guarantee of happiness; that is assured by the size of your heart.

People born on May 19 have a highly developed sense of fair play and an ability to put forward their case convincingly and credibly. They will speak out eloquently when they notice any injustice and act decisively to ensure positive changes are made.

One of the greatest strengths of these people is their natural ability to convince others that changes need to be made and action needs to be taken. Such is their persuasive power that after spending time with them others often find themselves feeling energized, focused and ready to commit themselves to a new course of action. There is a danger, however, that their magnetic and inspiring communicative skills can be used for unworthy causes. When this is the case, their charisma and eloquence can slip into dishonesty; they should avoid this path at all costs as it will only lead to frustration.

Until the age of thirty-two there is an emphasis in the lives of people born on this day on learning, writing, speech, and study, and, because this coincides with their student years, their talent for communication will be given plenty of opportunities to express itself and develop. In fact, education in some form is vital to bring out the best of their potential. During this time they will also begin to appreciate the powerful effect they have on others; as a consequence, they need to ensure they don't become manipulative or overbearing. After the age of thirty-two they become more focused on emotional intimacy, family and security; these years can be highly fulfilling and rewarding.

Inventive and original, people born on this day have a progressive philosophy in life and whatever they choose to focus their energies on, their arguments and ideals are always worth listening to. Once they learn to strike a balance between standing up for their own ideas and being receptive to the ideas of others, not only are they able to persuade others of the importance of their ideals, they can also become excellent representatives for others less fortunate than themselves.

On the dark side

Manipulative, frustrated, dishonest

At your best

Persuasive, fair, energetic

20 May

the birthday of
continuous momentum

Your greatest challenge is

learning to pace yourself

The way forward is ...

to understand that your desire to constantly seek out the new will lead you into random and inconsistent behavior, ultimately causing frustration not fulfillment.

People born on May 20 tend to be versatile, communicative and inventive. They generally respond to people and situations quickly and openly. When one of their highly original impulses strikes, not only do they talk about it a lot and update the whole world on their progress—they act on it.

However safe and serene they may appear, underneath they crave change, diversity and freedom of expression. When their fertile imagination has been activated they find it impossible to keep it to themselves, provoking both awe and exhaustion in others. The awe comes from their ability to convey excitement; the exhaustion from the speed with which they talk and move from one thing to another. They tend to stay up late and get up early, so there is never enough time in the day for them to do everything they want; but they will try regardless.

Outwardly focused with a huge range of interests, they run the risk of exhausting themselves when their pace becomes too manic. Others may also accuse them of only skimming the surface of life, rather than getting to grips with it. Until the age of thirty-one—when they are most likely to be constantly on the move, physically and mentally—they focus on learning, study and communication. After the age of thirty-two, however, they will concentrate more on emotional depth, family, home and security. Although they should never lose their wonderful energy, this would be the ideal time for them to get to know themselves better and commit to a project, person or place.

These people may often feel as if they simply can't switch off. It is important for their psychological growth, however, to learn that they don't constantly need to be on the go to find the fulfillment and excitement they crave. Once they learn to strike a balance between being and doing, these pioneering and stylish adventurers have the potential to be both a quick-witted energetic jack of all trades and an accomplished master of one; and this is a very rare combination indeed.

On the dark side

Undisciplined, verbose, superficial

At your best

Innovative, expressive, communicative

GEMINI

THE TWINS (MAY 21 – JUNE 20)

- **Element:** Air
- **Ruling planet:** Mercury, the messenger
- **Symbol:** The Twins
- **Tarot card:** The Lovers (choices)
- **Number:** 5
- **Favorable colors:** Orange, yellow, white
- **Key phrase:** Variety is the spice of life

Geminis are extraordinarily versatile people. As the first dual sign of the zodiac they have no problem doing lots of things at the same time—in fact they often prefer it that way. Their need to communicate with others is strong and a life without mobiles, texts, gossip and emails would be inconceivable for them. Highly creative but impossible to pin down, people born under the sun sign Gemini can be both frustrating and delightfully wonderful at the same time.

Personality potential

Gemini's ruler is Mercury, the light-footed messenger of the gods in ancient Greek mythology who traveled across the heavens delivering messages. This goes some way toward explaining why those born under this sun sign are forever on the move, eager to gather new knowledge and new experiences. They take great pleasure in knowing a little about a lot, although not a lot about one subject in particular, and live by their motto: variety is the spice of life.

Geminis learn through imitation. Highly versatile and adaptable, anyone who makes an impression on them becomes their role model. They are excellent communicators and can quickly dazzle people they meet with their charm, wit, intelligence and perception. In fact they can pick things up amazingly fast. If you put a Gemini in a new group of people or new situation they will blend in quickly without any trouble. One of the reasons why Geminis are so easily accepted into new situations is that they love to talk. They are genuinely curious about other people and know exactly the right thing to say. As well as being great talkers they are also highly charismatic and seem to have more than their fair share of good fortune. Part of the reason for their ability to attract good luck is their willingness to experiment and their firm belief that if one door closes there are countless other

doors to try. Their quest is always for new perspectives or alternatives, and with such versatile and active minds they can oscillate from genius one day to scatterbrain the next—hence the duality that defines the symbol of twins.

Staying with the theme of duality, Geminis can do two or more things at once with the greatest of ease; so, if you see one with a phone in each hand, don't be surprised. But it's not just multitasking and communicating at which these people excel. They are also masters of disguise and few people know their real motives. This makes them excellent teachers, motivators, politicians and experts in the field of human relationships. A Gemini knows how to talk even the most stubborn person round. In short, people born under the Gemini sun have a touch of the magician about them.

> **They are genuinely curious about other people and know exactly the right thing to say.**

Personality pitfalls

Although people born under this sign are ambitious and original thinkers, when they have a new idea they tend to dash off without waiting for a strategy for success. Their ability to adapt can sometimes help them overcome their lack of planning, but more often than not it can get them into trouble. Lack of planning and organization is not, however, their chief problem. Perhaps their worst fault is their superficiality. Their ability to quickly assimilate knowledge means that they often know a lot about everything but not enough about what really interests them. This character trait can also have a negative impact on their relationships—they have a lot of acquaintances but few real friends.

Silver-tongued Geminis are not incapable of bending the truth if it serves their purposes. They also have a tendency to gossip and their inability to keep secrets can upset those who have confided in them. There is no doubt that Geminis are great communicators and masters of language but they often use words as a way of talking themselves out of genuine emotions. This is because they live in the realm of thoughts and ideas, and real feelings—like love and sorrow—can deeply unsettle them. Inconsistency may be another problem. They may start one project with great enthusiasm but find it hard to maintain that level of enthusiasm to the end; this means that unfinished projects litter their path in life. This lack of focus will hamper any hope of a fulfilling life and, as fulfillment is what they are ultimately searching for and the reason why they seem to be flitting around so much, the result can be mood swings and despondency.

Symbol

The symbol of the twins eloquently represents the dual Gemini mind and personality. They have a sharp intellect that can see both sides of an argument but, instead of taking their time to decide where they stand, they tend to flit from one idea to another. Even though they usually believe what they say at the time they say it, it's not unusual for Geminis to change their mind from one day to the next.

Darkest secret

Geminis may appear to be the life and soul of the party but their charisma, social confidence and style can sometimes hide a deep-seated emptiness. It could be said that the Gemini's restless quest for new perspectives is really a quest for a part of themselves that they feel they have lost—the missing twin. Until they realize that the feeling of completeness they seek can only be found within, the more popular and in demand a Gemini is the more they are likely to feel desperately alone.

Love

Love is a blissful romantic ideal for Geminis. They long for a soulmate and will often have affairs in their quest to find him or her.

They don't really trust their emotions and, if they find themselves overwhelmed by feelings, they will try to rationalize and explain them logically. This can make them appear distant and at times untouchable. It can also stop their relationships moving forward from initial attraction to a deeper and more intense connection.

People born under the Gemini sun tend to do well with partners who are more cautious, level headed and serious than they are, because this complements their restlessness. Even though both Gemini men and women are born flirts, they demand complete faithfulness and devotion from their partner. They want their partners to be the dependable rocks they themselves find it hard to be. Shared interests are important, and they do also want their partner to be sharp and well informed so that spice can be added to the relationship with lively discussion and debate.

Love matches:
Aquarius, Libra and Sagittarius

The Gemini man

Men born under the sign of Gemini love to socialize and they will often dress in a striking manner. They won't talk much about their own feelings but they will be intelligent, witty and well informed. They can also be persuasive and there are few people who don't succumb to their charms.

True to his sign, the Gemini man is often restless and unpredictable, and you'll never be quite sure which personality he is going to be on any particular day. There is one thing, however, you can be sure of if you fall in love with a Gemini—life will never be boring. He will be able to say "I love you" in a thousand different ways. If you can survive his mood swings from being the most wonderful man in the world to becoming the most morose and sullen, you'll find yourself absolutely hypnotized by his immense knowledge and wide interests. He will always remain an enigma and for some unfathomable reason, however much in love with you he is, he will try to disguise it. Despite all this, being in a relationship with a Gemini man is inexplicably the most exciting, fun and easy thing in the world.

While it's true that the Gemini man has a tendency to flirt and needs two loves, this does not necessarily mean he needs two partners. What he needs is a partner who can offer him plenty of variety and romance. Sex is important but he wants more from a partner than just the physical. He wants love, warmth, loyalty, conversation and above all, companionship.

The Gemini woman

Gemini women have a reputation for being playful and fickle, especially when it comes to affairs of the heart. Their mind and their moods are constantly changing, but hidden underneath their detached exterior is a woman who is capable of intense passion. In other words, the Gemini woman isn't just one woman, she is several women and to win her heart you need to get all of them to fall in love with you.

Gemini women find it incredibly hard to commit themselves to one person at a time, and that's why they don't typically tend to settle down in a relationship until later in life when they have become more mature and self-aware. Until then they will present a different face to almost everyone they meet but few, if any, of the people they get close to will know them really well.

When the Gemini woman does finally come to a deeper understanding of her own restless nature and settle down, her partner will have not one but several wives to live with. She'll be moody one day, bright and breezy the next, quiet and thoughtful the day after, a beautiful hostess the day after that, and passionate, secretive and intense the following day—and so on and on. On the one hand all this sounds exhausting but on the other it sounds incredibly exciting. This just about sums up the Gemini woman. Her partner needs to be able to keep up with her thoughts and personality changes, but in return she will offer her partner companionship, devotion, loyalty, love, romance and—perhaps most important of all—hopes and dreams to last a lifetime.

Family

The typical Gemini child—if there is such a thing given their constantly changing personality—will often walk and talk at an early age. Their parents need to be fast, alert and ready not just to walk but to run and occasionally fly beside them. A young Gemini's mind is always active and they will want to know everything about everything. Patience is something they lack and they will need plenty to keep their active minds busy; this is because if boredom sets in they can become obnoxious and difficult to deal with. It's extremely important that they are encouraged to finish tasks they have started but don't assume that because they have many projects on the go that they are being scatterbrained. Gemini children have eclectic minds and work best when multitasking. At school, Gemini children thrive in a schoolroom environment that is spontaneous, but they don't tend to do so well in schools with a strong disciplinarian ethic. They are also very sociable at school and as soon as they get their hands on their own phone it will never stop ringing. When it comes to examinations and interviews they know how to talk the talk and walk the walk, but there is a tendency for their work to be opinion- rather than fact-based.

The Gemini parent is often very lively and open-minded, so there is a danger that they will try to fill their hours with a range of different activities and interests. This is fine if they have a child that enjoys versatility as much as they do, but not so great if their child is more a creature of routine. On the other hand, the Gemini parent may swing the other way and impose on his or her own child the very discipline and structure against which they themselves rebelled. They need to be careful that their sharp tongue does not become overly critical, and to understand that while the harsh words of a parent can scar a child for a lifetime, carefully chosen and loving words can help build a child's self-esteem for a lifetime.

Career

Geminis are so versatile and multitalented, and have such great communication skills, that they could do well in any career. Having said that, careers they tend to gravitate toward and excel in include the media, journalism, writing, advertising, entertainment, politics and photography. They are also natural salespeople and in business they can do very well as long as they can develop enough self-discipline and patience to see a task through to the very end. Solitary professions don't suit these sociable souls and they tend to do better when working with other people around them. They also need plenty of variety and challenge, and are ideally suited to jobs in which there is plenty of conversation, travel, action and quick return.

"Solitary professions don't suit these sociable souls..."

Health and leisure

Geminis seem to grow younger rather than older and they certainly aren't really into that "growing old gracefully" thing. In general they don't tend to suffer from many health problems, but when they do arise they are more often than not caused by stress and tension rather than physical reasons. Geminis can be very highly strung, possessing vast amounts of mental and physical energy that they need to need to use up. Sometimes, however, they can go overboard and, like a delicate butterfly, they can burn themselves out with restlessness. It's extremely important that they learn to listen to their body more and recognize the early signs of exhaustion.

Anxiety and nervous tension are areas of concern if they can't find ways to relax and wind down. Gemini rules the lungs, so those born under this sign also need to watch carefully for breathing problems, asthma and colds that linger on their chests. It's absolutely essential that they avoid smoking. Smoking is bad news health wise for anyone but particularly for a Gemini with their tendency for breathing problems. Relaxation, fresh air and plenty of gentle exercise are recommended. As far as diet is concerned, these people need to eat a light diet rich in fruits and vegetables, oily fish, legumes, nuts and seeds and other foods that support the nervous system.

Geminis love to move and they tend to move fast, but when it comes to exercise they can get easily bored with a weekly routine. Their best option is to cross train either individually or via a health club, and to combine a number of different forms of exercise from brisk walking, jogging, cycling and swimming to vigorous sports like squash. Activities such as yoga, which encourage them to relax and unwind both mentally and physically, are also recommended. Mental challenge is just as important as physical challenge for these lively individuals, so quizzes, crosswords and other exercises to stimulate their brain are recommended. Wearing, meditation on or surrounding themselves with the color green will encourage them to feel more harmonious and balanced.

Born between May 21 and May 31

People born between these dates are heavily under the influence of the planet Mercury, so they tend to be very social and creative. Several steps ahead of their time, their mental brilliance can be fascinating, controversial and—at times—exceptional.

Born between June 1 and June 11

These Geminis tend to be more objective with the clear vision needed to skip the details and get to the heart of the matter quickly or see the bigger picture. Their greatest joy is to see other people happy and, as a result, they may well devote themselves to a social cause.

Born between June 12 and June 20

Geminis born between these dates can be very resilient and tough but they can also be extremely level headed. Highly creative, they never fail to impress others with their wit, knowledge and insight into what is going on around them.

Life lessons

Geminis are witty, intelligent and well informed but with their gift of communication comes a tendency to talk too much at the wrong times. They would do well to learn the value of listening, silence and choosing the right moment to speak. They would also do well to understand the harm that reckless gossip can cause. Their fickleness may also alienate friends and loved ones as they have a tendency to say one thing and do another, or make a date and then cancel at the last moment. Being flirty with everyone can also make those who really love them feel as if they aren't special enough.

Although their non-conformist nature is one of their most appealing characteristics, it can also be one of the most infuriating when they refuse to respect authority or restrictions of any kind. When this non-conformity is combined with their notorious tendency to drop projects as soon as things get routine, the result can be indecisiveness and non-commitment. In fact, commitment is something most Geminis struggle with—whether it's commitment to a person, education, job and even

a family—and this flightiness can lead others to think that they aren't dependable or genuine. Some may even accuse Geminis of superficiality but this isn't strictly speaking true. At the time Geminis are one hundred percent genuine, but they simply want to experience everything that life has to offer; they find it hard to linger long on any one thing or with one person, when there are so many other things for them to learn and do.

Aside from learning to be more tactful and valuing the importance of rules and regulations, the greatest lesson for a Gemini to learn is that commitment doesn't have to mean restriction. In fact commitment can be the most liberating thing for a Gemini because with commitment comes true knowledge and true insight—the missing link they spend all their lives seeking.

Geminis would do well to repeat daily to themselves the mantra that it's quality not quantity that counts, and they can learn this kind of focus and commitment from other signs of the zodiac. Virgos can teach them to be more thoughtful and philosophical; Sagittarians, who are thinkers like Geminis but unlike Geminis can delve more deeply, can teach them the value of commitment and intellectual self-discipline. They could also learn the value of an emotional rather than an intellectual approach to life from Cancerians and Pisceans.

21 May

the birthday of
the can-do attitude

Your greatest challenge is

learning to balance giving and receiving

The way forward is ...

to understand that offering help to others and receiving support back is fundamental to psychological growth.

People born on May 21 are defined by their courage in the face of opposition and by their can-do attitude in the pursuit of their dreams. Their natural confidence may inspire jealousy in those who feel less in control of their lives but it gives them the head start they need to achieve their goals.

People born on this day have a refreshingly upbeat approach to life and when they are around things always seem much easier and challenges less daunting. In fact no challenge seems to be too much for them. This is because not only do they have wonderful ideas and talents, they also have the discipline to persevere. They are not just dreamers but also doers who roll up their sleeves and do whatever it takes to get the job done.

Whatever line of work these courageous people are involved in they are unlikely to be standing on the sidelines because they are at their happiest and their best when they are battling their way physically, mentally and emotionally toward progress. Less evolved types born on this day who find themselves unable to translate their dreams into reality are destined for unhappiness and frustration. It is very important for them to get into the driving seat of their lives because if they can find the strength to take action the chances are extremely good that they will succeed.

Until the age of thirty there is an emphasis in the lives of people born on this day on learning, study and communication and because of this they will probably have been an alert and quick learner at school or college. Their ability to learn quickly may have worked against them as they may have found themselves restless or bored with formal education or training and their early years may have been difficult as a result because others could not relate to their ingenious turn of mind. After the age of thirty, however, there is a turning point which shifts their perspective toward emotional security and stability and it is during these years that they are most likely to come into their own. As long as they are careful that their confidence does not turn into conceit there is very little that can stand in the way of their success.

On the dark side

Egoistic, defensive, frustrated

At your best

Bold, capable, confident

22 May

the birthday of
the inventor

Your greatest challenge is

avoiding obsessive or controlling behavior

The way forward is ...

to understand that the more you try to control people or situations, the more they want to break free.

People born on May 22 have exceptionally inquisitive and productive minds. Not only can they concentrate on one area in minute detail; they also abhor intellectual stagnation. This is an unusual and unique combination that gives them the potential to invent or discover something unique.

There is no doubt that people born on this day are creative and original thinkers; their biggest challenge is often deciding what it is that they want to create. It can sometimes take years for them to make up their minds; their twenties and much of their thirties are likely to be spent in intellectual exploration and experimentation. When they are involved in a specific project it will often take over their lives and, if their concentration is interrupted, they can become extremely irritable or unsettled, which may lead others to accuse them of being obsessive. It is extremely important that others give them the space to experiment and explore, and refrain from criticism, because before the age of thirty total devotion to one project is essential for their psychological and intellectual growth.

Typically by the age of thirty these people will have calmed down and learned to be less touchy when their concentration is disturbed. The late thirties and beyond are also the years when they are most likely to decide on what they want to contribute to the world and back it up with action. Once they have decided on a course of action, their single-mindedness will give them the drive, resilience and focus needed to realize their ambitions.

With a tendency to overreach themselves, they should never tone down their vision or ambition, but for their own happiness and fulfillment they should devote as much energy to finding ways to play to their strengths and minimize their weaknesses. This is because once they understand themselves better and are able to be more realistic in their quest for illumination and success, they have the potential to pioneer new and potentially life-changing, but also soundly researched, ideas.

On the dark side

Obsessive, touchy, manipulative

At your best

Inventive, productive, tenacious

23 May

the birthday of
the seductive solution

Your greatest challenge is

learning to say no

The way forward is ...

to understand that people will respect and approve of you more if you set down clear boundaries and let them know what your limits are.

There is something radiant about the positive and seductive energy of people born on May 23 that others find impossible to ignore. Their defining feature, however, isn't their charisma and sex appeal, but their ingenuity. They are gifted problem solvers who generously give a lot of their time and energy to help others resolve their problems in both practical and emotional ways.

As well as being inventive problem solvers, they are natural communicators. They can present a case convincingly and offer viable solutions. When faced with a dilemma they may find that they have brilliant eureka moments when the answer just pops into their mind. They have a natural flair for everything imaginative but instead of talking about creating, as they are prone to do, they need to get on and do it! This is because it is in activity rather than discussion that these intuitive individuals release their inventiveness.

They aren't motivated by a need to be the center of attention or to assume leadership, getting tremendous satisfaction from simply helping others solve professional and personal woes. The downside of this is that while they attack the problems of others with great energy and insight, they often neglect their own affairs. This can have negative consequences when others take advantage of their generosity and willingness to help. It is vital for their psychological growth that they learn to speak up for their own needs and interests; if they don't, this can lead to frustration and lack of fulfillment.

Until the age of twenty-nine there is an emphasis on information gathering, communication and learning; after the age of thirty they are likely to become more sensitive and security conscious. It is important during this turning point that they learn to say "no" to the demands of others and avoid sacrificing their needs completely to home, family and loved ones. They need to accept that people can and do value them for the energetic, innovative, positive, and inspiring person that they are, and not for what they can do for them.

On the dark side

Unaware, passive, self-effacing

At your best

Sensual, ingenious, convincing

24 May

Your greatest challenge is

not being a gossip

The way forward is ...

to understand that although gossip gets the attention of others, they will not respect and admire you unless you talk about others in a positive way.

People born on May 24 have a gift for expressing what others feel and for getting to the heart of the matter. Incredibly observant, they are commentators on what they see going on around them and will rarely hesitate to broadcast their often profound and insightful views.

With their love of observing and commenting, people born on this day often have a wealth of information about human nature. They are often obsessed with talking about the relationships of others, and others love their company and highly entertaining tales. Although they will always champion the underdog, they do need to be careful that they don't betray the confidences of others and that their witty insights don't dissolve into gossip. Despite being so eloquent about the affairs of others, they are often strangely reticent about discussing their own lives.

Their gift for incisive observation attracts the admiration of other sharp-witted people but they need to watch their tendency to alienate others with one cutting comment too many. They may also close their minds to conflicting opinions so it is important for them to learn the art of diplomacy and to respect the opinions of others. Until the age of twenty-eight they focus on learning and communication but around the age of twenty-nine they may prefer to look for emotional and professional security; the following thirty or so years are when they are likely to come into their own. Around the age of fifty-eight there is another turning point when they enter a period of increased authority, strength and confidence.

As long as these clever and witty people don't drain their energies with negative criticism and keep their minds positive and inquisitive, their natural vitality, drive, creativity and ability to clarify the most complicated of situations will keep them investigating new projects and invigorating old ones. They can see possibilities and connections that others might miss and this can take them far; and they will always be fascinating conversationalists.

On the dark side

Caustic, detached, egotistical

At your best

Caring, observant, expressive

209

25 May

the birthday of
the caring soldier

Your greatest challenge is

opening up to others about your feelings

The way forward is ...

to understand that opening up to others about the way you feel does not imply weakness or lack of moral fiber; everyone experiences inner conflicts.

Intelligence, imagination, compassion and courage are associated with those born on May 25. They are a study in paradox, sometimes being as much a puzzle to themselves as they are to others.

These people know how to fight for what they believe in. They have a strong sense of honor and personal responsibility to which they will cling regardless of the pressures imposed by those less principled. This does not mean they are intellectually rigid, for they often possess a sharp and inquisitive mind, allowing them to embrace new ideas. They are bold and courageous, but are also sensitive and willing to devote their energy and communication skills to improving the lot of those less fortunate. Although they have more than enough courage to go it alone, their favored approach is to inspire a group of like-minded individuals who are equally enthusiastic, principled and progressive.

With a tendency to be philosophically inclined, when it comes to the world of feelings, however, they can come across as cool and aloof. They have high expectations not only of themselves but also of others, and do need to learn to be more flexible and tolerant. They should therefore get in touch with their feelings and the feelings of others because if they don't, however successful they are in their professional life or in their ability to encourage social reform, they are likely to feel repressed and unfulfilled.

The childhood and teens of these people may have been emotionally isolating or difficult in some way but fortunately after the age of twenty-seven they focus on their emotional life, becoming aware of the need for a foundation or center to build from. They need to take advantage of these opportunities, because once they are able to ground themselves emotionally they will feel less frustrated. They will discover that their courage in the face of opposition and their compassion for others are not incompatible but highly compatible energies, being the key to their potential for making a difference and improving human life—be it in the global or personal sense.

On the dark side	At your best
Unforgiving, cold, repressed	Honorable, caring, bold

26 May

the birthday of
the solicitous adventurer

Your greatest challenge is

conforming to your own high standards

The way forward is ...

to understand that if you don't live what you preach, others will accuse you of hypocrisy, an accusation which will hurt and offend you deeply.

On the surface, people born on May 26 appear to be charismatic and popular but deep down they may dream of breaking away. Publicly they uphold convention, being vocal in their promotion of social values and their concern for others. Privately they tend to be a rebel against restrictions of all kinds.

It may seem paradoxical that for people born on this day it is their own talents, which they can use so effectively on behalf of others, that can impede their own search for fulfillment. If their firmly held beliefs and restless drive for new knowledge and experiences are in harmony, they can be startlingly progressive and innovative. But out of harmony they can result in double standards or impulsive, selfish and intolerant behavior.

The dynamism of those born on this day frequently inspires the imagination and admiration of others—but also their intense dislike. The fierce need these people have to express their individuality manifests in a highly visible struggle within themselves that gives them intense charisma, but can also lead them to disreputable, occasionally dangerous, causes and to unworthy people or situations.

Life may be something of a struggle for these complicated but fascinating people but they are unlikely to want it any other way. Part of them feels that conflict is essential for their psychological growth; in some respects they are right, but they should understand that self-knowledge can be gained during times of peace and contentment as well as times of danger. After the age of twenty-six they may focus on having a strong foundation or home and there are opportunities for them to get in touch with their feelings. They need to make the most of these as, contrary to their beliefs, feeling happy and fulfilled is a distinct possibility for them. Once they are able to gain a more profound level of self-knowledge, they have the potential not just to rise to positions of leadership but to impart their strong views through inspiring words and inspirational deeds.

On the dark side

Hypocritical, rebellious, escapist

At your best

Concerned, warm-hearted, decent

27 May

the birthday of
progressive action

Your greatest challenge is

to avoid hastily judging and condemning others

The way forward is ...

to understand that when you pass judgment on other people, you are sometimes passing judgment on yourself.

Although they are perceptive and creative thinkers, those born on May 27 are generally not interested in philosophical ideas but in sharing their knowledge with the wider world. Indeed their greatest desire is to find ways to benefit humanity as a whole, their favored approach being to take action to realize their progressive ideals.

Blessed with a healthy dose of self-confidence, they have the ability to keep their cool during the most difficult circumstances. Although very interested in the human condition and concerned for the well-being of others, they can detach emotionally. Others may criticize them for sometimes being cold and impersonal, but they instinctively realize that getting too emotionally involved in situations weakens their ability to offer effective help.

The steadiness of these people is complemented by their strength of purpose and infectious optimism. Their elegance and sophistication brighten every situation and they are generally well respected and liked by those they meet. Unfortunately, their close personal relationships may be less harmonious because they often devote most of their time and energy to work. Their strong self-belief draws success and opportunities to them; if self-belief is lacking, this may be because they have chosen a career not aligned to their talents. Fortunately, there are several pivotal moments in their lives which offer them opportunities to rethink their life; these will occur at age 25, age 30, age 40 and age 55. Although their greatest wish is to serve humanity, in the interests of their self-development they should take advantage of these opportunities to re-examine their motivations and strategies.

They find it hard to accept criticism, so their psychological progression depends on their being less controlling and taking on board alternative viewpoints in both their personal and their professional lives. Once they are more flexible in their approach, the prodigious energy and spirit of enterprise of these clever and passionate people will ensure their success as a guide and inspiration to others.

On the dark side

Detached, obsessive, selfish

At your best

Steady, dedicated, elegant

28 May

rejuvenation

Your greatest challenge is

coping with boredom

The way forward is ...

to understand that feeling bored can actually be a positive experience as it can teach you vital life skills such as patience, gratitude and self-sufficiency.

People born on May 28 are active, versatile, innovative and creative. Both at home and at work they are mentally sharp and physically agile, and they can think and act with lightning speed. They excel at concocting original schemes and are eager to see them produce results, before rushing onto the next.

Novelty, adventure and the excitement of the new are what these people crave, constantly seeking to reinvent themselves with traveling, visiting new places, meeting new people, and trying new things. Others find their silver-tongued charm hard to resist but they are doers as well as talkers, mastering any skill or discipline that is exciting enough to hold their interest. Competitive by nature, with a perfectionist streak and youthful assertiveness, they are well positioned for success.

They like to share their ideas with others but they can grow impatient when others seem slow to catch on. The problem lies in their choice of audience. They need to find a way to work independently from the mainstream in specialized areas where their flair, originality and versatility can be appreciated. It may take a while before they find their feet professionally and personally, perhaps moving from job to job or even from country to county, but when they do find their focus and an enlightened and adventurous audience, they usually succeed with spectacular flair and elegance.

Between the ages of twenty-four and fifty-four there are opportunities for them to find their place in life; after the age of fifty-five they may become more confident and creative, allowing them to become more powerful in public positions. Throughout their lives, however, their quest for inner security will lead them to explore many avenues of knowledge and they will feel a need to constantly renew themselves with novel situations and stimuli. Even so, they will eventually find that the greatest success comes when they slow down and simplify their life. In fact, reflection and learning to savor their success might be the most rejuvenating change of all.

On the dark side

Restless, impatient, hasty

At your best

Innovative, progressive, versatile

29 May

the birthday of
the plate spinner

Your greatest challenge is

knowing what you want to do

The way forward is ...

to keep pushing ahead and trying out new experiences until you find what's right for you, remembering that nothing you do is ever wasted.

Others are often drawn to the vibrant charm of people born on May 29. They are determined to find a career or a cause that fulfills them but they also believe in sharing their talents. Exhibiting both hedonistic and altruistic tendencies, they manage to juggle these opposites extremely effectively.

They are not necessarily motivated by money, wealth or social position but they do need an audience. If they don't have a following of some kind they can become very frustrated because they are always "switched on," entertaining others with amusing observations and stimulating conversation. They have a way with people and words, and enjoy employing their diplomatic skills to resolve conflicts between others. Unfortunately, their desire to please or entertain others can lead them to repress anger, with sudden and sometimes violent outbursts becoming almost inevitable. They should learn to deal with distressing issues or situations when they appear instead of letting them fester dangerously beneath the surface.

So determined are these people to experience all that life has to offer and to win as many admirers as possible that they may find themselves with dozens of projects on the go. Remarkably, they have the creativity and versatility to keep all these projects running smoothly, and others will constantly wonder how they manage to do it. Beneath their apparently languid approach to multitasking lies a fierce determination and desire to be tested as often as possible.

It will take some time for these people to settle on a fulfilling career; until then they may be something of a jack of all trades. They have a tendency to spread their energies too thinly but between the ages of twenty-three and fifty-three there are opportunities for them to find their direction and focus as they search for emotional security and fulfillment. Wherever they decide to direct their energies, however, their greatest wish is to improve the lives of others; once they find a way to make this a reality, they possess the charisma and leadership skills to make the world a better place.

On the dark side

Procrastinating, aggressive, frustrated

At your best

Vibrant, generous, mediating

30 May

the birthday of
mercurial sparkle

Your greatest challenge is

learning to focus your energies

The way forward is ...

to understand that scattering your energies all over the place is equivalent to scattering your potential.

People born on May 30 tend to be versatile, talkative and expressive with a mental quickness that ensures they shine in social situations. They possess an astute and agile mind, and the insight to take advantage of opportunities.

With a thirst for knowledge and a sharp intellect, they may be involved in many diverse activities. Although they have a talent to succeed in a variety of fields, they need to guard against becoming too restless or scattering their energies with diverse interests. Their challenge is to pick only one field of interest and to commit themselves to it for the long haul. As gifted, capable, expansive, and energetic as they are, their insatiable hunger for change can lead them to neglect their commitments and let others down if they get bored with routine or want to move on without seeing things through.

These people can also change mood rapidly, sometimes in a split second. They may suddenly explode with anger, impatience or frustration, only to be laughing and teasing the next; excitable and passionate one day, they may be cold and serious the day after. Although this adds to their sparkle and appeal, it can also work against them by unnerving those who may doubt their reliability and commitment. Fortunately, between the ages of twenty-two and fifty-two they may focus on emotional security and finding a secure home base, providing opportunities for them to become more responsible and understanding in their relationships.

Thanks to their mercurial sparkle, they can be both difficult and delightful, sometimes at exactly the same time. The greatest lesson for them to learn is the commitment that is essential for success in all aspects of their lives. When a little staying power is combined with their great communication skills, limitless imaginative powers, enthusiasm, and refusal to be bound by convention, these people can be blessed with great innovatory power and the capacity to inspire others with their magical vision.

On the dark side

Irresponsible, flighty, nervous

At your best

Fast, gifted, expansive

31 May

the birthday of
clarity

Your greatest challenge is

coping with rejection

The way forward is ...

to understand that there is no such thing as failure if you learn from your experience. In fact, the road to success is often paved with failure.

People born on this day are often known for their strong views and no-nonsense approach to life. They carry out their work and personal life with the minimum of fuss and are capable of adapting easily to changing situations. Although the image they project is often one of toughness, their greatest desire isn't to be feared or even admired, but for their intentions and their words to be clearly understood by everyone.

Because they want their message to be understood clearly, they are extremely efficient, no detail ever escaping them. The downside of leaving no room for misinterpretation is that they can tend to repeat themselves, and this can irritate others. They can also be obsessed with doing rather than reflecting. Underneath all this, however, is often an underlying confusion; this confusion is almost what keeps them constantly on the go and can make them explode with anger and frustration. The key to their success is to find some kind of balance between their restlessness and talent for adaptation, and their need for structure and clarity. Neither constant activity nor inaction will bring them fulfillment; this lies somewhere in between.

Between the ages of twenty-one and fifty-one they are likely to have a growing need for personal intimacy and emotional security. This can often be a challenging time for them because their overpowering mind rules their lives; they need to avoid the tendency to squash any sign of weakness and should remember that they, like all people, are a combination of weakness and strength. If they can express this, their loved ones will feel closer to them and others will relate to them more easily. After the age of fifty-two there is a turning point which suggests a period of high creativity, confidence, authority and strength.

Above all, these people have an air of authority and seriousness about them. Although they will benefit from letting their hair down occasionally, if they can direct their mind to being expansive rather than single-minded, they have the potential to achieve great success and possibly fame.

On the dark side

Compulsive, over-confident, restless

At your best

Confident, clear-sighted, capable

1 June

the birthday of
the enigmatic student

Your greatest challenge is

understanding yourself

The way forward is ...

to understand that acquiring self-knowledge is a lifetime's task, and there will be good days and bad days.

People adore the wit and humor of those born on June 1. They are often chatty, entertaining and fun to be around and even those who are less talkative will still have a mischievous sparkle in their eyes.

At work and in social settings they possess mercurial inquisitiveness, rarely concentrating on one subject alone because details bore them. There is one subject that never fails to fascinate them: human behavior. In all parts of their lives they tend to keep the focus on other people, often studying and imitating the styles of those at the top in the hope of achieving their success. Since feelings often follow behavior, this approach is often successful, leading them to success. The downside, however, is that they never get to know themselves or what their own talents, hopes and dreams are.

Their positive energy will attract many admirers; the danger is that they can be quite vain and may be tempted to flit from one admirer to another depending on who flatters them the most. This need for flattery is often the result of deep feelings of uncertainty and confusion. Despite their compulsive interest in others, they are private individuals who rarely reveal their deeper thoughts or feelings to others. They do need to get in touch with their own feelings and find what they want out of life; if they don't, they will find it impossible to attain their creative potential. Between the ages of twenty and fifty there will be opportunities for them to establish a sense of their own individuality; it is crucial during this time that they don't scatter their energies on causes and people unworthy of them. After the age of fifty they become more confident, assertive and self-assured.

If they can find the courage to trust their instincts they will be able to unite the enigmatic and melancholic aspects of their personality with those parts of themselves that are impulsive and charismatic. This will give them the focus and concentration they need to stop imitating others and realize their own unique potential.

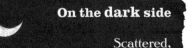

On the dark side

Scattered, impatient, vain

At your best

Discerning, popular, sociable

2 June

the birthday of

ingenuity

Your greatest challenge is

enjoying the ordinary

The way forward is ...

to understand that a fulfilling and happy life is not one of extremes but of steady, positive feelings about every aspect of your life, even chores and routine.

Analytical and intense, people born on June 2 have a talent for unraveling complicated situations. Their lives are rarely problem-free, but they would have it no other way. They are at their happiest when they are testing their ingenuity; if life won't present them with problems to overcome, their natural response is to seek them out.

Their lives rarely run smoothly but they thrive during times of crisis; as quick-witted individuals who can readily analyze and adapt to a situation, they often devise an effective solution or course of action. They can be the lifesavers who restore order, but their addiction to new stimuli or challenges can also work against them by unnecessarily complicating their lives and their relationships when things are running smoothly. Co-workers, for example, may resent their habit of playing devil's advocate and injecting difficulties into simple procedures; when a close relationship is going well they may develop bad habits like lateness or disorganization that threaten it.

The enthusiasm they have for problems and complications can attract them to people and causes that are troubled or unworthy. It is important that they remember the greatest challenge of all for them does not lie in the outside world but in getting to know themselves better. Between the ages of nineteen and forty-nine there are numerous opportunities for them to become more emotionally aware and tuned into themselves. They should take advantage of these because they offer great potential for fulfillment. After the age of fifty they enter a period of growing vitality and confidence.

If they can learn to focus less on external stimuli for a sense of fulfillment and more on their own talents and imaginative powers, their potential for success in whatever area of life they choose to focus on is limitless because they have highly developed intuitive powers. When directed to a cause that is worthy of them, these intuitive powers will lead them toward the satisfying sense of fulfillment that can only be gained from accessing their own unique and potentially spell-binding creativity.

On the dark side

Self-defeating, restless, complicated

At your best

Intuitive, inventive, adaptable

3 June

the birthday of original wit

Your greatest challenge is

avoiding sarcasm and negativity when things don't go your way

The way forward is ...

to cultivate a genuine respect for the rights of others.

Those born on June 3 have a wonderful way with words and their superb communication skills are the keys to their success, both personally and professionally. At work they use their persuasive powers to influence business negotiations and in social situations they use their sparkling wit to impress and entertain others, winning them many admirers.

Their ideas are always innovative and progressive; so much so that others may sometimes have problems understanding them. Not feeling understood can be an incredibly frustrating experience for them because they have plenty of important things to say and hate feeling misunderstood. Free spirits who need to express their individuality, if they feel their position is compromised or misrepresented they will defend their position passionately.

With a sharp wit and a fantastic sense of humor, their feelings run deep and they have a strong belief in the equality of all. But when disputes occur they are not afraid of using biting sarcasm to get their point of view across. Sometimes unaware that their comments can be so insensitive that they can greatly hurt others, it is important for them to become more sensitive to the effect their extreme words have on others. If they don't, others will shy away from them, a terrible punishment because one of their biggest fears is being ignored. Fortunately, between the ages of eighteen and forty-eight there are opportunities for them to become more sensitive to the feelings of others as there is an accent on personal relationships. After the age of forty-nine they have a strong need for self-expression and assertiveness.

Once they have learned to be more aware of the impact their words have on others and, ironically for such talented communicators, the impact that the seductive words of others have on them, there is very little to stop them reaching for the top. They will always be slightly eccentric or unconventional in their approach, but this originality is their driving force. Deep down they know that when they are true to themselves, life is infinitely more rewarding and fulfilling.

On the dark side

Argumentative, unclear, cutting

At your best

Expressive, articulate, witty

4 June

the birthday of the apprentice

Your greatest challenge is

acknowledging your emotions

The way forward is ...

to understand that every emotion, even so-called negative ones such as anger, fear and envy, has something important to tell you.

The intellectual powers of those born on this day are spectacular. The key to their success is an education or apprenticeship that can help nurture their quick minds and they are at their best when they are in the role of student acquiring new knowledge.

With an intense desire to learn and perfect themselves, they are always hungry for novel information or new challenges. Their natural curiosity is one of their greatest strengths but it can also turn into a weakness if they rely on it too much and neglect their emotional side. If trapped in the learning stage, they run the risk of losing some of their flexibility and identity by becoming totally absorbed with the project in hand. They can, moreover, explode with anger if their work is interrupted.

It is important for them to place more of an emphasis on the perceptive, feeling part of their nature, especially in close personal relationships. Fortunately, between the ages of seventeen and forty-seven there are plenty of opportunities for them to focus on the importance of their emotional well-being. They need to take advantage of these opportunities; if they neglect them they could end up becoming workaholics, with all the loneliness and lack of fulfillment that this lifestyle suggests. After the age of forty-eight they are likely to become more confident and there will be opportunities for them to realize their visions.

People born on this day have great leadership potential but until they grow in self-confidence they are often happiest working as part of a team, to which they will always be an asset given their excellent organizational and technical skills. Once they have learned to tune into their own and others' feelings, they will grow in confidence and discover a creative potential within themselves that may have been lying dormant. They should aim to cultivate and develop that potential, as not only will it help them progress from the apprentice stage to becoming more powerful in their own right, it is the key to their fulfillment as a human being.

On the dark side

Critical, stressed, unfulfilled

At your best

Intelligent, intuitive, empathetic

5 June

the birthday of
the intellectual juggler

Your greatest challenge is

learning to pace yourself

The way forward is ...

to understand that just because you are capable of doing lots of things at once doesn't mean you have to.

People born on June 5 can often be found successfully juggling ideas and projects simultaneously. They also have the ability to generate such innovative ideas that others either admire or fail to understand them. Indeed, their vision and soaring imagination seem unlimited in their scope.

With their unlimited energy, expansive mind, excellent conversation skills, and ability to get things done, they are always in demand. Born to stimulate others to think, they are always seeking to unearth some great discovery or mystery. The key to their success, however, lies in their ability to communicate effectively with others. If they are misunderstood, however, it is likely to wound them deeply and express itself in flashes of anger, irritation or nervous tension. Learning to be more patient and focused in the presentation of their thoughts and listening to what others have to say will help them get their point across more effectively.

Between the ages of sixteen and forty-six they may focus on emotional security, and security and home issues are likely to come to the fore. It is important during this time that they learn to guard against sudden anger, obstinacy and criticism in the way they communicate with others. Born worriers, they also need to learn to manage their own negativity and hold on to the dreams that inspire them when others perceive them as unrealistic or unfeasible. After the age of forty-seven there is a turning point which signals a period of growing self-confidence and strength, allowing them to become more outgoing and hopefully more measured in their approach to others.

These people have boundless energy and creativity; although they should never lose their vitality, they do need to learn how to channel it effectively. They also have the ability to multitask, but learning to become more focused will work to their advantage. Once they are able to find balance between their intellect and their instincts, they have the imaginative gifts, technical aptitude and steadfastness of focus needed to develop their novel ideas and share them successfully with others.

On the dark side

Anxious, chaotic, highly strung

At your best

Articulate, versatile, intelligent

6 June

anticipation

Your greatest challenge is

avoiding feeling misunderstood by others

The way forward is ...

to put yourself in your audience's shoes and to tailor the presentation of your vision to the interests of your audience.

Whenever people born on June 6 enter the room there is a sense of excitement and anticipation. They are people who know how to make things happen and others instinctively sense this. They have no problem communicating their progressive ideals and will work steadfastly to make them a reality, often gaining a following with their commitment to improve the lives of everyone.

Although these people are movers and shakers, they can take their ideals or vision to an extreme; this can manifest in unusual or dangerous behavior. More conventional people may find their wilder side expresses itself in extreme hobbies, unusual relationships, or strange and wonderful fantasies. Sometimes their dreams and ideals are so far-reaching that others may find them opaque; this can be deeply distressing to them as they live to share, inspire and reform. Learning to express themselves with greater simplicity will help them get their point across.

Although they should never rein in their wonderful energy, they should find some kind of balance so their more bizarre tendencies do not alienate others and isolate themselves. Fortunately, between the ages of fifteen and forty-five they are likely to be more restrained and security conscious, with a strong focus on their family, home and intimate personal life. However, when they reach the age of forty-six there is an increased need for self-expression and leadership; during this time they are likely to become more assertive and confident, taking more of a public role. It is important at this time that they understand how their actions serve as a role model for others and that a more balanced approach to life will help others relate to them.

Once they have found an audience they can relate to and who can relate to them, they more than live up to the anticipation that their progressive visions have created. The relief that they feel in finally being understood will encourage them to express their caring nature and, in their typically extreme way, their revolutionary determination to change the world.

On the dark side

Misunderstood, extreme, detached

At your best

Idealistic, visionary, artistic

7 June

the birthday of
the seduction

Your greatest challenge is

being on time

The way forward is ...

to understand that respecting other people by being punctual is the mark of a truly inspirational and charismatic person.

Many people think that the colorful individuals born on June 7 live in a land of make-believe; in fact it is an inner world full of great ideas and potential. Their enchanting verve and style captivates people's imagination and, more often than not, these seductive individuals are fashion icons or trendsetters.

Whatever they decide to do, it will be slightly ahead of its time. They instinctively know how to reach people with their creative energy; they enjoy the process of seduction and invest much energy in non-verbal signals. They often take great pains over their appearance and in many social situations their clothes, body language and eyes do the talking for them— sometimes too much talking, as they are not afraid of being shocking or sensational. They also have a fantastic sense of humor and fun, and life is always entertaining when they are around. Instinctively grasping the seductive powers of surprise and humor, they delight in shocking people and making them smile.

If they don't get in touch with their feelings, however, they run the risk of living life on a superficial level. When this happens, instead of being captivating and enchanting, others may start to think of them as unreliable, forgetful and unfocused and they could find themselves alone. Often possessing an instinct to run away, it is important therefore for them to try and probe their lives more deeply. Fortunately, before the age of forty-four there are significant opportunities for them to focus more on their inner life. After the age of forty-five there is a turning point which encourages greater self-expression and assertiveness; as long as they guard against self-absorption, these are the years they can really come into their own.

People born on this day have a rich inner life and they need to make sure that they don't subordinate this to material concerns or refuse to acknowledge or express it because they fear others might think them odd. They aren't odd—they're just full of unique and special potential.

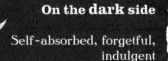

On the dark side

Self-absorbed, forgetful, indulgent

At your best

Trendsetting, visionary, entertaining

8 June

the birthday of

expectation

Your greatest challenge is

knowing how to relax

The way forward is ...

to understand that time out is not time wasted but time gained; you will return to your work with greater enthusiasm, energy and clarity.

People born on June 8 are honest and direct in their approach to life. They speak their mind and, because they have such high expectations of themselves and others, despise laziness or injustice in any form.

Although highly independent and quite happy to work alone, people born on this day will often find themselves in the position of leader. This is because they have a strong sense of fair play and understand the importance of adhering to rules—as long as these rules are their own. They also make great leaders because they set an inspiring example in their wholehearted dedication to their life's work, be that running a business, heading a team or raising a family. There is a danger, however, that their dedication and industriousness can tip over into workaholism.

Until the age of forty-three they focus on home and their emotional life. Their basic nature is to be personable and fun, so it is important during this time that they don't let their spontaneity disappear. In their attempt to be just, they should also make sure they don't become harsh or judgmental, placing impossible expectations of loyalty and dedication on themselves and others. After the age of forty-four they become more self-expressive and assertive, but they need to make sure that they do not become preachy toward others and overly zealous in their attitude to work. The key to their success and fulfillment both personally and professionally is to balance their emotional needs with their strong sense of responsibility. As they approach the age of seventy, they start to become more practical and analytical, and the emphasis turns toward serving others.

The integrity, industriousness and devotion that they are capable of enable them to blaze a pioneering trail through life and build a wide social circle. Once they can develop empathy and a greater tolerance for their own vulnerabilities and those of others, the high expectation of fulfillment that they have always had will be realized in their own success and happiness.

On the dark side

Workaholic, stressed, judgmental

At your best

Independent, honest, dedicated

9 June

the birthday of
unexpected opportunity

Your greatest challenge is

being consistent

The way forward is ...

to understand that consistency and responsibility are not limiting energies but extremely creative ones; without them, no project stands a chance.

People born on June 9 have a wonderful zest for life. They have limitless energy and others may find it hard to keep up with their ever-changing thoughts, feelings and emotions. Although they have quick minds and a logical orientation, everything about them is unexpected.

They have a quick temper but are quick to forgive. In their world view they are forthright and strong-willed, but in personal relationships they can be surprisingly passive and reserved. They are unconventional in their behavior but respectful toward authority. They are sympathetic and generous to those less fortunate, but sometimes insensitive and neglectful to their loved ones. Because they have so many different faces to present to the world they are endlessly fascinating individuals.

Action is a key word for them and they thrive on challenges and variety. Life can be a mad rush between one activity and another; they have little spare time, so great is their hunger for all that life has to offer. It is important for them occasionally to slow down and catch their breath. If they don't they may find that their lives descend into chaos. They should also aim to bring all aspects of their personality into an integrated whole; if they don't their lives will be governed by impulse rather than a clear sense of direction or purpose. Until the age of forty-two they focus on home, security and family; it is likely that they will spend longer than normal living with their parents or near their parents' home, being unwilling to branch out on their own. Around the age of forty-two, however, there is a turning point which emphasizes energy, power and self-confidence; these are the years when they can really come into their own.

Above all, people born on this day are spectacularly colorful and versatile individuals; if they can learn to harness their primitive instincts and channel their energies into mature goals that are worthy of them, they will find that life offers them a series of unexpected but well-deserved opportunities for happiness, success and fulfillment.

On the dark side

Immature, changeable, tactless

At your best

Youthful, direct, logical

10 June

the birthday of
dichotomy

Your greatest challenge is

being honest with yourself

The way forward is ...

to understand that overcoming the worries that plague your peace of mind is the only way to move forward.

People born on June 10 are gifted but extreme individuals with strongly held views they are not afraid to express. They have an abundance of talent and ideas, and boundless energy to put them to good use. Everything about them exudes vitality, confidence and charisma but, despite this, they can suffer from bouts of crippling insecurity and self-doubt.

They are experts at keeping up a happy front in both their professional and personal lives but underneath they have a serious and intense mind prone to negativity and worry. This dichotomy between public persona and personal fears splits their personality, making it hard for them to feel truly happy and fulfilled. They are unwilling to acknowledge their insecurities to others because it would mean admitting them to themselves. They would rather run, hide or lose themselves in either the confident persona they have created or in sex, passion or violence. But if they faced their inner demons and acknowledged them, they would find a sense of contentment and inner peace.

Until the age of forty-one they may focus on emotional security, home and family life; they should take advantage of these opportunities to get in touch with their feelings and build up a network of close friends to whom they can open up. After the age of forty-two they enter a period of increasing self- confidence, authority, strength and self-expression. If during this period they make sure they don't avoid problems or let other people walk all over them, these are the years where they are most likely to develop their talents successfully and really come into their own.

Above all, people born on this day should not underestimate their ability to cope in life because they are capable of bold and daring action once they confront their obstacles directly. The greatest challenge for them will be confronting their inner fears. Once they find the courage to do that, they will discover within themselves a powerhouse of creativity and star potential to achieve not just one, but all of their amazing dreams.

On the dark side

Erratic, confused, self-destructive

At your best

Gifted, warm, daring

11 June

Your greatest challenge is

dealing with domestic responsibilities

The way forward is ...

to understand that great fulfillment can only be found when all areas of their lives, including the domestic, are harmonized.

Disciplined, energetic, perceptive and optimistic, the ambitious people born on June 11 will often push their way toward their goals with surprising force, tearing down any obstacles in their path. Their driving force is always to push ahead, test their limits and expand their knowledge and experience.

With the enviable ability to lose themselves wholly in their work, their aim is to learn as much as possible in one specialist area and then move the goal posts by pioneering a breakthrough. Their sense of fair play and willingness to get their hands dirty makes them a much-sought-after team player. Less evolved individuals born on this day who find themselves lacking the support of others may find their self-absorption has slipped into arrogance or egotism. If they can change their approach to one of sensitivity and humility, they may find that others are more willing to seek them out.

Their remarkable zest for life and outstanding potential to make the important breakthrough means they have little time for those with less energy or enthusiasm. They despise being around negative or depressed people because they instinctively understand that a positive attitude increases their chances of success. But happiness and success are not always enough for them because their greatest desire is excellence; this is why they will often be found pushing their work or lifestyle to new heights. Although this winning attitude can take them to the very top, it can lead to emotional isolation when co-workers or friends find their constant pushing to be exhausting.

Fortunately, before the age of forty-one there are opportunities for them to develop a sense of emotional security. They should ensure they take advantage of these and don't neglect their friends and family. After the age of forty-two they become more confident and aggressive in their approach; if they have learned to recognize the damaging effect their obsessive tendencies can have on themselves and others, this is the period when they have the potential to achieve truly great breakthroughs not just in their careers but in their lives.

On the dark side

Stubborn, forceful, arrogant

At your best

Progressive, positive, disciplined

12 June

the birthday of
realistic positivity

Your greatest challenge is

facing your fears and insecurities

The way forward is ...

to understand that acknowledging you have fears and insecurities actually reduces their power over you. Once the enemy is understood, it is far easier to manage.

People born on this day tend to have a cheerful disposition and their optimistic, positive approach to life serves them well. Their strong belief in the power of good also has an uplifting effect on those around them, helping other people change for the better.

Extremely generous and supportive of others, their positivity is always tempered by realism. They support or value what they know they can achieve or what they believe others can achieve. Their aim is not to make things perfect, but better in the belief that the best way to help someone is to encourage them to help themselves. Occasionally this can manifest in judgmental words but their cruel-to-be-kind approach generally works.

The sunny disposition that the self-contained people born on this day present to the world bestows upon them the capacity not only to achieve great things but also to be pioneers in many aspects of their lives. They can't bear inertia and will push themselves to their limits, even devising new activities for friends and family or learning a new language or skill. The downside to all this cheerfulness is that it can sometimes be irritating to others, who may see them as lacking in depth. Although they can give the appearance of being superficial, inner conflicts often lie beneath their cheerful exterior. It is important for them not to try and bury these conflicts with external activities; if they do, it will lead to deep unhappiness.

Until the age of thirty-nine they focus on emotional security and need to take advantage of opportunities to learn about love and understanding. After the age of forty they become more self-confident and their personal capabilities are often recognized. During this time they need to make sure they surround themselves with people who challenge them intellectually or emotionally, and who encourage them to focus inwards. Once they have learned to understand themselves and others better and connect with their intuition, their infectious dynamism and creativity will be validated by remarkable achievements in all aspects of their lives.

On the dark side

Judgmental, unaware, superficial

At your best

Optimistic, decisive, generous

13 June

the birthday of
the wild dreamer

Your greatest challenge is

being sensible

The way forward is ...

to understand that sensible does not always mean being boring; it can also mean maximizing your chances of success by being focused and realistic about your objectives.

People born on June 13 live life according to their own rules and values. Often way ahead of their time, they can't bear routine and the everyday, and their wild streak will take them to places no one else would dare to visit.

Although following their highly creative and vivid imagination can lead them into danger, it can also make them great innovators and pioneers. They love to travel and explore, both externally and internally; their thirst for adventure can take them all over the world to exotic places or it can manifest itself in total absorption in their intellectual discoveries. They truly believe that the world is theirs for the taking and that they can achieve virtually anything they set their mind and heart on.

Many of these people realize their wild dreams and become highly successful in their chosen field. Those who are less evolved, however, may struggle to translate their dreams into reality. It is important for them to get in touch with their intuition as this will tell them which risks are achievable and which are likely to end in frustration. They also need positive people who encourage them to dream but who provide a healthy dose of realism and objectivity. Until the age of thirty-eight they focus on emotional security and should take advantage of opportunities to develop greater self-awareness and understanding. After the age of thirty-nine they will have more self-confidence and a greater recognition of their capabilities. During this period they should ensure their appetite for adventure does not endanger them; they need to think long and hard about what their wild schemes really entail.

Above all, people born on this day are adventurers and they should never try to dampen their powerful imagination and boundless energy with routine and repetition. However, if they are to maximize their potential to not just dream but actually realize the impossible, they should weigh up the pros and cons, studying what is possible and what is not before they leap in at the deep end.

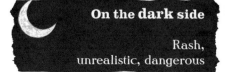

On the dark side

Rash, unrealistic, dangerous

At your best

Imaginative, intelligent, adventurous

14 June

the birthday of
the supervisor

Your greatest challenge is

resisting the urge to take charge

The way forward is ...

to understand that sometimes the only way for people to learn and grow is for them to make their own mistakes.

The bold individuals born on June 14 often have a powerful desire to take charge of people or situations, whether these are co-workers, friends or family, or projects that need to be supervised. Their instinctive urge to take control stems from their ability to observe what is going on around them and sum up quickly what needs to be done and who needs to do it.

The supreme confidence they have in their convictions is the result of their strong self-belief and their inability to stand on the sidelines when work needs to be done. It's no surprise that they often make inspirational and dynamic leaders, but their actions can sometimes be perceived as bossy and abrupt by those who prefer to make their own minds up. Unfortunately, when their methods or behavior are challenged they can become impatient and confrontational, and this can work against them, especially in their personal relationships. It is important for them to make a real effort to anticipate the reactions that their forcefulness can arouse in others.

Until the age of thirty-seven they may focus on their emotional security, and it is important during these years that they take advantage of opportunities to develop a greater awareness and consideration of the feelings of others. After the age of thirty-eight they enter a period of increased strength and confidence and, given their already well-developed self-confidence, they need to make sure that their direct approach does not tip over into arrogant certainty as this will alienate others from them.

Above all, they have clear-cut and strong opinions, together with a compulsion to take uncompromising direct action to achieve their far-sighted visions. They are also willing to work very hard, making considerable sacrifices for the people or causes close to their heart. Once they learn to respect the sensitivities of others, they have the potential not just to be outstanding supervisors but to make outstanding leaders and contributors to whatever field they choose to devote their prodigious energies, forthright opinions and powerful intellect.

On the dark side

Bossy, confrontational, abrupt

At your best

Persistent, authoritative, courageous

15 June

the birthday of
irresistible charm

Your greatest challenge is

believing in your own desirability

The way forward is ...

to understand that however many people you charm into loving or flattering you, the only way to feel truly desirable is to believe in yourself first.

June 15 people are blessed with natural charm. They can easily bring others around to their point of view, often using their seductive power to win the support of co-workers, friends and family and indeed anyone they meet. Their charm and their appeal are so strong that even the most cynical and suspicious of people find it hard to resist them.

What makes these people so charming is their genuine interest in others and their remarkable ability to guess what they are thinking or feeling. This makes others feel good, in that they feel they are on the same wavelength as these attractive individuals. Their outstanding people skills will often fast-forward them into positions of influence; if they do find themselves in such positions, they should devote their persuasive powers to worthy causes. If they don't, others may resent being conned into questionable courses of action. They also need to ensure they don't give others the wrong impression and charm them into believing a friendship exists when it doesn't. In all their dealings they should observe a strict code of ethics.

Until the age of thirty-six they may focus on emotional security; during this time they should ensure they are as honest with themselves and others as possible, and don't place being popular, wealthy or attractive over a sense of personal achievement. After the age of thirty-seven they become more confident and this may encourage them to use their people skills in a more assertive way. It is important during these years that they keep on the straight and narrow; if they do, they can direct their energy, intellect and inner power to influence others in productive and positive ways.

They have the potential to make great contributions to partnerships, groups and society as a whole, as long as they are aware of the power they have over others and make sure they are not manipulating them. If they truly believe in the cause they are promoting, their ambition and personal charm virtually guarantee their popularity, happiness and success.

On the dark side

Calculating, misleading, unstable

At your best

Seductive, attractive, intelligent

16 June

the birthday of
far-sighted astuteness

Your greatest challenge is

not being suspicious of everyone and everything

The way forward is ...

to understand that being too cautious can sometimes block creativity and spontaneity, key ingredients for your fulfillment and success.

Those born on June 16 combine within their personalities a unique blend of adventurousness and caution. Although they have a vivid imagination and innovative inclinations, they are also extremely astute, possessing a willingness to be flexible without losing their vision.

Often having big plans and an uncanny ability to pick up on lifestyle trends before they happen, they rarely throw caution to the winds by speculating wildly. They are far more likely to plot their course in life carefully, laying firm foundations for the future one brick at a time. They are at their happiest when they can take risks within a controlled environment where their goals are clear and where they can receive constant updates or feedback on their progress. They are at their least productive, however, when they fail to find a balance between their enterprising and prudent qualities, and suppress their risk-taking tendencies in order to play safe.

Until the age of thirty-five, emotional security is likely to play an important part in their lives; they need to remember to leave some room in their structured lifestyle for fun and games. After the age of thirty-six, they grow in confidence and often become more assertive and self-expressive. It's important during this period that they don't block their incredible enthusiasm, will-power and determination with indecision. They should be sure of what they wish for, as this is the time in their life when they are most likely to have the power to make their ideas a reality.

Equally practical and imaginative, they tend to derive the greatest comfort and satisfaction from non-material pleasures, such as strong relationships or the beauty found in nature and the arts. They often live their life according to a strict humanitarian code, giving them compassion for those less fortunate and contempt for those who abuse their power. When they have learned to be neither too impulsive nor too cautious, the strength of their desire for progress can be a remarkable power for good, not just for themselves but for all whose lives they touch.

On the dark side

Inflexible, indecisive, anxious

At your best

Earnest, patient, original

17 June

the birthday of
the influential example

Your
greatest
challenge is

explaining how
you feel

*The way
forward is ...*

to understand
that opening up
to others does
not weaken your
position; it
strengthens it,
because other
people will find
you easier to
relate to.

People born on June 17 are often strong and inspirational individuals who believe everyone has it within them to follow their dreams. A fascinating combination of creativity and structure, they know how to conform but also have a vivid imagination that they want to explore and, if possible, profit from.

Demanding a lot of themselves and the people they live and work with, whatever situation they are in they are likely to be excellent performers and a forceful presence. Although they set a terrific example to others and people are drawn to their vitality and masterful demeanor, if they find themselves in the role of mentor they may struggle. This is because they are often too wrapped up in their own goals, lacking the patience and understanding to listen to others.

There is a danger that they might stretch the truth if they feel it serves their purposes. This isn't motivated by a desire to deceive but simply so their arguments sound more plausible. But if they don't control this tendency to manipulate the truth, they can become known as untrustworthy. Such is their influence, however, that even if their exaggeration is uncovered, others may still continue blindly to follow their lead. It is important therefore for them to impose a strict ethical code upon themselves. Until the age of thirty-four they may focus on emotional relations, security and family; for their own happiness they need to ensure that they take advantage of opportunities to discover their feelings and learn how to express them to others. After the age of thirty-five they enter a period of strength, power and confidence; these are the years when they come into their own as inspirational leaders or pioneers.

Above all, the forceful but imaginative and progressive individuals born on this day are fired by progressive ideals. Once they develop an understanding of the effect that their intensity has on others, not only will this give their ideals a better chance of gaining acceptance, it will also bring them greater emotional fulfillment.

On the dark side

Impatient,
detached, untrustworthy

At your best

Influential,
physical, creative

18 June

the birthday of
perceptive congeniality

Your greatest challenge is

dealing with boredom

The way forward is ...

to understand that the answer to boredom is not in external stimulation but in the sense of excitement and change generated within.

People born on June 18 often have a charming manner and a likable vitality that uplifts everyone they meet. Their instant likability, however, conceals an insightful mind and a serious head for responsibility and business. They place as high a priority on meeting their personal, financial and professional goals as they do on being popular.

Whether they realize it or not, their personality has a lasting effect on others and, even if not physically present, their influence will be felt in some way. They possess a perceptive and highly intuitive mentality, and when this is combined with their sharp wit and quirky sense of fun they manage to get their point across effectively without causing offence. This makes it hard for others to forget them. Their ability to leave a lasting impact gives them potential for leadership, although they need to be careful that they don't abuse this power and become manipulative.

Although they enjoy attention, and popularity comes naturally to them, they are also good at reciprocating it, especially when it comes to helping others. They will often be indefatigable fighters for the rights of others and make witty and dramatic speakers and doers who refuse to tolerate injustice. Despite their sincerity and intelligence, they need to be entertained and can get easily bored. Their need for constant change, challenge and excitement can make them behave erratically and occasionally selfishly. They need to learn to be more consistent and disciplined in their approach to people and situations.

Until the age of thirty-two they may focus on emotional security but after the age of thirty-three they become more self-expressive and assertive. They should ensure that they don't fritter away their considerable talents during these years by a "grass is always greener" mentality. Once they learn to be grateful for what they already have, they will discover a capacity for spiritual achievement. This is the key to their creativity and their ability to make a positive impression on all those lucky enough to cross their path.

On the dark side

Egotistical, easily bored, erratic

At your best

Charming, powerful, intelligent

19 June

Your greatest challenge is

with being too confrontational

The way forward is ...

to understand that the direct approach simply won't work in every situation. The best way to get people on your side is often to approach them gently.

People born on June 19 are blessed with the ability to stimulate and uplift others. Their resolve and courage, along with their patience, tolerance and generally good intentions, serve as an inspiring example. Whether they realize it or not, they are catalysts spurring others into action and moving situations forward in the process.

They may choose to fight vociferously or to quietly hold firm, but whatever strategy they choose they rarely crumble under pressure. Their resolve comes from their most outstanding characteristic: their self-belief. They are rarely beset by feelings of doubt which can arouse both admiration and irritation. Indeed their huge personality can intimidate those less confident; however, their single-minded determination is not the result of blinkered obstinacy but rather of supreme confidence engendered by the knowledge that they have evaluated every viewpoint and arrived at the best conclusion. And their confidence is well founded, as they are blessed with incisive analytical skills, intellectual inquisitiveness and profound intuition.

Less evolved types born on this day may express themselves in controlling or dictatorial behavior, but life usually ends up teaching them the benefits of a less confrontational approach. Until the age of thirty-one they may focus on emotional security, home and family. After the age of thirty-two, however, they enter a period of greater self-expression and creativity, with added assertiveness and boldness. It is important during this period that they learn the art of diplomacy; if they do, these are the years that they come into their own. At the age of sixty-two they may feel a desire to be more methodical and to offer practical service to others.

Above all, people born on this day have the ability to empower others with their compassion, sparkling wit and youthful vitality. They may have a tendency to push themselves too hard, but as long as they maintain a sense of balance and perspective they have the potential to make their mark on the world by guiding, improving and energizing others.

On the dark side

Over-ambitious, unaware, inflexible

At your best

Energizing, courageous, persistent

20 June

the birthday of
excitement

Your greatest challenge is

avoiding extremes of emotion

The way forward is ...

to understand that the only way for you to find any real sense of fulfillment is to temper your reactions with a heavy dose of self-discipline.

People born on June 20 are affectionate and spontaneous with everyone they meet, because expressing their emotions comes naturally to them. Indifference is something they simply don't understand since, above all else, these people love and thrive on excitement.

Life is never dull when these popular people are around since everything elicits a passionate reaction from them. They are dramatic, charismatic, outgoing charmers who love to talk and adore being the center of attention. Excellent communication skills and an innovative mind crammed with insights make them vibrant, witty conversationalists. However, because they love excitement, they can sometimes provoke an argument for the sake of it. They can also be a little too needy of praise and if they don't get the reinforcement they crave, they may respond with attention-seeking or irrational behavior. It is important for them to surround themselves with warm-hearted but level-headed people who can give them the balance they need.

Until the age of thirty there is an emphasis on home, family and emotional security, and they should take advantage of opportunities to find a sense of inner balance. After the age of thirty-one, however, they will become more creative and confident, developing the assertiveness to be more adventurous. If they can get a grip on their passionate responses to situations and their ability to churn up strong emotions in others, these are the years when they can really come into their own.

Although people born on this day can sometimes create fireworks unnecessarily, more often than not they are a positive force. The atmosphere seems lighter when they are around because they help bring out the repressed emotions of others. Excitement and passion seem to follow them wherever they go and they also have considerable intuitive powers, helping them to enchant, persuade and influence others. If they can find a worthy cause and ensure that they occasionally check in with their reason as well as their emotions they can transform their creative and exciting dreams into reality.

On the dark side

Insecure, irrational, hypersensitive

At your best

Dynamic, exciting, rousing

CANCER

(JUNE 21 – JULY 22)

* **Element:** Water
* **Ruling planet:** The moon
* **Symbol:** The Crab
* **Tarot card:** The Chariot (resilience)
* **Number:** 2
* **Favorable colors:** Indigo, white, smoky grey
* **Key phrase:** When it's safe I will come out of my shell

Cancer is the first water sign and—like the unpredictable sea herself—Cancerians can be gentle and soothing one moment and stormy and snappy the next. They are perhaps the most sensitive of all the signs in the zodiac and the need to protect themselves and those they love from threat or danger is powerful. Although they may appear enigmatic and mysterious, beneath the surface there lurks a person who is highly intuitive, and truly loving and compassionate.

Personality potential

Both men and women born under the sign of Cancer tend to be compassionate and nurturing by nature. They truly care about the feelings of others and nothing matters more to them than giving and receiving love. Their motivation in life is the pursuit of happiness because they realize that the happier people are, the more productive and fulfilled they will be. Easy going, they often have a very distinctive laugh and will try to create a harmonious and welcoming atmosphere wherever they go.

Emotional, loving, intuitive, imaginative and sympathetic are all key words associated with Cancerians. They are also very protective of those they love and respect, and are extremely practical with money; if their compassion and intuition can flow harmoniously with their practicality it makes for a wonderful combination. The ruling planet for Cancer is the moon, the planet of emotions and intuition, and there is a strong tendency for them to let feelings be their guide through life. They will, however, make instinctive rather than impulsive decisions because their impulses are tempered by their practicality.

Home is of vital importance to Cancerians and any disruption will cause emotional distress. They are also prone to bouts of nostalgia and will cling to everything from the past. More often than not they will surround themselves with photographs of loved ones or objects which have very little material value but high personal value, either because they were gifts from friends or family, or because they are associated with an especially important personal memory. What others see as clutter Cancerians will hold onto tightly because these photographs and objects are important for their sense of security.

Perhaps one of the greatest strengths of people born under this sun sign is that they are highly intuitive when it comes to the needs of others. A Cancerian will instinctively sense what another person wants or needs before any words are even spoken. When this is combined with their nurturing nature it's easy to see why, in times of crisis, these people are often the lynchpin upon which everyone will depend or seek counsel from. Like a safe harbor in which boats can take shelter, Cancerians provide a safe and well-organized place for people both to escape and rest and also to draw strength and inspiration from.

> "Home is of vital importance to Cancerians and any disruption will cause emotional distress."

On the dark side

Those born under the sign of the crab can be incredibly moody and argumentative at times and, when they don't get their own way, they can behave like martyrs. The problem with this approach to life is that often the person who suffers the most is themselves. They are also the chief worriers of the zodiac, never "happy" unless they are worrying about someone or something.

Although their nature is compassionate and caring, it's important to not forget that the crab—the symbol for their sun sign—is covered by a tough, outer shell. Make no mistake that those born under this sign are fiercely ambitious. Success in life matters a great deal to them and, if need be, they will fight tough and hard for what they want. More often than not, how-ever, this fighting instinct doesn't get a chance to express itself in a positive way. This is because they are so tuned into other people's feelings and what is going on around them that it's hard for them to take a step back and actually define not just what they want, but who they are. Cancerians often suffer con-fusion and mood swings as a result of their sensitivity; with their feelings so dependent on the feelings of others, their emotional landscape is constantly shifting. Then, when the misunderstandings and expectations become too great, Cancerians will typically withdraw into their shell to process and make sense of things. This withdrawal can be particularly confusing and painful for friends and loved ones who may have grown to depend on a Cancerian's loving and nurturing presence in their lives.

Personality pitfalls for Cancerians therefore arise both out of their emotional sensibility and their inability to distinguish between their own feelings and those of others. When feeling threatened or vulnerable they will become self-defensive and possessive, grabbing onto what represents security to them and retreating into their hard shell.

Symbol

If you want a key to the personality of those born under Cancer, look no further than the symbol of the crab, with its soft, vulnerable interior and its hard, tough outer shell. The crab is a sensitive creature but the only way it can survive in a dangerous world is by surrounding itself with a hard shell. This can lead to both misunderstandings and vulnerability. For instance, Cancerians may decide to remain aloof for fear of get-ting hurt, but this can make them feel alone and rejected by others. Similarly, they may open up so much to others that there is never time for others to find out anything about them, and this can lead to feelings of loneliness and isolation.

Darkest secret

Cancerians are prone to constant fretting, and this fear of "what ifs" or nameless dangers can shatter their hopes and dreams. Nothing scares a Cancerian more than change or the unknown, and it's this fear of change which drives them to invest a huge amount of energy and time into relationships or projects that will give them a feeling of security. The problem is that the more they try to control their environment, the more insecure and vulnerable they tend to feel because the only thing that never changes in life is change.

Love

Cancerians have seemingly endless supplies of love and nurturing to give others, and although they can live by themselves they are far more fulfilled and happy in a relationship. If they do live alone, however, they will typically surround themselves with close friends. They make wonderfully caring and supportive partners, but all this love and emotion can sometimes come across as smothering. Emotional independence in others or not being needed anymore scares them and there could be issues of co–dependence in relationships if they don't learn to "let go."

Cancerians respond best to warmth and affection, and when they fall in love, they fall in love body, mind and soul. Romantic at heart, they will always put their loved ones first. All this is fine if their affection and dedication is reciprocated but if it's rejected they can retreat, deeply scarred and vulnerable, into their shell. Fear of rejection may also keep them in that shell for far longer than is healthy for them. Although they will tend to cling tightly to a relationship which shows signs of disintegrating, they are also capable of wandering off if they don't feel loved and appreciated in order to find someone else who is willing to give them the love and understanding they feel they deserve.

Love matches: Taurus, Cancer and Pisces

The Cancer man

Cancer men can be flirtatious so it will take time and patience to get to know them really well. They may appear aloof, but without warning their defenses may come down and a tender, warm smile and endearing laugher may break through. It's important to remember that, however moody, cautious, pessimistic or arrogant they may appear, their true nature is this softer, affectionate side. It's just that they often feel too vulnerable to show it.

This man isn't a mummy's boy, but the mother figure will be an important one in his life. He'll put his mother on a pedestal or have an image of what a mother should be like in his mind. Cancerians are either very close to their mothers or completely alienated and disappointed with them; either way, the relationship is never casual. So if you fall in love with a Cancer male you will have to understand the importance of the mother figure in his life. He will never, ever admit it, but a part of him adores being petted and mothered by females.

With his sensitive awareness of what others feel and his practical side—which ensures he won't be lacking in cash— this guy is never short of admirers but it may take a while before he really falls in love. This is because he sets very high standards and rarely compromises; so in the great majority of cases if a Cancerian asks a person out more than once it's a sign that he is genuinely enamored.

The Cancer woman

Like the waxing and waning moon Cancer women can be gentle, magical, enlightening and imaginative—and occasionally a little crazy. They may appear shy and sweet at first glance but over time they can flower into fascinating conversationalists with a wealth of hidden talents and a passionate sexuality.

If a Cancer woman falls in love there tend to be two different sides to her; one is modest and womanly, while the other is deeply affectionate, at times clingy. The latter can be wonderful if the affection is welcomed but suffocating if it isn't. Rejection and ridicule are a Cancer woman's greatest fears and this is why she will rarely make the first move in a relationship. She may also suffer from bouts of low self-esteem when she doesn't feel pretty or clever enough; if her partner can reassure her during these vulnerable moments she is theirs for life. Material comfort and security are important for this woman but she will not expect her partner to provide everything for her; she is more than willing to put in her fair share of hard work to give her family comfort and security.

Above all, there is nothing shallow or superficial about a Cancer woman and when she falls in love, it's generally for keeps. There is also no end to the heroic sacrifice this woman will make for those she loves. Her serenity and patience in the face of obstacles and setbacks—both her own and those of her loved ones—will never fail to soothe and inspire.

Family

Cancerian babies often appear very sensitive and intuitive. As babies, when their mother feels tense they will cry and scream for no reason, and when she feels relaxed they will babble gently and smile. Other changes in the home atmosphere will immediately be picked up and that is why Cancerian babies' moods are so unpredictable. They are often picky and slow eaters as infants, and will need coaxing to eat their fruit and vegetables. It's important, however, for parents not to be too authoritarian or to try to rush them when they eat because the Cancerian digestion is sensitive.

When they first start school Cancerian children may be shy and withdrawn, and it will typically take them a year or two to settle. Parents can help by encouraging them not to withdraw but to make new friends and join into activities and clubs that are school based. The best way to discipline a Cancerian child when they have broken a rule is not to send them to their room or withhold their pocket money, but to say they have upset or disappointed Mummy or Daddy. This approach will appeal to their sensitivity. Parents of young Cancerians should also encourage their children from an early age to tidy up after themselves, as people born under this sign have a tendency to untidiness and hoarding.

As parents, Cancerians often come into their own. Their need to nurture is instinctive, and they make loving and supportive parents. They do, however, need to make sure that they don't overprotect their children and fill them with unnecessary fears. As long as there are no clear signs of danger and threat, the Cancerian parent should learn to bite their tongue every time they want to say, "be careful," because children need to learn to take risks at school and in the playground. There is a danger that Cancerian parents might become so involved in their children's lives that they lose a sense of their own identity. They may particularly suffer when their children leave home, so it's important for them to keep their own interests going when they are raising their children.

Career

Cancerians enjoy challenge at work but it's important also that their work has some kind of continuity, because security is very important for them. Tenacious, determined and often shrewd, they have a talent for business where their powerful intuition can often serve them well. The caring professions will obviously attract them, given their powerful urge to nurture, and they make excellent doctors, nurses and social workers, as well as teachers and human resource workers. Work involving the past—in museums, antiques or as a historian—may also suit, as will careers involved with boating, and aquatic or ocean life. Cancerians love to cook, so they may gravitate toward careers in catering; they may also have an artistic side to them that seeks expression in music or the arts.

> **Fulfillment matters more to these people than making money...**

Fulfillment matters more to these people than making money; but having said that, they are often fairly good at making and keeping their money. Other careers that might work for them include gardening, animal breeding, counseling, psychotherapy, politics, journalism and the world of entertainment.

Health and leisure

Being so sensitive to the feelings of others, Cancerians need to watch their health. Cancer rules the breasts and stomach— breasts feed babies and stomachs are where we take in nourishment—so Cancerians need to keep a good balance between nurturing others and nurturing themselves. They can sometimes get so wrapped up in others that they forget to attend to their own needs. It's particularly important for them to make sure that their empathic nature doesn't draw people toward them who are negative energy drainers. They need to surround themselves with positive people and healthy situations that are life enhancing.

Rhythmical exercise—such as dancing, swimming and aerobics—is highly recommended to help keep their sensitivity balanced. As far as diet is concerned, they need to watch out for trigger foods that can upset their delicate digestion. A diet rich in oily fish, legumes, whole grains, fruits and vegetables normally works best for them. Fad diets should be avoided completely, as should any kind of dependence on recreational drugs, cigarettes and alcohol.

It's extremely important, given their vulnerable inner core, that Cancerians devote plenty of time to self-development, challenging negative thinking and building self-esteem. They need to understand that emotions such as fear, anger, guilt and sadness should not be ignored but listened to because they have something important to say. Getting in touch with their emotions is therefore crucial; if they can't do this alone they may benefit from counseling or therapy. Meditation, yoga and cognitive behavioral therapy are all recommended, as is spending plenty of time with life-enhancing people. Wearing, meditating on or surrounding themselves with the colors orange and yellow will increase feelings of warmth, security, enjoyment and self-confidence.

Born between June 21 and July 3

Cancerians born between these dates are under the double influence of the moon and all its changing moods. They tend to be highly emotional, intuitive and loving, but they might try to be less changeable and sentimental.

Born between July 4 and July 13

These people will often have deep and penetrating minds. This can make them brilliant but also rather intense in their approach to people and situations, so they need to learn when to back off and let go. They make very loyal and devoted friends.

Born between July 14 and July 22

Extremely compassionate and forgiving, these are the idealistic dreamers of the zodiac and people tend to gravitate toward them. This is fine as long as they learn to self-regulate, ensuring that they see to their own needs and self-development as well.

One of the Cancerian's greatest strengths—but also their greatest weakness—is their sensitivity, which can sometimes translate into oversensitivity. When a person they are close to is upset or moody, Cancerians tends to be upset and moody too. Therefore it's absolutely vital for Cancerians to learn to protect their sensitive nature and to distinguish between their feelings and those of others. If they don't, the result will be misunderstandings and despondency; but if they can learn to get a grip on their sensitivity and derive their feelings of emotional security from themselves rather than others, their reputation for being moody and unpredictable will disappear. Being emotionally manipulative is another Cancerian trait that can drag them and everybody else around them down. A Cancerian can cling onto a grudge longer than anyone else in the zodiac, and they need to understand that this is incredibly draining on their energy and achieves nothing. If they want to move forward they need to learn to let go.

Possessiveness, whether it's financial or romantic, can be limiting for those born under this sign since possessiveness is just another waste of their valuable energy. The sooner they learn that material things can't make them happy and that clinging onto a partner possessively won't assure them of their affection, the happier and more fulfilled they will be. Above all, Cancerians need to accept that there will always be a degree of unpredictability in life and in relationships.

Other signs of the zodiac can teach Cancerians how to let go of their desire to control everyone and everything. Arians have the light and energetic approach to life that Cancerians may lack, and they can also encourage them to let go of grudges and move on. Leos can inspire Cancerians to work on their self-esteem, Librans can help Cancerians balance their fluctuating emotions, and Virgos and Capricorns can help them be less subjective so that emotions don't get in the way of determination and achieving their goals in life.

21 June

the birthday of
rhapsody

Your greatest challenge is

not to become obsessive about your interests

The way forward is ...

to understand that sometimes when you throw yourself into things too deeply you lose a sense of perspective, excitement and enjoyment.

People born on June 21 tend to be intense, exciting and sensual individuals. Born on the longest and perhaps most magical day of the year, they are gregarious, sociable and relentlessly busy. They love every aspect of their lives with rarely the time to meet all their goals.

Fiercely individualistic, they detest pigeonholing of any kind and believe they can be a sex symbol, researcher, athlete, devoted parent, and talented artist all at the same time. Since it is almost impossible to achieve so much in one lifetime, they run the risk of driving themselves and others to exhaustion. They would not have it any other way, so determined are they to experience all the riches the world has to offer. They have terrific enthusiasm and determination to exceed, giving them the power and momentum not just to overcome obstacles but to grow stronger after surmounting them.

These highly sensual people take great delight in all that the world has to offer but they are not only devoted to physical and material pleasures; their thoughts and feelings are intense and passionate too. The big danger is that they can go to extremes, losing themselves in a world of sensation or obsession; they need to learn greater self-control. Until the age of thirty they may focus on emotional security, home and family, and they need to make sure they don't become too dictatorial and impatient with others. After the age of thirty they become more creative and confident, developing the assertiveness to be more adventurous. If they can learn to keep a sense of balance and focus, these are the years when they will realize that they can have it all—just not all at once.

Their inexhaustible thirst for adventure and external stimuli makes them not only interested but also extremely interesting individuals. Blessed with natural charisma, if they can learn to develop their introspective gifts of empathy and understanding, and avoid becoming obsessive about what excites them, their capacity for original and creative thought gives them genius potential.

On the dark side

Excessive, dictatorial, extreme

At your best

Sensual, exciting, intense

22 June

the birthday of
breathless anticipation

Your greatest challenge is

dealing with disillusionment

The way forward is ...

to understand that disappointment is likely if you credit others with qualities that they do not actually possess, so don't place unrealistic demands on yourself or others.

The romantic, affectionate and sensitive individuals born on June 22 tend to greet each new day, however ordinary, with breathless anticipation. For them every day is an optimistic new beginning where anything could happen; their imagination infuses everyday events and situations with excitement and potential.

Whether or not they realize it, people born on this day are constantly seeking their personal nirvana, be it the perfect love affair, lifestyle or a combination of both. Although they can be practical and will often excel in their careers, personal happiness typically takes precedence over professional success because they feel that if they have the love of a soul mate they can achieve virtually anything. Finding true love is therefore of paramount importance to their emotional and professional well-being, and they may sometimes pick unusual partners.

Until the age of thirty they focus on security, and if they don't marry young they may prefer to stay at home or build up a network of supportive friends. After the age of thirty, however, they will usually gain in confidence and perform with skill in their chosen field. In their middle years, if they have not already used the powerful energies of their birthday, they will get another opportunity to achieve success.

Although they can keep romance alive long after the routine of daily life has stripped away much of its mystery, they do need to look at the surface as well as the depths of the people they are attracted to. If they don't keep their feet on the ground by listening to other people's perceptions, they may find that they are left feeling isolated in their fantasy world and doomed to disappointment in love. However, such is their zest for life and enthusiasm for intellectual and sensory stimulation that they will not stay down for long, finding consolation in their professional interests, friends, hobbies, and, of course, their belief that today may just be the day when something or someone wonderful enters their lives.

On the dark side

Naïve, dreamy, confused

At your best

Imaginative, sensitive, romantic

23 June

the birthday of
the improver

Your greatest challenge is

resisting the tendency to gossip

The way forward is ...

to understand that if someone has told you something in confidence, you should resist the urge to share that information; it's not your information to share.

People born on June 23 tend to be highly sensitive and loving individuals who yearn to make the world around them a more beautiful place. With the vision of a peaceful world to inspire them, they devote their energy and intelligence to identifying areas that need improvements and then improving them.

They are extremely interested in the lives of others and are eager to help them in any way, be it emotionally, financially or practically. Not surprisingly they place great value on interpersonal relationships, treating both loved ones and strangers with great respect, consideration and warmth. Unfortunately, in their eagerness to connect with others they tend to become interfering and to repeat confidences. Although this is never done with malicious intent, it can make them appear untrustworthy, which they are not.

Up to the age of twenty-nine, they will be concerned with their home, family and their own emotional security; but after the age of thirty they are likely to be drawn into public situations which require them to be strong and confident. These are the years when they are likely to come into their own, realizing their dreams of improving the world in some way by enriching it with artistic endeavors or by bringing greater harmony, compassion and peace within human relationships.

They don't just love to study other people; they also love to share their ideas about how life can be improved in some way. Some of these ideas may be particularly wacky, especially those about love and sex, but generally such is their insight and charisma that others often find their lives improved or changed after spending time with them because they have an ability to make others feel secure and loved. They should, however, resist the tendency to pry uninvited into the affairs of others; but once they are able to be more discreet and open-minded, they have the creative potential and the practicality to implement their romantic ideals and to effect not just their own emotional fulfillment, but the happiness of all they meet.

On the dark side

Unreliable, unrealistic, over-involved

At your best

Devoted, enchanting, altruistic

24 June

the birthday of
inspired proficiency

Your greatest challenge is

learning to rely on others

The way forward is ...

to understand that a totally independent state of existence is impossible because no man or woman is an island.

People born on June 24 are often ambitious, hard working and strikingly independent. Leaders not followers, they like to choose their own path and will often be so successful that others follow their example. On whatever they choose to focus their energies, be it work, a cause or their family life, they tend to be extraordinarily proficient.

Blessed with keen intellects as well as innovative imaginations, the visions of these people can be startlingly original and their problem-solving ability inspired. Colleagues, friends and family know they can count on them because their approach is thorough. In addition, they are capable of remarkable feats of concentration and focus; when all this is combined with their energy and drive, they have enormous potential for success.

Despite the inspirational effect they have on others, they often perform best when they are largely undistracted. Although they recognize that they cannot obtain their objectives single-handedly, they tend to immerse themselves in work and neglect their personal life. They can also be remarkably insensitive to the emotional needs of others. It is important for them to become more self-aware and be alert to this tendency, because it will hinder their psychological growth and emotional fulfillment.

Up to the age of twenty-eight, issues relating to financial and emotional security can dominate their lives. However, after the age of twenty-nine they become more daring in their power and creativity. Crucial to their potential for success and happiness during this time is a need to curtail their urge for complete independence and apply empathy and sensitivity toward those closest to them. They should also choose a worthy career or vocation and not devote themselves to a cause that is ethically questionable. This is because if they choose a career that makes them feel they are making a positive, valuable or progressive contribution to the world, not only will they get the recognition they need and deserve from all those who play a part in their lives; they also will achieve something far more rewarding: personal fulfillment.

On the dark side

Tactless, confused, oblivious

At your best

Capable, independent, inspired

25 June

the birthday of
original sensitivity

Your greatest challenge is

not feeling overwhelmed by confusion

The way forward is ...

to understand that you have absorbed and internalized a variety of contradictory messages. You need to be more logical and objective in your approach.

People born on June 25 tend to be highly creative and sensitive. They react strongly to external influences, using their powerful intuition to draw clear-sighted conclusions or solutions. Others, however, don't just value them for their problem-solving abilities, but also for their fine minds and stunning originality of thought.

The sensitivity of these people makes them valuable team players because they sense what others need and enjoy helping them. Their heart definitely rules their head, and most of their actions are closely allied to their feelings and emotions; this can make them appear vacillating or contradictory. It is important for them to reconcile their emotional and mental responses because, if they do, they have the originality and ability to be effective instruments of progress. However, when their minds and hearts are unbalanced, it can result in insecurity, confusion, hypersensitivity, or inconsistent motivations.

This sensitivity will become less of a problem after the age of twenty-seven, when they become bolder and more self-assured in all areas of their lives. During this period, opportunities to develop greater self-awareness will arise and, if they can build their self-esteem and rely less on the approval of others, these are the years when they are capable of making outstanding contributions to the world. After the age of fifty-seven they are likely to apply greater patience and precision to their life skills, taking a more practical approach to life and fine-tuning their skills and creativity.

To achieve success, it is crucial for them to find a subject or cause that really captures their imagination, one that will keep them focused and perhaps help them develop as a specialist. If they fail to keep themselves mentally challenged, they run the risk of scattering their energies and suffering from frustration. However, if they learn to develop patience and discipline, they will soon see that along with their inspired creativity and powerful intuition, they also possess depth of thought and a mind capable of producing not just great, but truly inspirational work.

On the dark side

Over-sensitive, insecure, inconsistent

At your best

Creative, empathetic, sensitive

254

26 June

the birthday of
energetic fortitude

Your greatest challenge is

letting others fend for themselves

The way forward is ...

to understand that sometimes the best way for people to learn and grow is for them to make their own mistakes.

People born on June 26 tend to have an energetic, sturdy, resilient approach to life. They stand up well to attack and want those they love to lean on them; as a result others often wholly rely on them. Warm and sensual, they have great compassion and are good at taking control of people in need of guidance. They love life's comforts and are willing to work hard to provide these for themselves and those they love.

Another trait of these people is their prodigious energy, physical strength and stamina. Enjoying all kinds of physical, preferably sporting activity, their energetic approach will manifest itself in other areas of their lives, such as their work or hobbies. The area to which they will always devote most of their energy, however, will be the people around them. They are truly empathetic individuals whose intuitive response to the feelings of others arouses their urge to protect, guide and nurture. Not surprisingly, this tendency is pronounced if they have children; but whether they have a family or not, they will assume a mentoring role for colleagues and friends.

Whatever path in life they choose, they are at their best when they are part of a team or community. Their strong social orientation is perhaps their defining feature, but it has the potential to bring them both enormous fulfillment and enormous pain. This is because others may perceive their advice as an attempt to control their independence. It is extremely important for them to control their well-intentioned directional tendencies before it alienates others and smothers their own emotional needs.

Curiously, when it comes to their own personal life, hidden insecurities may manifest in unusual or compulsive behavior, such as an obsession with order and cleanliness. Fortunately, especially after the age of twenty-six, when there are opportunities for them to connect with their own emotions, they are able to discover courage and confidence within themselves. Once they have achieved this, they can display their own strong ideological beliefs and inspirational vision in a positive and self-assured way.

On the dark side

Over-protective, aggressive, compulsive

At your best

Energetic, resilient, sensual

27 June

the birthday of
protective conviction

Your greatest challenge is

dealing with criticism

The way forward is ...

to remember that constructive criticism can be enormously helpful because it can help you learn, improve and fine-tune your strategies.

People born on June 27 tend to be watchful, diligent and very capable of defending themselves and their interests from attack. They are competitive, driven and persuasive, and those who dare to criticize or argue with their convictions may find themselves out of their depth.

They feel they have a duty to guide and, if necessary, force others to follow the same uncompromising moral convictions that they themselves hold. The profound empathy they feel for those less fortunate arouses their fiercely protective instincts and a burning desire to effect social improvement. Such steadfastness does, however, have its drawbacks: they have a tendency to become inflexible and overly defensive when others try to offer their opinions or criticize them. If this happens, their favored response is to withdraw, shutting out everyone and everything in the process.

Emotions and family matters may occupy them into their mid-twenties, and they should take advantage of opportunities to become more sensitive to the feelings of others. Although they may appear self-assured, they may find that the solid confidence they seek is not forthcoming until after the age of twenty-five. It is important during these years that they keep their minds and hearts open, avoiding becoming too defensive or inflexible in their convictions, which could provoke unnecessary rifts in relationships and problems in their working life. After the age of fifty-five they become more practical, analytical and discerning. Remaining inquisitive and open-minded is the key to their happiness and success during this period.

The single-mindedness of these people can also mean that they miss out on opportunities to develop new assets or relationships. It is crucial for their psychological development that they remain open to the debates that their actions will engender, because learning to become more accommodating is the key to their personal happiness and fulfillment. It will unlock their intuition, giving them the inspiration they need to fulfill their progressive urge to effect real and significant improvements in the human condition.

On the dark side

Inflexible, defensive, isolated

At your best

Persuasive, protective, driven

28 June

the birthday of
the sprite

Your greatest challenge is

not always feeling you need to perform or deliver

The way forward is ...

to understand that you alone teach other people what to expect from you, so teach them to treat you with respect.

People born on June 28 are often focused and driven individuals, but they also have a sense of fun and lightness that permeates their lives. They can also laugh at themselves if the joke is on them and don't take themselves too seriously. Motivated and enterprising, they eagerly latch onto every opportunity to further their plans and endeavors.

They can typically be counted on to break the tension at any social gathering, their sharp wit turning the spotlight on them and winning them many admirers. Occasionally they can block their good fortune by taking easy shots that offend their targets, but they mainly aim to surprise and delight. Although they have a light-hearted quality about them, it's a mistake to underestimate their ability in the competitive world as underneath their fun-loving exterior they have an iron will and a facility to turn their visions into reality.

Sometimes they may be accused of disorganization because they like to be on the go; if they aren't moving, dancing or running they will probably be fidgeting, but the quality of the work they produce is anything but chaotic. Others will wonder how someone so lighthearted makes difficult tasks look so easy. What others don't realize is that they have worked as hard as everyone else, sometimes harder, but instead of complaining or reminding others of how tough things are, they simply get on with it and "effortlessly" generate quality results.

There is no denying that these people like to be the center of attention; their mischievous good humor well suits the spotlight. They do need to be aware, however, that their longing to be noticed may be the result of hidden fears and insecurities. In their early life they may have been painfully shy but after the age of twenty-three they gain a much-needed boost of strength and confidence. If they can take advantage of the opportunities to build their self-esteem, they have within them the determination to become an advisor or authority figure that others admire, respect and hope to emulate.

On the dark side

Chaotic, tactless, self-conscious

At your best

Warm, lively, delightful

29 June

the birthday of
the altruistic visionary

Your greatest challenge is

not giving too much of yourself

The way forward is ...

to understand that only after you know how to take care of yourself can you take care of others.

People born on June 29 are often highly intuitive and sensitive. They have a knack for anticipating other people's words, actions and reactions. This is because they have the rare ability to put themselves into another's shoes. As well as being intuitive, they also possess a dazzling imagination and the practical ability to transform their progressive visions into reality.

With their unique combination of altruistic intuition and imagination, these people give much to others and share their burdens. They are the people who will be a shoulder for their friends to cry on, a morale booster at work and a charity worker in their spare time. They will often be drawn to people who are lonely and insecure because they hope that offering their friendship will reinforce the self-esteem of those who feel fragile.

They often present a lighthearted, youthful and energetic face to the world, and others will love the fact that they rarely complain or drag people down with negativity. Their aim is always to uplift and help others, and while they may be accused of superficiality, underneath their charm and innocence they have all the drive and competitive edge they need to achieve their goals. They often have a talent for making money, and lots of it, although their competitive drive is motivated by a desire to share their vision and happiness with others, rather than gain personal success.

Although their dedication to bringing pleasure to others is admirable, they occasionally need to give themselves a boost as well. If their behavior becomes too self-sacrificing, they may suffer from bouts of indecision and anxiety about their own personal focus and motivation. Before the age of twenty they may be inclined to be shy or reserved but after twenty-three they will enjoy opportunities to develop their personal power and creativity. It is vital that they take advantage of these because in this period their intellect, imagination and understanding of the needs of others can help them make their own dreams, as well as the dreams of others, a practical reality.

On the dark side

Self-sacrificing, indecisive, superficial

At your best

Youthful, giving, intuitive

30 June

Your greatest challenge is

dealing with your insecurity

The way forward is ...

to understand that you are not alone. Everyone has doubts and fears, and building self-esteem is a lifetime's work-in-progress for all of us.

To those who don't know them well, people born on June 30 present something of a mystery. On the one hand they are driven and imaginative with a quirky sense of humor and flashes of fire when challenged; on the other hand, their tendency to keep their feelings to themselves puts them in the introvert category.

These people are indeed complicated, often appearing to be something they are not. It isn't just others who find it hard to second-guess them; they are often a mystery to themselves and unsure of their true identity. Despite their elusiveness, they have two distinctive personality traits. First, they are ambitious and highly motivated individuals with all the intelligence, imagination and tenacity to take them right to the top. Second, although they dislike public displays of affection, they are extremely giving and loving to their small group of friends.

They may incline more toward introversion in their early life, but around the age of twenty-two they may undergo a transformation of their power, creativity and confidence. Once they understand that strong emotional bonds of intimacy—so important to their feelings of self-worth—cannot be forged unless they open themselves up to others, these are the years when they are likely to achieve their personal and professional ambitions. After the age of fifty-two they tend to use their abilities to provide practical and inspirational service to others.

Often working hard to fulfill the expectations of others, be they employers, partners or family members, they may surprise people with bouts of apparent laziness. It's important that others allow them this time out and don't try to push them back into action prematurely. They need to recharge their batteries, and when they feel ready they will get back in the driving seat. When they reconcile the diverse aspects of their personality they have the potential not just to achieve outstanding personal and professional success, but to empower others with a sense of confidence and creativity.

On the dark side

Enigmatic, inconsistent, moody

At your best

Giving, motivated, interesting

1 July

the birthday of
delicate equilibrium

Your greatest challenge is

being consistent

The way forward is ...

to understand that when you're ruled by your impulses you're not in control of your life.

Charismatic, enterprising and determined to get ahead in life, people born on July 1 possess an adventurous spirit, a shrewd mind and a remarkable memory. Insightful, intuitive and imaginative, many of them are also great humanitarians capable of making tremendous sacrifices for others and for society as a whole.

Although they have the ability to be extroverts and are often genial and outgoing in public, in private they can be more moody and changeable than most realize. Balancing the introvert and extrovert, or feminine and masculine energies, within them, they are equally solitary and gregarious. They also have an unusual empathy for the issues, conflicts and insecurities experienced by the opposite sex, and as a result will be sought out by both male and female friends for their opinions or friendship. They love to give advice and offer support, especially if it's for those less fortunate; other people love them for their spontaneous generosity. Their volatile, artistic temperament can, however, cause them to act on impulse, alienating them from others when they say or do things they later regret.

Until the age of twenty-one they are likely to be extremely shy and lacking confidence in their own abilities, but after the age of twenty-two there are many opportunities for them to develop their strength, creativity and self-expression. They need to take advantage of these opportunities because if they don't, they may start to torture themselves with worry, anxiety and self-doubt. After the age of fifty-one their focus changes to a more pragmatic desire to be of service.

In many ways it could be said that they are their own worst enemies. They need to learn to reconcile their inner and outer selves so that they don't get trapped in only one half of their lives. When they do reach this delicate balance they will discover within themselves a rare and exquisite magic that can not only reach out and inspire others, but also enhance their own potential for happiness, success and good fortune in all areas of their lives.

On the dark side

Self-doubting, negative, impulsive

At your best

Warm, ambitious, charismatic

2 July

the birthday of
emotional intensity

Your greatest challenge is

addressing your own deepest needs

The way forward is ...

to understand that while the love of others may temper feelings of insecurity, the way to feel really fulfilled is to address your deepest needs.

People born on July 2 are deeply intuitive and imaginative individuals with the ability to utilize their marked determination, organizational skills and tenacity to great effect. They may, however, have often felt overwhelmed by their own emotional intensity and the key to their success or failure is the way they choose to deal with it.

They are also defined by their extraordinary sensitivity, a quality that leads them to empathize with those around them—especially those less fortunate—and which arouses in them strong feelings of natural justice that they are inclined to champion. They have a knack of reaching out to others and making them feel like family, but although their public persona is often colorful and capable, they may be plagued by private insecurities. They also constantly support friends and co-workers but find it hard to accept the support and praise they richly deserve from others.

It is important for them to get to grips with their fragile feelings and understand what motivates their self-sabotaging behavior; building their self-esteem is a crucial requirement for their psychological growth. Until the age of twenty they may be reserved but after the age of twenty-one they have opportunities to become more dynamic, positive and self-assured. They need to take advantage of these; if they do, their confidence will extend over the next thirty years, helping them achieve the positions of leadership or authority for which they are well qualified. After the age of fifty they become more discriminating and may desire to be practically useful and inspirational to others.

People born on this day can get carried away with unfounded emotions and fantasies either leading to introversion and an inability to express themselves, or to an exuberance that sometimes alarms others with its intensity. If, however, they can devote more time and energy to self-examination, looking at the effect their behavior has on themselves and others, they will find ways to balance their emotions, and this new-found stability will bring them greater happiness, success and fulfillment.

On the dark side

Insecure, touchy, uncertain

At your best

Capable, intuitive, exciting

3 July

the birthday of
the surveyor

Your greatest challenge is

not feeling lonely

The way forward is ...

to understand that you are in charge of the way that you feel. Other people are not excluding you, you are excluding yourself by holding back.

People born on July 3 are keen observers of everything that is going on around them. Their approach to life, however, is not that of the critic but of the philosopher or judge surveying what they see and coming up with an authoritative conclusion.

People born on this day have a very rational mind that helps them manage their emotions effectively. They want the world to be a better place but they usually conclude that emotions tend to hinder rather than help people progress, so they prefer to hide theirs. Although endlessly fascinated by people and the workings of the world, they tend to keep themselves detached because without emotions to cloud their judgment they think they can be more effective. They can charm virtually anyone with their calm, mild manner, and when they believe in a cause their progress is virtually unstoppable.

They are always curious to discover something new, but they should ensure this doesn't earn them the reputation of being interfering or nosy. Their curiosity may also lead them toward dubious or questionable people or causes but their rationality will help them steer clear of any wrongdoing or extremes of behavior. Until the age of nineteen they may focus on security and family, but after the age of twenty they may be offered opportunities to develop in confidence and to strengthen their performance in their chosen field. This can be an exciting time for them but they should remember that they belong to the same species as the creatures whose actions they love to survey. After the age of forty-nine they are likely to develop a more discriminating attitude and, although service to others is highlighted, they should make sure they don't become cynical or superior in their approach to others.

Once these people have been able to find a balance between detachment and involvement, they will find that their intuitive and intellectual talents combine to endow them with outstanding potential to become effective instruments of reform and progress.

On the dark side

Nosy, detached, superior

At your best

Observant, insightful, committed

4 July

the birthday of
dedication

Your greatest challenge is

staying objective

The way forward is ...

to understand that when your dedication to a cause makes it impossible for you to listen to alternative viewpoints, you run the danger of fanaticism.

People born on July 4 tend to identify strongly with groups and organizations, be they their family, co-workers, local community, country or even humanity as a whole. The creation of shared human bonds and goals is extremely important to them, and they will often dedicate themselves to defending people's wider interests.

Whatever path in life they choose, they will be at their happiest when they are surrounded by those who are working toward a common goal. Ironically, though, for those so focused on communal identification, they are also quite private individuals and prefer to keep their own feelings to themselves; opening up to others won't be easy for them. Despite their reserve, it's no coincidence that these people were born on US Independence Day. Their dedication and loyalty are matched only by their courageous spirit and desire to defend and protect those less fortunate. They are also extremely intuitive, but because this gift can make them feel as if they are different they may choose to repress it or only reveal it to those who know them well.

In the years leading up to the age of eighteen they will be concerned with home, family and security; after the age of nineteen they may find that they are increasingly drawn into public positions that require strength and confidence. During these years they should guard against inflexibility and uncritical belief in their cause. After the age of forty-eight they enter a new phase which brings practical issues to prominence, and they are likely to become more analytical, observant and methodical.

If they devote themselves to a cause that is worthy of them, they have the potential to rise all the way to the top, helping others rise to the top with them. The opposite is true if they make the wrong choice, so learning to make the right choices and decisions will be their major challenge. They will, however, be able to make the right choice with ease if they work with their intuition, investing time and energy to listening to their inner voice.

On the dark side

Biased, demanding, stubborn

At your best

Principled, courageous, generous

5 July

the birthday of
fireworks

Your greatest challenge is

concentrating for long periods of time

The way forward is ...

to understand that concentration is not something people are born with; it is a skill they learn and master.

Whatever situation they are in or whatever person or group of people they are with, people born on July 5 have a flair for injecting sparkle, energy and excitement into the atmosphere. Everything about them is vivid and colorful, and their charming manners and interesting conversation light up the workplace and social gatherings.

Thriving on constant variety and stimulation, their life never seems to stand still, and even if they are in a routine of some kind because of work or family commitments they will make sure that they have a hobby or interest to absorb them. They can, however, alienate others with their boundless energy and enthusiasm. Although they tend to have many admirers, some people may have trouble keeping up with their explosive pace; their wild shifts in mood may also frustrate those who admire them but doubt their reliability.

Before the age of eighteen, they may often have problems or difficulties with school or study. This is because their restless nature makes it hard for them to concentrate for long periods or conform to a schedule. Their vivid imagination may also make them feel different in some way, but they should cherish rather than repress it as later in life it may offer them an endless source of inspiration. After the age of eighteen their confidence increases; these are the years they are most likely to be adventurous and creative. It is important during this period that they learn to maintain a sense of stability, not frittering their energy and away in too many directions. After the age of forty-seven they may become more discriminating and efficient.

The key to their success is education and learning, as these will help develop the discipline and awareness they need to reach their true potential. Their desire to keep busy will always be a key characteristic, but when it is combined with a more centered existence their explosive ideas will finally come down from the drawing board and transform into accomplishments or achievements that are progressive and lasting in their impact.

On the dark side

Wild, erratic, unreliable

At your best

Exciting, entertaining, imaginative

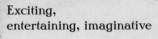

6 July

the birthday of passionate attachment

Your greatest challenge is

avoiding tunnel vision

The way forward is ...

to understand that human beings have complex emotional, physical, and intellectual needs; happiness and fulfillment can never be found through one avenue alone.

People born on July 6 are filled with infectious energy, vibrant optimism and dedicated enthusiasm about every aspect of their lives. It is impossible for them to be anything but passionate and intense about their relationships, responsibilities or career.

Compromise just doesn't make sense for these people. More than anything else they yearn to achieve their ideals and will dedicate themselves passionately to their personal quest, be it for the perfect love, career or lifestyle. Although they are reliable and dedicated, the passionate attachment that they have to their own ideas and plans can lead to problems with others. In some cases they can become so single-minded in their pursuit of their dreams that work may take over their life, their love life may dominate all their decisions, or they may devote every ounce of their energy to a cause. This is potentially dangerous as their happiness may depend on just one thing; if that is unachievable or there are setbacks, their behavior may become needy or obsessive. It is extremely important therefore that they learn to be less obsessive, broadening their interests and horizons to include not just one, but several potential sources of fulfillment.

After the age of sixteen they may have opportunities to become bolder and more self-assured; they need to take advantage of these to broaden their perspective. After the age of forty-six they are likely to become more health conscious, precise and discriminating; during these years it is important for them to manage their financial assets well as their passionate nature means that they may have a tendency to spend money faster than they make it.

Above all, people born on this day need to learn not to devote all their energy and enthusiasm to one area of their life. This is because when they finally manage to cultivate a more well-rounded approach to life they will find that they have all the talent and personal magnetism they need to see most of the passionate dreams that inspire them transformed into reality.

On the dark side

Obsessive, blinkered, needy

At your best

Passionate, attractive, intense

7 July

the birthday of
the beautiful dreamer

Your greatest challenge is

dealing with criticism or rejection

The way forward is ...

to take on board what is being said and learn from it. Criticism and rejection are simply stepping stones on the way to success.

People born on July 7 are the type of individuals whose soaring imagination will cause them to support projects deemed unfeasible and then surprise and confuse others showing that they are indeed feasible. The key to their ability to achieve the impossible is their rare combination of imagination and fierce determination.

They are beautiful dreamers in every sense, blessed with the creativity and idealism that many others lose when they become adults. People may describe them as naïve, not because they are unintelligent but because any form of deception is alien to them. Their openness and honesty is touching and endearing, but it will limit their rise professionally and socially. This is unlikely to bother them, however, because for them a life that isn't honest or where they can't be creative is a life not worth living.

Shyness and sensitivity may become less of a problem for them after the age of sixteen, when there are opportunities for them to become bolder and more assertive in all areas of their lives. At the age of forty-five they are likely to become more analytical and discriminating. They will never lose their remarkable imagination but these are the years when they are likely to fine-tune their creative talents, using their creative approach to life to lift others out of the mundane. Crucial to their success or failure, however, will be their willingness to step out from their dreams every now and again and see the world for what it really is.

The big threat to their happiness is the way they react to criticism or to those who misunderstand them. Instead of accepting that there will always be differences of opinion or learning from feedback, they may react strongly by crawling into a shell of resentment, self-pity and defeatism that is not conducive to psychological growth. However, once they develop the emotional maturity to be more objective, they have all the potential and passion not only to generate ambitious plans and see them realized, but to earn the support and admiration of others.

On the dark side

Disturbing, naïve, self-pitying

At your best

Imaginative, determined, creative

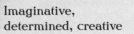

8 July

the birthday of mysterious pragmatism

Your greatest challenge is

learning to switch off or relax

The way forward is ...

to understand that regular down time is an essential ingredient for success, as it allows you to recharge your batteries and come back refreshed and re-energized.

People tend to admire those born on July 8 for their impressive pragmatism, fixity of purpose and dynamic energy, but the admiration they earn tends to be more of the respectful, awed variety rather than that born of affection. Such is their strength of will and uncompromising determination that they will stop at nothing to achieve their progressive aims.

They are often strong willed and motivated by the desire to make their mark on the world, tending to devote themselves to one single purpose and stick with it through thick and thin. Sometimes this one-track approach backfires, but more often than not they invest their time and energy wisely, bringing them considerable financial success. This sense of purpose can be so strong that it overrides their sense of right and wrong, so it is crucial for them to decide what their principles are and stick to them.

Despite their steadiness and fixity of purpose they are anything but an open book. Quite the opposite; they will often remain a mystery even to those closest to them. Of the many reasons for this one may be that they may have grown up never feeling quite good enough; because of this they may have grown emotionally defensive and doubly determined to achieve success in their career and relationships. This determination may lead to controlling or domineering behavior whenever they feel threatened or vulnerable. It is therefore important for their psychological growth that they get in touch with their emotions.

After the age of fifteen there are opportunities for them to use their talents and skills in a more confident way but they should ensure their driving interests don't alienate those closest to them. After the age of forty-four practical considerations become more important and these are the years when they are capable of achieving great things professionally and personally. If they can become more aware of the forceful influence they have on others, they can earn not just the respect but also the loyalty and affection of those they live and work with.

On the dark side

Defensive, dark, smothering

At your best

Steady, responsible, driven

9 July

Your greatest challenge is

accepting the word "no"

The way forward is ...

to understand that "no" can be an awful word to hear but the only way to move onward is to find ways to turn rejection into direction.

People born on July 9 are often a powerhouse of energy and enthusiasm. They love to taste all that life has to offer and put their heart and soul into everything that they do, whether it is work or a relationship. Endearingly curious and eager to learn, their wide-eyed wonder has an energizing and motivating effect on everyone they deal with.

The opportunist streak that they possess, when combined with their questing imagination and boundless energy, gives them great creative and innovative potential. Indeed, their conviction that there is so much yet to be discovered may lead them to explore concepts that others may dismiss as totally unfeasible or unacceptable. Despite their fierce originality, however, they are not unrealistic about the possibility of success and are able to supplement their intellect and intuition with persistence and effective practical skills. When their optimism and charisma are added to this combination, it's no surprise that they are often attractive and popular individuals.

Although they do tend to have a healthy self-esteem, they are not always so good at dealing with rejection or setbacks and they can also suffer from exhaustion. When they are feeling low, they may withdraw into bitterness, frustration or disillusionment; it is vital for their self-image that they find more constructive ways to deal with disappointment, using it as an incentive or a learning experience. When they hit their teenage years they will be presented with opportunities to develop more confidence to display their talents and skills; it is important for them to take advantage of these, ensuring that they believe in their potential for success, regardless of the setbacks they encounter. After the age of forty-three they are likely to become more discriminating, practical and perfectionist.

These people really do believe that anything is possible; if they can just learn to try another approach if the first fails, their enduring interest in investigating, exploring and pushing the boundaries of human knowledge gives them outstanding potential to blaze truly innovative trails throughout life.

On the dark side

Disillusioned, unrealistic, withdrawn

At your best

Vital, imaginative, persistent

10 July

the birthday of
the dark horse

overcoming your
shyness

*The way
forward is ...*

to forget what
you're thinking
and feeling, and
find out what
others are
thinking and
feeling. When you
put the attention
on others, shyness
will soon
disappear.

People born on July 10 learn lessons from the successes and defeats of those around them and plot their actions accordingly. Others may regard them as passive but they're not; they're steady and purposeful, only making a move when certain it will be successful or well received.

Sensitive to everything going on around them, once they have secured the background data they need for the best chance of success, they will embark on the quest to realize their goals with tenacity and determination, drawing upon their intellectual and organizational skills. Although motivation and perseverance are vital to their success, they are also quick learners with the self-confidence to be flexible in their approach.

People born on this day may often lead modest, steady lives but they are neither predictable nor dull. Quite the opposite; when people get to know them better, everything about them has the potential to surprise. For example, they are never afraid to speak their mind but when they do it is with tact and sensitivity. They may also surprise others with their incisive wit or devote their considerable energy to one specific goal, stepping aside at the last minute to allow others to take the credit. At certain points in their lives, their early forties especially, they are also likely to astonish people with a total change of lifestyle, but even though the change may come as a shock to others, to themselves it will all be part of a well-planned strategy.

It's not that they don't like to be in the limelight; they do. It's just that they will only step into it if it serves a purpose or highlights a cause they are promoting. Others may sometimes see them as shy and sensitive but beneath lies a steely determination to succeed that will reveal itself when the time is right. When they finally do decide to invest their energy into a worthy cause, everyone will wonder how they could have underestimated the creative and dynamic energy of this dark horse hiding behind a mild-mannered exterior.

On the dark side

Withdrawn,
passive, insecure

At your best

Curious,
purposeful, receptive

11 July

the birthday of
the innovative chameleon

Your greatest challenge is

telling it like it is

The way forward is ...

to understand that there is a huge difference between diplomacy and dishonesty.

People born on July 11 have an easy-going charm that appeals to other people, putting them at their ease. With the ability to effortlessly blend in no matter where they are or who they're with, they always seem to have the inside knowledge both professionally and socially.

The diplomatic skills of these people are extraordinary and they are often excellent at working around problems and side-stepping confrontations; this doesn't necessarily mean they are fickle or lazy. Quite the opposite. Although they are amiable and sensitive to the moods of others, they can be fiercely innovative and ambitious, with more than enough energy, intelligence and resourcefulness to reach their personal goals. It is just that, whether they realize it or not, their personality is defined by an intense interest in interpersonal relationships; this compels them to put the maximum effort into creating successful relationships with others.

Through their teenage years their confidence and creativity will gradually increase. During their twenties and thirties they will often find that they have unique access to information or insights into situations. If they choose to be discreet and stick to the truth, they will earn the respect and support of others; but if they choose to spread disinformation or fool others, they will earn a reputation for unreliability. After the age of forty-one there are opportunities to become more patient and discriminating; these may include providing practical service for others. They need to take advantage of these opportunities because the only way for them to find emotional fulfillment is through honesty, discretion and compassion toward others.

Throughout their lives they will find themselves in situations where their ability to put others at ease guarantees their popularity, giving them access to inside information. As long as they remember to center their lives on positive values such as honesty, respect, love, and responsibility, steering clear of play-acting or game-playing, these multi-talented individuals have the potential and versatility to produce excellent work, whatever they decide to do.

On the dark side

Opinionated, opaque, superficial

At your best

Sociable, knowledgeable, gregarious

12 July

the birthday of
the subtle initiator

Your greatest challenge is

accepting you may be wrong

The way forward is ...

to understand that truly great leaders are truly great because they have learned to adjust their opinions if life gives them reason to do so.

Those born on July 12 are characterized by their dualistic nature. On the one hand, they are profoundly empathetic and gentle creatures keenly sensitive to the emotions of those around them; on the other, they possess a compelling urge to initiate and direct the actions of others. Although these two aspects seem to conflict, they both stem from their intense altruism.

It's a mistake to dismiss these people as a pushover, because they hold profound convictions and refuse to redefine them. Their loyalty isn't limited to their convictions; they are a steadfast and generous friend, although their tendency to try and orchestrate the lives of others can become annoying. Sometimes they plant their suggestions in such a subtle way that other people will believe that they themselves have originated them. As a result they often have a powerful influence over others; the key to their success is whether they decide to exert this influence in a positive way that encourages others to grow independently, or in a negative way that fosters dependence.

They are such insightful and capable individuals that they will often step in without giving others a chance to get involved; this can earn them a reputation for being controlling, difficult and stubborn. However, if they can learn occasionally to take a step back and give others a turn, they will find that their chances of success and happiness increase. This isn't to say they should hide their talents. It's just that they are such strong-willed individuals that there's a tendency for others to be guided rather than inspired by them.

Until the age of forty there will be many opportunities for them to demonstrate their creativity and strong convictions. After the age of forty-one they may become more pragmatic and discerning. As long as they ensure that they nurture others without smothering them, this is the period when these empathetic but progressive individuals will do what they do best: initiate action that ensures the welfare of others and, by so doing, make their own special mark.

On the dark side

Stubborn, controlling, difficult

At your best

Persuasive, capable, disciplined

13 July

the birthday of
action man/woman

Your greatest challenge is

believing in yourself

The way forward is ...

to understand that like attracts like; self-doubt will attract misfortune and unhappiness. Change the way you think about yourself and you will attract joy, success and good fortune.

People born on July 13 tend to be courageous and daring risk-takers with a resilience that ensures they will always bounce back with their energy redoubled no matter how hard life knocks them down. This isn't to say they are blind optimists; rather their imagination never fails them, and if things can't or won't happen in one particular way they look for a new approach or strategy.

Fearless and focused, there is little that can intimidate them, except perhaps when it comes to affairs of the heart where they can be a little unsubtle and awkward. Their approach to life is action orientated, endowing them with an irresistible urge to achieve their targets. When their sharp mind, originality, inventiveness and prodigious energy are added, it results in an outstanding capacity to recognize a potentially advantageous opportunity, seize the moment and act incisively. Sometimes their risk-taking strategy backfires, but their refusal to admit defeat and willingness to look at alternative approaches maximizes their chances of success.

Taking risks and achieving success comes naturally to them because they tend to be blessed with self-confidence. There may, however, be those less evolved who lack this self-belief, and this is probably because they have taken a risk that backfired, affecting their confidence. It is vital for their personal fulfillment that they do not allow their negative self-belief to become a self-fulfilling prophecy. Getting involved may be their strength, but to be true to themselves they first need to change their thoughts about themselves. When they truly believe in their own potential, their chances of fulfillment and good fortune will increase significantly.

At the age of thirty-nine they come to a turning point; this is the time when they are most likely to be plagued by self-doubt. If, however, they can make this turning point work for rather than against them by becoming more orderly, discriminating and practical in their approach, they will find that their creativity and optimism return.

On the dark side

Reckless, inflexible, self-doubting

At your best

Daring, opportunist, resilient

14 July

the birthday of
the illusionist

Your greatest challenge is

reliability

The way forward is ...

to understand that however great is your ability to charm, the best way to earn the respect of others is to prove that you're honest, reliable and committed.

People born on July 14 tend to be seductive individuals blessed with intelligence and personal magnetism. They have the ability to cast a spell over others with their intense presence and excellent communication skills. Their charm can be gentle and subtle or bold and entertaining, but it will always match the occasion perfectly.

Whether they are talking to a large group or a small circle of close friends, these people know how to inspire confidence and, regardless of what cause or career they choose, they aim to convince and inspire others. They are masters of the art of illusion and their talent for developing believable and fascinating theories, strategies and stories is awesome. Possessing the drive and enthusiasm to make things happen, they can, despite their obvious gifts, get depressed or melancholy for no apparent reason.

Despite these sudden and unexplained episodes of melancholy, others tend to regard them with great affection and admiration. If they direct their thoughts and talents to a cause they believe in, they have the potential to achieve success. However, if they choose to manipulate the truth or devote themselves to an unworthy cause, they can become unscrupulous and untrustworthy. It is important, therefore, for them to understand the influence they have on others and not misuse their powers.

Until the age of thirty-eight, they are likely to grow steadily in confidence and creativity. Although winning the hearts of others by sensing their hidden motivations and promising to fulfill their desires will earn them popularity, if they want to hold the affection of others they must learn to balance this seductive gift with solid results. After the age of thirty-nine they will develop a more methodical and discriminating attitude, together with a desire to be of service to others; these are the years when they have opportunities to turn the illusions they create into reality. They need to take advantage of these because when they use their dynamic and seductive will-power to achieve rather than talk about their objectives, they are a force to be reckoned with.

On the dark side

Misleading, dark, unscrupulous

At your best

Persuasive, interesting, seductive

15 July

the birthday of stimulus

Your greatest challenge is

not being selfish

The way forward is ...

to understand that being selfish only brings short-term satisfaction; taking the feelings of others into consideration brings both short- and long-term satisfaction.

Whether they realize it or not, people born on July 15 have a powerful effect on others and a rare ability to exert their influence positively to help others move forward with their lives. When others do achieve impressive results, they do not hold back their praise, which only serves to increase their popularity: a wonderfully virtuous circle.

These people manage to combine their highly developed intellectual powers with an affinity and sensitivity toward both their environment and all those who live and work with them. This combination of emotional empathy and intellectual perspicacity, when combined with their strong powers of imagination and the profound effect they tend to have on others, endows them with the potential to bring about progressive change, enriching the lives of others.

From about the age of seven or eight, people born on this day are likely to begin manifesting their characteristic self-confidence and magnetic charm, but at around the age of thirty-seven there is a turning point which sees them becoming more pragmatic and realistic; they may find that their desire to be of service to others grows more intense, and these are the years when they can really come into their own. If they can learn to direct their prodigious energy and creativity toward the greater good, they are likely to bring about considerable change for the better.

An inner ambition or desire to achieve and make a positive difference in the world can extend to all parts of their lives, and their determination can be compelling and inspirational. If, however, they become materialistic or selfish and use their influence to manipulate others, they can be ruthless and disruptive. It is absolutely crucial for them, therefore, not just to think about what they want to accomplish in their lives, but also to consider what effect their behavior and their actions will have on others. To truly utilize their outstanding potential for leadership, they may have to recognize the awesome power of their commanding disposition.

On the dark side

Materialistic, manipulative, selfish

At your best

Influential, motivating, exciting

16 July

the birthday of

passionate logic

Your greatest challenge is

resisting the tendency to proselytize

The way forward is ...

to understand that compelling or forcing others to listen to your viewpoint will just alienate them.

People born on July 16 tend to have an impulsive, passionate nature. They dream adventurous and exciting dreams and more often than not these come true. Once they are inspired, their energy and enthusiasm is without equal, but they have another side, their logical side. This unusual combination of passion and logic makes them interesting, unusual and exceptional.

The demeanor of these people can be down to earth and pragmatic, but despite this they never lose sight of their dreams and passions. Whatever life path they choose, there will always be a conflict between their logic and their impulses, and this will come across in words that are rational but presented passionately or behavior that is impulsive but explained logically. When their logic and passion are in harmony, with neither gaining the upper hand, they are likely to feel at their happiest; but when one is more dominant than the other it can lead to unhappiness. For example, they may try to repress their emotions by becoming obsessive in their behavior; or they may try to bury their logic and become unrealistic or unfocused in their approach.

For the first thirty-five years of their lives people born on this day will often grow in confidence and capability; these are the years when emotions are most likely to take the lead. After the age of thirty-six, however, there is a shift toward logic and reason, and they are likely to have a more practical and discriminating attitude, with service to others becoming a more important part of their lives. After the age of sixty-six there is an emphasis on harmony and balance between the two conflicting sides of their personality.

The key to success and happiness for people born on this day is to allow neither their rational nor their impulsive side to take the lead. If they can find a way to balance the two, they will find that they have within them outstanding potential not just to achieve their own dreams but also to bring excitement into the lives of others.

On the dark side

Obsessive, unrealistic, unfocused

At your best

Intense, passionate, devoted

17 July

the birthday of the master

Your greatest challenge is

to stop procrastinating

The way forward is ...

to understand that not moving forward with your life is the same as moving backward.

People born on July 17 strive to rise to the very top in their chosen field and to have others acknowledge their mastery. Their independence, confidence and discipline make them extremely capable workers in whatever task they undertake, and they often greatly impress others with their focus, tenacity and professionalism.

Tending to present a serious, sometimes harsh face to the world, within their chosen sphere they are, however, passionate and creative; to those who know them well they have a wacky sense of humor. With a tendency to focus their energies on money and material concerns, they may end up in careers or situations that waste their talents. It is important, therefore, that they pay great attention to their choice of career as they will not find true fulfillment until they devote themselves to something that inspires them or speaks to their principles. They may also be guilty of procrastination. Although they are extremely good at working their way patiently up to the top, sometimes their rate of progress is so slow that it is detrimental to their creativity. They need to find the courage to speak up for themselves so that their talents can be exposed and given the recognition they deserve.

Until the age of thirty-six they are likely to win the respect of their associates and acquaintances with their confident, cool efficiency. After the age of thirty-seven, sometimes sooner, when there are opportunities for them to become more practical and discriminating, it is important that they direct their efforts toward gaining recognition for their creativity as well, so that well-deserved promotion does not pass them by.

If they make sure that their self-sufficiency does not make them seem unapproachable, they will be well on track to attain the targets they set for themselves without forfeiting the goodwill of others. They may also find that although their wish to have others acknowledge their mastery is granted, they find greater happiness and pleasure from their ability to bring cheer and inspiration to others with their generosity and creativity.

On the dark side

Serious, isolated, procrastinating

At your best

Self-sufficient, ambitious, capable

18 July

the birthday of the better way

Your greatest challenge is

recognizing your individual needs

The way forward is ...

to understand that making time for your own thoughts and interests is not incompatible with the needs of the people you are devoted to.

People born on July 18 appear to have limitless energy and enthusiasm. Throwing their heart, body and soul into whatever they do, they are admired for their dedication, conviction and determination to make their voice heard. They are unlikely to follow the conventional path in their personal or professional lives, and always aim to find a better way, speaking out boldly to let others know about it.

Although they can give the appearance of being extreme, eccentric or wild, there is often a method to their madness. Independent and innovative in their thinking, they also prefer to identify themselves with a group or common cause. The reasons for this include strong feelings of empathy with others, as well as a somewhat insecure need to ground themselves in the bonds of camaraderie that come from serving a common cause and receiving recognition.

Until the age of thirty-four they will be given opportunities to develop their daring as their power, confidence and creativity increase. They will often, however, choose to invest their considerable energies, intellectual talents and emotions in shared aims; it is important during this time that they don't allow their views or opinions to become extreme or inflexible. After the age of thirty-five they may become more discriminating, businesslike and efficient. The need to work with and serve others will be as strong as ever, but this time the emphasis will be on supplying creative and progressive solutions, making these people powerful figures in the community. Another turning point comes at the age of sixty-four when issues around beauty, harmony and emotional fulfillment are emphasized.

Although they are self-disciplined, intelligent and sociable, the true inspiration they seek will lie in the realms of emotional satisfaction. They will always be gifted problem solvers able to find a better way for others; but once they understand that the best way for themselves is the inner way and trusting their highly developed intuition, they will find that they attract countless opportunities for their own happiness and true fulfillment.

On the dark side

Insecure, extreme, wild

At your best

Bold, committed, driven

19 July

the birthday of energetic self-awareness

Your greatest challenge is

avoiding negative thinking

The way forward is ...

to understand that negative thinking is just as irrational as positive thinking. There are always two sides to the story, so aim for more realistic thinking.

People born on July 19 set themselves extremely high standards. From a very early age self-improvement will have been a key theme. They expect a great deal from themselves and others, but those who know them well will recognize that their harshest criticism is reserved for themselves.

These people are energetic and charming, and both physically and intellectually they need to keep their bodies and minds active. This is why they will often push themselves incredibly hard or jump from activity to activity. They need to keep moving and, above all, to feel that they are learning, growing and improving in all areas of their lives. In many ways they are among the most self-aware individuals of the year and when they have made any kind of mistake or oversight they will immediately acknowledge it, trying to find ways of improving their performance, behavior or attitude in the future. Others love them for their ability to learn and change, but their self-awareness does come at a price: a painful awareness of their own inadequacies.

People born on this day are prone to relentless self-criticism and they may often exaggerate their imagined shortcomings. When they are indulging in a bout of insecurity, mood swings and impatience are likely, so it is extremely important for their psychological growth that they understand the need to stay centered. Spending more time simply being instead of doing will help boost their self-esteem, giving them the objectivity and distance needed to manage their emotions effectively.

Until the age of thirty-three they will be presented with opportunities to develop their strength and confidence. After the age of thirty-four they are likely to become even more perfectionist in their approach to life. Because of their tendency to be harsh with themselves, they should ensure that they also bring more patience to their talents during these years, because if they do they will be able to make the most of their wonderful potential, becoming the creative and charismatic person they were always meant to be.

On the dark side

Impatient, insecure, moody

At your best

Energetic, self-aware, charming

20 July

the birthday of
evolution

Your greatest challenge is

feeling satisfied

The way forward is ...

to understand that moving onto the next challenge will not necessarily bring you the fulfillment you seek. The secret of fulfillment is within you, not without.

People born on July 20 love the journey of life. They thrive on movement, change and new experiences, being exhilarated rather than daunted by fresh challenges and situations. No matter how comfortable or secure their position in life, routine can be deadly to them and their restless spirit constantly seeks to move on and evolve.

These people rarely remain static for long, and their energy and intensity are boundless both physically and intellectually. Whether they are sporting types or not, they don't like sitting down for long; likewise whether they are academically inclined or not, they are inquisitive and constantly searching for novel experiences.

Not surprisingly, their natural exuberance and infectious optimism draw others to them, and friends may often take great pleasure in hearing about their adventures. Given the constant process of change that defines their lives, they run the risk of being unstable; but in many cases the opposite is true and they are all calmness and control. Courageous risk-takers, nothing really unsettles them but boredom, and they are far more likely to be anxious and unbalanced when their lives are too easy or stuck in a rut. Others may find their obsessive need for challenge and contrast hard to understand, but these people are at their happiest and their best when they are struggling.

Until the age of thirty-two, they will have many opportunities to use the sociable and dramatic part of their personality. Both at work and at home they are likely to be popular, poised and self-assured but slightly lacking in direction and focus. It may take them longer than normal to find their true vocation or direction in life. There is a change of emphasis after the age of thirty-two when they are inclined to be more orderly, practically motivated and methodical. During these years, if they can develop a greater sense of focus and find goals that provide them with enough adventure and challenge, they can direct their creativity and energy toward increasing their knowledge, as well as enriching the lives of others.

On the dark side

Unstable, scattered, restless

At your best

Adventurous, exciting, optimistic

279

21 July

the birthday of
daring

Your greatest challenge is

feeling that life
is moving fast
enough

*The way
forward is ...*

to focus more on
the spiritual
aspects of your
life; this will help
you move into the
deeper, more
profound aspects
of yourself.

Those born on July 21 are not afraid to go where no man or woman has ever gone before. Highly dynamic and innovative, their curiosity and understanding of what motivates others make them extremely good at assessing people and situations, and this unique combination of shrewdness and daring ambition draws both success and controversy their way.

Above all, they love being on the cutting edge of innovative projects and activities, possessing the vitality and ambition to be successful in creative endeavors. They move fast and usually prefer to be in the thick of battle rather than sitting on the sidelines. They tend to aim high and, even if things don't always work out exactly as planned, their jovial optimism and tragicomic sense of humor act as a buffer, providing them with a resilience that is second to none.

The drama and controversy of opposite points of view appeal greatly to the daring nature of these individuals. They make great debaters and conversationalists because they can see both sides of the argument. They love excitement, conflict and explosive situations, and are likely to be attracted to action games, racing cars, theme-park rides, diving, or any high-energy, adrenalin-pumping situation that provides drama and demands courage. Until the age of thirty there are many opportunities for them to develop their strength, creativity and confidence; these are the years during which they need to make sure their love of thrill-seeking does not encourage them to stir up trouble for the sake of it. After the age of thirty their focus will change to a more pragmatic and rational approach, with a desire for a life that is still very fast moving, but slightly more settled and orderly.

The greatest strengths of these people are to be found in their daring creativity and courage, and in their generosity and empathy toward others. Sometimes these qualities will combine and result in a rare and talented individual who can be counted among the most dynamic but also the most understanding of all people.

On the dark side

Thrill-seeking,
impatient, reckless

At your best

Bold,
interesting, exciting

22 July

the birthday of
brave compulsion

Your greatest challenge is

learning from your mistakes

The way forward is ...

to understand that making mistakes is an essential ingredient for success, helping you learn, grow and fine-tune your approach.

People born on July 22 are action orientated. They want to see progress, not talk about it. Although this compulsion to act can lead them into difficulties, it can also make them remarkable inovators.

In addition to their sharp intellect and prodigious physical and emotional energy, these people possess great sensitivity and creativity, although they sometimes take action without having fully thought through the potential consequences. However, when disaster strikes they are masters at coping with the often messy and complicated results. This is because from an early age they have realized the importance of self-sufficiency and have become extremely resilient as a result. Because they are impulse driven and action orientated, their lives will often fluctuate between periods of great success and periods of great disappointment, but so powerful are their self-belief and desire to win through that they never consider giving up.

One big problem for them is their refusal to acknowledge their own shortcomings. While their belief in the indestructibility of the human spirit is commendable, they don't take into account their vulnerabilities and the warning signs of potential problems. They may also have problems handling their anger and frustration, and this can manifest in controlling, dictatorial behavior or in repression with dangerous outbursts of rage. Until the age of twenty-nine there is an emphasis on creativity and sociability; during these years they need to make sure that they learn from both their failures and their successes. After the age of thirty there are opportunities for them to become more analytical, methodical and orderly. It is important for their psychological growth that they take advantage of these opportunities because attention to the details is the key to their success.

Above all, these people are natural optimists and, even though their actions can sometimes wear others out, their brave compulsion to re-energize and challenge themselves marks them out as inspirational leaders and survivors in their chosen fields.

On the dark side

Reckless, moody, inflexible

At your best

Bold, exciting, visionary

LEO

THE LION (JULY 23 – AUGUST 22)

- ✳ **Element:** Fire
- ✳ **Ruling planet:** Sun, the individual
- ✳ **Symbol:** The Lion
- ✳ **Tarot card:** Strength (passion)
- ✳ **Number:** 1
- ✳ **Favorable colors:** Yellow and orange
- ✳ **Key phrase:** I live every moment to the full

Sunny-natured and vital, Leos are eternal optimists who like to live every waking moment of their lives to the full. Their larger-than-life charismatic personalities ensure their popularity. Their nature is to be generous, outgoing, humorous and creative but they also have a streak of vanity about them, and their incredibly high standards can sometimes make them appear arrogant or dismissive of others.

Personality potential

It's not often that you will see a sad or gloomy Leo. These energetic individuals are ruled by the sun, the giver of life, and under normal circumstances Leos can be found bringing laugher and activity to everyone and everything they touch. They hate being miserable, and there is always a "buzz" of excitement and spontaneity when they are around. All the zodiac symbols revolve around the sun and Leos, being ruled by the sun, therefore believe that they are the center of the universe. With their knack of convincing others that they are very important people indeed, it's no surprise to find that plenty of politicians and actors are born under this sign.

Without doubt, Leos like to be the center of attention and this is typically the place where you will find them. Key words associated with Leos include creativity, bravery, generosity, energy and enthusiasm. They are also unusually resourceful people. Far-sighted and efficient, they can work their way toward a bright future, overcoming any obstacles they meet on the way. Their positive, up-beat attitude enables them to create opportunities out of rejection or disappointment. They aren't possessive of their success, however, and will generously share it with others. Other people need lots of energy and stamina to keep up with Leos, but they are always willing to share their sunshine with those they love and admire.

People born under the sun sign Leo are attracted to anything extraordinary. They love to explore new territory and

thrive on change. In addition, they are blessed with endless enthusiasm, energy and imagination, and all these qualities make them favorites with most people, especially children. Leos are also especially good at seeing the broader picture and, when this is combined with their ability to draw people toward them, it's easy to see why they are naturals for positions of authority in which their unflagging creativity and drive can fully express itself.

Above all, Leos have an inner sunshine which not only brightens their life but also illuminates the lives of anyone lucky enough to wander across their path. They like to live every waking moment to the full, and the generosity and genuine good nature of these creative spirits can light up not just the room they are in but also the world around them.

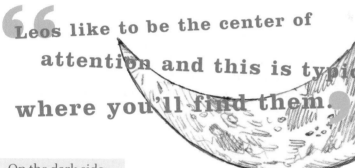

❝Leos like to be the center of attention and this is typically where you'll find them.❞

On the dark side

Leos like to be center stage and tend to demand adoration from others as a right. In many instances they do this in such a charming way that no one takes offence but they do need to be careful that their exuberant ego-led approach to life does not turn into domineering bossiness. Ego problems are common for sun-sign Leos. If you tell a Leo you agree with them or they are amazing you will see them grow an inch with pride and almost purr with contentment; but if you tell them that you disagree with them or that you don't think they are going about things in the right way, you will see them quickly deflate like a balloon. They are very sensitive to criticism of any kind and will take personally every negative thing that people say about them. This sounds contradictory considering that self-confidence is a key phrase for Leos, but often this self-confidence is more bluffing than reality. They are notorious for over-selling themselves, and their pride and boasting is a mask for their lack of confidence.

Sometimes they can come across as incredibly lazy but again this is down to vanity; if they aren't sure they can do something they would rather not do it at all and will feign indifference. In addition Leos often put more emphasis on looking the part rather than actually being the real deal. This desire to look good can make them extremely vulnerable to false praise and false criticism. Snobbery, pride and arrogance can weaken the brilliant strength of this sun sign. Perhaps their worst personality pitfall, however, is their misguided belief that they are always right. Leos can also be rather dogmatic and they desperately need to cultivate a more flexible mind as well as respect for the opinions of others.

Symbol

To get a picture of Leos at their best, imagine a playful lion cub and then a fully grown majestic king of the jungle. Like the lion that is their symbol, Leos have a noble but playful air about them that commands respect wherever they go or whatever situation they are in. But again, like the lions they are, they can also be overpowering, vicious and lethal if they are going in for the kill.

Darkest secret

Few would guess that underneath the noble, sunny exterior Leos display to the world is a vulnerable soul who seriously undervalues themselves, and craves love and recognition above all else. Without love, adoration and recognition the characteristic brightness of a Leo will fade. Winning is important to them but more important than that is being the one that everyone loves, respects and admires, and they will try to be that person at whatever cost.

Love

In love, Leos are typically playful and loving. They never tire of being told how wonderful they are and are very susceptible to flattery. They can also be surprisingly sensitive and can be hurt very easily by criticism, because they are often highly idealistic when it comes to affairs of the heart. Great pleasure is gained from sex but they don't necessarily want to be won over in a hasty manner. They like to be seduced by good wine, good food, good company and, of course, flattery.

Unfortunately, and especially when they are young, Leos have a habit of falling for the wrong type of person; but when they do eventually find the right person they don't tend to stray, but are steadfast and faithful. They prefer partners who are quieter than themselves, as they definitely like to be in charge in a relationship. But this isn't necessarily the best thing for them. They are often happier with the challenge of someone who isn't intimidated by their posturing and attention seeking, and who maintains their own independent interests and friendships outside the relationship.

Love matches: Aries, Libra and Sagittarius

The Leo man

If you want to find a Leo man you'll most likely find him sur-rounded by a circle of admirers or on the stage. The secret of winning his friendship or his heart is fairly simple—be his audience. Even if he is one of the quieter types born under this sign, he will still respond to adoration and flattery.

Love is a vital ingredient for a Leo man to feel happy and fulfilled, and if it's missing from his life he will slump into despondency and even depression. He needs to be worshipped to feel alive, and when he does find the partner of his dreams he will make a passionate and generous lover. But there is a drawback, and that is his jealousy and possessiveness. He expects his partner to belong to him body, mind and soul but ironically he'll grow restless if his partner is totally sub-servient. A delicate balancing act therefore needs to be struck between provocative challenge and submission. Another draw-back is that the Leo man is a born flirt. Even if he is deeply in love, this won't stop him appreciating beauty and his eyes will frequently wander. But as long as his partner is keeping him satisfied with plenty of romance and affection he is unlikely to stray.

Whether or not the Leo man is truly the King of the Jungle or just a pretender is open to debate, but there is no doubt that this man was born to command and to be respected by those who follow his rules. He's also capable of magnificent strength, devotion and courage on behalf of the people he loves or a cause he believes in.

The Leo woman

Many Leo women have the ability to light up a room when they walk into it. Vivacious, intelligent, clever and sexy, they rarely go unnoticed and are instinctively generous and friendly. They are also natural leaders and will often be the social lead-ers of their group. It can be quite daunting for a potential part-ner to know how to approach the Leo woman as her self-con-fidence and popularity seem to know no bounds. The secret is to flatter her as, like the male Leo, flattery is her secret weak-ness. It's also important that her partner does not stifle her. This woman cannot bear confinement. She needs to make her own decisions and lead her own life.

The Leo woman is many wonderful things but above all she is a proud lion—vain but magnificent. Despite all her airs and

graces, however, deep down a Leo woman is deeply vulnerable. If a partner is unfaithful to her or leaves her, they can leave behind a deeply hurt person and it may take several months or even years for her to rebuild her self-esteem and recover from the deep hurt. She may become very wary about risking her heart again.

Anyone in a relationship with a Leo woman will have to learn not to be jealous when she is in a room surrounded by a group of admirers. This doesn't mean that she is falling out of love, because in her mind it's only natural for other people to admire and respect her, and she needs constant reassurance that she is still desirable.

Family

Leo babies and children tend to have delightfully sunny, optimistic dispositions and they can also be extremely playful and, at times, mischievous. From an early age the classic Leo trait of attention seeking will appear. Their natural leadership potential will also shine through fairly early in their lives when they are with other groups of children, but parents should be alert to signs of bossiness and egotism as these will alienate them from their peer group. The same applies to their siblings or their place in the family if they have no siblings. Leo children will soon try to take charge or manage the family dynamic. It's important to remember, however, that this apparent self-confidence isn't really as powerful or strong as it may appear; as a result it's actually quite easy to put a Leo child in their place. Adults who need to reprimand them need to do it in a positive and affectionate way otherwise their self-confidence could be dented. The best way to parent a Leo child is not through criticism or anger but through gentle guidance and loving reassurance. At school, Leos are often extremely popular and it's important that they are given plenty of freedom to run off and burn up their explosive physical and mental energy.

Parents of Leo children should try to encourage them to listen more as this will help them keep an open mind and make them less likely to become inflexible in their opinions when they grow up. Leo children also have a very stubborn streak and this should be discouraged. They need to understand that there is always more than one way to achieve a goal.

It's not unusual for Leo parents to be more like friends and playmates to their children than anything else. This is fine to a certain extent, but as their children grow older they need a parent who can set boundaries for them rather than a friend to play with. Leo parents will certainly encourage their children to reach their full potential but there is a danger that they will set standards or goals that are unreachable. It's important for them to understand that although challenge is healthy and motivating, pushing their children toward perfection and piling on the pressure is unhealthy and damaging.

Career

Leos can excel in many careers but they are particularly suited to careers in which they can use their imaginative, creative abilities and their sense of drama. The world of media and entertainment is an obvious choice but they may also be drawn to the world of fashion and advertising, or jobs in which there is an element of glamour or luxury, or that require them to be center stage in some way. They may be fine surgeons or lawyers, for example. Other career choices could include politics, public relations, journalism, building, architecture or new product development.

Leos make great managers and bosses, but they do need to subdue any autocratic tendencies if they are to retain the

"Their ideal working environment will have an air of luxury about it..."

loyalty and respect of their employees. Their ideal working environment will have an air of luxury about it and, as well as being convenient and comfortable, it will be a place that inspires admiration. Leos will often take up causes and lead charities, playing the role of savior or hero and putting great plans for the future in place. They can also shine as entrepreneurs, picking trends before others do and pioneering the way for others to follow. During times of crisis or uncertainty at work Leos really come into their own, displaying the courage and strength that is needed to help them and others overcome setbacks and forge ahead.

Health and leisure

Leos tend to be fairly robust physically but as Leo rules the heart a heart-healthy, low cholesterol diet is advised as is lots of exercise. They don't tend to get ill often but if they do their need for attention and affection from friends and loved ones can be overwhelming. Being incredibly independent they often find it hard to accept the advice of a doctor, but it's important for them to understand that occasionally they need to relinquish control and give it to someone with greater knowledge than themselves. Their backs are also vulnerable and should be carefully exercised as well to prevent inflexibility or stiffening. Exercise with a creative element such as dancing, ice skating, martial arts and gymnastics are especially rewarding.

As far as leisure activities are concerned, Leos may struggle. They detest the word amateur and if they take up a leisure interest more often than not it will be pursued to professional standards. Their dedication is admirable but they need to learn that you don't have to be brilliant at something to enjoy it.

Leos do have a love for the good life and a great weakness for good food and wine. This can lead to weight problems if they aren't careful, so moderation is advised. As well as healthy eating and regular exercise, it's also extremely important for

them to make sure they set aside time each day for rest and relaxation. Otherwise they are in danger of burning themselves out. They need to be aware that health and happiness can only be experienced when all aspects of their lives—body, heart, mind and spirit—are in balance, so finding ways to regularly renew and strengthen these four key areas of their lives will be extremely beneficial. Getting plenty of fresh air, spending time with friends and loved ones, and sticking to a regular sleep, exercise and meal routine will help them feel more secure, especially during times of stress. Wearing, meditating on and surrounding themselves with calming colors like green, blue and purple will encourage them to seek this balance.

Born between July 23 and August 3

People born between these dates are natural leaders and everyone will look to them for guidance and security. There is a danger that they can become autocratic and too harsh on themselves and others, demanding nothing less than perfection—which is, of course, impossible.

Born between August 4 and August 14

These Leos tend to be more adventurous. They love to travel and long to explore the world and other cultures. Mostly easygoing, they have a lucky streak and seem to attract friends and good fortune wherever they go.

Born between August 15 and August 22

The fighting spirit of these people is admirable and there is little doubt that once they set their sights on something nothing will stand in their way. They do, however, need to be careful that their fierce ambition does not encourage them to walk over the feelings of others as they climb the ladder of success.

Life lessons

While Leos have no problem accepting power, they can have problems understanding the responsibility that goes with that power. One of their greatest challenges in life therefore is to get their fulfillment and energy from their own sense of personal empowerment rather than through power over others. Proud and regal, when Leos get the attention and affection they feel they deserve they are playful, energetic and optimistic. They crave the spotlight like no one else, but problems occur when their audience isn't there or isn't appreciative, or when they get criticized. Others may see this craving for attention as supreme egotism but underneath all that there is a very deep-seated insecurity. Leos should try to understand why they need to be the center of attention; the answer is that they rely far too much on outward approval for their feelings of worth and validity.

If they can just accept that they don't need to be amazing to be loved and appreciated, and that being a loving, content human being is enough, Leos will be able to find the fulfillment and happiness they deserve. They also need to understand that to be human is to make mistakes; being fallible doesn't disappoint other people—it helps form a connection with them. And finally, Leos need to spend less time looking in the mirror and more time looking within. Good looks will eventually fade, but inner strength and beauty just get better and stronger with age. While it's true that appearances matter, it's also true that there are far more important indications of character than the clothes a person is wearing or the amount of money in their wallet. And really Leos have no need to get so hung up on outward show because they possesses incredible strength of character, kindness, dignity and compassion. Developing these traits will bring them a great deal more happiness than looks and fashion.

Other signs of the zodiac can help Leos learn some important life lessons. Virgos can teach Leos about quiet discipline, patience and hard work behind the scenes. Scorpios can teach Leos to look beneath the surface for hidden treasures and true fulfillment, and Leos can learn from Aquarians about working tirelessly to make the world a better place without the need for outward show or recognition.

23 July

Your greatest challenge is

avoiding being taken advantage of

The way forward is ...

to understand that there is a difference between compassion and stupidity. You are not stupid, so make sure you are only there for those who appreciate you.

People born on July 23 are often warm and sympathetic individuals and the first choice of shoulder for others to cry on. They have a gift for helping others resolve their inner conflicts and a strong desire to help them progress—be it professionally, materially or spirituality—and are prepared to devote their considerable energies to this cause.

Above all, their greatest wish is to see others liberated from their doubts, fears, anxieties and misfortunes. Other people recognize this selfless orientation and will gravitate readily to their warmth and compassion. For example, their office will always be the one where people stop to chat about what is going on, or their home the one where people like to congregate or settle disputes. But as well as being giving and supportive they have a quick and piercing mind. They can be a little conservative in their views, but underneath they are bursting with creativity and are excellent at learning new skills.

Sometimes, however, their approach to life can be a little too cerebral and they may hide their own feelings. Ironically, for someone who is always there to listen to others, when it comes to their own feelings they can be incredibly shy. It is important for their psychological growth that they learn to pay as much attention to their own feelings as they do to the feelings of others, because their feelings have important messages to tell them.

After the age of thirty there is a turning point when they are likely to become more practical, analytical and discerning in their approach to life. In the years ahead their lives can be positive, fulfilling and powerful if they take advantage of the opportunities presented to them to pay attention to their feelings and grow in emotional confidence. Once they stop trying to be everyone's liberator and pay sufficient attention to their own need for liberation and fulfillment, their strength of conviction, vigor, creativity, and orientation toward the common good augur well for outstanding success both personally and professionally.

On the dark side

Self-sacrificing, directionless, repressed

At your best

Generous, compassionate, creative

24 July

the birthday of
charismatic uncertainty

Your greatest challenge is

feeling happy on your own

The way forward is ...

to celebrate your aloneness. The idea of aloneness carries with it a wonderful quality of freedom, as you're free from what other people might think.

People born on July 24 are among the most original and exciting of the year. They have an invigorating presence that surprises and shocks everyone they meet, and their charisma is so intense that others find themselves irresistibly drawn in.

They are exciting and adventurous, and others tend to cluster around them in the hope of understanding them better and perhaps catching some of their magic and energy. Sometimes they may express the dangerous side of their personality by taking up an extreme sport, dating someone wholly inappropriate or accepting a job that involves a huge amount of retraining or risk to their professional status. They are able to do this because they are often more concerned with the thrill of taking on a new challenge than they are with the consequences of their actions. They are here to have an amazing time and that is what matters most to them.

Although they may give the impression of being fearless, what they fear most of all is routine, the mundane and not moving forward with their lives. They need to learn that some of the greatest adventures lie within, and that getting to know themselves better will be an endless source of excitement and discovery. After the age of thirty there is a turning point in their lives when opportunities will be presented to them to draw more pleasure from being of service and doing their job well. They need to take advantage of these opportunities because their real source of fulfillment is to motivate and help others.

Whatever they choose to devote their dynamic creativity to, they will always find themselves attracted to the far out and the unusual. Whether they realize it or not, their actions are often designed to attract the admiration or attention of others. Once they discover that others will notice and admire them just as much, if not more, when they demonstrate their quieter, but no less effective, gifts for sensitivity and creativity, they have the potential not just to motivate others but to truly amaze and inspire them.

On the dark side

Selfish, obsessive, fickle

At your best

Innovative, hypnotic, inspirational

25 July

the birthday of
pure intention

Your greatest challenge is

learning to like yourself

The way forward is ...

to understand that human beings weren't meant to be perfect. It is okay to have weaknesses, make mistakes and have room for improvement.

Those born on July 25 are motivated by a passionate desire to realize their progressive ideals. Whatever their motivation may be—professional recognition or the accumulation of wealth—they will always strive to do the right thing, their actions always being governed by a personal code of conduct that forbids them from doing anything that disadvantages others.

These people have a code of honor or a set of strongly held principles which they live by. These principles give them a sense of purpose and are more important to them than success itself. They are more interested in the reasons for a person's behavior than the outcome of their actions, and winning and losing matters less to them than discipline, integrity and sincerity. Those who are success orientated may find this approach to life limiting, but to people born on this day it is liberating because it means that no experience, even the ones they fail in, is ever wasted.

With much to teach others, they have the potential to be a shining example of maturity and integrity, but curiously they are often unwilling to ask for the same level of honest commitment from others as they are willing to give themselves. This is because personal integrity is their guiding force in life and they believe that this must be the same for others. Unfortunately, this approach can be a little naïve and they may find that others often disappoint them or let them down.

After the age of twenty-eight they are likely to develop their analytical skills and to become more practical, discerning and efficient. It is important during this period that they don't become too perfectionist in their approach, because it will block their creativity. In fact, throughout their lives they need to be a little less harsh on themselves because if they learn to be more accepting of themselves they will find that it isn't just their integrity that makes others smile with appreciation; it is also their creativity, charm and unwavering devotion to their remarkably progressive vision.

On the dark side

Self-critical, struggling, naïve

At your best

Noble, dignified, warm

26 July

the birthday of self-assurance

Your greatest challenge is

not being overconfident

The way forward is ...

to understand that for self-confidence to work it needs to be appealing, not overpowering. People need to feel motivated by you, not cornered or embarrassed.

People born on July 26 tend to be charming and strong individuals with an almost unshakable belief in themselves. Without doubting their ability to judge situations and people, they will offer their opinions unstintingly as fact, expecting others to agree and acknowledge them as such.

Other people tend to listen when these dominant personalities speak because they have an air of authority and experience about them which others respect and admire. They also don't speculate widely and pointlessly on a wide variety of subjects but focus their energies on one particular field of interest in which they have immersed themselves and about which they have earned the right to speak with authority. They don't believe in fabricating the truth, and others can be sure that what they are saying is the honest and blunt truth, however painful it may be to hear.

They can also display incredible moments of insight; this can be reflected in a humorous outlook that expresses profound wisdom behind the joker's façade. Such is the astuteness, wit and insight of their pronouncements that others sometimes put them on a pedestal and more often than not they are very happy sitting there. Unfortunately, their elevated status can come at a cost; they may find that they lose touch with their spontaneity and feelings, becoming isolated from the very group whose admiration, affection and respect they crave.

From the age of twenty-seven they have an increasing desire for more practical order, efficiency and analysis in their lives. In the years that follow, it is important for their psychological growth that they don't become over-confident and should be more sensitive not just to their own feelings but to those of others. This is because once they can accept that they are a part of the world and not removed from it, and that others have feelings just like themselves, they can use their formidable intelligence, insight and passion to formulate spectacular and authoritative strategies for success in all aspects of their lives.

On the dark side

Over-confident, tactless, uncompromising

At your best

Honest, authoritative, confident

27 July

the birthday of the director

Your greatest challenge is

finding peace of mind

The way forward is ...

to be as honest with yourself as possible, because this will help you find inner peace and realize your full potential.

People born on July 27 are blessed with energy, passion and authority as well as highly developed practical and organizational skills—a formidable combination which often casts them in the role of linchpin around which others revolve. In fact, these dynamic individuals can often be found successfully organizing, managing or directing others in some way.

They make wonderful directors of those around them, in command both of the bigger picture needed for victory and of the strategies that will make it possible. Fueled by the desire to make progress, they rarely do things by halves and will throw themselves into the pursuit of their professional and personal vision with single-minded determination and dedication. Their style is often so authoritative and powerful that it can mislead others into assuming that they are as tough as nails; but the truth is they are not.

Underneath they are actually quite vulnerable and this will manifest in their inability to make decisions on their own behalf. While they are superb at managing what is best for others, when it comes to their own concerns they can be hesitant and indecisive. They may, for example, be able to advise others on the best career strategy but be unable to decide which direction their own career should take.

After the age of twenty-six they often become more analytical, practical and efficient; it is important for them to make sure they channel this emphasis positively and don't procrastinate in an unworthy career or lifestyle that does not utilize their full creative potential. They are natural leaders, and others tend to do things the way these people want, but for their own psychological growth and emotional fulfillment it is vital that they focus their energies on making the right decisions for themselves. This is because with a little more self-awareness and honesty these creative and determined thinkers can produce original thoughts and, with a clear personal vision, they will be able to turn their wonderful ideas into a tangible reality that guarantees both personal and professional success.

On the dark side

Insecure, distant, procrastinating

At your best

Authoritative, generous, confident

28 July

the birthday of
the independent spirit

Your
greatest
challenge is

asking others
for help

*The way
forward is ...*

to understand that
working
cooperatively
toward a goal with
people you trust
does not weaken
your position, it
strengthens it.

People born on July 28 are fiercely independent and competitive. They love to work independently, and although they have superb communication skills they prefer to lead by example than by hollow words. They relish testing themselves against challenges and their urge to win is so powerful that they find it almost impossible to admit defeat.

The dominating characteristic of these people at first appears to be an urge to win at all costs, but this competitive streak is fueled by their intense desire to appear self-reliant. From an early age this independent spirit will probably have manifested itself in a refusal to conform or acknowledge authority they do not respect, and throughout their lives they will always value independence of thought and action above all else.

Other people tend to be awed by this self-assurance and although it can lead people born on this day to considerable achievements it can also lead to loneliness and, ultimately, disappointment. This is because the admiration that these people earn for their courage, confidence and willingness to break new ground is merely admiration; what they crave is the affection of others. There is often a reason for this lack. The single-minded, independent and combative approach that they are characterized by is, unfortunately, more likely to alienate those they seek to impress, who perceive them as being selfish or lacking in consideration for others. This is unfair as they can be kind, generous, intuitive and warm; but until they forge lasting emotional connections with others, their creativity and potential may be misunderstood.

Fortunately, from the age of twenty-five there are opportunities for them to become more discriminating, practical and thoughtful with their time and energy, as well as the image they present to others. If they can take advantage of these opportunities to let others see what a modest, thoughtful and generous person they are, this will assure them the popularity and affectionate recognition they need to truly enjoy their undoubted talents and seemingly endless winning streak.

On the dark side

Insensitive,
detached, selfish

At your best

Resolute,
independent, dynamic

29 July

the birthday of
the partisan leader

Your greatest challenge is

using your own judgment

The way forward is ...

to understand that subordinating your individuality to the needs of the group often leads to emotional problems and resentment.

People born on July 29 tend to be energetic and positive individuals dedicated to fostering community awareness. Their ambitions are directed less toward achieving their own success and more toward benefiting the social group to which they belong, be this their family, their local community, their work, their country or the world as a whole.

Within their own social group, these people tend to gravitate toward leadership positions and, because they are strong willed with clear-cut goals and the organizational talents to motivate others, they can be inspirational. Their willingness to nurture and assume responsibility for those around them—combined with the generosity, loyalty and pride they display toward those in their charge—generally earns them affection, respect and gratitude.

Although their dedication and commitment to the social group they belong to is nothing but admirable, their intense communal bias does not leave them much room for those closest to them, such as partners and family, or for their own independent interests. This is ironic considering that many of these people like nothing better than to encourage self-reliance in others, even though this self-reliance does need to be within a framework of community awareness.

It's important for them to make time for themselves and for their own psychological development, especially between the ages of twenty-four and fifty-four, during which their mental focus becomes more analytical and practical, and the desire to be of service to others takes center stage. These are the years when they are likely to make outstanding contributions to their community or even humanity as a whole, but they need to make sure they don't regard their own personal needs and ambitions as less important than those of the community. This is because by demonstrating to others that their community supports their individuality rather than suppresses it, they can give their community the most powerful and liberating endorsement of all.

On the dark side

Conformist, restricted, generalizing

At your best

Generous, loyal, cooperative

30 July

the birthday of
the robust explorer

Your greatest challenge is

seeing beyond the material

The way forward is ...

to understand that focusing on material satisfaction without a spiritual dimension is a recipe for frustration, loneliness and unhappiness, however rich or successful you are.

People born on July 30 tend to be practical and down-to-earth individuals. They set ambitious material goals for themselves and love exploring all aspects of the physical world. Sensual and robust, they are often comfortable in their bodies, and their forceful, self-confident manner usually takes them to the top in their careers. Money and status, and all the privilege and pleasure they can bring, matter a great deal to them.

Although friends and family will often take second place to material goals, their relationships are conducted with steady equanimity and a concern for the physical and emotional well-being of friends and loved ones. They are fair and ethical in their dealings with others, and are almost always true to their word. They hate playing games of any kind and can be extremely generous with their material assets. In fact, one of the reasons they devote so much energy to increasing their earning power is that they enjoy being able to offer material support to those close to them.

Despite their morality, reliability and generosity, their target-orientated ambitions tend to exclude recognition of the importance of personal emotional and spiritual fulfillment. Unless they learn to cultivate an interest in their psychological growth, any victories they achieve in the material world will seem strangely hollow. Between the ages of twenty-three and fifty-three there is an emphasis in their lives on practicality and, given that they are already biased toward the material, it is crucial that they try to see beyond the material world they love so much. After the age of fifty-four there is a turning point which highlights their growing need for intimate relationships, creativity and harmony.

Above all, these extraordinarily robust individuals are motivated by a desire to achieve concrete progress in life, and they have all the determination and star quality they need to succeed. Their journey toward success, however, will be considerably happier and more rewarding if they can learn to appreciate and put a high value on the things in life that money can't buy.

On the dark side

Materialistic, mundane, repressed

At your best

Generous, sensual, ambitious

31 July

the birthday of
the descriptive artist

Your greatest challenge is

not being cynical

The way forward is ...

to understand that the pessimistic approach to life is just as unrealistic and unreliable as the optimistic because it means you focus too much on one perspective.

People born on July 31 are eloquent observers of the human condition. They always seem to be researching or digging around for information, possessing the ability to share or describe people and situations with remarkable accuracy and insight.

Nothing seems to escape their attention, even their own faults, which they are quick to correct. Their communication skills are superb and their insightful observations are often laced with a keen sense of humor. Those less comfortable with social interaction may prefer to use the medium of writing, music, art, or painting to make their contribution, but whether they become artists or not they often have a well-developed esthetic sense, loving to surround themselves with beautiful objects and attractive people.

Their highly developed concern for exploring, describing and occasionally idolizing aspects of human existence, combined with their logical train of thought, tenacity and devotion to their work, suggest that these people can make significant contributions to the store of human knowledge. They are not, however, the types to allow their observations to isolate them from the world around them; if they do make a breakthrough, they are often eager to share their insights and their triumphs.

Work matters greatly to them and they may throw themselves so wholeheartedly into it that they have little time to spare for friends and family. If they are to become emotionally fulfilled, they need to strike a better work–life balance. They also need to watch their tendency to think negatively. Their observations of the harsh realities of life may have led them toward pessimism but they need to ensure this does not become a destructive force in their lives, especially between the ages of twenty-two and fifty-two when there is an added emphasis on practicality and realism. If, however, they can keep their generous spirit alive with uplifting thoughts and compassion, they may be able to transform their high ideals of emotional fulfillment and dreams of beauty into reality.

On the dark side

Work obsessed, anxious, detached

At your best

Articulate, artistic, hard working

1 August

the birthday of

independence

Your greatest challenge is

learning to compromise

The way forward is ...

to understand that compromise is not a step back but a way to break out of deadlock so that everyone can move forward.

Independent in thought and behavior, people born on August 1 will often speak out passionately about their beliefs and when confronted with criticism, setbacks or disappointments they will rarely give up on those beliefs. Because they find it hard to function in a subordinate position they are best suited to roles where they can function independently or take a leadership role.

When these people see opportunities for improvement they will not hesitate to take them. Self-reliant, they hope others will see the wisdom of their ideas but they will never force others to accept their point of view, believing wisely that people need to be ready for the truth to hear it. They will, however, subtly try to influence people with their excellent, sometimes dark, sense of humor, and their insights that are merciless but accurate.

Those born on this day prize self-sufficiency above all else and, although this can help them bring about great progress through their energy and organizational skills, it can also bring them great unhappiness. They may, for example, cut themselves off from the love and support of others, a tendency which will leave them feeling emotionally isolated, wounding those who wish to offer them help. They can also take their independence to the extreme by becoming stubborn and inflexible in their beliefs; this can block their psychological growth and their chances of achieving success.

It is important, therefore, for them to learn to compromise and to be aware of the negative effect their intensity can have on others. Between the ages of twenty-one and fifty-one they will enter a period of increased emphasis on work, efficiency and order during which they are likely to gain an enhanced awareness of practical problem solving. Whatever their age, if they can recognize the need to be less detached and more sensitive to the feelings of others, so that workable compromises can be reached, these strong and independent individualists will surprise themselves and others with flashes of outstanding and truly inspired creativity.

On the dark side

Detached, unbending, difficult

At your best

Independent, original, influential

2 August

the birthday of
extreme clarity

Your greatest challenge is

falling in love

The way forward is ...

to stop confusing love with admiration. When it comes to affairs of the heart there are no rules or regulations, except that you and your partner should be yourselves.

People born on August 2 tend to be straightforward, and their clarity of vision makes it easy for them to identify their goals in life and then direct their prodigious energy, tenacity and organizational skills to their realization. What you see is what you get with these people; developing their talents and being respected is far more important to them than being liked as a person.

Often supremely confident in their ability to reach their professional goals, rarely will they be thrown off track. Their confidence is the result of their ability to realistically assess their abilities and know exactly what their strengths and weaknesses are. And because they rarely set goals that are out of their reach, more often than not they achieve them. Sometimes in their journey toward success they may appear to change course, earning them a chameleon-like reputation, but this is just a demonstration of their flexibility and creativity. They never lose sight of their ultimate goals and are simply experimenting with different ways to get there.

Despite their toughness and determination, the more sensitive people born on this day can be hurt by the criticism of others but are unlikely to show it. Their nature is to be non-conformist and their straight-ahead vision can lead to harshness toward others. In fact, they need to be extremely careful that the hard shell with which they surround themselves does not lead to a hardening of their attitudes. Fortunately, between the ages of twenty-two and fifty-two, although there is an emphasis on order, analysis, efficiency and logic in their lives, they may also feel the need to become more introspective. If they can use this opportunity to get in touch with their feelings and the feelings of others, their quality of life will improve immeasurably.

Blessed with a strong personality, clarity of vision and a unique approach to life, they have outstanding potential and, as long as they make sure they never lose touch with their intuition and sensitivity, their success and happiness are often assured.

On the dark side

Uncompromising, selfish, ruthless

At your best

Focused, versatile, determined

3 August

the birthday of
the heroic rescuer

Your greatest challenge is

avoiding dangerous thrill-seeking

The way forward is ...

to understand that you don't need to put yourself at risk to feel alive. The journey within is the most exciting and fulfilling exploration you will ever undertake.

People born on August 3 are fiercely energetic people primarily driven by their constant need for excitement, the stimulation from testing themselves against a variety of challenges, their desire to receive the admiration and respect of others, and last, but by no means least, their wish to cast themselves in the role of the heroic rescuer.

Their adventurous compulsion and heroic instinct to protect and rescue others can lead them to act impulsively and dangerously, but can also help them seize opportunities while others stand back and hesitate. They tend to believe that their ability to overcome risk and uncertainty gives them the right to get involved in other people's problems and offer their help, support and judgments. This is not always the case. Although friends and colleagues value their loyalty, and their willingness to throw themselves in and help out, they may tire of their constant need to give advice. These people need to learn to back off, allowing others the freedom to make and learn from their own mistakes.

Another danger for people born on this day is their susceptibility to flattery and praise, as this can lead them to an overinflated sense of their own worth, isolating them both from others and from reality. From the age of nineteen there is an increasing desire for practical order, analysis and efficiency in their lives, and some may find that their urge to seek out danger for danger's sake eases somewhat over the years. From the age of forty-nine there is a change of emphasis in their lives when relationships and creativity are likely to take center stage.

Whatever age they are, however, they will always fantasize about rescuing or inspiring others with their heroics; if they can learn to seek a balance between their fantasies and reality—so that they don't endanger themselves for no reason or rescue others who don't actually want rescuing—their sudden flashes of insight and outstanding displays of courage can, like the heroes that they are, both impress and inspire others.

On the dark side

Interfering,
self-important, reckless

At your best

Loyal,
adventurous, idealistic

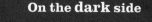

4 August

the birthday of
the rebel

Your greatest challenge is

dealing with authority

The way forward is ...

to understand that freedom and independence are not automatically superior to acceptance, cooperation and diplomacy.

Those born on August 4 are rebellious free spirits who definitely prefer to take the path less traveled, even if there is nothing really wrong with the path everyone else seems to be taking. Their intense dislike of being restrained in any way, combined with their hatred of complacency and the unthinking acceptance of the status quo, often leads them to behave, think, act, or dress somewhat perversely or to defend unconventional opinions.

These people are intelligent, compassionate and strong-willed, and their resistance to any kind of restraint endows them with radical and pioneering potential. When they channel their energies positively they have the ability to enlighten and enliven others, but others should be very careful not to challenge their need for independence because autonomy of thought is of the utmost importance to them. So averse are they to submitting to the authority or directions of others that from an early age they may reject well-intentioned attempts to help them, fearing that some sinister motive lurks behind people's helpful exterior. Taken to an extreme, this can make them fiercely independent but also incredibly lonely figures.

From childhood, people born on this day are likely to have enjoyed being at the center of things. At the age of eighteen, however, they enter a thirty-year period during which there are opportunities for them to become more conscientious, thoughtful, discriminating and efficient in their working environment. They need to take advantage of these opportunities to learn the art of diplomacy and compromise, as this will make life much easier.

When they are forty-eight they will reach another turning point that puts the emphasis on creativity and relationships. If, throughout their lives, they can learn to distinguish between independence and self-sabotaging behavior—being perverse for the sake of it—they will find that instead of becoming misunderstood, restless loners, they have the potential to become responsible rebels on whom others know they can depend for inspiration, guidance and radical but always exceptional insight.

On the dark side

Disruptive, perverse, undiplomatic

At your best

Original, courageous, striking

5 August

the birthday of steely determination

Your greatest challenge is

controlling your temper

The way forward is ...

to understand the damage that your loss of control can cause, reminding yourself that you are in charge of your feelings, not the other way around.

The focus and steely determination people born on August 5 are blessed with, combined with their ability to keep their cool, instills in others a sense of admiration. This often turns to awe when their resolute sense of purpose, striking originality and incredible energy help them achieve their goals.

These people dream big dreams, but what makes them stand out is that they are prepared to give everything they have to make these dreams happen. At their happiest and best they are natural optimists and, although their lack of caution can lead them into trouble, they have no problems taking calculated risks or betting against the odds. Not surprisingly their fixity of purpose can antagonize others, but criticism rarely deters them, rather energizing them and spurring them on to prove everybody wrong.

They have the potential to achieve success in any sphere that holds their interest; but more often than not underneath their impressive self-discipline there are intense and powerful emotions which, if they are crossed in any way, can explode in dramatic outbursts of temper. The volatile tendency that is characteristic of these people can be unsettling to those around them, and it is important for them to be gentler with both themselves and others.

After the age of seventeen, and for the next thirty years, there is an increased need for practical order and stability in their lives and they will be more inclined to analyze things practically and look for ways to reshape their lives. The key to their success during these years will be to ease up a little on the expectations they place on both themselves and others. After the age of forty-seven there is a turning point which emphasizes the growing importance of relationships, creativity and harmony. Throughout their lives it is important for these strong and determined personalities to learn to trust rather than repress their feelings. This is because working with their intuition will help them build up the confidence and faith they need to achieve their inspired dreams.

On the dark side

Insensitive, volatile, harsh

At your best

Determined, optimistic, original

6 August

the birthday of
high expectations

Your greatest challenge is

coping with routine

The way forward is ...

to understand that routine is not always a deadening force; it can provide a safe and secure structure in which creativity can be nurtured.

People born on August 6 have a lust for life, especially things that are uncommon and exciting. Their fascination with what is unique leads them to seek out the extraordinary and attracts interesting experiences their way.

They work hard and play hard, and big projects and grand schemes are their hallmark. If they are allowed to retain decision-making powers and the independence that is so important to them, their sharp mind, ability to take decisive action and unwavering determination augur well for professional success in whatever field they choose to devote their prodigious energies. In their private lives they understand the importance of secure bonds with friends and loved ones, but their commitment to their work may make it hard for them to live up to their ideal of devoting equal time to both work and home.

The urge for people born on this day to participate fully in every area of their lives can make it hard for them to deal with the more mundane aspects of life. This is because, whether they realize it or not, they are forever searching for something extraordinary or unusual. When life does not live up to their expectations they can become moody, despondent and restless. The key to success and happiness for them is to find ways to combine their passion for the unique and unusual with the routine of daily life.

After the age of sixteen and for the next thirty years there is an increased emphasis on order and practical problem solving, and they may become more discriminating with their time and energy. Another turning point occurs after the age of forty-six when they may focus more on relationships and the opportunity to develop any latent artistic, musical, literary, or creative talent. In fact it is in the realm of creative expression that they may eventually find the fulfillment they have always been seeking, as this will give them the opportunity to discover that the fantastic and the extraordinary really can be found in the most ordinary things.

On the dark side

Reckless, obsessive, unfocused

At your best

Exciting, creative, ambitious

7 August

the birthday of
the undercover visionary

Your greatest challenge is

declaring how you really feel

The way forward is ...

to understand that, unlike you, most people are not mind readers and sometimes things need to be spelled out to make your intentions clear.

People born on August 7 have fascinating, many-faceted personalities with many hidden talents which they are often surprisingly reluctant to reveal. Their secretive nature allows them to surprise and amaze people with sudden and unexpected flashes of insight, or outstanding contributions and achievements.

They are attracted to what is secret or unknown, and their own life mirrors this attraction. Not only do they love to uncover mysteries or secrets—they are often fans of detective stories—there is also something secret or enigmatic about them; even their closest friends may find it hard to really get to know them. Although they are sociable, witty and charming they tend to dwell in a realm of private feelings and fantasies that they seldom, and sometimes never, share. When this is taken to extremes they can even become reclusive or antisocial in their behavior, but they are more likely to find a compromise and will assume an outwardly confident and extroverted personality while at the same time enjoying a hidden fantasy life.

After the age of fifteen they are likely to feel an increased need for practical order in their day-to-day existence, and for the next thirty years they will be more inclined to analyze things, looking for ways to restructure and improve their lives. They should take advantage of this opportunity to find a way to integrate their hidden personality into their social world. They also need to guard against lethargy and becoming too closed or fixed, and should avoid resting in some comfortable routine that does not challenge them to achieve their full potential. After the age of forty-five there is a significant turning point which sees them recognizing the growing importance of relationships, creativity and harmony; these are the years during which they are most likely to open up to others about their feelings.

However, the sooner they find the confidence to open up, the better. The hidden but potentially outstanding originality, creativity and intellect of these fascinating people should never, ever be underestimated.

On the dark side

Reclusive, repressed, insecure

At your best

Charming, intelligent, insightful

8 August

the birthday of
versatility

Your greatest challenge is

setting yourself realistic goals

The way forward is ...

to understand that it is great to be bold but you also need to be realistic and aim for what you know you can achieve.

Other people tend to think that success comes easily to people born on August 8 because they appear to be naturally good at everything they do. Their success, however, is the result of their sharp intellect and strong work ethic. It is also a result of their exceptional versatility and ability to learn new skills from scratch.

Although they are versatile and will probably play many roles and sample many careers in their lives, they are not flighty by nature. Quite the opposite, in fact; when they are engaged in a particular project their focus is intense and their discipline inspirational. It is just that when they have learned all they feel they can learn or gained the recognition they feel they deserve, they like to move on to the next challenge, even if it is totally unrelated to the one they devoted themselves to previously. This ability to change direction and immerse themselves in different projects both confuses and surprises others, especially when these people change direction when they appear to be at the height of their success or capability.

Until the age of forty-four there is an emphasis in their lives on order, problem solving and being more discriminating with their time and energy. It is particularly important during this period that their versatility does not lead them to make career or life choices that are unrealistic or simply unsuitable. After the age of forty-four there is a significant turning point which stimulates their need for balance and harmony, and heightens their awareness of partnerships and relationships in general.

During this period in their lives the key to their happiness will be to develop more emotional depth and find ways to stamp their individuality on the world around them. Having said that, they should not try to suppress their characteristic versatility because, once they find a cause that is worthy of them, their affinity with diversity and love of fresh challenges will continue to be the key to their success.

On the dark side

Unrealistic, perfectionist, unaware

At your best

Versatile, energetic, talented

9 August

the birthday of
the mentor

Your greatest challenge is

allowing others to make their own decisions

The way forward is ...

to understand that sometimes the best way for people to learn and grow is to allow them to make their own decisions and mistakes.

People born on August 9 are dynamic and determined achievers. Their presence is authoritative and others tend to look to them for guidance. Although they are extremely ambitious they can also be patient, inspiring and hands-on mentors to those who want to learn.

They are at their happiest and their best when they are giving advice to others. They feel qualified to take on the role of mentor because they have a good understanding of human psychology and what motivates or demotivates others. They have a wealth of ideas and insights about how people can improve or enjoy their life more, and are extremely generous with their advice and support. However, because they love to be looked up to and consulted when decisions need to be made, they can get upset if others ignore them, or assert their own independence and follow their own advice. It is extremely important for the psychological growth and emotional fulfillment of people born on this day that they ensure their concern for others does not turn into a need to control them.

Until the age of forty-three they will find that life presents them with opportunities to be conscientious, discriminating and efficient in the working environment. During these years they need to be especially careful not to let their controlling tendencies exert an unhealthy amount of influence over the lives of others. Learning to listen to others and understanding things from their point of view will help them with this. After the age of forty-four there is a turning point which brings a strong emphasis on social relationships and partnerships, and after the age of seventy their focus is on deep emotional transformation.

Whatever age they are, however, if these wise and generous individuals can learn to let go of their need to tell others what to do all the time and listen to their own inner guidance instead, they have the potential to be not just a mentor but a creative, inspiring, confident, charming, and successful role model as well.

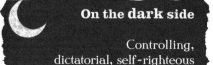

On the dark side

Controlling, dictatorial, self-righteous

At your best

Authoritative, influential, insightful

10 August

the birthday of
expressive charm

Your greatest challenge is

coping with rejection

The way forward is ...

to try to find out why things didn't work out. The answer could help you change your approach and improve your chances of success.

People born on August 10 like nothing better than to please others or to win their approval. As a result they are often highly appreciated and admired, both at home and at work. They understand the importance of communication, utilizing their impressive vocal skills to persuade and influence others. In fact, their charming and energetic public persona is often cultivated with the sole purpose of impressing and delighting others.

Orientated toward others, these people seek to communicate their ideas to as many people as they can and, because their greatest desire is to be of benefit to others, their ideas are often progressive and original. Once they have convinced themselves of the merit of a course of action, they will pursue it with tenacity and courage. Determined to make their voice heard and to draw the attention of others to what they have to say, they are hard to ignore.

However, because they put such a high priority on what others think of them they will often put on a happy face, regardless of how they are feeling. Although this makes them very popular, it can deny others the chance to get to know the real person behind the mask. They spend very little time getting to know themselves and what they really want out of life, and their lack of self-awareness can make them place unrealistic expectations on themselves.

Until the age of forty-two they will often place great emphasis on order, work and efficiency. These are years when they are most likely to focus on how much they are appreciated and, because of this, they can suffer greatly when they encounter rejection or setbacks. Discovering what their strengths and weaknesses are will help them gain in confidence and resilience. After the age of forty-three there is a turning point which places more emphasis on relationships and creativity and, if they can learn to open up emotionally to themselves and others, these are the years when they are likely to develop the necessary self-confidence and conviction to ensure that their message becomes an effective instrument of progress.

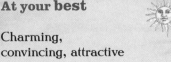

On the dark side

Unaware, vulnerable, confused

At your best

Charming, convincing, attractive

11 August

Your greatest challenge is

being considered in your words and behavior

The way forward is ...

to understand that just because you feel or think something does not mean you have to act on it.

People born on August 11 are astute observers and communicators with a powerful desire to uncover the truth or hidden but essential knowledge or insight. In any situation they are in, both at home and at work, they have the ability to go directly to the root causes of the issues.

These people seek clarity and are always quick to detect manipulative behavior in those around them. They aren't shy about confronting others with their version of the truth either, even if it hurts. In fact, they like nothing more than to reveal to others the insights they have uncovered and are often at their happiest and their best in front of an audience. Not surprisingly, they can be harsh and judgmental at times and their sharp criticism can distance them from others; but they are also quick to point out the good in people and are as lavish in their praise as they are with their criticism, winning themselves many admirers in the process.

The clear-sighted observation with which they are blessed, when combined with their resourcefulness, courage and determination, augurs well for success, but their love of exposing hypocrisy, although refreshing, can lead them into confrontation with those who seek to maintain the status quo. In addition, their inability to accept others at face value can lead to relationship problems. Until the age of forty-one there is an emphasis in their lives on practicality and efficiency, and they need to be careful that they don't become too discriminating or critical of those around them. After the age of forty-two, however, there is a turning point when they may want to become more involved in personal matters and may move from concentrating on practical considerations to more creative, esthetic ones.

Throughout their lives if they can learn to moderate their tendency toward brutal honesty and develop greater tolerance of others' imperfections, they will not only retain the affection of those closest to them, they will also gain the attention, affection, approval and respect of the wider audience that they crave.

On the dark side

Argumentative, hurtful, attention seeking

At your best

Insightful, powerful, intelligent

12 August

the birthday of
the historian

Your greatest challenge is

learning to relax

The way forward is ...

to understand that time out from your frantic pace is not time wasted but time gained; you recharge your batteries so no longer run on empty.

People born on August 12 have a strong desire to make progress by leading others along an innovative path. At the same time they respect and value existing knowledge and convention. In some respects, they are like a historian in that they gather as much information as they can and subject it to logical evaluation before deciding on the best way to proceed.

When their intelligence and clarity of purpose are combined with their resourcefulness and tenacity, they often impress others with their abilities. They can often be virtuosos in their chosen field, whether that is conducting orchestras, writing books, raising a family, or designing a building. Not afraid of hard work and able to toil at a frenetic pace, they draw on both the latest research and traditional knowledge to create spectacular results. Not surprisingly, they have high expectations of themselves and the knowledge that they have thoroughly investigated every aspect of their belief gives them almost unshakable self-belief. Despite the potential success that such personality traits appear to offer, these people can, however, run the risk of alienating those they seek to influence by their inflated ego or harsh words of criticism. Although they should not compromise on their self-belief, learning to share will encourage others to listen to and support them more.

Until the age of forty there is an emphasis on efficiency and practicality, and they need to be especially careful during this period not to become too strict or emotionally detached from others. After the age of forty-one they may focus on relationships and a need to bring more beauty, harmony, creativity and balance into their lives. This can draw them toward such activities as writing, art, music, or any of the creative arts.

Throughout their lives, if they can learn to assess the potentially damaging effect their forceful approach can have on others and develop greater tolerance and patience, this will not only help them achieve their aims more successfully, it will add an additional and infinitely more rewarding dimension to their lives.

On the dark side

Tyrannical, overly serious, judgmental

At your best

Energetic, innovative, knowledgeable

13 August

the birthday of
the sharpshooter

Your greatest challenge is

coping with your anger and impatience

The way forward is ...

to step outside yourself when your emotions reach boiling point. This will remind you that you alone are in charge of your feelings.

People born on August 13 are no strangers to conflict and controversy. They are sharpshooters who always aim true, and their urge to break with convention compels them to take on challenges or make waves, whatever situation they are in.

The unconventional vision, resilience and tenacity of purpose that are key characteristics of these people can earn both the admiration and the disapproval of others. This is because despite the wounding criticism of those who regard their rebellious notions as ridiculous or fanciful, they always remain faithful to their beliefs. If life doesn't go their way, they refuse to be crushed by disappointment. And as their unusual imagination is supported by solid analytical skills, more often than not those who start out disagreeing with or disapproving of them will end up admiring their bravery, even if not agreeing with their standpoint.

Until the age of thirty-nine there is an emphasis in their lives on practical order and efficiency. It is important during these years that they keep their authoritarian tendencies and their temper in check. After the age of forty there is a significant turning point when they are likely to become more amiable and collaborative, placing greater emphasis on personal relationships. Whatever age they are, it is important for them to understand that although aiming true and flouting convention will guarantee that they are a force to be reckoned with, they will not guarantee that they always triumph.

As risk takers, they have all the courage, discipline and energy to attract success; what they sometimes lack is perfect timing. They need to learn when to cut their losses and move on, when to be patient, and when to pounce. The only way for them to learn this skill is to develop their intuition. Once they are able to recognize and connect with their intuition, they will not only be able to identify their target and take aim, they will finally be able to shoot and, by so doing, make progressive and characteristically unconventional contributions to society.

On the dark side

Brash, insensitive, unrealistic

At your best

Ambitious, resilient, courageous

14 August

reflection

Your greatest challenge is

attaining self-awareness

The way forward is ...

to understand that you will never fully understand other people until you understand yourself first.

Those born on August 14 are among the most perceptive individuals of the year. Their primary focus is on what is going on around them and, because they are blessed with clarity of vision, they have a gift for assessing the motivations of others and the impulses that govern their behavior. Nothing escapes their penetrating gaze. They never hesitate to say what others may be reluctant to say and in many ways become a mirror for others; through them, others see themselves as they really are.

These people are inspired by a desire to get to the truth of a situation and because they like to express their thoughts in a direct, sometimes brutally honest manner, it is not surprising that they often end up in deep water. Fortunately they understand the importance of humor, and this considerably softens the impact of their judgments, but it is important to understand the powerful influence they can have on others and to use it wisely.

Although their insights and perceptions often stimulate others to think more deeply about themselves, when it comes to their own personality they are surprisingly unaware. Instead of reflecting the views of others they would benefit enormously from some quiet reflection of their own so as to discover their own strengths and weaknesses. If they are able to do this, they will realize that they have a talent for entertaining and informing the world with the biting accuracy of their comments. They will also find out, however, that their tendency to observe rather than participate in human dramas often leaves them feeling emotionally isolated and is the cause of much of their unhappiness and confusion.

Fortunately, around the age of thirty-eight there is a turning point which places more emphasis on relationships and creativity; but throughout their lives, if they can remember that communication is not just about words, language and behavior but also about connection, their strong sense of purpose and undoubted creativity ensure that nothing can stop them from achieving their tremendous potential.

On the dark side

Critical, unaware, distant

At your best

Perceptive, honest, amusing

15 August

the birthday of
the regal presence

Your greatest challenge is

coping with coming second

The way forward is ...

to understand that however much you feel you deserve it, you simply cannot come first every time. You will often learn more from your "failures" than your successes.

People born on August 15 tend to be blessed with great self-confidence and courage, giving them a commanding or imposing presence whatever situation they are in. Others look to them for leadership and enjoy basking in their regal presence.

These people have such great self-belief that even if they find themselves in a situation where they are out of their depth they will still be able to convince others that they are the right person for the job or responsibility. Their optimism and ambition are magnanimous enough to include all those close to them, as well as co-workers, and they will never be reluctant to share their success. They are powerful role models but sometimes others may feel that they are losing themselves and their identity in the mighty shadow of these people.

It is important for them to learn to cooperate with their fellow human beings and to grant other people a chance to give their opinion or make their contribution. If they don't do this, they run they risk of becoming controlling in their domination. Until the age of thirty-seven there is an emphasis in their lives on practical order and efficiency, particularly in their working lives, and they need to make sure that their need for adoration does not lead to an inflated ego. They also should ensure that they listen very carefully to what other people are trying to tell them, as listening will earn them greater support and respect than commanding.

After the age of thirty-eight there is a turning point that highlights the importance of relationships and creativity, and this can stimulate them to develop any latent musical, artistic or literary talents. Throughout their lives, however, the key to their success will be their ability to empathize with others and to recognize that the right to personal autonomy is not their sole preserve. Once they are able to develop this awareness, not only will they be able to realize their ambitious and progressive visions, they will be able to lead and inspire others.

On the dark side

Aggressive, egotistical, insensitive

At your best

Generous, imposing, decisive

16 August

the birthday of
the powerhouse

Your greatest challenge is

resisting the desire for revenge

The way forward is ...

to understand that revenge isn't sweet. People don't like to be associated with those who are bitter or motivated by anger.

Seductive and magnetic, people born on August 16 are at their happiest when they can broadcast their unconventional convictions to as large an audience as possible. Their main priority in life seems to be to attract attention to themselves and, because they are such a powerhouse of energy, ambition and enthusiasm, they are often impossible to ignore.

Once they have decided on their sphere of influence, they will seek to triumph over any obstacles or people that stand in their way. Their drive to achieve power and recognition is so strong that they can be vindictive and destructive toward those that oppose them, and the desire for revenge is a destructively powerful force in their lives. Yet behind the brash and confrontational exterior that these people adopt there is a more determined self that directs their attention-seeking behavior but is entirely different to the image they project. Although their behavior appears to be geared toward material gain and career success, their more profound motivation is found in the attainment of personal happiness. As a result their private life is just that: private. This is the one area of their lives in which they can take off their public persona and be themselves.

Until the age of thirty-six there is an emphasis on being practical and building a structure for themselves, particularly in their work environment. These are the years when they tend to be at their most ruthless and they need to be careful that their enormous potential for creativity does not transform into driven exhibitionism. After the age of thirty-seven they may start to place more importance on relationships and the emphasis will be on quality rather than quantity when it comes to displaying their creativity.

Throughout their lives if they can listen to their powerful conscience and make sure their don't act in ways that are hurtful to others or lose touch with the simple pleasures of life, they have the potential not just to seduce others with their magnetic style, but to surprise them with their extraordinary achievements.

On the dark side

Ruthless, exhibitionist, excessive

At your best

Seductive, motivated, energetic

17 August

the birthday of
the dormant volcano

Your greatest challenge is

controlling your temper

The way forward is ...

to understand that you should be the one in control of your emotions, not the other way around.

People born on August 17 may present a calm, composed exterior to the world but, like a dormant volcano, underneath fiery emotions fester and smolder. The quest for success for these people is relentless and, because they are so strong-willed, they either win a loyal following of devoted fans or create a legion of implacable enemies.

These people attract the attention of others with their intensity and self-sufficiency. On the one hand independent and creative types with great energy, imagination and determination not to be bound by convention, on the other they are serious thinkers with the ability to focus on progressive, occasionally idiosyncratic ideals. This combination of vigor, self-confidence and purpose ensures that any contribution they make has great impact. Although they make fine leaders, possessing the resilience and self-belief to recover from virtually any setback, their Achilles' heel is their argumentative, stubborn nature. They can be extremely defensive and aggressive, and their occasional rages can terrify those around them.

Until the age of thirty-five there is an emphasis in their lives on practicality and creating an effective working environment; these are the years when their untamed energy can be at its most explosive and undirected. Learning to think before they speak and act and listening more to the advice of others will help them gain the control and sense of direction they need to earn the respect of others. After the age of thirty-six there is a significant turning point that highlights their social relationships and partnerships; during these years their already powerful creative energies are highlighted even more, and this is the period during which they can really come into their own.

Throughout their lives the key to their success will be putting the emphasis on self-control. If they can find ways to harness and direct their incredible energies to a cause that is worthy of them, when their volcanic creativity erupts it will not cause chaos and destruction but enlighten, inspire and guide others with its dynamic originality.

On the dark side

Argumentative, defensive, out of control

At your best

Intense, self-confident, powerful

18 August

the birthday of
the deep heart

Your greatest challenge is

avoiding getting wrapped up in other people's problems

The way forward is ...

to learn to distance yourself more from what you see going on around you.

People born on August 18 are among the most sensitive and tolerant of the year. Emotionally deep, they seem to experience both joy and pain at a more intense level than anyone else. However, this sensitivity doesn't unsettle them since they believe that feelings hold the key to their personal fulfillment.

Not surprisingly, they are not only sensitive to their own emotions but to the emotions of others, and others will often seek them out for advice and support, sensing a person who will not only listen to their problems but who will also take these on board. Not only do these people feel a pronounced sense of responsibility toward others, their urge to benevolently guide and protect others is also strong. Although this wins them many friends and supporters, it can also cause confusion about what their real needs and feelings are, limiting their potential to think and act independently. Once they have the maturity and the self-confidence to connect with their own feelings and be more objective when it comes to the feelings of others, they will discover that they have an innovative and original mindset that gives them the potential to be the masters in any chosen field.

Until the age of thirty-four there is an increasing emphasis on practicality and a need for order in their lives and it is important during these years that they find ways to connect with other people without losing themselves in them. Learning not to over-extend themselves and to find a place in their hearts for optimism alongside their realism will help them recharge their batteries. After the age of thirty-five their awareness of relationships is highlighted and they may be stimulated to develop a number of innate artistic interests.

If they can find a way to protect and nurture their sensitivity and vivid imagination without becoming self-involved, they will find that these are the years when they are most likely to inspire others with their idealism, determination, compassion and progressive vision.

On the dark side

Over-sensitive, avoidant, struggling

At your best

Sensitive, creative, generous

19 August

the birthday of
the editor

Your greatest challenge is

revealing the real you

The way forward is ...

to understand that people tend to relate better to a person's vulnerabilities than they do to their strengths, so appearing too smooth can work against you.

People born on August 19 present a deceptively smooth façade to the world, but behind all this is a more serious person—one who has a definite agenda and will push ahead determinedly until this is achieved. The thoughts and feelings they present to others may be genuine but they never reveal the whole story, having carefully edited their ideas and opinions before presenting them.

They prefer to reveal to others only the information which they feel will impress or enlighten them. Image is extremely important—sometimes more important than performance. With such meticulous attention to detail and presentation, more often than not these people find that their work or ideas inspire enthusiasm in others, who tend to follow wherever they lead. There is a risk, however, that with such effort put into their image they lose touch with their real feelings and fall prey to delusions of grandeur or invincibility.

Deep-seated insecurities rarely lurk beneath the façade of people born on this day. Quite the opposite; they tend to be very aware of their own worth, and this is one of the reasons why they need to hide any trace of weakness. Sometimes this struggle to maintain their image can prevent them taking the risks necessary for their psychological growth and they run the risk of procrastinating when they should be moving forward.

Until the age of thirty-three there is a growing importance in their lives on paying attention to detail. It is extremely important during these years that they are more open and generous with their feelings because they will find that their complexity, rather than being a weakness, is a strength, helping others relate to them better. After the age of thirty-four there is a turning point when they are likely to become even more sociable and creative. If they can remind themselves that to err is human, these dynamic and bright individuals will find ways to combine their courage, originality, popularity, and endearing complexity to achieve brilliant and inspiring results.

On the dark side

Secretive, bland, indecisive

At your best

Charismatic, influential, confident

20 August

the birthday of
thoughtful mystery

Your greatest challenge is

coming to terms with your past

The way forward is ...

to stop letting your past destroy your present. Concentrate your energies on the new beginnings and wonders that the present can bring instead.

Those born on August 20 are complex, self-contained individuals whom others often find very hard to understand. The reason for this is the air of thoughtful mystery that tends to surround them.

Although people born on this day need time alone this does not mean they are lonely. Quite the opposite, they are orientated toward and genuinely concerned for the well-being of others and their intelligent humor often lightens the atmosphere. It's just that, even in their most relaxed and happy moments, there is always a tinge of thoughtfulness about them which others may interpret as sadness. It can sometimes seem as if they are struggling with dark and deep secrets, but more often than not they aren't really sure why they find it difficult to share their complex imagination with others.

Struggling and overcoming their personal fears are therefore key driving forces for the melancholic but beautiful people born on this day, and sometimes the struggle can become so intense that they long to be able to forget themselves. They may seek solace in addictive pursuits or by losing themselves in their work, but neither approach will bring them long-term happiness and fulfillment. Although their need to understand and explore their past is a dominant and overpowering force in their lives, learning to focus their energies on the here and now will be the way forward.

Until the age of thirty-one there is an emphasis in the lives of August 20 people on order and practicality. They may find themselves continually analyzing things to improve them and their chances of happiness will improve if they shift the focus of this self-improvement from the past to the present. After the age of thirty-two there is a turning point which puts the spotlight on relationships and, if they can find ways to stand up for themselves and express their dynamic creativity and originality in the here and now, not only will they solve their personal mystery—they will also discover a magical way to live.

On the dark side

Escapist, lonely, conflicted

At your best

Thoughtful, imaginative, intelligent

21 August

Your greatest challenge is

resisting the temptation to "fit in"

The way forward is ...

to celebrate the fact that your inspired originality, however much you try to hide it, is destined to attract attention.

However hard they try to fit in or lose themselves in the crowd, people born on August 21 will always attract attention. Their appeal is so powerful and bright that it refuses to blend in or conform.

These people tend to stand out but not because others reject or ridicule them. They stand out because there is something incredibly likable and appealing about them; they may be beautiful to look at, they may have a seductive voice or they may be extremely athletic or intelligent. Whatever the secret of their appeal, the curious thing about these people is that a part of them longs to withdraw and not attract attention. They often resent feeling like a square peg in a round hole, but as long as they are unable to accept or embrace their uniqueness they will find that their opportunities for success and fulfillment are limited. However, once they are mature enough to celebrate who they are, they can put their natural appeal to work so that the attention they gather can be redirected as they wish.

Until the age of thirty there will be an emphasis in their lives on practicality and perfectionism, and these are the years when they are most likely to deny or repress their individuality. After the age of thirty-one, however, there is a turning point that brings a growing awareness of relationships. Their creative abilities might be enhanced as well, and these are the years when they are likely to feel more comfortable with themselves and their exceptional talents.

Above all, they are extraordinarily imaginative, and because they are also blessed with resourcefulness and formidable practical skills to develop their visions they have trail-blazing potential. The only roadblock for them is their tendency to repress their deep creativity and originality, but when they realize that far more satisfaction can be gained from expression and involvement than from detachment and distance, and that people love them for being fresh and original, they have a world of opportunities for success and happiness at their feet.

On the dark side

Withdrawn, confused, elusive

At your best

Interesting, appealing, purposeful

22 August

the birthday of
the commander

Your greatest challenge is

being open to the advice of others

The way forward is ...

to understand that not listening objectively to others can lose you allies and destroy your potential to be successful.

Whatever talents they are blessed with, August 22 people will not hesitate in exploiting them to the full. They believe that hard work is the secret of success, not luck or fate, and they like to be the master and commander of their own destinies. Not surprisingly, for people with such remarkable self-control they are also far happier giving orders and commanding others than they are receiving them.

As well as being commanding, people born on this day are also extraordinarily creative. Their imagination is broad enough to cover a wealth of possibilities, and so powerful is their charisma that they are able to inspire others to execute their inspirations alongside them. They have a talent for making work seem exciting, bringing flair to even the most mundane chores. In keeping with their authoritative presence they typically display a tough and outspoken exterior to others, and they can be extremely stubborn in their refusal to change their opinion once it is formed. Behind their combative exterior there is, however, a surprisingly sensitive side, although they are unlikely to allow anyone to see it.

Until the age of thirty there is an emphasis in their lives on practical order, and during these years they are likely to lay the foundation stones for their far-seeing and carefully constructed game plans for realizing their ambitions. It is extremely important during these years that they remain as open to advice and suggestion as possible. After the age of thirty there is a significant turning point when their natural talent for leadership is likely to come to the fore and the urge to do things their way—sometimes regardless of the potential cost to others and themselves—will dominate. Fortunately, however, there is also an emphasis on relationships and creativity. If they can find ways to incorporate their love of discovery and adventure into their lives so that they can be creative as well as commanding they have outstanding potential, not just for leadership positions, but for fulfillment and happiness in all areas of their lives.

On the dark side

Controlling, inflexible, shut down

At your best

Influential, courageous, hard working

VIRGO

THE VIRGIN
(AUGUST 23 – SEPTEMBER 22)

* **Element:** Earth
* **Ruling planet:** Mercury, the communicator
* **Symbol:** The Virgin
* **Tarot card:** The Hermit (inner strength)
* **Number:** 5
* **Favorable colors:** Yellow, green, brown
* **Key phrase:** Busy is better than bored

Virgos are perhaps the most misunderstood signs of the zodiac. They have a reputation for being detailed, sensible, organized, meticulous, practical, efficient and analytical. While this reputation is well deserved it's important to point out that they also have razor-sharp perception, probing minds and an innate creativity. The Virgo drive to create perfection reflects their keen sense of aesthetic order; but there is always a danger that this drive for perfectionism can breed narrow-mindedness and fussiness.

Personality potential

Virgos tend to be reliable, intelligent, hard working, systematic and considerate. One of their greatest talents is their innate ability to get to the bottom of problems, find the missing link or to keep working at something until they eventually achieve a breakthrough. There's also something incredibly refined about their approach to life—these people are the fine-tuners of the zodiac, giving attention to the important details that other more hasty signs often forget.

The Virgo love affair with detail can often be reflected in their living or working environment, through their choice of design and décor, or through their clothing—they are typically impeccably dressed and fragrant smelling. Personal hygiene matters a great deal to them. They wouldn't dream of turning up anywhere looking anything less than their best. Although they are one of the few signs who have the potential to be multi-talented because they can use both sides of their brain at the same time—the creative and the analytical—they tend to be extremely modest and will feel uncomfortable in the limelight. They are quite happy to work quietly in the background or be the second in command. To them the approval or admiration of others means far less than the joy and satisfaction they get in creating order and making sure that a job is well done or a mission accomplished.

Virgos are ruled by the plant Mercury so stimulating and intelligent conversation is very important to them—they often make great writers, teachers, counselors, journalists, interviewers and debaters. From an early age they are also often interested in the visual and decorative arts and crafts, antiques and fine music, opera and ballet.

Above all, Virgos are efficient and, because they can be relied on to get the job done, other signs of the zodiac tend to rely on them. Graced with integrity, practical creativity, discipline, common sense, refinement and an eye for the important details, this sign rarely lets other people down. Virgos never shirk responsibility or an opportunity to be of service because their instinct to serve, help others and make sure everything runs smoothly is strong. It's often the case that these quiet, modest souls have far more power and influence than they themselves would believe possible.

> "They are one of the few signs who have the potential to be multitalented..."

On the dark side

As admirable as their drive for perfection is, their need for every detail to be in place can make many Virgos highly critical and fussy. They can be as hard on themselves as they are on others and all too easily set impossibly high standards that de-motivate rather than inspire others. And, although they are talkative and able to express their ideas clearly, they can at times over-elaborate and give painstaking attention to unnecessary details, meaning that they lose sight of the bigger picture. Their perfectionism also leads to a lack of confidence, so they will often look to others for approval. But even if they get that approval they are so self-critical that they will doubt any praise or love they are given. In fact, the Virgo craving for constant approval can make them one of the most needy sun signs of the zodiac.

Virgos may avoid trying something new because they fear making mistakes and this will limit their range of experience, earning them a reputation for being narrow-minded. They also have a rather unpleasant self-righteous and relentless air about them, and carping criticism of others can be one of their worst faults. Coupled with their tendency to believe they are always right and that nobody can do things as well as they can, there may also be a tendency toward prudishness. They will condemn anything which does not meet their exacting standards of wholesomeness. But ironically, on rare occasions these may be double standards since some Virgos find themselves secretly attracted to voyeurism or the seedier side of life.

Symbol

The symbol for Virgo is the virgin but don't make the mistake of thinking that those born under this sun sign are innocent. Although there is often an untouchable quality about Virgos they are no strangers to the ways of the world. Virgin, in this instance, means pure and perfect, and that can relate to sex and passion too. In other words, these people set themselves the very highest standards. It's quality rather than quantity they desire, and their approach to love and to life is refined and meticulous.

Darkest secret

People born under this sign have a reputation for being critical and others in their lives may fear that they can never live up to their high standards. But what these people don't know is that the Virgo tendency to nag often masks a secret terror that they themselves are simply not good enough, attractive enough or likeable enough.

Love

Lack of confidence can be the biggest barrier to happiness in relationships for Virgos. They may often question why others would want to spend time with them. This modesty and humility can be endearing, especially in a young Virgo, but over time if the problem isn't dealt with it can lead to problems. It's crucial that Virgos learn to love themselves more because if they can't do this, no amount of love, compliments and affection from a partner will convince them that they are lovable.

Virgo's tendency to be critical of their partners is one that they would do well to curb. When it comes to the physical aspect of love, partners may feel that those born under this sun sign are holding something back. There is always a part of them that remains untouchable and this mysterious quality can give them great sex appeal; but it can also stop them fully expressing themselves and feeling fulfilled emotionally and sexually. Learning to relax with their partner and allowing themselves to be loved for who they are, warts and all, is the key to their happiness in love, and indeed life.

Love matches:
Capricorn, Scorpio and Taurus

The Virgo man

The Virgo man is typically in constant motion; either physical or mentally, or both. He never sits still and it's vital that his abundant energy finds a positive outlet otherwise it's likely to be wasted in restlessness. When it comes to affairs of the heart, this man won't sweep you off your feet. He lives on a practical level and he certainly won't give himself over to mushy promises and sentimentality. This doesn't mean, however, that love isn't important to him. Love matters a great deal but the way he chooses to express his love is in his unselfish devotion, rather than through grand romantic gestures.

He may present a detached and icy exterior to the world but there are ways to win over his heart. In love—as with everything in life—he will seek quality rather than quantity, setting his sights on an accomplished and intelligent partner with a subtle rather than a blatant attractiveness. He'll probably have very few real love affairs and, if a relationship doesn't work out, he will bury himself in hard work and be doubly cautious about committing his heart again. In fact, many Virgos can live with celibacy far more easily than other people. There are a lot of Virgo bachelors around—single not because they have to be but through choice.

Although his displays of affection are never obvious and he will take his time finding the right partner, because he is highly critical and enormously particular, he can be a master of the art of subtle seduction. More often than not, the object of his desire will find his controlled but powerful masculinity impossible to resist. Then, once he has decided he has found "the one," he will declare his love with touching simplicity and do everything in his power to ensure that his love is returned. He is capable of enormous sacrifice for the person he loves, and his love will burn constantly and dependably over the years, never fluctuating as it can do for other signs.

The Virgo woman

At first glance the Virgo woman may appear fragile and vulnerable, but underneath her fluttering, shy exterior is a woman made of steel. She may be pure minded but she is not naïve, and her practicality and common sense make her extremely independent. She may be many things but she is

no clinging vine and is more than capable of opening her own doors. She may not be given to outward displays of affection or spontaneous romantic gestures but her heart is far warmer than most people suspect. If she appears distant it's important to remember that her emotions are controlled, not non-existent.

Although she can be painstakingly meticulous about details and good manners—and presentation matter a great deal to her—she can also be the kindest, most generous and, if she is truly in love, the most affectionate woman in the world. Her perfectionism can be irritating at times, but there's something very endearing about this woman's modest manners; her organized approach will have a positive effect on all those who cross her path. When people get to know her better, they will also discover a sharp wit and a lovely sense of humor—her laugh really is music to the ears.

Above all, Virgo women value honesty and truth in a relationship and they are the souls of discretion. People can trust them not just with their hearts but with their secrets and their dreams. If these dreams fade over time, the Virgo woman will help dust them off so they are shiny and bright again. In short, this woman is a rare treasure whose presence graces and enriches the hearts and lives of all those she touches.

Family

Keen to please and often a "teacher's pet," the chances are a Virgo child will be tidy, well organized, clean, and a willing and hard worker at school. You're unlikely to find folded and messy workbooks in their school bag and their handwriting will be beautifully formed. Virgo children have abundant energy, and their hands and their brains need to be given lots to do to keep them occupied and challenged. "Busy is better than bored" is their motto. When they start a new school it might be a good idea to familiarize them with the restrooms first, as knowing there is a place for them to go and wash their hands and tidy up matters a great deal to them. School playtimes may be daunting for them and they may at times prefer to stand apart from the crowd. They are extremely sensitive to being made fun of. Parents should try to encourage them to develop their self-esteem with praise and with repeated reassurances that it's okay to make mistakes. It will also be helpful for them to develop hobbies, activities and interests that they can share with other children. Examination time may be particularly stressful for Virgo teens, given their tendency to worry; so, as soon as examinations appear on the horizon, parents should encourage them to master study and revision skills because the better prepared they are, the less intense their worrying will be.

As parents, Virgos are often extremely hard working. They will devote long hours at work to give their family the very best and then, when they are at home, they will work long hours to make sure their home runs efficiently. Sometimes there may be an obsession with hygiene and cleanliness; this can be detrimental because children need to be exposed to a certain level of germs and infections as they grow up to help build up the strength of their immune system. Many Virgos bring their work home with them and this can destroy their work–life balance. They need to learn where to draw the line, otherwise they will miss out on spending quality time with the people that matter most to them in life.

Career

Virgos are interested in the details and are typically apprehensive about taking the lead, so they often work best under supervision. When given instructions they will follow them to the letter and to their best of their abilities, which makes them excellent assistants and deputies. They often take great pride in being the real backbone of any organization or commercial venture. Many also make brilliant and inspirational teachers and linguists, and others do themselves proud in the armed services and the caring and medical professions. Their eye for detail may also lead them to careers in journalism, editing, publishing, science, pharmacy or the arts.

> **They do need to watch their tendency to be overcritical and overcautious.**

Other possible career choices include crafts, design, charity work, administration, law, research, accountancy and any occupation which enables them to handle complicated details. The ideal working environment for a Virgo will be calm, organized, tidy and quiet, decorated in neutral but tasteful colors and with the most up-to-date equipment. As employees they are typically courteous, reliable and thorough, with a quick, analytical mind, but they do need to watch their tendency to be overcritical and overcautious. They are an asset to any organization because they love to work hard, but they are not overly ambitious and getting to the top is not their main consideration.

Health and leisure

Virgo rules the intestines, digestive system and hands, and most Virgos have lovely hands. They often look younger than their years and their fastidious approach to life means that unhealthy habits are kept to a minimum. Their drive toward perfection, however, can cause physical tension, digestive problems and allergies. It's therefore crucial for Virgos to learn how to relax and unwind. The more relaxed a Virgo is, the healthier they tend to be.

When it comes to diet, Virgos tend to be fussy eaters. The phrase "You are what you eat" is ingrained in their psyche, and they are likely to be extremely well informed and conscientious about what they choose to put into their mouths. Having said that, they are also prone to cravings for food and to bouts of comfort eating. Because their usual diet is typically simple and healthy, these bouts of overindulgence in fatty, sugary food can cause digestive problems. If they were less strict in their approach to food in the first place, they may find that they

don't get as many food cravings. As far as diet is concerned, Virgos should go for mainly whole foods and for foods that are high in fiber as these will boost their digestion. They should also follow the 80/20 rule, which means that as long as they eat healthily 80 per cent of the time they can allow themselves the occasional indulgence—when an indulgence is not forbidden, food cravings are less likely. Virgos also need to learn to distinguish between real hunger and the hunger that is caused by loneliness, anger and fear. Waiting 15 minutes before eating when they get a craving will help, as will distracting themselves with a walk around the block or chatting to a friend. If the craving is not food related it tends to pass.

Fresh air and regular exercise are essential for Virgos as these will boost their mood and their spirits. Unfortunately, being such hard workers, Virgos often tend to sacrifice these healthy pursuits; but it's important for them to ensure that exercise and regular "me time" is scheduled into their life along with everything else. Meditation, yoga or activities such as gardening that have a meditative quality about them are especially good if they are prone to worry. Wearing, meditating on and surrounding themselves with the color orange will encourage them to work on building their self-confidence.

Born between August 23 and September 3

People born on these days really hate to be in the spotlight and cringe with embarrassment if singled out in the crowd. They prefer to be the quiet achievers who remain in the background but are the lynch pin that keeps everyone and everything running smoothly without fuss.

Born between September 4 and September 14

These Virgos bring a clear and concise viewpoint to any situation. They have a quick mind but, although they are extremely practical and logical, they also have brilliant flashes of intuition from time to time.

Born between September 15 and September 22

There is something touchingly youthful, pure and innocent about these people. They will always remain young and active, both physically and mentally, and like to live every day of their lives to the full.

Life lessons

With their love of helping others and their efficient and organized approach, Virgos are perhaps the most unselfish signs of the zodiac but it's important for them to make sure that they do not become too servile. They also need to be careful that the high standards they apply to themselves and to others do not make them overly critical and pedantic. Perfection is their ideal but they will never be truly happy until they learn that it's an impossible ideal, and that only by making mistakes and being imperfect can people learn and grow.

Virgos pay excessive attention to detail but all this crossing of the T's and dotting of the I's may be drawing their focus away from the bigger picture and from what really matters. Their analytical mind is both a blessing and a curse, and they need to learn to distinguish between what does merit close scrutiny and hypercriticism (for example a criticism that is unfair or a partner not pulling their weight in a relationship) and what doesn't (such as the color used on a presentation folder or the way a person loads the dishwasher).

Being born worriers, Virgos are in real danger of worrying themselves to an early death. They are often hypochondriacs and—given the strong link between mind and body—their fear of falling ill can lead to real medical conditions. Given the strong link between what a person thinks and the reality they create for themselves, the situations or worries they dread can tend to manifest in their lives. And even if the worst doesn't actually happen, there isn't much fun in worrying more about life than living it. It's been said before but it's so important for Virgos it should be said again: Virgos need to learn to relax and let go of their need for perfection.

Other signs of the zodiac can give them help and inspiration. For instance, Arians can help them see the bigger picture, and Sagittarians can help Virgos see the deeper truths that they often miss or simply do not comprehend. Pisceans and Geminis can encourage Virgos to be less critical; Cancerians can help them understand better the reasons why people make mistakes, and Leos can encourage them to use their sharp, incisive mind for fun and creativity.

23 August

the birthday of
sparkling accuracy

Your greatest challenge is

avoiding preoccupation with your own interests

The way forward is ...

to understand that there's nothing wrong with self-involvement as long as you aren't insensitive to the feelings of others.

People born on August 23 have a tremendous store of energy, and when it is directed to something that holds their interest, their intensity and commitment sparkle. They pay as much attention to the process as the product, whether they are preparing an assignment, arranging flowers or deciding what to wear. The accurate eye, incredible focus and attention to detail that define them are invaluable to colleagues, friends and family alike, and everyone counts on them to keep everything organized and running smoothly.

The intensity of their commitment to accuracy can make them lose sight of the bigger picture from time to time. It is important for them, however, never to lose sight of their progressive and ambitious goals because they have the resourcefulness, tenacity, technical abilities and, if they trust themselves more, the creativity to see their visions realized.

Another danger for these people is that they can become so wrapped up in their interests and their work that any kind of interruption or setback can lead to outbursts of anger; others may therefore perceive them as aggressive, neglectful or in extreme cases selfish. This is unfair, as August 23 people are inherently kind and always willing to help those in need. It's just that they have a strong tendency to immerse themselves in the solitary pursuit of intellectual concerns, and although this gives them incredible potential for professional success, they run the risk of unintentionally upsetting or neglecting others.

After the age of thirty there is less emphasis on practicality, efficiency, problem solving, and order in the lives of people born on this day, and opportunities will arise to focus more on relationships, and explore the possibility of creative and artistic outlets. It is important for them to take advantage of these opportunities and not to be confused by the apparent emotional complexities they create in their lives, because, paradoxically, it is the complexities that hold the key to their fulfillment and happiness.

On the dark side

Obsessive, selfish, detached

At your best

Intense, accurate, stylish

338

24 August

Your greatest challenge is

listening to your intuition

The way forward is ...

to understand that knowledge and information can only take you so far; sometimes the only way forward is to let go and trust your instincts.

People born on August 24 are blessed with a sharp and questioning mind that is at its best when untangling mysteries, uncovering the truth or making new discoveries. They don't like to take anything at face value, and even the opinions of experts or their most trusted friends will not stop them searching through the evidence to catch what others might have missed and to discover their version of the truth.

Their questioning mind makes them hard to manipulate, and people may rely heavily on them for advice and insight. Indeed, they often have a reputation for being someone whose opinion and approval others can trust. They could be said to mistrust anything or anyone that appears simple or straightforward, so strong is their belief that hidden complexities lie beneath the surface. Paradoxically, although their self-image is of being very simple and direct, what they do not realize is that they are just as complex as the subjects of their investigation, if not more so. Although they never miss the facts, they can have a tendency to miss out in their observations what is subtle or unspoken, and their accuracy and creativity would be enhanced if they learned to develop their intuition.

Until the age of twenty-nine there is an emphasis in their lives on practicality and efficiency, but after the age of thirty there is a turning point when they may focus on relationships and opportunities to develop their latent creative potential. They need to take advantage of these opportunities, using sharp-witted intellectual skills and their creative potential, as these will boost their chances of success professionally and personally.

Throughout their lives, intense inner forces may cause them to alternate between extremes of uncertainty and a sense of being special. If they can cultivate positive thinking, trust their deeper intuition and learn to manage worry positively, these gifted and astute discoverers, who leave no stone unturned in their quest for knowledge, have the potential to enrich the lives of others with the fruits of their observations.

On the dark side

Stifling, over-critical, suspicious

At your best

Observant, insightful, thorough

339

25 August

the birthday of
the live wire

Your greatest challenge is

resisting the need to prove yourself all the time

The way forward is ...

to understand that only you can give yourself a sense of self-worth.

People born on August 25 are difficult to ignore. Their polished image and excellent social skills get them noticed wherever they go, success seeming to come easily to them. Others often think of them as self-assured, attractive, clever, accomplished and charismatic. In short, they are real live wires and life always seems more interesting and dynamic when they are around.

Although they are seductive, outgoing and vital on the outside, these people seldom feel like this on the inside, and they will drive themselves extremely hard to prove to others that they are really self-assured and accomplished. They rarely let down their guard and if they feel threatened or insecure in any way they may over-emphasize their polished public image to compensate. Unfortunately, this can lead to conceited, arrogant or superficial words or behavior that can alienate the very people they seek to impress. It is vital for people born on this day to focus less on charming others to win their approval and more on cultivating their own sense of self-worth.

From childhood people born on this day may have been inclined to analyze situations practically in order to understand and improve them. As they grow older they may devote a great deal of energy to cultivating and projecting their public image. After the age of twenty-eight, however, there is a turning point and over the next thirty years they become more aware of the importance of close relationships and partnerships. Creative abilities are also enhanced during this time. After the age of fifty-eight there is another turning point which brings an emphasis on greater self-awareness and personal power. In some respects, these may be the years when they feel at their happiest and their best because the focus is on their individuality.

However, whatever age they are, if they can find the courage to discover and develop their real talents and sharp intellect, they will find that the accomplished, clever, attractive and creative persona they have created isn't a mask any more but a reality.

On the dark side

Insecure, superficial, vain

At your best

Charismatic, exciting, sociable

26 August

the birthday of
star potential

Your greatest challenge is

asserting yourself

The way forward is ...

to understand that there is a difference between assertiveness and being aggressive. Assertive people are respectful, whereas aggressive people ignore the needs of others.

People born on August 26 tend to feel most comfortable when they are the power or support behind the throne. Although their star potential is undoubted, they often choose the role of understudy, second in command or advisor, gaining quiet satisfaction from the knowledge that the success of others is largely down to their support.

Usually setting high standards for themselves in whatever line of work they select for themselves, they will often master their skills so well that their work is often of an exceptionally high standard. Yet if their admirable talents are thrown into the limelight, even if the recognition is well earned and well deserved, they will feel ill at ease and may resort to self-deprecating behavior to underplay their talents. This is because nothing matters more to them than the satisfaction and happiness of everyone they are living and working with. If their own profile gets too high they feel that this might have a detrimental effect on others.

Until the age of twenty-seven the selfless tendencies of these people will be highlighted, and they need to make sure this does not lead to unhappiness and resentment. After the age of twenty-eight there is a turning point which puts the emphasis on diplomacy, partnerships and relationships; these are the years when they are most likely to step into the role of supportive advisor, guide or partner. If they are content to remain in this role they can feel incredibly fulfilled, but if they are not content and long to strike out on their own they can feel frustrated. Fortunately, during this time they are also likely to gain an enhanced sense of balance and harmony that helps them develop their creativity.

If they can learn to stand up for themselves, these are the years when their undeniable star potential and capacity for independent and original thought will finally reveal themselves to the world, to guide and inspire others in a supportive role, or enlighten and surprise others in a leadership role.

On the dark side

Self-effacing, passive, frustrated

At your best

Inspiring, supportive, resourceful

27 August

Your greatest challenge is

to overcome negative thinking

The way forward is ...

to realize you cannot help the world by focusing on negative things. As you focus on the world's negative events you are only adding to them.

People born on August 27 have much to give the world and may often be found helping others or doing charity work. They have a huge humanitarian spirit and from an early age may have felt that they need to heal the world in some way. The key to their happiness will depend on whether or not they can allow the world to give back to them as well.

They are generous, special spirits and they are at their happiest and best when making others happy, or improving others' lives in some way by performing a valuable service. Self-sacrificing, they drive themselves incredibly hard and expect others to offer the same level of devotion and commitment to their ideals as they have. Their generous urge means that they are universally admired and respected, but their success can be limited by their tendency to be easily disillusioned, seeing the world as an unhappy, negative place. Developing optimism and positive thinking will help them balance giving and receiving, and turn their life from a struggle into an adventure.

Until the age of twenty-five there is an emphasis on being mentally focused and discriminating, and they can help themselves considerably during these years if they think and worry a little less about the common good and get involved more in making a difference. In fact, the positive energy that practical involvement gives them will help them find their way in life. After the age of twenty-five there is a turning point when there is an increased need for partnership or relationships with others, with the possibility of exploring literary, artistic or creative outlets in some form.

Whatever age they are, however, they are always likely to be universal in their approach to life and, if they are able to find an outlet for their humanitarianism and spirituality, they might not only find deeper fulfillment—they might also find that their generosity and kindness are repaid many times over.

On the dark side

Driven, depressive, aloof

At your best

Generous, altruistic, hard working

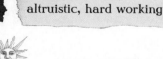

28 August

Your greatest challenge is

becoming more flexible

The way forward is ...

to understand that those who are inflexible and stubborn don't tend to grow psychologically or progress as fast as those who understand the importance of compromise.

People born on August 28 are blessed with superb communication skills. They are extremely convincing speakers and know how to get others to listen to them and, even if they don't agree with them, to admire them. Although they are also skilled crafts workers with excellent organizational skills, one of their greatest strengths is their debating skill.

Their informed comments on a huge range of subjects are likely to have the backing and validation of detailed research or personal experience. This is why others don't just trust and rely upon their pronouncements, but also expect them to have a word or two to say about anything. They are highly principled, and the word dishonesty simply isn't in their impressive vocabulary. Although their knowledge is extensive and they can back it up with facts, they possess a tendency to become so convinced of the truth of their arguments that they start to believe that they alone have the answer. It is vital for their psychological growth that they don't abuse their superior intellect by shutting out alternative viewpoints or by manipulating others with the strength of their convictions.

When they reach the age of twenty-five they will enter a thirty-year period of increased emphasis on partnerships, both personally and professionally. This is the time when they may also develop a greater sense of esthetic beauty and may want to develop their latent creativity. It is important during these years for them to keep themselves motivated and their minds stimulated with constant challenges; settling into a mundane routine in which no questions are asked is damaging for them. After the age of fifty-five there is another turning point when they are likely to seek deeper meaning in their lives, becoming more reflective and thoughtful.

Whatever age they are, as soon as they can accept that there should always be more questions than answers, they have the potential not just to become convincing and influential debaters, but to be brilliant advisors with original, imaginative and innovative contributions to offer the world.

On the dark side

Inflexible, strict, blinkered

At your best

Articulate, respected, knowledgeable

29 August

the birthday of
the improviser

Your greatest challenge is

going with the flow

The way forward is ...

to understand that sometimes life can't be controlled; you simply have to relax and trust that something good will come to you.

People born on August 29 are blessed with an incredible imagination that can take them to the pinnacle of success in their personal and professional life. Reluctant to be confined by the limits of convention, they prefer to analyze all existing information, reappraise it and then present their findings in a new and original manner. As such, they are the great improvisers and re-interpreters of the year.

Although they are wonderfully creative and artistic in their approach, they also thrive on routine and structure. A recurring theme for them is their attempt to impose control or structure upon every situation. As such they are not just positive thinkers but also positive doers; once they have set down their ambitious goals, they move toward implementing them with a self-discipline and practicality that inspire amazement in their friends and colleagues alike. Paradoxically, the one area of their lives where they find it hard to improvise or impose structure is their emotional life. Frequently, they will subordinate their private to their professional life, preferring to devote their energies to an environment in which they don't feel so threatened. It would be beneficial for them, therefore, to reappraise their priorities.

From childhood they will probably have demonstrated their practical and analytical skills, impressing others with their ability to find their way around problems by thinking up new solutions. After the age of twenty-four there will be opportunities for them to focus on their relationships, and it is important for them to take advantage of these opportunities as their need for a fulfilling personal life is strong, however much they try to escape. There will also be an emphasis on creativity during these years.

Whatever age they are, if they can learn that sometimes the best solution to a problem is to stop trying so hard to solve or understand it and to simply trust, they will be able to present to others the fruits of their research in reinterpretations that are both innovative and inspiring.

On the dark side

Withdrawn, impatient, lonely

At your best

Innovative, structured, imaginative

30 August

Your greatest challenge is

to outgrow your tendency to be overbearing

The way forward is ...

to understand that not everyone is as self-sufficient or as capable as you; help others grow by giving them more responsibility.

People born on August 30 often play a leading and protective role in both their professional and personal lives. Friends, family and co-workers look to them for stability, guidance, support and a sense of direction, and because they are often intelligent, capable and insightful individuals, they are well qualified to assume this responsibility.

Self-reliant and strongly focused on their goals, people born on this day seem destined for success and recognition in whatever field they choose to specialize. Their mercurial minds also bestow on them marked curiosity, as well as the desire to impose order and structure in both their professional and personal life. Because they often have such a responsible and self-possessed air about them, they run the risk of becoming a magnet for needy people. Although they relish guiding and protecting, it is important for them to understand the difference between those who genuinely need their help and those who are lazy and irresponsible. They must also ensure that their need to control others does not make others overly dependent on them.

From their childhood, they are likely to have been interested in studying situations and people in order to understand, improve and direct them. After the age of twenty-three and for the next thirty years, there is a turning point which places an increased emphasis on partnerships, both personally and professionally. This is also a time when they have an increased sense of beauty and harmony, and may want to develop their creativity. It is important during these years that they don't get obsessed with the material aspects of their lives by placing too much emphasis on money making, practical problem solving, directing and organizing at the expense of their emotional and spiritual needs.

This is because, whatever age they are, the more they get in touch with their feelings and the feelings of others, and the more they can connect with and use the spiritual power or intuitive wisdom within them, the more power, happiness and fulfillment they will attract to themselves.

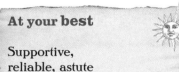

On the dark side

Controlling, inflexible, overburdened

At your best

Supportive, reliable, astute

31 August

the birthday of
dynamic approval

Your greatest challenge is

to escape dependency on the approval of others

The way forward is ...

to understand that if you rely on the attention or approval of others for feelings of self-worth, you will not be in control of your life.

People born on August 31 are blessed with abundant energy and enthusiasm. There is often something attractive and fun about them that draws others to them effortlessly, and they typically climb the ladder of success to leadership positions with great ease.

They tend to make life appear very easy but there's a price to pay for their popularity and success. Although extremely astute when it comes to understanding what makes others tick—and therefore able to influence the thoughts and moods of others—when it comes to their personal development they may be completely in the dark. Unaware of what their real needs are, they may rely heavily on the attention or approval of others for feelings of self-worth. Ultimately this is a dangerous strategy as it puts control of their happiness in the hands of others. It is only when they are able to lessen their need for public attention that they will grow psychologically and, although they are dynamic with few problems either socially or professionally, their "success" in life may have an empty feel about it.

After the age of twenty-two there is an increased emphasis on social relationships for the next thirty years of their lives. It is important for them not to lose themselves in work or other people during this period. Their happiness and fulfillment depend on their ability to look within for guidance and approval; if they are unable to do this they may end up feeling stressed, confused and frustrated. Fortunately, there is also an emphasis during this time on developing their creativity, and they need to take advantage of the opportunities life presents them to think and act more independently.

After the age of fifty-two there is a powerful turning point that signifies a need for emotional change, making them more self-reliant and in control. Whatever age they are, the sooner they learn to depend less on the approval of others and more on their intuition, the greater their chances of finding true happiness and lasting fulfillment.

On the dark side

Needy, frustrated, stressed

At your best

Energetic, dynamic, astute

1 September

the birthday of
the survivor

Your
greatest
challenge is

knowing when to
stop

*The way
forward is ...*

to understand the
principle of less is
more. Sometimes
it is beneficial to
hold back or quit
while you are
ahead.

People born on September 1 are often obsessed with their work, but this does not mean they are boring and uninspiring. Quite the opposite; they simply find work demanding and fulfilling and will carry out their responsibilities with an infectious enthusiasm and excitement. They also like nothing more than to have their skills or abilities tested and challenged, and are very open to suggestions for improvement. In fact, they have the mental and physical toughness to survive even the most taxing of circumstances, standing their ground with pride in the face of adversity. This makes them the true survivors of the year.

With a tendency to take their work and themselves very seriously, they would benefit greatly from more fun and laughter in their lives, although their energy, enthusiasm, industriousness, and insatiable curiosity for everyone and everything more than compensate. Being so dedicated and full of enjoyment of their work, it's not surprising that many of them excel in their careers; but sometimes their love of challenge and refusal to give up can work against them. For example, they may find themselves putting up with things that they shouldn't be putting up with simply because they are unable to move on, find it hard to admit defeat or don't know when to cut their losses.

After the age of twenty-one, the following thirty years present opportunities for them to develop stronger relationships with those around them, strengthening their intuition; they should take advantage of these opportunities as these will help them improve their timing, so that they can enhance their chances of success by knowing when to hang on and when to quit. During these years they may swing between modesty and confidence, but when they are positive and enthusiastic about a project they have the ability to motivate and energize others.

Whatever age they are, however, their extraordinary mental and physical toughness and fixity of purpose in the pursuit of their goals endow them with the potential for extraordinary and inspiring accomplishments.

On the dark side

Insistent, over-
worked, overly serious

At your best

Courageous,
resilient, hard working

347

2 September

the birthday of
the egalitarian

Your greatest challenge is

putting yourself first

The way forward is ...

to understand that, just like everyone else, you have a right to be noticed for your accomplishments.

People born on September 2 are idealistic and lively individuals with an egalitarian view of the world. They are usually the first to defend the rights of everyone, and when presenting their opinions they make sure they are understood by everyone, no matter what their background or level of education.

They cannot tolerate pretension or unnecessary complications of any kind, placing a high value on simplicity of language, behavior and action. Other people always know where they stand with them and they also know that, whatever the circumstances or situation, they will be given a fair hearing and a fair chance to prove themselves. In fact, these people place such a high value on egalitarianism and fair play that when in direct competition with others they will quite happily take a step back and allow others to race ahead, even if they are well qualified for the job or due for advancement. It is important for them to understand that pushing ahead when their talents merit it does not mean they are becoming pretentious or ego-centered; it simply means that they are placing a value on themselves.

After the age of twenty they will have an increased need for partnership and relating to others for the next thirty years, and again it is important for them not to undervalue themselves and realize that equal relationships with others can be indispensable to achieving their high ideals of fairness, honesty, inclusion and respect. There are also opportunities during this time for them to develop their creativity; they should take advantage of these to inject some inspiration into their working life. After the age of fifty-one there is a turning point when they are more likely to get in touch with their personal power.

Whatever age they are, the sooner they realize that they don't live to work but work to live, the more fulfilling their lives will be, and the greater their chances of discovering their outstanding potential for exerting a beneficial and inspirational influence on others.

On the dark side

Workaholic, passive, uninspired

At your best

Fair, direct, vital

348

3 September

Your greatest challenge is

to overcome your fear of failure

The way forward is ...

to understand that failure is a vital ingredient for success because it shows you what works, and what doesn't.

Those born on September 3 are remarkably determined individuals, a quality that those who do not know them well may not appreciate until a situation arises to encourage them to be more confrontational. Generally, they prefer a gentler, conciliatory approach, believing that more can be achieved through communication than combat. This personal style can be highly effective but it can cause others to underestimate them or misjudge their iron will.

They are blessed with a sharp and independent mind, and a highly developed sense of justice and fair play, as well as great technical and organizational skills. Their desire for excellence will drive them to succeed personally and professionally and, although everything about them reflects this drive for perfection, their easy-going style and unassuming personality make it hard for others to resent them.

After the age of nineteen and for the next thirty years, they will become gradually more aware of the importance of relationships and partnerships. Their creative abilities will be enhanced too during this period, and some of these highly developed people may produce work that is way ahead of its time. Unfortunately, they are not always very good at demystifying their ideas and visions, sometimes taking it for granted that others are on the same wavelength when they clearly are not. Taking the time to simplify and explain their thoughts or methods to others will make all the difference. After the age of forty-nine there is a turning point which brings a strong emphasis on a deeper need for change, transformation and personal power.

Throughout their lives, however, if they can develop their self-confidence and overcome their fear of failure by understanding that no failure is a failure if you learn from it, they may just find that their novel ideas—combined with the iron will so artfully hidden behind their easy-going appeal—will not only help them outshine others, but make them influential agents of advancement and true progress.

On the dark side

Procrastinating, passive, self-doubting

At your best

Determined, socially adept, original

4 September

the birthday of

the master planner

Your greatest challenge is

valuing tradition

The way forward is ...

to understand that the past is not just something to be torn down; it is also there to be learned from and understood.

People born on September 4 are the master planners of the year. They bring process and precision to everything they do, and are forever planning, organizing, designing and putting systems in place for a more productive future. Others will typically look to them not only for the last word on due process, but also for the first word on planning ahead.

With a natural understanding of how systems, procedures, buildings, establishments and just about everything else work, efficiency is very important to them and they are brilliant at finding short cuts or better ways of doing things. They can delight in exposing, criticizing or tearing down the Achilles' heel or fatal flaw in a project to make their point. Their knowledge is so great that they should ensure they put it to good use and do not divert their focus to unworthy causes. Unfortunately, the less highly developed and luckily very rare individuals born on this day can make formidable conmen or women.

After the age of eighteen there is an increased need for partnership and relating for these people; their sense of harmony and beauty is likely to be enhanced during this period. It is important during these years that their focus on planning for the future does not close their eyes to the possibility of happiness in the present. After the age of forty-nine there is a significant turning point which will highlight a growing emphasis on emotional and spiritual regeneration, as well as joint finances or corporate business activity.

Throughout their lives, the key to their success and happiness will not necessarily lie in material gain or career advancement, but in developing their spirituality, a goal that may confuse or frighten them. Once they understand, however, that spiritual growth—rather like material progress—is something that needs their concentration, dedication and passion, they will be able to realize their perceptive and inspirational hopes for the future in the most powerful way possible—in the present.

On the dark side

Disrespectful, demanding, fussy

At your best

Responsible, thorough, constructive

350

5 September

the birthday of
the extraordinary mind

Your greatest challenge is

to give up self-sabotaging behavior

The way forward is ...

to start thinking about what triggers self-sabotaging habits and what you are gaining from them. Remind yourself that you are not your behavior and you can change these habits.

People born on September 5 are blessed with an extraordinary imagination, and the fantastic schemes and magical ideas they present to the world are always full of potential. Friends, family and co-workers are inspired by their innovative problem-solving skills, contagious wit, affectionate generosity and infectious enthusiasm.

Magnetic, fast-moving and fast-thinking, these people are fueled by their desire to realize their own individual dreams, which are not just for their own benefit but for the benefit of humanity. However, despite their genuine desire to help others, their righteous energy may fail to realistically assess their chances of success and thereby unintentionally sabotage their best plans and efforts. It is important for them to learn how to improve their judgment so that they minimize the chances of failure, as well as actively taking steps to reduce the number of mistakes they make. One way they can do this is to learn to distinguish between what is realistically attainable and what is fantasy. If they stay with reality and strive to make things better, not perfect, they are likely to succeed in most of what they put their minds to.

From an early age they may have been rather reclusive and solitary figures, but around the age of seventeen, and for the next thirty years, there is a turning point when they grow more socially orientated with a strong need to be popular and appreciated. Professional and personal relationships will also start to play a more important part in their lives, and these are the years when their extraordinarily creative potential is likely to come to the fore. If they can learn to harness that creativity so that it is grounded in reality rather than in unattainable fantasy, their potential for success, fulfillment and recognition is outstanding. Whatever age they are, however, these people are blessed with positive, expansive energy and magical sparkle and—if a bit of good judgment is added to the mix—they are likely to get most, if not all, of what they most desire.

On the dark side

Irresponsible, self-destructive, over the top

At your best

Energetic, creative, fun

6 September

the birthday of destiny

Your greatest challenge is

coping with the unforeseen

The way forward is ...

to understand that since there will always be aspects of your life out of your control, you should always allow room in your plans for the unexpected.

Despite their best efforts to plan and organize their lives, people born on September 6 seem destined to be confronted by the unexpected. Nothing ever seems to settle into a comfortable routine for them and, although this can make them feel anxious and fill them with self-doubt, deep down they would have it no other way.

After the age of sixteen until the age of forty-six these people will feel a strong need for partnership; after the age of forty-seven there is a turning point when the evaluation of their own personal power comes to the fore, and these are the years when they are likely to feel less anxious and more confident. The older they get, the more they are likely to believe that destiny plays a hand in shaping their lives, the situations in which they find themselves and the people they meet.

The upside of their belief in destiny is that they soon develop the ability to focus their creativity and intensity on the details of the present moment, which is the recipe for a happy life. They can also be incredibly supportive and appreciative not just of the present moment but of all the people in their lives, making those around them feel good about themselves. The downside is that not enough thought or energy is put into planning or preparing for what might lie ahead; they can forget that their thoughts, actions and behavior today also create their future.

With their energy focused on the present moment and their belief that no person, word, action, or situation is trivial or unimportant, these people are both compassionate and fatalistic. As long as they make sure that their tendency to think negatively does not attract misfortune, that their belief in destiny does not make them over-cautious and that their giving nature does not prevent them taking from others as well, they have the potential to become highly developed, expressive, progressive, and truly inspirational souls.

On the dark side

Self-doubting, passive, fatalistic

At your best

Sympathetic, committed, passionate

7 September

the birthday of
tenacity

Your greatest challenge is

showing yourself and others mercy

The way forward is ...

to understand that until you can learn to ease up on yourself and others, your successes will feel hollow because you cannot fully enjoy them.

People born on September 7 are blessed with remarkable tenacity. When they decide on a course of action, nothing can stand in their way. Their ambitious professional goals matter more than anything else; however many obstacles stand in their way they will not give up until they have achieved their objectives, even if this means making enemies along the way.

Although they can be ruthless in their determination to succeed they can also be fiercely loyal, protective and supportive to friends and family. Those close to them respect their determination to succeed, their passion for helping those less fortunate and their inner strength, but they may also be fearful of getting on the wrong side of them. Unfortunately, this means that friendships tend to linger at the first-base stage and they may find themselves with numerous acquaintances but few real friends.

Fortunately there are opportunities for them to rectify this situation, especially between the ages of fifteen and forty-five, when there is an emphasis on social life and relationships, both personal and professional, as well as a desire to develop their creative potential. They should take advantage of these opportunities by being a little more flexible in their relationships and approach to life, and by recognizing that professional success, however rewarding, will not give them the same fulfillment as positive relationships with others and themselves.

After the age of forty-six there is a turning point which encourages them to seek deeper meaning in their lives, placing the emphasis on personal transformation and finding inner harmony. If they can learn to work with this by looking within—rather than to work or other people—to find fulfillment, they will find the contentment for which they have always longed. They will also find that their tenacity, compassion for the underdog and courage in the face of adversity help them push the bounds of human knowledge and endeavor forward so that everyone, themselves included, can benefit.

On the dark side

Ruthless, inflexible, unforgiving

At your best

Determined, courageous, ambitious

8 September

the birthday of
complicated superiority

Your greatest challenge is

being yourself

The way forward is ...

to understand that you, like everyone else, are human— a mass of contradictions.

Most people born on September 8 have a very black-and-white view of the world. This makes it all the more surprising that, although others are quick to acknowledge their intellectual superiority, they often come across as complicated or enigmatic individuals. This is because instead of showing others their true selves, they will often take on the identity of the cause or group they're representing.

The fierce determination and conviction to set others on the right path, combined with their excellent communication skills, earns these people great respect from others, although this may not extend to affection. Problems—and occasionally bitter confrontation—can occur, however, when others do not agree with them. They are often so convinced of the superior merits of their position that they will often dismiss any conflicting viewpoint; this can not only gain them enemies but earn them a reputation for being narrow minded. It is crucial, therefore, for them to appreciate the negative effect their superior attitude can have on others, even those whose interests they are passionate about promoting.

Between the ages of fourteen and forty-five they will gradually become more aware of the importance of social relationships and their creative abilities will be enhanced. These years can be dynamic ones if they can learn to be a little less bossy and a little more sensitive toward others. After the age of forty-five there is a turning point when they are likely to become more self-aware; now the emphasis is on power, intensity and personal transformation. During these years, and indeed during any time in their lives, they are likely to have successfully assumed leadership positions or to have become an integral part of a leadership group.

Nothing is more important to their psychological growth during these years than their ability to show tolerance toward others, because although these advanced souls do often know what is best for others and for the world, other people and the world may not yet be ready to listen.

On the dark side

Difficult, unyielding, proud

At your best

Influential, progressive, committed

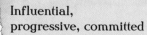

9 September

the birthday of
the missing link

Your greatest challenge is

to stop worrying

The way forward is ...

to understand that often your biggest worry is fear and the greatest antidote to fear is boldness. Whenever you act with boldness, you unlock your unused powers of creativity.

Although people born on September 9 have wonderfully inquisitive, original and sharp minds, they tend to come across as serious individuals with a strong sense of responsibility toward others. For reasons they themselves may not be able to understand, they often find themselves drawn to complicated and difficult situations. Part of the reason for this may be that they often feel as if something is missing from their lives, regardless of how successful, admired or settled they appear to be.

They may often have been searching for something to fulfill them—although they aren't sure exactly what—from an early age. As a result they are irresistibly drawn to people or situations that are challenging, complex or difficult. These people might not be the best for their personal development, and this incompatibility can cause them to become very anxious and insecure.

It is important for them to understand that the missing link they are seeking will never be found externally but by looking within and getting in touch with their spiritual needs. This may help them find a balance between their quest for excitement and the more meaningful aspects of life. Introspection may be a frightening prospect for them at first, and some may prefer to indulge in reckless or wild behavior rather than face it. But looking within is the only way for them to understand that the only person holding them back from their potential for success and fulfillment is themselves.

Between the ages of thirteen and forty-three there is an emphasis on socializing, partnership and relating to others, and these are the years when they are most likely to find themselves drawn toward complicated or destructive situations or relationships. After the age of forty-four there is a turning point that will highlight a growing emphasis on emotional and spiritual regeneration. This can spur them to new heights because, when driven by will, enthusiasm and self-belief, these people will not only find the missing link they have always been looking for, they will be able to achieve miracles.

On the dark side

Unfocused, reckless, anxious

At your best

Curious, responsible, committed

10 September

the birthday of
inspired responsibility

Your greatest challenge is

following your heart

The way forward is ...

to understand that your needs and wants are just as important and as fascinating as those of others.

People born on September 10 tend to have strong wills and opinions. Focused, thoughtful and concerned about the welfare of others, their ability to categorize and notice every detail means that the aura surrounding them is one of concerned but resourceful responsibility.

Gifted with versatility and inner strength, they know how to survive and use their strengths to help others become more positive and independent. They take responsibility seriously but a part of them also longs to be free; the challenge they face throughout their lives is balancing these two drives. Between the ages of twelve and forty-two the emphasis tends to be on other people, particularly their strong need to be appreciated and relied upon. They are likely to learn early in life the importance of diplomacy and of accepting other people's weaknesses. As a result, other people tend to rely on them for a sense of stability but it is important that they don't allow others to take advantage of them while they wait patiently in the wings. Key to their psychological growth during this period will be their ability to develop their own creativity and individuality.

After the age of forty-two there is a turning point when their personal power is likely to become enhanced and there are opportunities for them to become more self-reliant. It is important that they take advantage of these opportunities, as they have a tendency to put the needs and talents of others before their own. They need to learn that their own needs and talents are just as valuable.

In fact, throughout their lives the sooner these multi-talented and innovative, occasionally revolutionary thinkers discover a sense of self-worth, the better. This is because when they start to listen to their hearts as well as their heads, an aura of glamour will be added to the aura of stability and responsibility they already exude. This will mean that when they walk into a room other people will look up, take notice and want to hear every inspired word they say.

On the dark side

Passive, unfulfilled, uninspired

At your best

Capable, influential, responsible

11 September

Your greatest challenge is

to avoid becoming fixated on one issue

The way forward is ...

to understand that a balanced workload and approach is a far more effective, rewarding and healthy way to deal with life.

People born on September 11 think independently and clearly, and they will often shock or surprise others with their unconventional views. As well as being fiercely opinionated, they are also incredibly compassionate and their urge to help others may be so strong that it may take a radical form: either by passionately defending traditional views or by defiantly rebelling against them.

Whatever position they choose to defend, they will defend it passionately or take risks to prove their conviction. They can sometimes come across as extremely serious or critical, but behind this outward show of boldness and courage there is also a part of them that longs for stability or an authority figure to guide them. There may often be a silent battle or conflict going on within themselves that manifests itself in sudden mood swings of intense highs followed by intense lows.

Between the ages of eleven and forty-one there is an emphasis on relationships, and opportunities will be presented to explore their creativity. It is important that they take advantage of these because successful relationships will give them the sense of perspective they occasionally lack, and developing literary, artistic or creative interests will help them connect with their intuition, the key to their psychological growth. After the age of forty-two there is a turning point when they may undergo some kind of personal transformation, making them more self-reliant and in control.

If they can listen to their intuition rather than their conviction, become more tolerant and, most important of all, find a cause that is worthy of them, they will find that they no longer want to surprise or shock others with radical words and deeds. They want to realize their full potential and, by so doing, encourage others to do the same. In this way these determined and imaginative individuals will be making their own extraordinary mark on the world and fulfilling their destiny as the progressive revolutionaries or traditionalists of their age.

On the dark side

Judgmental, controlling, inflexible

At your best

Idealistic, imaginative, passionate

12 September

the birthday of the motivator

Your greatest challenge is

avoiding information overload

The way forward is ...

to understand that occasionally you need to take time out to be alone. Private time recharges your batteries and gives a sense of the bigger picture.

People born on September 12 have bags of charisma, energy and strong ideals. They are also blessed with a strong desire to share their knowledge with the less fortunate and to encourage others to be the best that they can be. Excellent motivators, these are the people others tend to look up to and admire.

Driven by a desire to motivate, serve and educate others, they can fight hard and long for a cause they believe in. They rarely lack courage and are unfailingly responsive to the needs of friends, family and those less fortunate than themselves. Others tend to look to them for encouragement and support, and if their leadership skills are not advanced they will align themselves with someone powerful. At some point in their lives, however, they need to determine whether their desire to encourage and boost others is rooted in a deep-seated need to control rather than inspire. If it is the former, they run the risk of becoming a dictator or being ruled by one; but if it is the latter, their potential to positively shape the thoughts and behavior of others is extraordinary.

Until the age of forty they may find that their energies are directed toward chasing popularity; as a result they may overload themselves with work and commitments. During these years they will learn a lot about their motivations through close relationships with others. After the age of forty, however, there is a powerful turning point that will highlight the importance for them of evaluating what their unique contribution to the world will be. These are the years when they are likely to be more discerning.

Whatever age they are, however, they should realize that listening to their inner voice and picking and choosing to whom and what they want to devote their considerable talents and energies is the secret of their success. Time to reflect gives them the ability to make a real and positive difference, not just to the lives of others, but to the world around them.

On the dark side

Unreliable, controlling, over-eager

At your best

Encouraging, optimistic, fearless

13 September

the birthday of
ardent concentration

Your greatest challenge is

opening up emotionally

The way forward is ...

to understand that emotions are not meant to be suppressed; they are meant to be listened to, accepted and managed.

People born on September 13 tend to dedicate themselves passionately to their work or the task in hand. Their powers of concentration are unrivalled and their determination awesome. In fact, many born on this day have the ability to confront and rise successfully above any challenge that life throws at them.

One of the reasons they are such strong individuals is their powerful self-belief. They care greatly about being true to themselves regardless of what the current trends may be, and although their straightforward, uncomplicated but highly idiosyncratic approach can win them many admirers, it can also make them the butt of many jokes. This isn't likely to worry them, however, because they know that sooner or later others will see that their methods were right.

Although they are very advanced when it comes to willpower and concentration, in affairs of the heart they may not be able to demonstrate the same level of commitment or passion. It is important for them to make sure they don't suppress their emotions because it is only when they have learned to acknowledge, accept and manage their emotions that they will be able to grow psychologically. If they are unable to face their emotions, they run the risk of becoming uncompromising, controlling and ruthless. For those with such potential for creativity and sensitivity, this would be a tragedy.

Fortunately, until the age of thirty-nine there will be opportunities for them to develop and learn from close personal relationships. After the age of forty there is a turning point which puts the emphasis firmly on seeking a deeper meaning to their life and placing more emphasis on the power of personal transformation. Whatever age they are the sooner they learn to listen to their heart as passionately as they do to their heads, the sooner they will be able to devote their considerable talents to a cause that is worthy of them, lead by example and dedicate themselves to making the world a much better place.

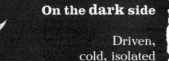

On the dark side

Driven, cold, isolated

At your best

Dedicated, intense, resilient

14 September

the birthday of
the problem solver

Your greatest challenge is

to learn tact

The way forward is ...

to put yourself in someone else's shoes and think how your opinions or behavior will impact them.

People born on September 14 are typically the first port of call when others want to find a solution or understand a situation better. Their critical abilities, creativity and problem-solving skills are exceptional and, because they are not afraid to rock the boat, uncover the underlying causes and tell it like it is, they have a reputation for being innovative and progressive thinkers.

Compromises or half-way solutions are not in their vocabulary and their goal is always to work for improvement. Although their ability to evaluate and suggest ways to improve can make them powerful agents of change and progress, it can also earn them a number of enemies because one skill they need to fine-tune is tact. They don't mean to offend other people; quite the opposite, as they often have the best interests of others at heart. It is just that they are so insightful, straightforward and direct that they don't understand that sometimes people aren't ready to hear the blunt, unadorned truth; they need it to be sugar coated or revealed subtly.

Until the age of thirty-eight there are numerous opportunities for them to become more diplomatic and tactful when relating to others, and to develop their creativity. They should take advantage of these opportunities because successful relationships with others and a flexible approach to situations and people will be the keys to their professional and personal success. After the age of thirty-nine there is a powerful turning point when they are likely to be more self-reliant. It is important at this stage that they understand the powerful influence their words and actions have on others. Listening to the silent voice of guidance in their head before they respond or react will help them interact productively and positively with others.

Whatever age they are, however, once these energetic and constructive individuals have found a cause that is worthy of them, they have the potential not just to turn things upside down but to make sure everyone—including themselves—flies high and lands the right side up.

On the dark side

Confrontational, tactless, controlling

At your best

Creative, influential, constructive

15 September

the birthday of
the specialist

Your greatest challenge is

to transcend materialism

The way forward is ...

to understand that money is not necessarily a guarantee of happiness or success. However much you possess, without a spiritual or loving center you will feel unsatisfied.

People born on September 15 put a lot of effort into succeeding. Whatever line of work they choose to devote their considerable energies to, the chances are they will specialize in it, and their ability to master their chosen skill sets them apart.

Other people tend to admire these people for their technical skills and for their depth of knowledge about their chosen field of interest. Such is their devotion to their work that they can appear solitary figures; even though friends may not be high on their list of priorities, loved ones and family certainly are. The potential for people born on this day to excel professionally is outstanding, but the key to their success will lie not in their determination or technical skills but in their ability to wait for the right opportunity to present itself. If they jump before they have fine-tuned their skills or achieved mastery, they may find that their ambition has robbed them of success; but if they bide their time, slowly building up their store of experience and knowledge, they will reach the heights for which they seem destined.

There is no denying that these people like money, and lots of it. They also tend to equate status with financial reward, which can be damaging to their creativity and their integrity, so it is important for them to resist the urge to compromise or take short cuts to the top. Until the age of thirty-seven there are opportunities for them to develop the close personal relationships they need to give them a sense of perspective. After the age of thirty-eight there is a turning point which highlights a growing emphasis on emotional and spiritual regeneration, as well as joint finances or corporate business activity.

If they have learned by then to get a grip on their ambition and materialism, these are the years when they can really come into their own and step into the role for which they seem destined—that of the respected and, in some cases, world-renowned specialist.

On the dark side

Materialistic, selfish, self-indulgent

At your best

Detailed, motivated, ambitious

16 September

the birthday of

vitality

Your greatest challenge is

getting others on your side

The way forward is ...

to understand that the way to get others on your side is to emphasize what they can gain by offering their support.

People born on September 16 are passionate and enthusiastic individuals whose infectious joie de vivre enchants all those with whom they come into contact. Although they are lively and passionate, this does not mean they are also impulsive and impatient individuals; quite the opposite, they also have the discipline and patience to focus their outstanding energy on a particular skill or project.

These people are motivated by a desire to learn, master and then go beyond what has already been achieved. They are typically passionate about what they do and keen to recruit others to their cause. In addition, they can be courageous risk-takers not afraid to stand up for what they believe in or to fight their corner. Occasionally their passionate nature can lead to rebelliousness and they rarely respond well to any form of authority; a character trait which will have been noticed from childhood. Above all, though, they are bursting with vitality and energy, thriving on competition and challenge. Fiercely independent, they may find it hard to work with a group of people but in time they do learn the art of compromise and that giving their opinion gently yields far better results for them than their previous blunt, unsparing or attention-grabbing way.

Until the age of thirty-six they will find that relationships play an important part in their lives. They may also want to be popular and appreciated, but this may prove elusive until they learn to control their impulsive candor. From the age of thirty-seven there is an important turning point when their need for self-reliance is enhanced and the emphasis is on personal transformation.

It is extremely important for them to take advantage of any opportunities life offers them to become more in control of their energy, because once they learn to aim their passion in the right direction these big-hearted individuals will not only make a name for themselves, they will find true happiness by passing on their inspiration and happiness to others.

On the dark side

Rebellious, difficult, impulsive

At your best

Energetic, enthusiastic, warm hearted

17 September

Your greatest challenge is

being spontaneous

The way forward is ...

to understand that sometimes thinking gets in the way of living.

People born on September 17 are strong, tough and determined individuals with a clear sense of right and wrong. They possess a heroic spirit, stamina, courage and no fear of hard work. In fact they can easily take on tasks that make others cringe and perform them with little effort.

Control is important for people born on this day, and in anything they do their steady discipline and commitment to the smallest detail shine through. They can be imaginative but their preference is to organize their approach and their thinking logically; the facts, justice, fair play, tradition and maintaining the status quo matter greatly to them. There is a fun side to them but it takes a lot to reveal it spontaneously; the downside of this is that they can come across as serious and heavy, but the upside is that when they do open up, others can be assured of their absolute sincerity.

Until the age of thirty-five there are opportunities for them to develop the more creative side of their personality, forging relationships with others both professionally and socially. They should take advantage of these opportunities to be less self-contained and more expressive, as they offer tremendous potential for happiness. After the age of thirty-six there is a turning point which stimulates them to seek a deeper meaning to their life and emphasizes the power of personal transformation.

Whatever age they are, they often do well financially in life, and enjoying a good standard of living is one of their first priorities. They will probably achieve their material goals, but to reach their full potential they should ensure they don't neglect their spiritual and emotional life; money alone will not completely satisfy them. Above all they are determined people, so when they do realize the true value of things money can't buy, their steady and resilient star won't just light their own path. It will inspire others to take a more disciplined, responsible, compassionate and honest approach to work and to life.

On the dark side

Controlling, workaholic, heavy

At your best

Persistent, fair, resilient

18 September

the birthday of
elusive devotion

Your greatest challenge is

dealing with conflict

The way forward is ...

to be assertive without being aggressive. Assertiveness skills, such as standing up for yourself, can be learned.

There is something quite feline about people born on September 18; like a cat, they can be devoted and available one moment, independent and elusive the next. Although they can be sociable and are often extremely attractive individuals, few will get to know them very well; even getting close to them is no guarantee that they will commit in any way.

So strong is their need for absolute freedom that these people will often change their minds or hearts at the last moment, leaving those around them feeling confused. Although this unpredictability adds to the attractive air of mystery they create around themselves, part of the reason they tend to vanish or isolate themselves from time to time is that they tend to have a low stress threshold, feeling that the best way for them to deal with conflict is to withdraw and reflect in private. Problems, however, arise when the need to withdraw and regroup becomes a need to hide or escape; they need to learn that conflict, although unpleasant, is essential for their psychological growth.

Until the age of thirty-four they will be presented with many opportunities to develop their friendly and sociable side, and they should take advantage of these, because left to their own devices they run the risk of being over-serious in their approach to life. After the age of thirty-five there is a turning point that brings an emphasis on their deep emotional need for change, intensity and personal power. During these years their powers of concentration are likely to be exceptional, and when they find a cause that is worthy of them their absolute devotion to it will attract incredible success and fulfillment their way.

Throughout their lives, however, as long as they make sure that they don't become so devoted or absorbed in their work or thoughts that they lose a sense of direction or their own identity, these highly advanced and unusual individuals will find their own unique way to contribute new knowledge and insight to the world.

On the dark side

Unpredictable, aloof, negative

At your best

Disciplined, profound, devoted

19 September

the birthday of
the immaculate presentation

Your greatest challenge is

seeing beyond the material

The way forward is ...

to accept that, however frustrating, true beauty, true meaning and true fulfillment can only be found in things that are intangible.

People born on September 19 have their own unique style and a great awareness of the way they present themselves to the world. More often than not their appearance will be immaculate and elegant, but even if they appear casual or sloppy they will have spent time considering how their appearance will affect others. They believe that the world is a stage and that we are all players, but this doesn't make them cynical. Quite the opposite; they relish any opportunity to perform or play a role.

Spending an excessive amount of time worrying about their appearance, a running theme throughout their lives will be a wish to change something about their body or personal style. Other people may find this preoccupation with outward show frustrating and superficial, but many of these people do understand that inner beauty is just as important as outer beauty. They have the balanced perspective they need to attract success and find fulfillment. Unfortunately, there are a few people born on this day who run the risk of losing themselves in a world of superficiality.

Until the age of thirty-two there is an emphasis on relationships and socializing; during these years they need to make sure that they don't forget who and what really matters to them. After the age of thirty-three there is a significant turning point when issues concerning their sense of personal power become more prominent, and there may be an accent on transformation. During these years they will be presented with opportunities to give their lives more meaningful depth and, in addition to connecting with their intuition, the key to their psychological growth will be testing themselves out in a variety of different situations.

Overcoming personal and professional challenges will give them the confidence they need to step into the one role they have always been destined to play, but perhaps didn't realize it. This is the role of the profound, resilient and refined sage sought out by others for advice and inspiration.

On the dark side

Superficial, changeable, materialistic

At your best

Wise, experienced, resilient

20 September

the birthday of
the charming controller

Your greatest challenge is

learning to look before you leap

The way forward is ...

to understand that calculated, not impulsive, risk-taking is the key to success. You need to weigh up the pros and cons before you leap in.

People born on September 20 are often blessed with great charm, their outgoing personality tending to attract those in need of guidance. They are natural leaders and are at their happiest when guiding or controlling individuals or a group in a well-thought-out project.

The organizational skills of these people are often in great demand but because they can have problems saying "no" they may sometimes take on more than they can cope with. They are independent and resourceful, and like to pride themselves on being able to seek the best way to manage a situation. More often than not they are the most capable person on hand, but there will be times when even their best efforts don't succeed. How they cope with these setbacks or "failures" is the key to their psychological growth. If they can learn from their mistakes and move forward with increased awareness, their potential for success both personally and professionally is outstanding; but if they go on repeating the same mistakes or refuse to acknowledge where their words or actions may have been at fault, they will block their progress.

Until the age of thirty-one they will often feel a need to be popular and admired. They will stand a better chance of winning friends and allies if they don't overpower others with their opinions. After the age of thirty-two there is a turning point when their sense of personal power will increase and opportunities will be presented to them to become more self-reliant. During these years nothing will be more important for them than their ability to learn the art of caution and patience; this is because they have a tendency to leap before they look.

Although they should never lose their energetic and passionate spirit, their chances of happiness and fulfillment will increase once they have learned that the best way they can make their innovative and significant contribution to the world is to advise, organize and inspire not just others but themselves.

On the dark side

Condescending, controlling, superficial

At your best

Organized, practical, intelligent

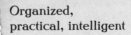

21 September

the birthday of
the sensation seeker

Your greatest challenge is

finding your own sense of direction

The way forward is ...

to understand that organizations or people can't give you a sense of purpose; the only way is to find out who you are.

People born on September 21 are fascinated by all things unusual, unexpected, erratic and, on occasion, dark. They have the wonderful ability to inject an air of mystery and suspense into even the most mundane of occasions.

Because they are hungry to learn or experience the unusual or complex, these people may be drawn to explore novel or bizarre subjects that those with less imagination would avoid. Highly sensual, they often feel compelled to seek out new sensations and to share their discoveries or viewpoints with others. Their messages are often profound but frequently misunderstood, and this can make them feel lonely and frustrated. Part of the reason others are sometimes unconvinced by their approach or theories is that they tend to lose themselves in their current obsession, leaving others with no sense of who they are and what they really believe in. It is therefore extremely important for them to try to stay true to their principles and keep a sense of personal identity.

Until the age of thirty-one they tend to gain much of their self-esteem and respect from their relationships with others, and they therefore need to learn to trust their own judgment. They also need to ensure that their sensation-seeking impulses do not lead them astray into a murky underworld of disreputable danger and strangeness. After the age of thirty-two there is an important turning point in their lives when there will be opportunities for them to feel more in control of their life. It is vital for their psychological growth that they take advantage of these opportunities to move from the passenger seat to the driving seat of their lives.

This is because once they are able to discover within themselves the mystery, wonder, sensation and excitement that so enthralls them in the world around them, their attraction to the unconventional, new and different gives them the potential to become progressive and inspired instruments of human advancement.

On the dark side

Sensationalist, unaware, unfocused

At your best

Curious, progressive, interesting

367

22 September

the birthday of
the master builder

Your greatest challenge is

learning to relax

The way forward is ...

to understand that downtime is not time wasted but time gained because you give yourself an opportunity not just to rest but also to recharge.

People born on September 22 tend to be multi-talented, hardworking and intelligent individuals with excellent communication skills and their own slightly eccentric but wonderfully endearing personal style. They are at their happiest and their best when they are creating or building, and such is their love of challenge that no sooner have they completed one project than they will jump to the next and then the next and so on, without a hint of a pause in between.

From an early age these people may have felt that they were here for a reason, and this explains their restless urge to constantly challenge themselves and make their mark on the world around them. Whatever it is that they feel called to do, they will follow their vision no matter how disruptive or difficult.

They may sometimes find that their ideals of fairness and equality and their superior intelligence clash with those in authority over them; this is potentially dangerous for them as enemies are not conducive to professional or personal success. Learning to compromise and play the game when necessary will be difficult for them but it will make their transition to success smoother.

Until they reach the age of thirty, relationships for these people are likely to be important, as will the need for harmonious surroundings in both private and professional spheres. Establishing a work–life balance so that they have enough time to spend on themselves and their friendships will be important during these years. After the age of thirty there is a turning point when they start to become more emotionally self-reliant and in control. If they can learn to be more flexible in their thinking, these are the years when they are likely to come into their own. This is because once they have learned to balance their restlessness with plenty of quality time out to recharge and connect with their intuition, amazing opportunities to build a career and a life of great and unique creativity will come their way.

On the dark side

Workaholic, stubborn, isolated

At your best

Progressive, hardworking, individual

LIBRA

THE SCALES
(SEPTEMBER 23 – OCTOBER 22)

* ❋ **Element:** Air
* ❋ **Ruling planet:** Venus, the lover
* ❋ **Symbol:** The Scales
* ❋ **Tarot card:** Justice (discernment)
* ❋ **Number:** 6
* ❋ **Favorable colors:** Green, purple, pink
* ❋ **Key phrase:** There are decisions to be made

Peace and harmony are right at the top of the list of priorities for a Libran. They strive to create harmony in the world around them and will sometimes make great personal sacrifices to achieve it. They have the amazing ability to see every side of an argument, and their open-mindedness and appreciation of beauty will win them much respect. However, when forced to make a decision the chances are they will sit on the fence until the problem goes away by itself, rather than commit themselves to one side or the other.

Personality potential

Charming, co-operative, sociable, idealistic and brilliantly diplomatic, whether they are conventionally attractive or not Librans will often have an air of grace and beauty about them. In arguments they won't typically confront others; their preference is always to play peacemaker or negotiator. They have a deep dislike of hurting other people, and this compassionate side of their personality may make some people think of them as a pushover. This couldn't be further from the truth. They may adapt, adjust and compromise to keep the peace but underneath their character is tough. If you push them too far they will slowly but surely fade out of your life; their withdrawal will be so cleverly subtle that you will barely notice it until it's too late to reel them back in again.

The Libran unwillingness to get off the fence is not because they don't have a point of view or because they can't argue that point of view, but because they have too much dignity and maturity to ram their viewpoint down everybody else's throats. They truly believe that negotiation is the answer and that it's always possible to find a compromise between opposing viewpoints so that both sides feel satisfied. Small wonder they make great solicitors, negotiators and mediators or flourish in any line of work in which their role is to keep the balance or maintain the status quo. Their powers of mediation and negotiation are beyond compare. Tactful and diplomatic, they can smooth everything down to find a middle ground.

Librans are often blessed with impeccable good taste, possessing the ability to create harmony and bring beauty to any surroundings. They like to see everything beautiful and everyone happy, and will often cast themselves in the role of matchmaker.

Above all, Librans strive for balance in all things and, since much of the secret of success and happiness in life is through moderation, Librans not only have a knack for making life look easy; they also have a knack for attracting success and happiness their way.

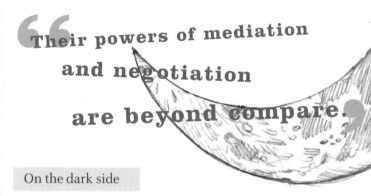

"Their powers of mediation and negotiation are beyond compare."

On the dark side

It really is one of the hardest things in the world for a Libran to make a decision or decide where they stand regarding a particular debate or situation. And it's not just the big decisions that Librans struggle with—it's any decision. Afraid of limiting their options, their mind keeps changing this way and that, resulting in indecisiveness. What they don't realize is that by not making their mind up they actually lose opportunities and limit their choices.

Librans are at their happiest and their best when in a close, loving relationship; but if this is denied to them they will suffer more than any other sign of the zodiac. Dependency is another issue for them because their need to be in a relationship can sometimes be so strong that they will make too many compromises. Complete happiness for them means sharing their lives, but until they can learn to be happy and fulfilled by their own company, the completeness they seek in a relationship will remain elusive.

Laziness and self-indulgence are two negative character traits associated with this sign; the more they refuse to step out of their comfort zone and take a risk by making a decision, the more they are likely to slip into laziness. For such a peace-loving sign it's surprising that they can sometimes be rather selfish and self-absorbed and, if need be, lie and cheat to get what they want.

Symbol

Libra is the only sign in the zodiac that has a symbol which is an inanimate object. This isn't to say that Librans are emotionally cold but they do have a remarkable ability to cast aside their own feelings, see every side of the argument and strive for balance in all things—hence the symbol of the scales. The scales represent justice in life and the Libran journey is a constant search for peace, balance and harmony not just for themselves, but for everyone.

Darkest secret

They may often look calm and collected as if they are able to cope with just about anything, but the Achilles' heel of any Libran is their fear of being abandoned and alone. They will therefore often rely on the approval of others for a sense of self-worth. Intelligent and gullible, easygoing and petulant, cautious and reckless, like the scales that are their symbol Librans will tip their behavior one way and then another to get the attention, approval and the companionship they crave.

Love

Librans rarely have problems attracting partners or friends and are usually surrounded by admirers. Generous by nature, they love to share and are also excellent listeners. Their talent for friendship means that they often have friends from all walks of life but, as generous and warm-hearted as they are, they do lack one thing—a sense of humor.

When it comes to affairs of the heart, Librans only feel truly fulfilled when they are in a rewarding relationship. Their usual indecision does not express itself fully in relationships; they can be impulsive and romantic, and they are capable of being decisive about who they want to welcome into their life. Curiously, in a close relationship they may also be quick to provoke arguments, which is surprising given their peace-loving nature. All this is designed to test their partner's affections, and it's a dangerous strategy that sometimes backfires.

Love matches: Aries, Leo and Sagittarius

The Libran man

A Libran man can give advice and answers for just about everything. His logical, intelligent arguments never fail to impress, and his charm and his smile are irresistible. On the face of it this man seems perfect but there will also be times

when his Libran scales tip back and forward and he starts to contradict himself. Making up his mind is tough for him and, even when he does appear to make a decision, he may change it immediately for fear of making a mistake. All this can drive his friends and loved ones to distraction, but such is his power that when they try to confront him with his inconsistencies he melts them with his genuine regret and beautiful words.

When it comes to romance the Libran man is the king of all the signs of the zodiac. He could write books about the art of romance and the art of seduction. He'll use his casual charm and intelligent charisma to win over even the most resistant of potential partners. Then, when he has won them over, he may not be sure what to do and there may be a lengthy engagement period during which he weighs up his options. When he finally decides to take the leap he will be a devoted, passionate and charming partner; but since the art of romance comes so easily to him he will always remain a flirt. His partner will just have to learn to live with this, as asking a Libran man not to flirt is like telling him not to breathe—even if he is happily married he will always be a speculator.

Friendship and love can often get extremely confused for Libran men. They will often have many friends of the opposite sex because they are so good at understanding what women think and feel. Fortunately, the Libran male loves harmony so he is unlikely to stray if his current relationship gives him what he needs—intelligent conversation and companionship, and plenty of physical affection.

The Libran woman

The typical Libra woman—if there is such a creature, as she is so multifaceted—is dainty, fragrant smelling and seductive. She often loves luxurious clothes and perfumes, and in many cases will be very aware of her good looks. But with all her femininity and sweet grace there is plenty of the masculine about her. Like an iron fist in a velvet glove, you're unlikely to see the tougher side of her personality when you first get to know her; but in time it will be impossible for her to hide forever her sharp mind and self-sufficient spirit. This woman is in fact one of the most capable women of the zodiac. She can cope with just about anything and is more than a match for any man or woman.

Above all, the Libran woman is fair and her commitment to finding a solution that works for everyone makes her invaluable in family discussions or during times of crisis. In fact,

she'll come into her own during family emergencies or crises and she'll be the one who keeps everything afloat. When there are disagreements she will never believe that her opinion is the correct or only one—she has too much respect for the opinions of others. Although living alone doesn't suit her, when she is in a relationship she will not slip into a dependent role and will contribute more than her fair share both emotionally and financially. As tough as steel but as soft as velvet, on the outside the Libran woman is a hard act to follow. She's an amazing combination of sweetness and strength and, whenever she walks into a person's life or heart, the chances are high that they won't ever want her to leave.

Family

Libran babies and children are often easy on the eye and easy to please. Everyone finds them charming and loveable, but parents should keep their eyes open for any tendency toward laziness and procrastination because this will hold them back later in life. The greatest thing a parent can do with a Libran child is encourage them to be decisive and, when faced with a decision, to make their mind up. They should also help them understand that if the wrong decision is made it's not a tragedy or a character flaw but a learning experience. No mistake is ever a mistake if you learn from it. Above all, Librans need to find the confidence to think and make decisions for themselves.

Librans tend to enjoy their schooldays as long as they feel they are being fairly treated by their teachers and their friends. Logical and analytical, they may lean toward mathematics and science. They also have real creative and artistic potential and encouraging this early in life will help them trust and believe in it later in life. Parents need to be especially careful that their Libran child does not try to talk them into spoiling them. Firm boundaries need to be set down because when a Libran child knows what they can or cannot do arguments are less likely— and Librans get very upset by arguments of any kind.

Libran parents are gentle and loving but their tendency to dither over important decisions for their child's upbringing— for example choice of school—may be detrimental. In addition their tendency to dither over less important decisions, such as the supper menu, can infuriate their child. They also need to make sure they don't settle for the easiest option and the path of least resistance when parenting. Tough love won't come easy to them but sometimes tough love is an essential ingredient for good parenting.

Career

Librans love to be surrounded by luxury and comfort so they will often go after careers which give them the kind of money that can finance a luxurious lifestyle. Any profession that calls for diplomacy and tact will suit them, and the fashion and cosmetics industry will also appeal. They are ambitious and hate being ordered about, so they often aspire to be in charge or to run their own businesses. They may not, however, be suited to top jobs where they have to work in isolation as they work better when surrounded by a team of people. Other occupations

They are ambitious and hate being ordered about...

that may suit them include the legal professions, diplomacy, management consultancy, civil rights campaigning, banking, veterinary science, therapy or any kind of partnership. The Libran love of aesthetics may also point toward a career in interior design or a career as a graphic artist, image consultant, personal shopping assistant, art dealer or anything involving music.

The Libran manager or boss tends to have a reputation for being approachable and fair because they are likely to consider all opinions before making a decision. They will also create a restful, harmonious working environment for their staff. The Libran employee will often be honest, hardworking and a superb team player.

Health and leisure

Librans are ruled by the planet Venus and this gives them a taste for the good things in life. They especially like rich, sweet food, but this urge should be resisted as they have a tendency toward weight gain if they overindulge. They would feel much fitter, healthier and lighter on a healthy, balanced diet rich in simple, nutritious foods, such as whole grains, fruits and vegetables. They would also benefit from cooking their food from scratch and from chewing their food slowly to boost their digestive health. The kidneys are linked to the sign Libra and, to ensure these organs of detoxification are running efficiently, plenty of fiber is advised to prevent constipation and bloating. The classic Libran indecisiveness can make them prone to tension headaches and migraines, so learning to relax and unwind—and how to make decisions—is crucial for their health and well-being. Quiet time spent alone will help them get in touch with their feelings and figure out where they think their life should be heading, but if these headaches and other symptoms of stress persist they should visit their doctor.

Looking good matters a great deal to people born under this sun sign, and if they drink and smoke they need to question why they indulge in activities that damage their health as well as their looks. Although they may have exercised when they were at school, once they leave school or college they may ease up or completely give up on physical activity. When this sedentary lifestyle is coupled with their love of food and wine it can lead to weight gain, especially around the waist. It's extremely important therefore for them to increase their activity levels to help them lose weight and reduce the increased risk of heart disease and diabetes associated with weight gain

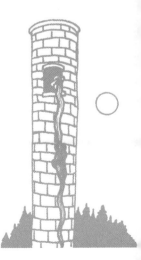

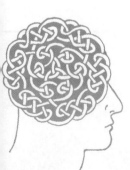

around the middle. Regular exercise is important, especially long walks in the fresh air where they can organize their thoughts.

Retirement can be a challenge for most Librans as the working life is so rewarding for them. It's therefore vital for them to ensure they have plenty of hobbies and interests outside work so that they aren't completely defined by their job. Learning techniques taught by cognitive therapy will help them challenge any tendency toward negative thinking. Yellow is the color of optimism and self-confidence, and meditating on it will encourage them to have more faith in their own decisions.

Born between September 23 and October 3

Librans born between these dates have all the sensuous qualities of Venus enriching their lives. They tend to be beautiful, artistic, caring and full of generosity and warmth. They are never short of admirers, although they sometimes may have too many.

Born between October 4 and October 13

There is a touch of the loveable eccentric about these Librans. They are spontaneous and fun, and anyone who knows them needs to expect the unexpected from them.

Born between October 14 and October 22

These people have a sprightly and youthful approach to life, and are forever on the hunt for new knowledge and information. Their inquisitive minds make them the eternal students of the zodiac and they never tire of learning something they didn't know before.

Life lessons

Librans are quick to grasp ideas and possess an innate creativity that yearns to express itself in producing works of art or unusual or original things. Unfortunately, their indecisiveness can limit the expression of this creativity so it's important that they try to incorporate their creativity into their lives because if they do they will be richly rewarded.

Justice and equality are among a Libran's greatest concerns, but partnerships and friendships matter more to them. This makes them delightful hosts—as well as social butterflies—and they are rarely without a lover; but it can also make being on their own extremely hard for them, even if it's only for one evening. This stands as one of the greatest challenges in their lives. To find true happiness and fulfillment they need to learn to stop looking to other people for completeness. Although Librans are right in assuming that companionship and team efforts are incredibly rewarding, they are wrong in assuming that time spent alone is time wasted or that if their efforts are not being acknowledged and praised by others they are not worth doing. Librans first of all need to learn to be happy alone and after that they should learn that they don't actually have to rely on the support of others—they are complete as themselves. Furthermore, the approval of others is fickle and not to be relied on. At the end of the day, the only person they can really count on is themselves.

Indecisiveness and a relaxed relationship with the truth are other areas Librans need to work on. They have a tendency to bend and twist to suit the opinions or needs of others, and will sometimes resort to manipulation just to keep things running smoothly. In the end, this always backfires on them and the balance they were trying so hard to achieve is upset. If only Libra would learn that it's impossible to make everyone happy all of the time and be liked by everyone. Sometimes it's important to take a stand.

Libra can look to other signs of the zodiac for help and inspiration. Arians can teach them to be bolder and more courageous with their decision making and to place less importance on the opinions of others. Cancerians and Scorpios can encourage them to notice and listen to their feelings, even when these feelings are dark and uncomfortable. And Leos can encourage them not to be afraid of striking out alone but to enjoy the challenge and rewards that going solo offers.

23 September

the birthday of
the unassuming warrior

Your greatest challenge is

communicating the strength of your convictions

The way forward is ...

to understand that abandoning your personal beliefs if they might create conflict is counterproductive because it causes conflict within you.

People born on September 23 tend to be charming but unassuming individuals with an appreciation of beauty, and a great deal of personal integrity and reliability. Behind all this, however, is a character of steely determination. They may appear gentle on the outside but from early in life they will have faced a series of challenges, setbacks and conflicts, most of which they have overcome and gained spiritual strength from.

Many of these people will be unaware of just how evolved, inspirational and creative they really are; as a result they may underplay their talents. For example, because they are often people of few words, others may step in to speak their part and take the credit; because they treat everyone with generosity and loyalty, they can become a target for those who are manipulative or simply lazy.

Most of the time, they approach daily life with pure, almost childlike pleasure, and if something or someone captivates their attention, their enthusiasm and zeal can become infectious. However, there will also be times when they don't feel that enthusiasm and run the risk of slipping into despondency or, in extreme cases, depression. This is because they are such honest people that they find it hard to pretend an interest. The key to their happiness, therefore, is to find a vocation, lifestyle or relationship that inspires and fulfills them.

Before the age of thirty they are likely to be concerned with relationship issues, but after the age of thirty there is a turning point that highlights a growing emphasis on deep emotional change. They may also be involved in joint finances or dealing with other people's money. After the age of sixty they may become more freedom loving and adventurous. Whatever age they are, however, once they figure out what works for them and what stops them moving forward, they have the inquisitive minds, the creativity and, above all, the fighting spirit to realize their cherished dreams and command not just the attention but the respect of all those with whom they come into contact.

On the dark side

Unassertive, unmotivated, addicted

At your best

Charming, honest, passionate

24 September

Your greatest challenge is

staying in one place for long enough

The way forward is ...

to understand that however many times you move or change direction you take the same personality with you.

People born on September 24 tend to be hard to catch or pin down because they are nomads at heart. If their restlessness doesn't manifest externally in a love of travel or movement, they will be travelers in their minds, constantly reading, thinking and jumping to original conclusions.

Their desire to seek out the new will be a dominant theme in their lives, alongside their powerful desire to love and to be loved. Although they will naturally express themselves in different ways, they often tend to be orientated by an urge to discover and an urge to help others with their resourceful and creative efforts. Considerate and empathetic, they have the almost psychic ability to detect unhappiness in others, even if that unhappiness is unspoken, and this is followed up by a desire to relieve feelings of distress.

Despite their concern for the well-being of others, they also find it hard to commit to a settled existence. A part of them longs to feel secure but another part of them is always wondering whether the grass really is greener on the other side. As a result they vacillate a great deal. The key to their psychological growth will be when they are able not just to choose goals that inspire them, but to stick to them.

Before the age of twenty-eight they are likely to experiment in their social life, forming friendships and relationships with people from a wide variety of different backgrounds. There may also be numerous career changes or a spell of professional uncertainty. After the age of twenty-nine there is a turning point which highlights issues concerning emotional change, creating a desire to find deeper meaning to their lives. This is an extremely powerful and positive influence for them, because once they learn that discipline, perseverance and commitment can be liberating rather than restrictive, these versatile, progressive, humanitarian and multi-talented people will discover within themselves the potential for tremendous power, which can both move and inspire others.

On the dark side

Unsettled, detached, unfocused

At your best

Concerned, giving, creative

383

25 September

the birthday of
complexity

Your
greatest
challenge is

overcoming your
cynicism

*The way
forward is ...*

to understand that
the cynic's view of
the world is just as
unrealistic as the
optimist's; try to
strike a happy
medium between
the two.

People born on September 25 are among the most complex individuals of the year. On the one hand they are extremely empathetic and can easily identify with others, but on the other they are fiercely independent and critical of what they see going on around them, being keen to set themselves apart from others.

One of the reasons they are often so complex is that they have a fairly black-and-white view of the world, but a part of them longs to live in a world of color. They tend to achieve great success in life, but more often than not this is because they work hard for it and they expect others to do the same. They can therefore become openly resentful of those who seem to attain success without putting in as much effort as they believe is necessary. It is important for them to learn to manage this tendency to criticize or judge because their words can wound others deeply.

Until the age of twenty-seven people born on this day are likely to be concerned with developing their social skills, creative talents and opportunities for material or financial success. After the age of twenty-eight there is a powerful turning point that emphasizes a growing need for personal transformation, change and power. After the age of fifty-eight there is another turning point, which indicates that they are likely to become more adventurous and freedom loving.

Whatever age they are, behind their soberness these people possess an amazing imagination, dynamic creativity and ability to shine or stand out in the crowd, because other people are always drawn toward complexity. The key to their psychological growth is to embrace and acknowledge their wonderful complexity. This is because when they learn to trust their intuition, think universally and acknowledge that life can never be explained in black and white, they have the potential to be not just the most complex but the most progressive, visionary and truly inspired individuals of the year.

On the dark side

Negative,
hurtful, resentful

At your best

Interesting,
caring, progressive

26 September

the birthday of
the perfection seeker

Your greatest challenge is

coping when mistakes are made

The way forward is ...

to understand that sometimes mistakes are important, even necessary, because they point you in a different, sometimes better direction.

Tenacity is the first name of people born on September 26 and discipline the second, but their last name is perfectionist. They demand nothing short of excellence from themselves and others, and simply cannot understand those with less drive.

The careers of these goal-orientated people are of supreme importance to them and, as a result, they often take on far too much. They possess, nevertheless, the ability to thrive under pressure and to inspire the admiration of others when they achieve what seemed to have been impossible. Not surprisingly, with such inspired ambition, determination, self-discipline and focus, their career potential is of the highest order and more often than not they can and do rise to the very top. The downside is that their absorption in their work can become obsessive and compulsive; this is damaging to their psychological growth because it makes them ignore not only their own emotional needs, but those of their loved ones.

Before the age of twenty-six they are likely to be concerned with issues regarding money, but there will also be opportunities for them to develop strong relationships with others. They should take advantage of these opportunities because the support and company of others will help them keep a much-needed sense of perspective. After the age of twenty-seven the focus shifts to emotional change and intensity, and these are the years when they are most likely to become devoted or committed to their careers. During these years their potential for success is outstanding but for their psychological growth they need to make sure they take regular time out to ensure they nurture their relationships and find time for outside interests.

These people will always be driven, focused and occasionally bossy, but once they are able to moderate their obsession with work their tenacity and superior powers of concentration will yield results that can not only benefit others considerably but are also the subject of awed, if somewhat bemused, admiration.

On the dark side

Compulsive, workaholic, controlling

At your best

Disciplined, driven, influential

27 September

the birthday of
the paradox

Your greatest challenge is

being true to yourself

The way forward is ...

to understand that until you are true to who you are, life will forever feel confusing and overwhelming.

Although people born on September 27 often fail to recognize it, they have the ability to make a lasting and positive impression on all those they meet. This is because they are extremely versatile and sensitive to the feelings of others, and like nothing better than to bring harmony to any situation. Paradoxically, however, underneath their sociable and relatively normal persona they may often be riddled with doubts, insecurities, contradictions and hidden fears. Learning to develop faith in their abilities, which are considerable, is crucial to their success and happiness in life.

These people are far deeper and complex than anyone, themselves included, realizes. This may be due to the fact that they set very high standards for themselves—failure simply isn't an option for them—but also because professional success tends to take priority in their lives over fulfillment. As a result they may find themselves mixing with groups of people or working in careers that are wholly unsuitable for them, although few would notice their discomfort. Until they get in touch with their feelings and find a path in life that is fulfilling, nagging feelings of depression and despondency will haunt them.

Before the age of twenty-six people born on this day are likely to be preoccupied with fine-tuning their people skills and carving themselves opportunities for career success. After the age of twenty-seven there is a shift in emphasis when issues concerning emotional change and transformation come to the fore; these are the years when they need to be alert to the way that their choice of career shapes their character.

As long as people born on this day believe that professional or material success is the only option, happiness and fulfillment will be elusive. However, once they understand that their hidden feelings and insecurities are not their enemies but their teachers trying to lead them to a fuller awareness of their potential, there is nothing these determined, driven, multi-talented and vigorous individuals cannot achieve, if they set their inquisitive and highly creative minds to it.

On the dark side

Conflicted, insecure, frustrated

At your best

Charismatic, ambitious, successful

28 September

the birthday of

the seducer

Your greatest challenge is

to tolerate boredom

The way forward is ...

to understand that boredom is not necessarily something you should try to avoid; your need for constant stimulation may be holding back your personal development.

Other people are often drawn to the magnetic and highly seductive people born on September 28. Whether they are attractive or not, they have the ability to wrap almost anyone they want around their little finger.

Many of them seek and find personal fulfillment through affairs of the heart, indulgence of the senses and the pursuit of beauty in all its forms. They are also highly imaginative and sensitive, with a strong desire to bring harmony and beauty to the world. However, they run the risk of believing that their ability to seduce others with their interesting and enlivening aura is enough to bring good fortune their way. They should understand that although charm will get them far, if they want to go all the way they need discipline, insight and hard work.

Until the age of twenty-four they are likely to be concerned with issues regarding relationships, but after the age of twenty-five there is an important turning point that emphasizes a need for emotional change, personal power and transformation in their lives. How they respond to the opportunities life presents them to back up their charm with substance will determine how successful they are personally and professionally. If they can move away from complacency, making practical decisions about how to realize their goals and backing these decisions up with hard work, they have the potential for success. If, however, the thrill of the chase becomes a dominant force, their potential creativity will be blocked by game playing, power struggles and procrastination.

These people will always have the ability to charm the birds off the trees but the key to their success and happiness, whatever age they are, will never be their seductive warmth but their will-power. This is because when they can take control of their passions and steer their energies in a clear direction, not only will they continue to seduce everyone who crosses their path, they will also be able to realize the ideals of beauty and harmony that are powerfully linked to their emotional fulfillment.

On the dark side

Manipulative, impulsive, destructive

At your best

Charming, magnetic, exciting

29 September

the birthday of
the maverick

Your greatest challenge is

coping with feeling like you don't fit in

The way forward is ...

to celebrate rather than feel ashamed of your uniqueness— going your own way is your destiny.

People born on September 29 are mavericks at heart. At every possible opportunity they will question authority and convention, and if they find themselves disagreeing with rules and regulations they are not afraid to spark a rebellion.

Real livewires, life is never dull when these people are around. They are rebellious by nature, but this isn't because they lack discipline or self-control. Quite the opposite; they are capable individuals with the ability to startle others with their talents but, despite their intelligence and talents, they can also be rather unpredictable at times. They may, for example, suffer from bouts of low confidence because, however many followers they have, a part of them never really feels accepted. This sense of not belonging can make them swing between extroversion and introversion with confusing speed.

Until the age of twenty-three their emphasis will be on relationships, and during these years their incessant need to be on the cutting edge of things may earn them more enemies than friends. The friends they do have, however, will remain loyal for life. Their intense desire to be of service to others during these years, and indeed throughout their lives, may also make them subordinate their personal needs; but it is important for them to strike a more even balance between their different emotional drives because if they don't they may end up feeling unsatisfied, however great their success and popularity.

After the age of twenty-four there is a turning point which places the emphasis on emotional change. In the years that follow they will gradually begin to realize that, although they can compromise and work productively with others, they are not—and never will be—team players. The sooner they learn to listen to their intuition, go their own way and use their own methods, the sooner they will realize their outstanding potential for success and fulfillment. By the same token, others will celebrate rather than criticize the tenacity and originality of these inspirational leaders and talented organizers, together with the contributions they can make to society.

On the dark side

Rebellious, insecure, disruptive

At your best

Exciting, capable, bold

30 September

Your greatest challenge is

accepting that you might be wrong

The way forward is ...

to understand that without an awareness of your own fallibility, you will never be able to uncover the truth in yourself or any situation.

People born on September 30 tend to be focused and knowledgeable individuals with a strong desire to champion or reveal the truth. They have an uncanny ability for identifying intellectual or social rights and wrongs and suggesting progressive alternatives to bring about change or improvement.

These people are driven by the urge to expose injustice or unfairness in any form and, because they understand that revealing the truth as they see it can put them in the line of fire, they tend to create a tough and courageous exterior for themselves which inspires both respect and apprehension in those around them: respect, because others know that once these highly attractive and persuasive people are on the scene, they have the insight and star quality to attract support and success; apprehension, because their uncompromising sense of fairness and strong need to expose those who do not live up to their high moral standards can easily flip into judgmental or aggressive behavior. It is important, therefore, for them to understand that although pointing out the failings of those around them can clear the air, it can also have an uncomfortable effect on all concerned.

After the age of twenty-three there is a turning point that highlights issues of emotional intensity, change and transformation for these people; but whatever age they are, their challenge is not just to be more open and accepting in their beliefs, but to express as much interest in discovering the truth of their own lives as they do in uncovering the truth in others and in the world around them.

This is because once they are able to acknowledge their own vulnerabilities they can move beyond self-righteousness to greater tolerance of human weaknesses. When their tolerance is combined with their remarkable courage and impressive resourcefulness, not only can they ensure that justice is done and falsehood is exposed, they can also discover within themselves the ability to motivate and inspire others to work alongside them to create progressive and inspirational solutions for a fairer and better world.

On the dark side

Self-righteous, critical, smug

At your best

Knowledgeable, fair, influential

1 October

the birthday of
unusual capability

Your greatest challenge is

mastering the art of delegation

The way forward is ...

to understand that trying to be on top of everything confuses the bigger picture with unnecessary details, limiting your potential for success.

Although they are extraordinarily intelligent and capable individuals, people born on October 1 will often stand out in some way. Sometimes it will be the dignified way they carry themselves, or in their remarkable dedication and devotion to a cause they believe in, but whatever it is there is always something special and unique about them that makes others look or think twice.

On some occasions they can come across as stern, even proud, but to those who know them well they are incredibly warm and open-hearted. The cool front they present to the world is often a form of defense they have built up over the years as they learned how to overcome challenges and setbacks, but eventually their perseverance and dedication have earned them the just reward of rising to the top. Sadly, some of them may find that once they have reached the pinnacle of success they have aimed for all their lives, it isn't as rewarding as they hoped. The way for them to deal with this predicament is to worry less and live a little more; to feel truly successful and fulfilled they need to inject more laughter and fun into their lives.

Before the age of twenty-one they are likely to be concerned with developing their social and relationship skills, but after the age of twenty-two there is a turning point in which issues concerning personal power take center stage. It is absolutely crucial in the years that follow that they don't take themselves and their careers too seriously, and get a sense of perspective.

Above all, these people need to think big, aim high and set high standards for themselves. Their strength is the dedication they show to a purpose or goal, and as long as they don't isolate themselves from others with their perfectionist tendencies, they will not only be able to make a positive contribution to the world by transforming what is rough and ready into a smooth and progressive system, they will also discover within themselves an unusually large capacity for real happiness.

On the dark side

Obsessive, intimidating, isolated

At your best

Dedicated, stylish, original

2 October

the birthday of
the graceful conversationalist

Your greatest challenge is

taming your tendency to be confrontational

The way forward is ...

to understand that the best form of attack is often a surprise, undercover one—being more tactful and tolerant will improve your chances of success.

In whatever situation they find themselves, the favored approach of people born on October 2 is a direct one. They like to talk, think and act quickly and decisively, and the graceful ease and certainty with which they go about their business endow them with tremendous potential.

These people will not hesitate to let others know exactly where they stand, but what impresses others most about them is that they are compelling conversationalists with considerable knowledge on a wide variety of subjects. It will not be unusual to find them deep in conversation with a sparkle in their eye because they love to stimulate their minds with intelligent talk. Although they enjoy talking, they also understand the importance of listening and are forever hungry for new information and ideas, eager to hear what others have to contribute. In fact, they tend to be more at home in the world of ideas and words than in the world of feelings and emotions.

Although the lively, inquisitive and candid approach of these people is refreshing and exciting for some people, for those more sensitive they can come across as unfeeling, ruthless and upsetting. It is therefore important for their psychological growth and their professional development that they learn to express their disagreement or disapproval in ways that are not overly negative or confrontational.

At the age of twenty they will reach a turning point that highlights a growing need for emotional change and personal transformation. In the years that follow they are likely to become more committed and decisive, and it is essential that they are more sensitive in their relationships with others and don't hide behind a mask of cynicism. This is because when they are able to lean toward the positive rather than the negative, and can encourage rather than discourage people with their intelligent insights, these charming conversationalists have the potential not just to entertain and enlighten, but to enlist and direct the support of others in the collective pursuit of their inspirational cause.

On the dark side

Cutting, angry, undemonstrative

At your best

Charming, interesting, charismatic

3 October

the birthday of the cutting edge

Your greatest challenge is

valuing tradition

The way forward is ...

to understand that just because something is new does not automatically mean it is better.

People born on October 3 love to be surrounded by all that is new and original. They are eager to explore the latest trends and technologies, and in some cases to set the trends as well. They are enthusiastic and up to date, so the place to find them is always right at the cutting edge.

These people hate to be out of fashion or not looking the part, and more often than not others will comment on how well presented they are. This doesn't mean, however, that they blindly follow the latest fashion or trend. Quite the opposite; they are highly original, hating to be categorized, and will usually add their own unique twist to new trends. There is a strong drive within them always to be one step ahead of everyone else, setting the pace so that others can follow. In fact, giving an example to others is what these gregarious people love to do more than anything else. They feel comfortable in the limelight and are good at playing their part to an adoring audience. Their greatest fear is to be ignored and, worse still, to be left out. Fortunately, with their talent and charisma this rarely occurs.

Although they can be the life and soul of their set, there is a part of these people that longs to hide or is reluctant to reveal their true feelings. It is important for them to listen carefully to what their feelings are telling them, because they have a tendency toward superficiality, and superficiality is no recipe for lasting happiness. After the age of twenty there will be opportunities for them to find deeper meaning to their lives and it is important for them to seize these opportunities.

This is because once they realize that the latest is not necessarily the best, and that their emotional development matters far more than being seen, their energy, dedication, style and originality will take them to the only cutting edge that really matters—and the only place where true happiness and success can be found—that of personal fulfillment.

On the dark side

Superficial, materialistic, pretentious

At your best

Original, sociable, exciting

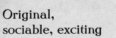

4 October

the birthday of
edgy congeniality

Your greatest challenge is

overcoming complacency

The way forward is ...

to understand that until you start testing yourself in new situations you won't learn much about yourself and what really makes you happy.

The desire for a harmonious environment that drives people born on October 4 makes them among the most agreeable and popular people of the year. They have sensual, esthetic tastes and love to surround themselves with pleasant people and beautiful things.

In whatever situation they are in, these people tend to come across as relaxed and at ease with themselves; this is in part due to their love of the good things in life, their naturally non-confrontational personality and their gift for getting along with just about anybody. This doesn't mean they don't have strong opinions; if pressed they can certainly be passionate and forthright in their beliefs. It's just that they like to present their case in a way that is not offensive to others and in a manner that is laced with humor, humility and tact, believing that this approach is more likely to get people on their side. They also have an astute way of looking at the world and a strong sense of realism about what is achievable and what is not.

After the age of nineteen, and lasting for the following thirty years, there is an important turning point for people born on this day that highlights a growing need for personal change, intensity and transformation. During these years they will feel a strong need to create a life of pleasure and harmony; with their congenial personality this is often just what they manage to create for themselves and others. However, they will also find that time and again life throws obstacles, challenges and conflicts in their path. The way they respond to these challenges will to some extent determine their success or failure personally and professionally.

If they can discover within themselves a fighting spirit and a determination to do their things their way, these remarkably gregarious, sensual but always level-headed and peace-loving people will find not only that they are extremely popular with others, but that others look to them for advice, guidance and inspiration about how to make the world a more beautiful place.

On the dark side

Superficial, indulgent, complacent

At your best

Agreeable, tasteful, popular

5 October

the birthday of
dignified altruism

Your greatest challenge is

keeping a sense of perspective

The way forward is ...

to understand that getting carried away in your devotion to a cause is counterproductive; losing your perspective means losing your ability to make an effective contribution.

People born on October 5 tend to put others or the cause they are promoting first and themselves second. They can't do enough to help, and so powerful is their conviction that others often find themselves persuaded to do good deeds as well. In addition, they also have a highly developed sense of fair play and are passionate in the defense of the rights of all, especially those who are less fortunate. As a result they often come across as unusually dignified as well as altruistic individuals.

In every situation in which they find themselves these people bring their concern for others and their strong sense of ethical responsibility. Their willingness to not just talk but take action earns them the respect and loyalty of those around them. Occasionally, however, they can lose their sense of perspective and get so wrapped up in their righteous propensity that they can become impatient and aggressive, failing to consider the consequences of their methods or the alternative viewpoints of others.

After the age of nineteen there is a turning point for people born on this day which emphasizes a growing need for emotional change and regeneration. This influence will continue for the next thirty years and during this time there will be opportunities for them to express their social instincts and make their mark. But if they are serious about being effective instruments of progress it is vital for them to learn to keep their cool, pay attention to the details and not get carried away with their own power. After the age of forty-nine there is another turning point which puts the spotlight on expanding their mind through study and travel.

Whatever age they are, these people will always be shining examples to others of joyful dedication to the ideals of justice and generosity of spirit. And once they learn to constructively direct rather than give free rein to their passion for altruism, they have the potential to become leading figures in humanitarian, spiritual or social reform.

On the dark side

Neglectful, extreme, impatient

At your best

Altruistic, gracious, warm hearted

394

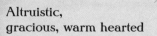

6 October

the birthday of
the romantic adventurer

Your greatest challenge is

being realistic

The way forward is ...

to understand that optimism can be as damaging as negativity, because there is good and bad in every situation and person.

People born on October 6 live each day as if it were the last. As a result they are one of the most alive and spontaneous individuals of the year. Every day for them is an adventure and an opportunity to fall in love with anyone or anything.

Romantic adventurers at heart, these people are driven by an irresistible urge to savor as many stimulations and sensations as life has to offer. They adore novelty and will waste no time in gathering as much information as possible before moving on to the next big adventure. Although their need to be stimulated is strong, they are not selfish people because their need to identify with and help others by means of their discoveries is equally strong.

After the age of seventeen they will reach a turning point in their lives, finding a growing need for emotional intensity, personal power and transformation. During this time there will be many opportunities for them to deepen their emotional commitment to others and they need to take advantage of these. This is because although they are often highly valued by their friends as a delight to have around, others may grow tired of their endless optimism and seeming inability to take into account the darker, more complex and deeper aspects of life. It is almost as if a part of them is like the romantic star of a story, with their character lacking depth and definition. However, once they start to understand that life cannot always be sunshine and roses and that suffering—however distressing—is essential to psychological growth, their life will become infinitely more exciting and rewarding.

After the age of forty-seven people born on this day are likely to become more freedom loving and willing to take risks emotionally and professionally; there may be opportunities for them to expand their minds and lives by traveling or studying. Whatever age they are, however, their versatile, energetic and inspirational contribution to the world draws luck and success to them, exerting a magnetic attraction on those around them.

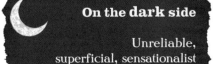

On the dark side

Unreliable, superficial, sensationalist

At your best

Adventurous, energetic, spontaneous

7 October

the birthday of
acquired taste

Your greatest challenge is

surrendering your stubbornness

The way forward is ...

to understand that stubbornness is very different from conviction; conviction is defending your principles, stubbornness is obstinately refusing to see another person's point of view.

October 7 people tend to be energetic and strong-minded individuals. They often have a reputation for speaking with deep-seated certainty and commitment to their set of beliefs. Indeed, reactions to them can be extreme—others either love them or hate them—but whether people agree or disagree with them they rarely fail to be impressed by their determination and strong will.

Although they could be described as an acquired taste, these people are rarely concerned about their impact on others since they believe that progress or improvements can't be made without someone rocking the boat or challenging the status quo. They would certainly prefer to win followers rather than enemies, but so strong is their belief in their ideals and their urge to pioneer progress that they have all the courage necessary to survive any opposition or criticism along the way.

From the age of sixteen there is a turning point for people born on this day that emphasizes for the next thirty years of their lives a growing need for emotional change, power and regeneration. During these years the key to their success is their ability to unite their ambition and drive with their awareness of the importance of diplomacy and cooperation. Another turning point occurs at the age of forty-six when they are likely to become more idealistic and optimistic, perhaps wishing to take more risks in their life or challenge their mind through study, travel or retraining. Whatever age they are, they need to keep their minds open, their rebelliousness under control and, most importantly, they need to understand that their way is not the only way.

Above all, people born on this day are strong-minded individuals. Once they are able to internalize their tremendous will-power so that it can improve their focus and effectiveness, rather than externalizing it in confrontational behavior, they have the potential to be among the world's truly brilliant innovators.

On the dark side

Stubborn, isolated, blinkered

At your best

Committed, resilient, fascinating

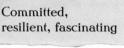

8 October

the birthday of
the free spirit

Your greatest challenge is

keeping your feet on the ground

The way forward is ...

to understand that when your soaring visions don't take reality into account, they can isolate you from the very people you seek to inspire.

From an early age, people born on October 8 may have felt a need to fly beyond the realms of existing knowledge. Their imagination is so creative that others may have regarded them as either highly original or slightly weird. But even those who find it hard to relate to or understand their wild creativity will be forced to admit that they are secretly envious of their ability to somehow disengage from the routine aspects of daily life.

These people may appear flighty and inconsistent because they are easily distracted and don't always show much common sense, but they have a powerful intellect and incredible insight into what motivates others. Unfortunately, that insight somehow doesn't always include an understanding of themselves and, because they have such an experimental approach to life, they can hop from one person or experience to another forever searching for excitement, freedom and inspiration. Although this makes them rather interesting and magnetic people, until they are able to understand why they find it hard to commit or face the realities of life they will feel restless and unsatisfied.

Before the age of forty-five these people will be presented with opportunities to discover more about themselves and what it is they actually want from life. Key to their personal and professional success during this period will be their ability to inject a heavy dose of discipline into their lives. After the age of forty-six there is a turning point which puts the emphasis on freedom and a desire to expand their horizons and take more risks. It is very important in the years that follow that they discover within themselves the adventure and excitement they crave, rather than relying on constant change to keep themselves from becoming bored.

With their active imagination, excellent communication skills and love of life they will often find themselves at the forefront of new ideas and trends. But only when they are able to unite their powerful emotions with a degree of will-power can they fulfill their destiny as a dynamic force for progress.

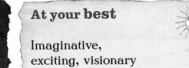

On the dark side

Easily distracted, lightweight, eccentric

At your best

Imaginative, exciting, visionary

9 October

the birthday of
the psychologist

Your greatest challenge is

tempering your eagerness to please

The way forward is ...

to understand that people will respect you more not less if you develop your self-esteem.

Very little escapes the attention of people born on October 9. Acutely observant, they are fascinated by all aspects of human behavior and interaction. In addition, they are extremely perceptive individuals with the ability to spot weaknesses or failings in others; but because they are also extremely sensitive, their insights and imaginative solutions will not offend but inspire others.

As natural psychologists, these people are extremely inquisitive individuals. They are fascinated by everyone they meet and every new situation they are in; when this open-mindedness is combined with their intelligence and energetic style, it is small wonder they are often very popular. They have many talents and will probably experiment with several different professions before they settle into the kind of work which can utilize them all. Although it may take a while—and there may be lots of stops and starts professionally—they do tend to find their feet eventually. Their personal life may be quite a different story. This is because the perception and insight that are the trademarks of these people somehow do not translate into self-awareness.

Until the age of forty-four there is an emphasis on issues concerning change and the transformation of their personal motivation. These are the years when they are most likely to look outside of themselves for a sense of purpose and identity, perhaps in their career or in their relationships with others. These are also the years when their eagerness to please can overshadow their will-power; it is vital for them to listen to and trust their intuition, which more often than not has been right all along. After the age of forty-five there is a turning point where they are likely to become more adventurous and freedom loving, and their genuine enjoyment of life will shine through clearly.

If they have learned to stand up for themselves and their dreams, this is the period during which these intelligent, intuitive and highly imaginative dreamers will finally be able to turn their visions of progress and improvement into a reality.

On the dark side

Passive, needy, jealous

At your best

Imaginative, insightful, popular

1O October

the birthday of
the overseer

Your greatest challenge is

asking for help

The way forward is ...

to understand that asking for help is not a sign of weakness but one of strength and self-belief. It shows that you believe you are worth helping.

People born on October 10 despise chaos and disorder, and are at their happiest and their best when they can bring order and harmony to unproductive situations. In many respects they take more pleasure in their natural role of overseer, organizing and implementing improvements, than they do in seeing the rewards of their efforts.

Their career is extremely important to people born on this day and they want to find a vocation that is both fulfilling and meaningful. When it comes to their personal lives they will often display the same love of order at home as they do at work, running their houses or their families with smooth and effortless efficiency. Although they can sometimes come across as slightly serious and self-contained, they have an attractive sincerity that draws others to them. For example, they don't smile very much but when they do it can warm even the coldest heart with its sincerity. They are intelligent and articulate, but small talk is definitely not for them; as far as they are concerned, a conversation that is not meaningful in some way is a waste of time.

Until the age of forty-three there is an emphasis in their lives on issues concerning emotional sensitivity, personal power and transformation; in many ways the first part of their lives can be the most challenging for them. If, during these years, they allow their tendency to be logical and circumspect to overshadow their need to be emotionally spontaneous and creative, they run the risk of becoming overly serious and unfulfilled. If, however, they can open their minds, their hearts and their wallets, they can begin to lay the foundation stone for a life that is more balanced and fulfilling. After the age of forty-four there is a turning point which puts the spotlight on travel and new experiences.

Whatever age they are, however, the sooner they discover within themselves their adventurous spirit, the sooner they can become the inspired and progressive leaders they are destined to be.

On the dark side

Unimaginative, unfulfilled, obsessive

At your best

Detailed, authoritative, constructive

11 October

the birthday of
social elegance

Your greatest challenge is

harnessing your ambition

The way forward is ...

to understand that popularity does not guarantee fulfillment; for a more rewarding life you need to set yourself personal goals.

People born on October 11 tend to be attractive and popular people. They are masters of the art of socializing, at their happiest and best when they are at the center of a group of colleagues or friends. Their style is easygoing and elegant, and their likable personality enables them to mix with people of all ages and all walks of life.

Others may envy the ease with which they merge into a group, strike up a conversation with a newcomer, advance up the career ladder, and ascend into the highest social circles. But underneath their graceful exterior, people born on this day may feel as if something important is missing. It's important for them to listen to this feeling because what's missing is personal ambition. Although their upbeat personality attracts popularity and position, they tend to drift into these positions rather than having clearly defined personal goals. As a result they may feel as if they have very little control over their lives; their aversion to conflict or challenge is even more damaging, because a little challenge and suffering in their lives will help them learn and grow emotionally.

Until the age of forty-two there is an emphasis in their lives on emotional change and a need for personal power. During these years they need to take advantage of opportunities to challenge themselves professionally and personally, because challenge is the key to their success. After the age of forty-three there is a turning point when they are likely to widen their interests, feel more free, and seek inspiration through study, relationships or travel. Again the key to their success and fulfillment will be their willingness to take calculated risks and embrace challenge.

This is because once they discover within themselves a drive to achieve and the courage to avoid the temptation of always taking the safest or most popular route, their outstanding grace, humanity and intellect will ensure that they don't just appear to be leading a charmed life—they will actually feel as if they are living it.

On the dark side

Superficial, unfulfilled, passive

At your best

Sociable, charming, popular

400

12 October

the birthday of

effusive complexity

Your greatest challenge is

getting over yourself

The way forward is ...

to understand that although you may be at the center of your world, this does not mean that you are at the center of everyone else's.

Heads turn when the larger-than-life personalities of people born on October 12 enter a room. They are determined to have their opinions heard and, if speaking loudly won't do the trick, they are not above resorting to outrageous tactics to get the attention they feel they deserve. Although they are attention seekers, they have a heart as expansive as their head, and their tantrums are just as likely to be on behalf of others as themselves. It is this curious mixture of wholehearted generosity and extreme self-indulgence that makes them such complex individuals.

This combination of characteristics can manifest itself in a number of different ways for people born on this day. Some may subordinate their pleasure-loving and sensation-seeking side in their dedication to serving others in an imaginative way, while others may be more non-conformist individuals with their own inimitable and expansive way of engaging with life. Common to them all, however, will be their infectious appetite for life, and their desire to inspire and invigorate others by their own passionate example.

Until the age of forty-one there will be an emphasis in their lives on emotional change, power and transformation. During these years their chances of success and happiness will improve significantly if they can learn to become less addicted to attention or the desire to seek a reaction from others, and become more focused on their personal ideals and goals in life. After the age of forty-two there is a significant turning point which will stimulate them to expand their perspective; they may, for example, have more contact with foreign people or places, or take up a new interest.

Whatever age they are, however, the key to their psychological growth and fulfillment will be their ability to take the feelings of others into account. Once they have found a balance between giving and taking, they will find that the reaction they provoke in others moves beyond surprise to respect, and in some cases awe.

On the dark side

Selfish, attention-seeking, outrageous

At your best

Dramatic, warm-hearted, exciting

401

13 October

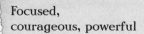

the birthday of
the polished diamond

Your greatest challenge is

learning to relax

The way forward is ...

to understand that regular time out gives you the sense of perspective you need to make better judgments.

As natural leaders, people born October 13 take their jobs and their lives very seriously indeed. Their total focus on their goals, their always polished performance and uncompromising strength inspire either devotion and awe, or hostility, sometimes fear, in others.

Those born on this day aren't people to fool around with, and their vigor and determination can shock almost everyone out of their lethargy. When they set their minds on something, nothing, including their own emotional and physical health, will stand in their way. Blessed with a sharp mind that cannot help but uncover and expose the weaknesses or failings of others, they are able to come up with ingenious solutions designed to inspire or benefit others. Not surprisingly, they are perfectionists; the tough and near-impossible expectations they place on themselves and others can make it very hard for them—and anyone who lives or works with them—to relax.

Until the age of forty, these people will experience a growing emphasis on issues concerning power, change and transformation of their personal motivation. These are the years when they are most likely to be harsh and unrelenting in the pursuit of their goals. Although this means they will succeed in whatever career they choose, personal happiness may be elusive unless they learn to ease up on themselves a little and open up to those they trust. They need to remind themselves that they are human and have emotions just like everyone else. After the age of forty-one there is a massive turning point, indicating a more optimistic and freedom-loving perspective. They may expand their mind through study, travel or new interests.

If they can learn to be less critical of themselves and others, allowing themselves to be directed by their inner voice rather than by pressure to perform, these are the years when they can really come into their own. Their driving urge to assist progress will not only bring about progressive and significant benefits to others, but also earn them their natural place in the spotlight.

On the dark side

Stressed, cold, critical

At your best

Focused, courageous, powerful

14 October

the birthday of
the middle path

Your greatest challenge is

putting yourself on the line

The way forward is ...

to understand that if you don't ever take a risk in life you can deprive yourself of opportunities for psychological growth.

People born on October 14 tend to be the steady rock to which friends and colleagues run for shelter when life gets stormy. They have a wonderfully calming influence and their ability to counter extreme situations with practicality and common sense often propels them into positions of authority.

Striving to achieve moderation and balance, doing the right thing in whatever situation they find themselves is the driving force of these people. They usually find the middle way, giving not just their own lives but the lives of those they live and work with great influence, stability and structure. Friends trust them to pull them back to reality when they are going to extremes, and colleagues trust them to be the voice of reason and common sense. Their greatest strength, however, can also become their greatest weakness if taken to extremes. This is because too much common sense and moderation can cause their behavior to become imbalanced with the result that they either don't take risks at all or they give themselves completely to self-indulgent behavior. Either way the results are a disaster for their psychological growth and well-being.

Until the age of thirty-nine there is a growing emphasis on personal power and transformation; during these years they need to listen as much to their intuition as they do to their common sense to decide what is appropriate to a situation. They also need to learn to let mistakes from the past go, as they have a tendency to blame themselves or other things and get stuck in the past, rather than looking ahead to the future. After the age of forty there is a significant turning point when they may wish to expand their mind through new experiences, the study of philosophy and spirituality, or traveling abroad.

Whatever age they are, if they can learn to look ahead with positive expectancy and find the middle way in all things, they have the potential to become imaginative and inspirational managers with a powerful and important message of moderation in all things.

On the dark side

Excessive, overly cautious, passive

At your best

Temperate, composed, reliable

15 October

Your greatest challenge is

to compromise

The way forward is ...

to understand that compromise is not a backward step but a victory for both your way and someone else's.

People born on October 15 will often exert a hypnotic or seductive power over others and the key to their success will be the way in which they use this provocative influence. If they use it positively they can play a crucial role in the lives of others, helping them to develop a sense of their own individuality and power. If, however, they use it recklessly they can agitate others, exciting negativity with behavior that is sensationalist and attention-seeking.

Whether or not they are aware of their powerful influence over others, these people cannot bear to have their independent will constrained in any way; but this does not mean they are selfish. Quite the opposite. They often feel a strong connection to others, and friends treasure their thoughtfulness. It's just that their greatest wish is to make a positive contribution to the world. Being multi-talented, their potential for success is great and they will almost certainly make their mark; but even when they do earn the respect of others, they can become over-confident or attention-seeking in the process. It is therefore extremely important for them to appreciate how vulnerable others are to their charms, and to find ways to be a positive rather than a negative role model.

Until the age of thirty-eight there is a growing emphasis in their lives on issues regarding emotional change and personal power. During this period they would benefit greatly from the study of psychology. They already have a natural understanding of human nature, but investigating more deeply would provide them with the answers to many unanswered questions about themselves and others. After the age of thirty-nine a turning point occurs where they are likely to expand their mental perspective and become more adventurous in their approach.

During these years if they can learn to moderate their urge constantly to act as an independent agent and always remember that others look to them for guidance, insight and inspiration, they can become not only a positive role model but also a powerful agent of progress.

On the dark side

Provocative, over-confident, selfish

At your best

Charming, influential, intelligent

16 October

the birthday of
the breakthrough

Your greatest challenge is

being consistent

The way forward is ...

to understand that, although your spontaneity is one of your greatest strengths, to earn the respect of others you have to prove that you are worthy.

People born on October 16 are often blessed with a sharp mind and highly developed critical faculties. They love to observe and analyze everything and everyone they encounter, and human behavior provides them with an endless supply of material. Although they are perceptive and intelligent, their greatest talent is their ability to break through layers of confusion to expose failings and weaknesses with objective and brutal honesty.

They enjoy the company of others but their wit, independence and tendency to direct their criticism of others from a distance, for example in writing or in social campaigning, sets them apart from others. They are motivated by a desire to enlighten or inform, but the uncomfortable accuracy of their observations and the frank way in which they can express them may offend and alienate those they seek to educate. They place a high value on justice, striving for honesty and equality in all their dealings. When they get their own way—which they frequently do—they are models of charm, poise and magnanimity; but when their voice is ignored they can become defensive and moody, and will often refuse to accept failure or compromise.

Until the age of thirty-seven there will be an emphasis on issues concerning emotional sensitivity and power; these are the years when they are most likely to be stubborn and trying in the face of opposition. After the age of thirty-eight there is a significant turning point when they are likely to widen their perspective on life and may wish to expand their horizons through travel, study and finding adventure. They should take advantage of opportunities to work cooperatively with others and form partnerships during these years, as this will attract considerable success and good fortune their way, both personally and professionally.

Whatever age they are, however, their brilliant and unconventional minds and ability to cut to the core of any subject will eventually lead them toward self-analysis, and this is when they will make the most important and empowering breakthrough of all.

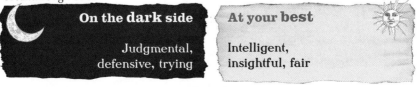

On the dark side

Judgmental, defensive, trying

At your best

Intelligent, insightful, fair

17 October

the birthday of the lucky escape

Your greatest challenge is

to overcome a tendency to embellish

The way forward is ...

to understand that embellishing the truth doesn't make you appear more exciting or interesting; it just makes you appear attention-seeking.

A central theme for people born on October 17 is the ability to pick themselves up when things don't work out and start again without complaint. Although they know how to be responsible, taking chances is a way of life to them and their life appears to others to be a delicate balancing act where lucky escapes, gambling or risk-taking are the order of the day.

The fearlessness of people born on this day inspires the respect and admiration of others, although their example may not perhaps be the best one to copy. This is because these people are perhaps the only individuals of the year with enough self-assurance, resilience and stamina to cope with the demands, disappointments, successes and highs and lows of such a lifestyle. They are also not above embellishing the truth if they feel it will get them the attention they deserve. Although this never fails to entertain others, it can be dangerous for their emotional well-being, especially when they risk losing touch with what is fact and what is fantasy in their lives. Self-deception can be a big problem.

In their late twenties and early thirties they may experience an intense longing to find deeper meaning in their lives. This can send them either in the direction of greater risk-taking or more positively in the direction of greater self-awareness and a realization that what really needs to be balanced in their lives is their emotional life. Once they are able to step out from behind the image they have created for themselves to reveal their true self to others, they will find that their life takes on a whole new and positive meaning and direction.

Typically in their late thirties and forties they do finally find a balance between their impulsive and cautious natures, and as long as they stay positive, developing patience and tolerance, they will be able to combine their dynamic courage with the perseverance they need to achieve the clear potential for success and happiness associated with this birthday.

On the dark side

Reckless, image-conscious, dishonest

At your best

Adventurous, courageous, resilient

18 October

the birthday of
vulnerable expectation

Your greatest challenge is

believing in yourself

The way forward is ...

to understand that from the moment of conception you were already a winner. Look at any baby; self-belief is your birth right.

People born on October 18 often have a regal, dignified air about them; from their early years expectations will have been high for them to achieve great success. As the years go by, more often than not they do fulfill those expectations by rising to the top; but although they long to make their mark on the world, another part of them longs to run away and hide.

With all the imagination, intellect and talent to blaze exciting trails in life, their need for the approval of others can crush their self-esteem and stop them developing to their full potential. Perhaps in childhood they were criticized or neglected too much; lasting feelings of inadequacy and insecurity continue to haunt them, however successful they are. It is therefore vital for their psychological growth that they work on rebuilding their vulnerable self-esteem. If they don't, they will be like reeds blown in the wind, flying high when others applaud them but falling down when the praise or support isn't there.

From the age of five until the age of thirty-five there is a growing emphasis for people born on this day on emotional change, power and transformation, and opportunities will be presented to them to take control of their lives. They must take advantage of these by becoming more proactive and saying "no" to others who seek to take advantage of them. Once they get a handle on their insecurities and realize their own worth, there is nothing they cannot achieve. When they approach their forties and beyond, there is another turning point when life will call upon them to be more adventurous, and it is more important than ever for them to leave self-doubt aside.

This is because once they see what everybody else sees and realize what creative, courageous and inspirational individuals they really are, they have the potential not just to promote the happiness of themselves and others but to be an inspirational force for the common good.

On the dark side

Self-sacrificing, stressed, approval-seeking

At your best

Dignified, inspirational, giving

19 October

the birthday of
the peaceful activist

Your greatest challenge is

allowing others to take the lead

The way forward is ...

to understand that the mark of a truly evolved person is often their ability to feel comfortable in a supporting role.

On the surface people born on October 19 appear peace loving and conventional, but underneath the surface—just waiting to appear at the first sign of conflict—is a great deal of independence and originality.

When things are going well for these lively people they can be wonderful team players, and their charm and optimism never fail to lift the spirits of all they are involved with. Rarely seen without a smile on their face, they will work long and hard to maintain the status quo. The moment that status quo is threatened or conflict arises, however, their toughness and independence as well as their explosive temper can surprise and shock even those who know them well. Indeed it is during difficult times that they tend to stand out, revealing their strength of character and both the best and the worst of themselves. Deep down, people born on this day are battlers and they just need a battle or a conflict to expose their crusading spirit. Once this is exposed, other people learn never to underestimate them again. Fortunately, their chosen weapon isn't intimidation but persuasion and logical presentation of their ideas; but if they are pushed in a corner they have it within themselves to lash out with wounding words and actions.

Until their mid thirties people born on this day are likely to be presented with opportunities for emotional growth, change and transformation. These are important character-building years where learning to control their temper and injecting enthusiasm into their life without conflict as a stimulus will be invaluable to their psychological growth. As they head toward forty there is another turning point where they may become more adventurous, possibly desiring to travel or seek more education.

Once again if they can learn to control their rebellious tendencies and direct their enormous vigor, optimism and courage toward a worthy cause, they have the potential to discover, shed light on and reverse injustices and by so doing bring the world closer to its natural peace-loving state.

On the dark side

Rebellious, tactless, possessive

At your best

Independent, energetic, courageous

20 October

the birthday of
the double life

Your greatest challenge is

admitting mistakes

The way forward is ...

to understand that the person who can admit they have made a mistake is not someone people disapprove of, but someone people can identify with and respect.

People born on October 20 are something of a paradox, with two distinctively different sides to their personality. One side is the quintessential professional who spreads a message of harmony and collaboration. The other side is one of unpredictability, but also great artistry and an appreciation of sensuality, beauty and creativity.

Generally, people born on this day find a way to accommodate both sides of their personality, perhaps by pursuing conventional careers and indulging their artistic tastes as a hobby, or by placing an emphasis on matters of personal style. Indeed, their appearance is rarely a trivial concern for them and, however conventional their career choice, they will always find a way to express their individuality through their clothes, hairstyle or fashion sense.

The double life that they tend to lead also shows up in the way that they interact with others. They like to think they put the focus on others and are born democrats, but it is only a matter of time before they take center stage or a leadership role—this is the place they were born to be. This isn't to say they are scheming or insincere. Quite the opposite, they are extremely giving and caring individuals. It is just that their creativity and originality are so powerful it is impossible for them to contain or subordinate them for long.

In their twenties they may experience a growing emphasis on emotional change, personal power and regeneration, and they may struggle to find a way to express themselves creatively in their professional life. In their mid to late thirties there is, however, a turning point when they will become more adventurous. These are the years when it is absolutely crucial for them to find ways to reconcile their rational capacity with their creative, often artistic impulses. If they are able to find this delicate balance they will continue to lead a double life; the difference is that it will no longer feel conflicting and complicated, but completely natural and fulfilling.

On the dark side

Unfulfilled, confused, egocentric

At your best

Creative, fair minded, enthusiastic

21 October

the birthday of
eloquent charm

Your greatest challenge is

managing your emotions

The way forward is ...

to understand that you, not your anger, your fear or even your excitement, are in charge of the way you feel.

As well as being charming, intelligent and multi-talented, people born on October 21 are also skilled communicators. Indeed their eloquence, whether verbal or written, is one of their greatest assets; used wisely it can help them win friends and influence the right people.

These people are very good at talking or writing down their thoughts, and although they may not be aware of it at the time their pronouncements will often make a lasting impact on those around them. As well as being articulate they are natural entertainers; people find themselves drawn not just to their stories but to their easygoing nature, emotional spontaneity and upbeat lightheartedness. Rarely unsettled by the attention they receive, they themselves would be the first to admit that they enjoy occupying center stage. Being accepted and well thought of by others means a great deal to them, but there is more to them than just being a social butterfly. They would like nothing more than to indulge their strong pleasure-seeking tendencies and share their enjoyment with a group of like-minded individuals. But they are also extremely perceptive, realistic and somewhat critical individuals who recognize the unfeasibility of such an agreeable lifestyle, and the importance of trying to improve the injustices and misfortunes of the world.

Despite their ability to subordinate their more selfish urges for the greater good, these people remain profoundly emotional creatures with a powerful desire to see their creative ideals realized. Before the age of thirty-two they are likely to lack in self-confidence and be conservative in their approach to life; but after the age of thirty-three there is a turning point which will stimulate them to be more adventurous, confident and freedom loving. It is important for them to realize during these years that although acting on impulse is exciting it can also be dangerous.

Whatever age they are, these outspoken, dynamic but eloquent and sensitive individuals will find fulfillment when they dedicate their gifts to healing, spirituality and an ideal of justice or beauty.

On the dark side

Addictive, flighty, unfulfilled

At your best

Charming, articulate, influential

22 October

the birthday of
the golden aura

Your greatest challenge is

not being in control

The way forward is ...

to understand that sometimes going with the flow or allowing events to unfold is the most empowering choice you can make.

Even if they wanted to, people born on October 22 could not fade into the background, so compelling is their presence and the seductive power they seem to have over others. In fact, throughout their lives all eyes seem to be drawn to their golden aura.

Although they do not object to being the focus of attention, a part of them longs to be recognized for their talents and capabilities rather than for their appearance or their ability to incite feelings of excitement or desire in others. Indeed these people have many hidden talents, including intelligence, intuition, discernment and compassion for those less fortunate. Unfortunately, people don't often give them an opportunity to reveal or express these talents because it is enough for them to simply bask in their attractive and compelling presence. Not being taken seriously can therefore be a huge problem for people born on this day and they will often feel that they have to work twice as hard as anyone else to prove themselves.

Over the years they find ways to project the power of their intentions onto others but unfortunately they do not always do so in a constructive way. For example, they have a masterful control over their emotions and if they choose to they can also influence the way others feel. Their powers of projection are unsurpassed and it is therefore extremely important for them to use these powers wisely, making sure that their attempts to control situations do not end up hurting others and damaging themselves emotionally.

Before the age of thirty their tendency to manipulate others emotionally may come to the fore, but after this age there is a powerful turning point where they are likely to become less controlling and more optimistic, open-minded and adventurous. These are the years when they can really come into their own. When directed positively, their golden aura, or inner strength, can finally manifest itself as healing or creative ability, as well as the urge to help create a fairer world.

On the dark side

Manipulative, superficial, disturbing

At your best

Seductive, charismatic, exciting

SCORPIO

THE SCORPION
(OCTOBER 23–NOVEMBER 21)

* **Element:** Water
* **Ruling planets:** Mars, the warrior and Pluto, the destroyer
* **Symbol:** The Scorpion
* **Tarot card:** Death (regeneration)
* **Number:** 9
* **Favorable colors:** Red, purple, black
* **Key phrase:** I will renew myself

principal characteristic is a relentless, restless energy that can wear anyone and anything down with its persistence. At their best, Scorpios are dynamic achievers but if they can't get what or who they want or if their incredible energy is blocked or restricted in some way they will display their worst characteristics: jealously, resentfulness, negativity and stinging sarcasm.

Personality potential

Of all the signs of the zodiac, Scorpios are probably the ones with the most negative connotations because of the negative and self-destructive traits of their symbol—the scorpion—are so obvious. But these connotations simply are not true. It's just that the creativity and energy associated with this sign can sometimes be so strong that they seem overpowering and over-intense. However, once they find a way to express their creativity and utilize their energy productively, they have the potential to achieve truly great things.

There are many sides to a Scorpio and every day new sides of their personality will reveal themselves, but two aspects of their personality are revealed most frequently. First there is the silent-but-deadly scorpion that takes delight in catching a person off-guard; then there is the phoenix, the magical and mystical bird that dies but is reborn with renewed strength, wisdom and potential to start again. It's no coincidence that the Tarot card linked to the sun sign Scorpio is the card of death. This card often scares people the most in a reading; but if they take the time to look beneath the surface they will discover that although death does mean endings, it also means new beginnings, and all the promise and potential of a new life or fresh start. It's not surprising, either, that the sign of Scorpio rules the genitals—the organs of reproduction—and that the planet Mars, the warrior, and the planet Pluto, the

planet of rebirth, transformation and hidden knowledge, also exert a strong influence over those born under this sign.

Scorpios are fascinated by the unknown and the unanswerable mysteries of life. Their intense stare seems to look right into a person's soul, and their astute, original mind has the ability to combine logic with intuition so that they can immediately get right to the heart of the matter or the root of a problem. They are often magnetic personalities and excellent strategists who seem to be able to hypnotize other people to do exactly whatever they want. Wherever or however they choose to direct their awesome energy, they have enormous resilience and staying power as well as the potential to overcome obstacles and attract outstanding success their way.

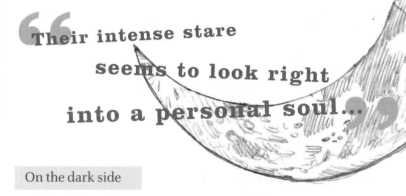

" Their intense stare seems to look right into a personal soul... "

On the dark side

Words often linked to Scorpios include jealousy, sarcasm, vindictiveness, possessiveness and stubbornness. There is no denying that the potential for these negative personality traits exists within this sign, like a sting in the tail. The most curious thing is that Scorpios are often the first to admit these ugly traits in themselves but, instead of taking control of them, they often allow them to dominate or drive them. In other words, they often sting themselves in the tail with their compulsiveness and obsessiveness and are therefore their own worst enemy. There is a masochistic side to them that can hurt them far harder than any criticism or rejection by other people.

Scorpios can be relentlessly self-critical and their suspicious personality will often dwell on past hurts, allowing resentments and negativity to build up. They also tend to judge the present by past experiences and, if they have been hurt in the past, they can be very reluctant to trust again. Often their feelings of insecurity are masked by arrogant, dismissive behavior, but if a Scorpio is betrayed in some way, this is the sign most likely neither to forgive nor forget.

Scorpios are also the master manipulators of the zodiac, and they will never hesitate to use the knowledge they have gained with their probing insight and their dangerous charm to help them get to where they want. Perhaps their worst personality pitfall, though, is their deep and dark jealousy. Scorpios can smolder with resentment and eat themselves up with negative feelings if they think others have more or are doing better than they are.

Symbol

The scorpion is a dangerous, dark, silent and terrifying creature with a lethal sting in its tail. When cornered, the scorpion will sting itself to death rather than face defeat or humiliation. Like the scorpion, those born under this sun sign have the potential to destroy anyone or anything that obstructs their path, and they also have the potential to self-destruct when they feel that their life isn't going according to plan.

Darkest secret

The darkest secrets of Scorpios will typically remain a mystery because their nature is to keep things about themselves hidden. Unwilling to open up emotionally, they can often feel incredibly isolated and alone—as if they are an observer rather than an active participant in their own lives. Deep within every Scorpio there's a deep need to be loved and accepted; but if they can't find ways to transcend their intractable and impenetrable heart, they may find that this need isn't fulfilled.

Love

There's a secretive air about those born under this sun sign that can make them extremely difficult to get to know, but their intuitive personality never has a problem understanding other people. As a result they will always have plenty of acquaintances and admirers but only a select few people will know a Scorpio really well—and even fewer, if any, will get really close to them emotionally. This isn't to say that it's impossible for a Scorpio to fall in love. They are capable of deep affection but all too often they mistake passion and sex for love. The real test for a Scorpio's heart is after the honeymoon period. When things settle more into a routine they may struggle to transform a sexual relationship into something deep and longer lasting.

If there is a Scorpio in your life they will almost certainly try to control you in some way and, if they see you confiding in anyone else, their insecurity will be awakened. Many of the problems Scorpios face in their lives revolve around their intense emotions, in particular love and jealousy. Prone to bouts of lovesickness, infatuation and impulse, it's often the case that common sense, reason and logic disappear and reckless, dangerous and self-destructive behavior takes their place.

Love matches:
Virgo, Capricorn and Pisces

The Scorpio man

On the surface a Scorpio man can often appear calm, confident and in control, but if there was only one word to sum up a Scorpio man that word would be "passion." Not just passion in the bedroom, but passionate intensity about everything and everyone involved in their life. If you find emotional intensity unsettling, then a relationship with a Scorpio man isn't for you.

People tend to either love or dislike Scorpio men. It's impossible to be neutral about them and they will always make an impression with their hypnotic intensity. They are an enigma in every sense of the word and can be passionate one moment but full of common sense the next, philosophical one day then earthy and sensual the next. Full of surprises, it's impossible to second guess them and that's exactly how they like it. They delight in unsettling people and encouraging them to let down their guard. Then once you've let down your guard they'll either move in for the kill or scuttle away in search of another conquest.

Coming second is not in the Scorpio man's vocabulary. Losing is not only painful for him, it can kill a part of him. He doesn't just want to win in life, he *has* to win, and it's the same in relationships. He'll want to control you and if he catches his partner's eyes wandering his jealousy will know no bounds. However, he has a completely different set of rules for himself. You've got to give him space. You'll have to put up with his flirtations. Although this sounds very unfair, the fact is that you need to be very brave and strong to fall in love with a Scorpio. Once he's hypnotized you, however, you'll soar higher and further with him in physical, emotional and intellectual expression than you would ever have thought possible.

The Scorpio woman

Magnetic, proud, confident, mysterious and deep are key words for the Scorpio woman. The chances are she'll also be strikingly beautiful and seductive but, as stunning as she is, the Scorpio woman harbors a secret resentment. In her mind, being a woman brings its joys but also its restrictions. She may, for example, find the role of being a girlfriend challenging. She'll want to be the one making the move and—if it comes to marriage—she'll be the one who wants to pop the question. Then if children come on the scene, although she can

make a wonderful mother, she'll struggle with the limitations that having a family can make on her career.

Sexy and aggressive, it's not that this woman wishes she was more like a man. She just longs for more freedom and a life without limitation. She'll be the woman pushing the boundaries at work and, when it comes to relationships, she'll have no time for girlie mind games—she'll want to cut right to the chase. She does, however, know how to play the game of life well and will often disguise her true intentions behind a mysterious, enigmatic exterior. She's a mistress of the art of getting other people to do exactly what she wants without them even realizing it. Before you know it you'll be hopelessly caught in her spell. This woman is many things, but above all she is powerful.

Being so strong, a Scorpio woman can't stand weakness in others. In relationships she will look for a partner who is ambitious and intelligent, like she is; although she will try to dominate, when she is truly in love she secretly wants her partner to dominate her. She's deeply passionate and sexual, but in times of crisis her calm, inner strength will shine through. Although she is touchingly honest in her affections, her partner will never feel they completely understand her—but that's all part of her magic.

Family

Scorpio children often have the reputation for being sulky or moody. Instead of shouting and screaming when they don't get what they want, they may just go quiet and refuse to participate. It's extremely important for parents to encourage their little Scorpio to talk about what is bothering them because if this habit can be learned early in life it will save them a lot of grief and unhappiness later on. Intelligent and curious, these children also need to have plenty of interests and hobbies to keep them stimulated because if they get bored they can become restless physically and volatile emotionally. Their curiosity can sometimes lead them to explore or want to talk about areas of life that their parents feel uncomfortable discussing, such as death, sex, drugs and disease. Instead of telling them they are not old enough—which will simply make them more curious—parents should try to find ways to openly discuss taboo subjects in a safe way.

Scorpio children often have endless supplies of energy and should be encouraged to use this up with active participation in sports, dance and gymnastics. There will always be a secretive aspect to their personality and they may, for example, keep a secret diary or have a secret place where they like to go when the world feels overwhelming. Parents should be aware of their need for secrecy and should monitor it to make sure they are safe but they should not try to invade it.

Scorpio parents are often fairly strict and set high standards for their children—sometimes too high. They may often try to encourage their child to follow the same road in life they have followed but need to learn to let go if a child wants to follow a different path. Their children's development is fascinating to them but they need to ensure that they don't get obsessive about knowing everything their child is doing, thinking and feeling. Children have a need for space and freedom too. As far as disciplining their children is concerned, Scorpio parents must understand that being strict and authoritarian has its merits, but that most children thrive better when rules and regulations guide, rather than dictate their lives.

Career

Work matters more to Scorpios for a sense of personal fulfillment than for perhaps any other sign. They are willing to work extremely hard and long to carve themselves a career that will

" The reason work is so important to a Scorpio is that they need to feel challenged... "

give them both emotional and financial security. Periods of unemployment, career confusion or sudden retirement can be deeply unsettling for them because there is no outlet for their restless energy. Others may tell them to relax, unwind and enjoy the time to themselves but Scorpios are far happier when they are doing; for this reason they may often seek out unpaid work rather than not working at all. The reason work is so important for Scorpios is that they need to feel challenged; they must have something to pressure them emotionally, financially and intellectually.

Once Scorpios set their mind on a career there is little to stop them succeeding but they are particularly well suited to careers that involve research and detection. They make great criminologists, spies, detectives and journalists. They may also be drawn to jobs that allow them to take things apart and study them, such as a mechanic or scientist. Other career options may include surgery, pathology, psychology, psychiatry, stockbroking or market analysis, undertaking, insurance, therapy, nuclear weapons design, computing, diving, law enforcement or business.

Health and leisure

Scorpios have a tendency toward self-indulgence as far as food and drink is concerned, and this can often lead to digestive upsets or constipation. It's especially important therefore for Scorpios to aim for a healthy, balanced diet with the emphasis on moderation in all things. As far as alcohol, smoking, drugs and gambling are concerned, they should be avoided at all costs given the addictive tendencies of this sun sign. They have seemingly endless reserves of energy so regular exercise is a must, but they must be careful not to overdo it as over-training can lead to injuries and strain.

Although Scorpios do need to slow down when they start pushing themselves too long and too hard, doing nothing

neither suits them nor is healthy for them. Whether they are eight or eighty, those born under this sun sign need a compelling interest or lots of activities to keep them challenged, motivated and active, both physically and mentally. Leisure activities that particularly attract Scorpios are likely to include the martial arts, jogging and anything to do with water such as swimming, diving, snorkeling and water sports. The thrill-seeking aspect of their personality may be drawn toward speed racing, extreme sports and mystery thrillers, and the intense side of their personality may be attracted to magic and the occult arts as well as the mysteries of metaphysics and self-improvement courses. Because they can find it hard to open up emotionally to others, Scorpios often bottle up their emotions; this can have a damaging effect so, if they have no close friends in whom to confide, counseling or therapy is advised. Wearing, meditating on and surrounding themselves with the color blue will encourage them to keep a sense of perspective in life and be more calm, cool and collected when emotions start to overwhelm them.

Born between October 23 and October 31

Determination is the key word for people born between these dates. Some may regard them as insensitive and obsessive because they push forward so single-mindedly, but for them there are no half measures in life. They want to be the best, and they won't let anything stand in the way.

Born between November 1 and November 10

People born in the first couple of weeks of November are not afraid of obstacles or challenges in any way. In fact they positively thrive on them and love nothing better than trying to prove that no one can stop them—and as a result, more often than not, no one can.

Born between November 11 and 21

If these people are cornered or put in a compromising situation, they won't give in until they get what they want. Born fighters and seekers of justice, they know how to crush their opposition and do what they do best—win.

Life lessons

Deep, emotional and intense, Scorpios know what stimulates others but it isn't so easy to know what exactly it's that they themselves want. Their drive in life is to connect with others—and in close relationships to control others—but underneath that drive to connect there's often a deep-seated fear of being abandoned and left alone. Perhaps the most important life lesson for a Scorpio is to learn to let go of their fear of abandonment. Just because people need space or want to express their independence in some way does not necessarily mean that they are distancing themselves.

Scorpios are obsessed with finding out secrets and they need to learn the value of privacy and trust in a relationship. One reason they may find trusting others so hard is that they find it really hard to trust themselves. The first step for them must therefore be to learn to get a handle on their own emotions. They need to learn to forgive themselves when they mess up and to take charge of negative emotions—such as jealousy, anger and fear—rather than let them take over. Once Scorpios discover that it's they themselves rather than other people that make them feel a certain way, life will get much easier for them because it puts them in the driving seat rather than being at the mercy of the whims and inconsistencies of others.

Gaining emotional self-confidence is a tough lesson to learn, but in their struggle for fulfillment and happiness Scorpios can get help and inspiration from other signs of the zodiac. Aquarians have the inner calm and emotional self-control that many Scorpios lack. Arians can encourage them to express their emotions honestly and Cancerians can encourage them to be open to others rather than bottle their feelings up. Leos can teach them to be warm and open-hearted rather than secretive and suspicious, and Libras can help them discover the contentment that comes when there is a balance in their life between giving and receiving, holding fast and letting go.

23 October

the birthday of
the maelstrom

Your greatest challenge is

loving unconditionally

The way forward is ...

to understand that there is no greater power on earth than the power of unconditional love.

People born on October 23 run on high-octane energy. Life is exciting when they are around because they seem to create a maelstrom around whatever situation they are in. Others admire their lively charm, intelligence and courage, but may sometimes wonder why they seem to want to make life so difficult for themselves.

These people have a low boredom threshold and they find themselves drawn to conflict, excitement and tension as ways to challenge themselves. Others may find this need to stir things up inexplicable but to these people it is simply the way they love to live. For them, life on the sidelines or life that has settled into an easy routine, no matter how successful or enjoyable, isn't a life worth living. Their compulsive zest for stimulation and ambition for improvement forces them to make groundbreaking advances or—if that's not possible—to experience or learn something new.

Above all, they need to be active, and even the calmer people born on this day will find that during times of crisis they really come into their own. Before the age of thirty they are likely to be concerned with issues of personal power; because there is a tendency for them to cling possessively to power when they feel they have earned it, they need to make sure power and control do not go to their head. After the age of thirty there is a turning point when they are likely to become even more adventurous, and they will have a strong desire to expand the horizons of their life. It is important in the years that follow that they find a balance between their need to test and challenge themselves, and their need to seek stability and harmony.

Whatever path in life they choose, change and instability will always be a feature. Once they understand, however, that they don't necessarily need a crisis to feel alive, their ability to respond instantly to stimulating opportunities for growth and improvement makes them among the most independent, progressive and compassionate individuals of the year.

On the dark side

Confused, temperamental, restless

At your best

Exciting, charismatic, inspiring

24 October

Your greatest challenge is

going with the flow

The way forward is ...

to see that certain things in life cannot be controlled; the most empowering choice you can make is to stand back and leave things alone.

People born on October 24 have an irresistible intensity about them that draws others to them. They are ruled by extreme emotions that they battle to control, but one of their greatest strengths—and the reason others tend to admire or aspire to be like them—is that they can play it cool, even when they feel totally insecure or out of control on the inside.

These people get absorbed in their work and feel compelled to present, often with dramatic flair, their discoveries or revelations to the world. This doesn't mean they are exhibitionists. It just means that they take their profession, craft or work extremely seriously and pride themselves on their accomplishments. Their intensity about what they do means that others can't help but be magnetically drawn into their world.

The upside of all this intensity is that they have enormous potential to shine in their careers, perhaps rising to the very top. In their personal life it means that they can fall passionately in love with someone to the exclusion of all else. The downside is that they can neglect their family and their emotional life in preference for their work. They can also become rather controlling, jealous and interfering, and this can alienate them from the support of those who can give them a much-needed sense of perspective.

Fortunately, around the age of twenty-nine there is a turning point which highlights a need for freedom and a more expansive outlook on life. They will be presented with opportunities to broaden their horizons through a quest for truth, education or travel. It is important for their psychological growth that they take advantage of these opportunities to diversify and explore, because it will help keep them in touch with the joy of life. Whatever age they are they should never lose their ability to devote themselves with enthusiasm to their work; when this is balanced with greater tolerance, flexibility and open-mindedness, they have outstanding potential not just to realize their ambitions but to enjoy the fruits of them as well.

On the dark side

Obsessive, jealous, stressed

At your best

Hypnotic, dramatic, authoritative

25 October

the birthday of
tangible results

Your greatest challenge is

putting the needs of others above your own

The way forward is ...

to understand that helping and supporting others earns you their lasting loyalty and respect.

People born on October 25 are forceful and tenacious, and their actions and behavior are driven by the urge to give concrete expression or provide tangible results for the original visions that inspire them. In other words, the driving force of people born on this day is their desire to translate their progressive dreams into reality.

Although they are articulate and intelligent, these people don't have much time for small talk. Results are what matter to them and, "Actions speak louder than words" is their motto. Others may accuse them of not being visionary enough, but this is not the case. They have dreams and visions, and respect the dreams of others, but ideas mean nothing to them unless they can somehow be substantiated in the real world.

Quiet and straightforward with a result-based, no-nonsense approach to life, they can often be a comforting presence in the lives of those around them. This doesn't mean they are necessarily compassionate and supportive; indeed they are not the most caring and sharing individuals of the year. It means that for most of the time they are a steadying and reassuring presence and a role model of self-belief, determination, focus and organization. Unfortunately, though, there are also times when they can be critical and intolerant, and this can earn them potentially dangerous enemies.

When these people enter their late twenties there is a turning point where they are likely to become more expansive in their outlook. This may involve taking more risks or expanding their horizons through philosophy, study or travel. While they should never lose sight of their goals, they need to take advantage of the opportunities life offers them to open their heart and spread their wings. This is because by actively involving themselves in new experiences and relationships, they can keep their spirit of adventure and romance alive. In this way they can achieve their goal of bringing about tangible progress, not just on their own path to happiness and fulfillment, but also in the lives of others.

On the dark side

Intolerant, self-centered, workaholic

At your best

Dependable, driven, practical

26 October

the birthday of
the powerful planner

Your greatest challenge is

accepting your limitations

The way forward is ...

to understand that accepting your limitations helps you appreciate, value and focus your attention on your strengths.

The goal-orientated individuals born on October 26 are perhaps the most hardworking individuals of the entire year. They are ambitious and conscientious but their motivation isn't money or success but power, and they are at their best when they are organizing and managing others.

Although these people are hungry for power, this is not to say that they are lonely, power-crazed egomaniacs. Quite the opposite; they simply believe that organizing people to work collectively is the most effective way to achieve progress. And with their ability to focus on the distant goal, while at the same time orchestrating the collective effort of others, they are gifted and inspired leaders whose dedication and authority inspire respect. More often than not, they will be found planning events, serving on committees or putting structures in place for community reform. Their desire to manage people, to plan and put systems in place extends as much to their personal life as it does to their professional life, and they will expend a lot of energy trying to get others to think along the same lines as them. If others agree with them then their loving, affectionate qualities surface; the opposite is true if others disagree with them, and they can be extremely cold and disinterested to the unconverted.

Before the age of twenty-six people born on this day may find that their progress is blocked by crippling shyness, but after the age of twenty-six there is a turning point that offers them opportunities to grow in confidence and self-belief. They may become more optimistic and may wish to expand their mental outlook, perhaps through learning or through contact with foreign places or people. Whatever career path they eventually choose, they will often find themselves coordinating and directing others.

Outstanding professional success is strongly associated with this birthday. However, to ensure that this magic extends to their personal life as well, they need to trust their intuition more and remember that the greater good is not always served by suppression of originality, and that includes their own.

On the dark side

Obsessive, rigid, dull

At your best

Cooperative, organized, perceptive

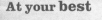

427

27 October

the birthday of
the galvanizer

Your greatest challenge is

overcoming your impatience

The way forward is ...

to understand that lots of people miss out on good fortune because they aren't patient enough to wait for serendipity to visit.

People born on October 27 are emotional individuals. They tend to react instantly and spontaneously to anyone or anything they encounter. Acting on their impulses comes as second nature to them, and their ability to excite and galvanize others with the intensity of their emotions gives them outstanding potential to lead and motivate others.

Impossible to ignore, these people are at their happiest and their best when they are expressing their thoughts and feelings, and influencing or directing those around them. Their decisions and opinions are undoubtedly driven by emotion, but they also have the intellect, communication and practical skills they need to see their goals realized. Once their imagination or heart has been touched they are, quite literally, unstoppable.

Given their impulsive nature, it is not surprising that they are also prone to mood swings, and a recurring theme in their life will be intense highs followed by intense lows. One of the reasons for this unpredictability is that beneath their outspoken, expressive exterior there is often a fragile and vulnerable side that simply isn't getting the nurturing or respect it needs. This is especially the case if getting the approval of others matters more to these people than anything else. It is therefore extremely important that they work on building their self-esteem, learning to listen more to their intuition as their inner wisdom will be able to gently warn them when their emotions are blocking their potential for luck and happiness.

Before the age of twenty-five the emotional impulsiveness of people born on this day will be heightened, but after the age of twenty-six they are likely to become less sensitive, and more independent and adventurous. Whatever age they are, however, they will always follow their heart rather than their head, and they will feel things more deeply than other people. The key to their success will be to direct their emotional intensity and energy positively so that they don't just galvanize but light up both their own lives and the lives of others.

On the dark side

Reckless, insecure, scattered

At your best

Exciting, energetic, intelligent

428

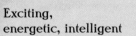

28 October

the birthday of

preparation

Your greatest challenge is

taking a risk

The way forward is ...

to understand that when a risk is calculated, it is not reckless but a way to move forward with your life.

People born on October 28 tend to be very committed to their career and therefore the choice of career is of utmost importance to them. They may take a while to find their vocation, but once they do they nearly always reach the top of the field. This is in part due to the incredible effort they are willing to put in and their eye for detail. One of their biggest fears is being caught unprepared but this is largely unfounded as they are among the most organized and well-prepared individuals of the year.

They will often be completely absorbed in their work to the extent that they don't have much of a life outside. Although this means that they nearly always reach the very top of their field, which more often than not is dedicated to improving or educating others, there is a heavy price to pay. They may come across as overly serious or preoccupied and, if they haven't got friends and family to give them a sense of perspective, they are in danger of becoming emotionally isolated, completely losing their spontaneity and ability to have fun.

Until the age of twenty-five they are likely to be at their most serious and intense but after this age there is a turning point that highlights a need for freedom. Opportunities will be presented to them to expand their horizons, whether through travel, further education or study, and it is important that they take advantage of these because they offer them the chance to become a more fully rounded and fulfilled human being, rather than a human working.

Above all, these people are inquisitive individuals with an insatiable desire to explore. Fascinated with the tiny details that can make all the difference, their logical mind gives them the potential to make pioneering contributions to the world. And if they can learn to expend as much energy discovering and preparing themselves for the wonderful adventures life has to offer outside work, they will also be able to create lasting connections with the world.

On the dark side

Workaholic, detached, confused

At your best

Dedicated, detailed, inquisitive

29 October

the birthday of
the chess master

Your greatest challenge is

letting others know where they stand

The way forward is ...

to understand that although secrecy can be an extremely effective strategy for professional success, the same is not true in your personal life.

People born on October 29 are highly accomplished tacticians and strategists prepared for any scenario, but this is not to say they are predictable in any way. They are in fact extremely independent and innovative individuals, bursting with new ideas and energy. It's just that one of the reasons they invest so much energy in preparing and planning for potential outcomes is that, like a chess master, they appreciate the element of surprise and the benefits of keeping others in the dark about their true intentions.

Secrecy and surprise are recurring themes in the lives of these people. They are secretive in both their professional and personal lives, so others never really understand what makes them tick, and are surprised by their sudden changes of direction. For example, they can be caring and considerate one moment, then cold and self-absorbed the next; or needy and insecure in one situation, and confident and dynamic in another.

All of this only makes sense when the bigger picture of their lives is taken into account, and in this bigger picture is a pronounced desire to organize and direct others toward their personal goals or ideals. To some this may appear manipulative but to people born on this day unpredictability is an empowering tactic to strengthen their personal and strategic position; when applied to their professional life it can be extremely useful. Problems arise, however, when they use the same tactic in their personal life as it can make others feel excluded or mistrusted.

Before the age of twenty-three, people born on this day may be shy or reserved and it may take a lot to draw them out of themselves. After the age of twenty-four, however, there is a turning point when they become more optimistic and adventurous, and this may lead them to open up and take more chances emotionally. Whatever age they are, they should make a huge effort to reveal more to others because, although outstanding professional success is assured, personal success is more elusive until they can connect more honestly and openly.

On the dark side

Devious,
secretive, detached

At your best

Innovative,
masterful, thorough

30 October

the birthday of
the deep-sea diver

Your greatest challenge is

staying in touch

The way forward is ...

to understand that networking is an important part of attracting success; to stay alive, contacts and friendships need to be nurtured on a regular basis.

People born on October 30 like to immerse themselves fully in whatever project, situation or relationship captures their vivid imagination. Like deep-sea divers, they throw themselves in at the deep end and their whole world is taken over by their current interest or concern.

Whatever it is that engages the interest of these people, it will often monopolize all their attention. The upside of this is that their energy, absorption and one hundred per cent dedication give them great potential for success in whatever field they have chosen to plunge into. Their infectious enthusiasm and charismatic charm encourage others to take the plunge with them. They are also not afraid to deal with the mundane aspects of the goal to which they have committed, and this practicality—combined with their logical and progressive intellect and excellent communication skills—makes them natural organizers and motivators of others. The downside, however, is that, as well as neglecting other important areas of their lives, when a particular challenge has been overcome or their current passion has settled into a routine they tend to lose interest. This can leave their disillusioned followers without a motivated leader.

Before the age of twenty-three they are largely concerned with the development of their personal power and how to handle their strong feelings. They may come across during this period as rather intense and serious individuals. However, after the age of twenty-four there is a turning point which emphasizes a growing need for more optimism and expansion in their lives. They need to take full advantage of opportunities to study, travel and expand their horizons.

Whatever age they are, these fascinating and sincere individuals will always have a strong spirit of enterprise. When they are able to expand and diversify their life from a one-dimensional to a multi-dimensional focus, not only will they fulfill their potential as inspirational teachers, managers and leaders, they will finally be able to come out of the water and breathe.

On the dark side

Obsessive, neglectful, distant

At your best

Fascinating, charismatic, passionate

31 October

the birthday of
the indomitable cooperator

Your greatest challenge is

concentrating your energy

The way forward is ...

to understand that concentration is the most important ingredient for success; without it you will become confused and uncertain.

People born on October 31 have all the talent, originality, intellect and creativity they need to excel in whatever field they choose, but their natural modesty often prevents them from stepping forward to take the credit. They much prefer to guide and praise others; as a result, people tend to rely on them for support, comfort and inspiration.

Although people born on this day are accommodating by nature, they are not so self-effacing that they don't know how to accept praise when they feel that they have genuinely earned it. In fact, when they sense that injustice has been done, toward themselves or others, their indomitable fighting spirit will emerge, and they can display remarkable courage and resilience. Their outspokenness and willingness to take risks will indeed surprise those who may have wrongly pigeonholed them as gentle, unassuming souls.

These people will give their all to a cause or ideal in which they believe, and when their indomitable will is combined with their logical turn of mind, excellent communication skills and superior organizational skills, they are a force to be reckoned with. The only chink in their armor is that they can get bogged down with details, and this can lead to confusion and despondency. It's important for them to always keep their ultimate goal or the bigger picture in mind, and not to get sidetracked along the way.

After the age of twenty-two there will be a growing need for people born on this day to expand their horizons, whether through further education or contact with foreign people and places. It's important for them to take advantage of opportunities for new sights and experiences, as these will energize them. However, they need to bear in mind that they work better when they have a plan for what they want to achieve, and if they can stick to it—and move from the passenger seat to the driving seat of their life—they will be able to satisfy their strong desire to contribute something of lasting value to the world.

On the dark side

Passive, self-effacing, confused

At your best

Sympathetic, supportive, indomitable

1 November

the birthday of
the quarterback

Your greatest challenge is

self-knowledge

The way forward is ...

to understand that having opinions or education does not necessarily make you self-aware. You need to take the time to reflect and look within.

The greatest fear for people born on November 1 is a life without variety and challenge. They despise inaction and lack of progress, being stimulated by progressive, even radical concepts. Doers, rather than thinkers, offense rather than defense, as soon as they have completed one challenge they throw themselves wholeheartedly into the next.

These people are up for any challenge life can throw at them because the excitement and uncertainty taxing situations offer them make them feel alive. If they find a way to satisfy their hunger for adventure and stimulation, their boundless energy and vital spark give them the power and potential to make things happen. If, however, they find themselves in an environment where they do not need to be in battle mode, they can sink into despondency, even depression.

They tend to be honest and outspoken individuals, willing to offer their opinion on anything. Although their self-confidence is admirable, it does not always help them achieve their goals because one thing they can lack is good judgment. They may, for example, take dangerous risks or underestimate or misinterpret people and situations, and their inability to listen to the sound advice of others, even those who are experts in their field, can work against them. In other words, they make excellent quarterbacks, but very poor defenders, and in tough situations their lack of defensive strategy can leave them wide open to attack.

Until the age of twenty-one they may come across as intense and serious, but after the age of twenty-two they break out of their shell and their adventurous nature shines through. They want to take more chances and challenge themselves in new areas to build up their sense of purpose. Whatever age they are, their courageous spirit and expansive outlook give them remarkable potential to extend the bounds of human knowledge. But to become the inspirational and influential force they are destined to be, self-knowledge and a powerful dose of common sense are crucial.

On the dark side

Foolish,
unaware, restless

At your best

Inventive,
exciting, energetic

2 November

the birthday of regeneration

Your greatest challenge is

resisting the temptation to interfere

The way forward is ...

to understand that change for the sake of change serves no purpose but unsettles and confuses both yourself and others.

Like a serpent that sheds its skin, people born on November 2 often appear to be in the process of change, rebirth or renewal. Nothing gets them more excited in life than a new start.

But it isn't only their own lives that are constantly changing and evolving; they can also play an integral part in changing the lives of others in some way or in altering the course of events. For example, they may play a significant role in changing the structure of a business or they may encourage others to change the direction of their lives in some way, perhaps by leaving a relationship or by expanding their horizons with travel. As self-awareness doesn't tend to be strong in these people, many of them will not realize just how influential they can be. It is important therefore for them to guard against advising change for the sake of change.

Ironically, despite their love of change and regeneration, the one area of life they may be surprisingly resistant to change is themselves. Many of them simply aren't aware of their real needs and, instead of focusing on their inner life, they will direct their energy outwards with constant fresh starts or changes of direction. It's only when they can learn to listen to the quiet still voice within them that they will begin to realize that too much change is counterproductive.

After the age of twenty, they enter a thirty-year period when there is an emphasis on expansion and adventure in their lives. This may come through study, education or travel. After the age of fifty there is a turning point which highlights the need for greater order, structure and realism in achieving their goals. Whatever their age or stage in life it will be an exciting one, but for the lasting success and outstanding creative potential associated with this birthday to be unlocked they need to understand that, although regeneration is a necessary process for psychological growth, it is not a goal in itself.

On the dark side

Scattered, restless, unaware

At your best

Energizing, influential, flexible

434

3 November

the birthday of
the marathon runner

Your greatest challenge is

finishing second

The way forward is ...

to understand that people tend to learn more about themselves during times of disappointment and defeat than they do in times of victory.

People born on November 3 have all the strength and staying power of a long-distance runner. They are ambitious and energetic but know how to bide their time and go the distance to achieve their goals.

With the ability to keep calm under the most intense pressure, they can earn the reputation for being extremely cool, sometimes ruthless, customers. At times they may appear to be hesitant or passive, but all the while they are simply waiting for the right moment to strike out and achieve their goals. If there is one thing, however, that can unsettle the masterful self-control of these people it is defeat or failure. They are terrible losers and, instead of trying to find alternative solutions, they may waste tremendous energy on self-recrimination and in some cases this can lead to depression.

Although they can be overwhelmingly negative at times, the upside is that when things are going well they can be energetic, charismatic, pleasure loving and stimulating. Those lucky enough to catch them in one of these moods will be enchanted and uplifted. They can also be compassionate and supportive during these moments, with a deep understanding of the feelings of others. Unfortunately, when it comes to understanding themselves they lack similar insight, so they should look deep within to understand why the need to win can sometimes overpower their need to feel happy.

Despite being moody and intense as a teenager, after the age of twenty they will acquire a more optimistic and expansive outlook; this may lead them to broaden their horizons to seek truth, travel or study. After the age of forty-nine there is another turning point when financial and emotional stability is likely to take center stage. Throughout their lives they will always be highly competitive warriors, but once they understand that the only battle really worth winning is the one within themselves they can apply their progressive intellect, superb communication skills and almost superhuman endurance to the only cause that's always a winner—one that furthers the common good.

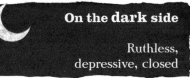

On the dark side

Ruthless, depressive, closed

At your best

Persistent, focused, progressive

4 November

the birthday of
the ice breaker

Your greatest challenge is

being less provocative

The way forward is ...

to understand that being controversial is not the only way to make people notice or remember you.

Although they can sometimes come across as conformist and sincere, as soon as people born on November 4 start interacting with others their provocative nature shines through. They have a talent for uncovering hidden weaknesses and insecurities in people and situations, and for luring everyone they meet into their tangled web of controversy and excitement.

They are extremely persuasive individuals, and in their minds they know that they have the ability to win over almost anyone to their point of view. This is not to say they are manipulative. Quite the opposite; they are principled and honest. It is just that it is almost impossible for them to believe there are any alternatives to the truth as they see it.

Above all, these people are ice breakers wherever they find themselves. They make full use of the element of surprise and are somehow able to articulate what is unspoken or unacceptable in the most humorous or convincing way, so that others are lured into either agreeing with them or at least reviewing their own position. Unfortunately, however, their shock tactics can work against them. They may, for example, find that the situations they have stirred up have got out of hand or the views they are expressing have truly overwhelmed or offended.

Until the age of eighteen, they may have come across as shy or intense. After the age of nineteen, however, that slowly recedes and is replaced by a growing need for freedom and the desire to expand their horizons through study, education or travel. After the age of forty-eight there is another turning point when the emphasis is on financial and emotional security. Whatever age they are, the key to success is to use their common sense and become more aware of the way their stance toward life is affecting others and, ultimately, themselves. When greater self-awareness and self-discipline are combined with their intuitive perception and natural leadership qualities, they are capable of achieving not controversial or shocking but truly spectacular results in life.

On the dark side

Overwhelming, provocative, tactless

At your best

Magnetic, exciting, supportive

5 November

the birthday of
the representative

Your greatest challenge is

self-reliance

The way forward is ...

to understand that as long as you rely on others for a sense of self-worth, you will not be in control of your life; they will be.

People born on November 5 like to be at the center of things; this is often where you will find them. They are the ones others tend to turn to if they want to be in the know, not just because they can be assured of an honest and informed response but because consciously or unconsciously they are representatives of the social group, family or occupation they belong to.

As information gatherers, these people keep up to date with what is current, not because they are gossips or busy bodies, but because their forte is spotting cutting-edge trends before anyone else. Sometimes their mind seems to be focused in another dimension because it is suffering from information overload, but despite their occasional absent-mindedness they are determined individuals and real power-houses who get things accomplished. Their realism means that they refuse to let their idealism get in the way of practical considerations.

Until the age of seventeen they may have presented a somewhat withdrawn or intense persona, but after the age of eighteen there is a dramatic change which sees them becoming more confident and outgoing. This may lead them to expand their mental outlook and to develop their characteristic fascination with what's going on around them. After the age of forty-eight they become more organized and industrious, with a greater understanding of their goals in life. The key to their success, whatever their age or stage in life, will not be their ability to adapt to what is going on around them, but their ability to control and direct it.

The lesson in life they need to learn is that until they are as fascinated in their own self-development as they are in keeping up with what other people are doing, the outstanding potential for personal achievement associated with this birthday will remain elusive. However, once they start to become more self-aware, not only will they find greater happiness, they will also be able to use their incredible insight and knowledge to represent and to benefit others.

On the dark side

Deluded, gossipy, over-accommodating

At your best

Inquisitive, up to date, honest

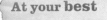

437

6 November

the birthday of
the energetic over-achiever

Your greatest challenge is

handling disappointment

The way forward is ...

to understand that unless you know what it feels like to lose or miss out, you will not be able to fully appreciate what it feels like to succeed.

Vibrant and stimulating, people born on November 6 have boundless energy and the ability to create an enthusiastic environment wherever they go, stimulating and motivating others with their infectious, limitless and honest enthusiasm.

Driven and ambitious, with a can-do attitude, these people typically refuse to be sidetracked or blocked from the goals that excite them by limitations or obstacles. Although this gives them incredible potential for success there is a danger, however, that they can get ahead of themselves with their enthusiasm and become too confident of success without the necessary plans or back-up. Sometimes their aims can appear so far reaching that others simply brand them as unfeasible; although they will often shake off criticism with humor, a part of them feels deeply hurt that others don't believe in them enough.

Surrounding themselves with people who are as optimistic and upbeat as themselves will lift their spirits, but it is also important for them to make sure that they inject a heavy dose of realism into their lives. A realistic outlook is not a negative one but one that takes into account both the upsides and the downsides of a situation.

After the age of sixteen, people born on this day start to develop their characteristic enthusiasm, energy and drive, and they are likely to be positive and expansive in their outlook. This may lead them to further education or travel, or stimulate them to be adventurous and take chances. This influence continues until the age of forty-six, when they become more realistic, practical and organized in their approach to life, with a strong need for order in their lives. Given the fact that realism is an important ingredient for their psychological growth, these are the years when they will finally be able to come to terms with the fact that there will always be positive and negative outcomes to consider. This rational outlook will empower them on their dedicated quest to enlighten others and realize their innovative visions.

On the dark side

Over-confident, driven, despondent

At your best

Optimistic, energetic, uplifting

7 November

the birthday of
the curious adventurer

Your greatest challenge is

to be decisive

The way forward is ...

to understand that your mind will present you with all sorts of excuses not to move forward with your life, but inaction will keep you stuck.

People born on November 7 tend to be inquisitive and progressive types with an adventurous, pioneering spirit. They relish any opportunity to learn and discover something new, and to test their skills in demanding challenges.

There is very little that they don't want to learn about or understand better. Their curiosity is limitless and nothing gives them more satisfaction than being able to figure out what makes a person tick or how something works. In addition they are extremely ambitious and driven individuals who thrive on variety and change; being caught in a mundane, routine existence is their personal nightmare. Although the potential for remarkable success in exploring the outermost parameters of human knowledge is great for these people, the biggest threat to their potential is their lack of focus. In some ways their greatest strength—their inquisitive spirit—is also their greatest weakness, because their constant need to struggle, learn and challenge can stop them setting achievable goals for themselves.

Until the age of forty-five they are likely to be at their most restless and may have a burning urge to study, travel and expand their horizons in as many new directions as possible. After the age of forty-five, however, there is an important turning point when—with a strong need for order and structure—they are likely to become more realistic, practical and organized in order to achieve their goals in life.

This is not to say that the first part of their lives is chaotic, because if they set themselves personal goals and pursue them actively they can achieve great success. It is just that for many of these people the second part of their lives tends to be the most fulfilling and rewarding. This is because they can build on the incredible knowledge and experience they have gained in their youth and use it as a launching pad to work toward realizing their goals—those that they believe will be of great benefit not just to themselves and those they live and work with, but to the wider world.

On the dark side

Scattered, restless, unfocused

At your best

Inquisitive, pioneering, refreshing

8 November

the birthday of
dark fascination

Your greatest challenge is

developing a sense of humor

The way forward is ...

to understand that if you take yourself too seriously you will lose the sense of perspective and objectivity you need to make good judgments.

Although they are blessed with imaginative and progressive minds, people born on November 8 can come across as serious or intense. They tend to be attracted to unusual subjects that others would consider borderline, shadowy or dark. In some cases their interests may even be considered peculiar or, at the very least, out of the ordinary.

They are brilliant at concentrating their energy on achieving their goals, and this, combined with their courage and ambition, augurs well for professional success. Many will attract money their way, rise to the top of their career or make a comfortable standard of living an important goal in their lives. Sometimes the desire to achieve materially can be so strong that it becomes overpowering in its intensity; it is important for these people to remember what is truly important in life.

It is their curiosity which draws these people to the shadowy aspects of life, and a part of them longs to push the boundaries of knowledge and experience to their limits. If they are able to maintain objectivity they have the potential to be innovating pioneers; but if they can't keep their distance, there is a real risk of their becoming too closely identified with the darker aspects of the world and the shadow side of themselves.

Until the age of thirty-three, the urge for these people to explore the unconventional is at its strongest; during these years they need to remember that, as fascinating as the unconventional is, there is also much to be learned from what is routine. After the age of thirty-four there is a turning point when they start to become more practical, disciplined and goal-orientated in the realization of their objectives. Whatever age they are, however, the key to their success is their ability to confront their inner fears rather than seeking it outside. When they can do this, their hunger to explore the meaning of life will inevitably draw them away from the darkness within to the light of understanding, compassion, love, and what is truly important in life.

On the dark side

Obsessed, overly serious, addictive

At your best

Deep, driven, inquisitive

9 November

the birthday of
temptation

Your greatest challenge is

resisting temptation

The way forward is ...

to understand that the forbidden often seems tempting just because it is forbidden.

Many times during their lives people born on November 9 will find themselves in situations that test and challenge their resolve. Temptation and the moral issues it uncovers for them are a constant factor in their lives.

The pursuit of physical and material pleasure is a powerful drive for these people. The great majority of the time they do find a balance between satisfying their urges and doing the right thing, but occasionally they can dip into behavior that is morally questionable. This isn't to say that they are amoral. Quite the opposite; they are honest and well-intentioned individuals. It's just that sometimes they can get so caught up in the enticement of the moment that they lose a sense of perspective and of right and wrong.

Not surprisingly, these people are risk-takers, and this gives them the potential to go all the way to the top. Unfortunately, they aren't always good at dealing with rejection and, instead of treating it as a learning experience, they are likely to isolate themselves with resentment and self-pity. Learning to become more resilient or to roll with the blows by tapping into their inner strength is therefore essential for their psychological growth.

Until the age of forty-two, they are most likely to feel a need to expand their horizons, take risks and seek out new challenges. Developing a more positive attitude will encourage them to seek out opportunities that can enlighten rather than confuse or disorientate them. After the age of forty-three there is a turning point when they are likely to become more industrious and practical, needing a strong sense of order and structure in their lives. Making sure that the spiritual side of their life is not neglected is absolutely crucial during these years, because when they are able to connect with their inner wisdom they will not only be able to resist the temptations that block their chances of good fortune, they will be able to rise above these and achieve remarkable success both professionally and personally.

On the dark side

Materialistic, thoughtless, seedy

At your best

Interesting, curious, seductive

10 November

the birthday of
awareness

Your greatest challenge is

developing self-confidence

The way forward is ...

to understand that you are as confident as you believe yourself to be; change your thoughts about yourself and you can change your world.

People born on November 10 are among the most self-aware of the year. From an early age they will have got to know their strengths and weaknesses very well, and as a result they have a realistic idea of what is or is not achievable for them. This self-knowledge gives them a huge advantage in the game of life and, when combined with their curiosity, intelligence and originality of thought, their potential for success is considerable.

These people don't simply have a unique understanding of themselves; they also have a natural understanding of how objects, strategies or methods work. For example, they are the first person to whom others will turn when things break down, because to others they are the fixers and menders in life.

There is, however, one subject of which people born on this day have very little understanding and awareness, and that is other people. Individual and group dynamics are a mystery to them, so when it comes to socializing and networking they may feel out of their depth. They need to learn that, however good they are at their job, if they don't have the right connections or social skills to promote themselves there is a strong likelihood that they will not get the recognition or success they deserve. Working on their self-confidence and social skills is therefore a top priority.

Fortunately, until the age of forty-two there are opportunities for them to step outside themselves and reach out to others; they should take these opportunities, however hard or frightening they may appear, because becoming unhealthily self-absorbed is a real risk to their chances of happiness and fulfillment. After the age of forty-three there is another turning point when they are likely to become more practical, disciplined and goal orientated; again, if they can learn to overcome their shyness, put the spotlight on others instead of themselves and resist the temptation to hold back when they should be pushing forward, they will be able to make the most of their remarkable creative potential and achieve almost anything.

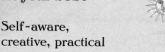

On the dark side

Shy, passive,
self-absorbed

At your best

Self-aware,
creative, practical

11 November

the birthday of
the painted veil

Your greatest challenge is

overcoming inertia

The way forward is ...

to understand that you are letting fear or laziness take control of your actions. Change this by regaining control of your life.

People born on November 11 will often present an energetic, bright and cheerful face to the world, but to those who know them better this is more often than not a veil masking an intense and original but sometimes troubled personality.

These charismatic individuals know how to appear attractive to others and as a result they tend to get their own way, often without others realizing it because veiling their powerful ambition is, they believe, the best way to win others to their point of view. Above all, they are complex characters with the ability to surprise others with their hidden talents and unexpected sides to their character. Unfortunately, they are often extremely confused about what their motivations are, what they want out of life and in which direction they should be heading. This can obviously have a confusing effect on others, presenting a straightforward, energetic persona and clear-cut goals on the one hand, but manifesting a propensity for anxiety and uncertainty on the other. It is only when they are able to reconcile these two sides of their personality that their potential for success and happiness can finally be unveiled.

Until the age of forty there is a growing need for optimism and expansion through study, travel or a personal quest for meaning in life. If they can find a way to be more assertive in stating what their needs are, and be more flexible and creative when setbacks occur, the promise they may have showed from an early age will manifest. After the age of forty there is a turning point when they are likely to become more pragmatic and realistic in their approach to life.

It is more important than ever during these years that they don't allow hidden fears and insecurities to plunge them into procrastination, resentment and obscurity. This would be a tragedy because, if they can summon the courage to lift their veils, they are destined to shine, contributing their talents and energies to the greater good.

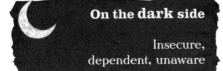

On the dark side

Insecure, dependent, unaware

At your best

Enthusiastic, inspiring, generous

12 November

the birthday of

mesmerizing prerogative

Your greatest challenge is

taking responsibility

The way forward is ...

to understand that until you can own up to the part you play in shaping your destiny, life will feel confusing and out of control.

People born on November 12 feel it is their right to attract attention or get whatever they want from others and from life. With such powerful expectations, the chances should be good for their success and happiness. Unfortunately, in some cases the opposite is true.

These people have the potential to be the most mesmerizing and seductive individuals of the year. In some cases others don't just listen to or even follow them, but worship the fact that they can bring excitement and beauty into their lives. Their boldness and imagination are outstanding, but unfortunately they aren't always the positive force they seem to have been destined to be from an early age. This is because they have a tendency to flout not just convention but moral and ethical codes to get what they want. In some cases the ends may justify the means, but there will also be times when they do not; their success may depend on how subtle they are in bending the rules, and how considerate and kind they are toward others.

Despite their golden aura, in many ways they are complex individuals able to bring beauty and harmony to the world, but possessing deep internal conflicts between their strong, sometimes dark and always confusing emotions. These conflicts may prevent them from realizing their goals and it is only after great personal struggle that they are finally in a position to claim their victory.

Until the age of thirty-nine there is an emphasis in their lives on adventure and freedom, and they may wish to explore and expand their mental outlook through study or travel. After the age of forty there is a turning point when they are likely to take a more disciplined and practical approach. Whatever age they are, the key to their success will be their ability to remember the importance of the emotional well-being that is vital to their happiness. When they are able to do that, happiness and success won't just be their prerogative—they will be their reality.

On the dark side

Selfish, amoral, troubled

At your best

Illuminating, magnetic, generous

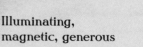

13 November

the birthday of
conversion

Your greatest challenge is

changing your mind

The way forward is ...

to understand that refusing to acknowledge alternative viewpoints or possibilities blocks the possibility of change and progress.

People born on November 13 are highly observant, with strong and passionate convictions. They can absorb all kinds of data, subject it to rigorous analysis and then pronounce their strong opinions. At some point they may have undergone a powerful conversion of some kind which now influences all their beliefs and opinions.

The views that these people present to the world tend to be well informed but their personal conviction will always shine through. The conversion that they may have undergone will not necessarily have been religious, it could simply be a specific way of looking at the world; but whatever it was, there is a tendency for them to gather information to support their beliefs rather than the other way around. This is not to say that they are not logical or reasonable. Quite the opposite; their opinions will always be well presented and clearly thought out. It's just that they are so optimistic and passionate in their beliefs that they find it impossible to acknowledge that there can be any other truth than their own.

Until the age of thirty-eight they tend to be at their most zealous, with a strong emphasis on idealism and optimism. It is extremely important during these years that they don't become inflexible and authoritarian, and make a real effort to take on board what other people are saying to them. After the age of thirty-nine there is a turning point when they start to have a more determined and disciplined approach to life. During these years it's crucial that they don't allow their idealism to slip into dogmatism. If they can learn to be more flexible in their beliefs, they are less likely to alienate or offend others and attract misfortune.

Whatever age they are, getting to know themselves better will help them see that having strong opinions is not the same as having a sense of self. With a more flexible and open mind they will discover within themselves the potential to promote their cause or their opinions in a remarkable way.

On the dark side

Dogmatic, authoritarian, blinkered

At your best

Passionate, determined, spiritual

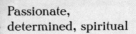

14 November

the birthday of

the guide

Your greatest challenge is

being sensitive to the feelings of others

The way forward is ...

to understand that the truth presented tactfully can be motivational but the truth presented harshly can make others defensive.

People born on November 14 have an intense and earnest air about them, others immediately sensing their conviction and self-reliance. They are driven by their desire to fully understand what life presents them with but most of all by their urge to guide others toward improvement.

Tending to observe others with a degree of affectionate distance, this gives these people the detachment and objectivity they need to guide and improve the lives of others. More often than not the insights and advice they offer are embraced wholeheartedly by colleagues, friends and loved ones, but sometimes they can be too meddling. It is important for them to understand that there are situations in which their advice will not necessarily be welcome and occasions where their judgments will not be appreciated.

Until the age of thirty-seven there will be opportunities for people born on this day to become more expansive in their outlook and, because of their tendency to connect with others on an intellectual rather than an emotional level, they should try to integrate more with others and with society as a whole. It is also important during this time that they evaluate their choice of career intensely and if need be make changes, because it might significantly impact their psychological growth. After the age of thirty-eight there is a turning point when they may become more realistic, persevering and security conscious, seeking more structure and order.

Whatever career they choose, they tend to see themselves as teachers or guides and have all the passion, integrity and intellect they need to be a positive force in the lives of others. However, it is not until they are able to turn the spotlight on their own needs, in particular their own need for guidance and support, that they will be able to balance their orientation toward others with their own needs. Ironically, it is only when they can find what gives their own life meaning and fulfillment that they can truly assist others, becoming the inspirational guide and role model they were destined to be.

On the dark side

Interfering, controlling, frustrated

At your best

Intelligent, observant, helpful

15 November

Your greatest challenge is

really trusting other people

The way forward is ...

to appreciate that people tend to respond to your expectations of them; approach them in the spirit of trust and they are likely to return the favor.

People born on November 15 have an air of the unexpected about them. Smooth and slick but with the deadly accuracy of a cobra, they can strike out suddenly and unexpectedly in defense or attack.

These people never have a straightforward existence and their life appears to be a series of unforeseen encounters, challenges or confrontations; but instead of crumbling under this kind of intensity, they thrive on it. In fact, these people are unlikely to avoid any kind of conflict or challenge, and once engaged in an argument they will never be the first to back down. They are brilliant at defending themselves and finding the weak spot in their opponent's arguments or situation— they are enemies to be truly feared. They also know how to wait until the moment is right to strike; when they do, their timing is typically perfect.

What these people often fail to appreciate is that not every situation in their lives is a battle. They can be suspicious or covert when they don't need to be and this can alienate others or create negativity when there is no cause for it. Sometimes, too, their love of challenge and change can make them create conflict just for the sake of it to enjoy the "excitement" it generates.

Until the age of thirty-six their risk-taking tendencies will be at their most intense and there will be many opportunities for them to take chances, some of which will pay off, some of which won't. After the age of thirty-seven, however, there is a significant turning point when they may start to become more disciplined and realistic. This is a positive development but, whatever age they are, injecting a healthy dose of optimism and self-belief into their lives to balance out their undercover tendencies will give them the courage to keep their spirit of adventure alive. It might also give them sufficient confidence and trust to put down their sword so that their heart of gold, and clear potential for happiness, success and fulfillment, can come out into the open.

On the dark side

Wary, volatile, defensive

At your best

Courageous, exciting, brilliant

16 November

the birthday of
the authority

Your greatest challenge is

resisting the urge to control everything

The way forward is ...

to understand that true leaders or directors empower others to make their own decisions.

People born on November 16 have a naturally authoritative manner and, because they are also intelligent, perceptive and display a remarkable strength of purpose, their command is rarely questioned. In addition, they usually have the best interests of everyone at heart. As a result, people learn to listen to what they have to say and more often than not follow their advice or instructions.

Fiercely individualistic and independent, these people may have challenged the status quo as children or teenagers. As they grow older, however, they often reach the conclusion that they can be more effective agents for change if they work within the system to try and change it for the better, rather than being a lone voice on the outside. They are particularly well suited to leadership roles where they can exert a powerful or informative influence over others.

Those around them generally respect their conviction and genuine desire to promote the common good, as well as the tact they display when enlisting support for their aims. There will be times, however, when their urge to enlighten and inspire others is so strong that their behavior becomes controlling, manipulative or intolerant, and they stubbornly refuse to acknowledge any other way forward but their way.

Until the age of thirty-five they are likely to want to expand their horizons through study or travel. After the age of thirty-six they reach a turning point where they start to take a more practical, ordered and realistic approach to life. Whatever age they are, it is important for them to make sure that they use their natural authority wisely and don't abuse the position of trust they tend to earn for themselves. If they can remember always to keep the interests of others in their mind and to respect others' right to hold different opinions to their own, not only will they become a voice of unquestionable authority, they also have the creativity and imagination to become a voice of insight, inspiration and wisdom.

On the dark side

Self-involved, controlling, judgmental

At your best

Authoritative, influential, understanding

17 November

the birthday of
the facilitator

Your greatest challenge is

setting yourself clear goals

The way forward is ...

to remember that going with the flow or following the herd can sometimes lead you over the cliff.

People born on November 17 are extremely intuitive and sensitive, with a powerful orientation toward others. Many times in their lives they will find themselves in the important role of integrator or facilitator.

One of the reasons these people are so good at encouraging others to work better together or ensuring that everyone gets on and things run smoothly is that they have a real understanding of the importance of compromise. Perhaps in their own lives they have had to learn the hard way that in the real world everyone can't get exactly what they want and that there is always a certain amount of trade-off. For example, they may have given up their dreams of performing to teach instead, or have scaled down their career to devote more time to their family. Whatever the nature of the compromise, they have convinced themselves that greater satisfaction can be found by placing the interests of others above their own.

This rightfully earns them great respect from others, but the downside is that they can become overly dependent on the satisfaction they get from helping others. They may also have a tendency to over-identify with the concerns of others, neglecting their own interests and psychological growth in the process. Until the age of thirty-four these people are more likely to take chances but after the age of thirty-five they reach a turning point when they start to become more progressive, determined and serious in their approach to life. After the age of sixty-five they begin to place more emphasis on friendship and independence.

Whatever age they are, it is crucial that they don't shut down emotionally and over-identify with the role of facilitator. As valuable and important as that role is, nothing is more valuable and important for their psychological growth—and for their ability to unlock the outstanding potential for success and happiness associated with this birthday—than their acknowledgment of and willingness to express their own dynamic creativity, independence and sense of purpose.

On the dark side

Unfocused,
self-sacrificing, aloof

At your best

Helpful,
inspiring, charming

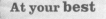

18 November

the birthday of
sensitive exuberance

Your greatest challenge is

being decisive

The way forward is ...

to ask yourself when choosing between options what you really want to happen, not what others expect. Once you are attuned to your feelings, decision making gets a whole lot easier.

Like a ray of warm sunshine, the exuberant, energetic individuals born on November 18 have the ability to enliven any situation with their good cheer, optimism and humor. They are refreshingly upbeat in their approach to everyone and everything, and not surprisingly their company is much sought after.

Not only do they enjoy being the center of attention, they are also fiercely ambitious, making them natural candidates for leadership. Those who do not know them well, however, would be surprised to discover that underneath the happy face they present to the world there can be a lot of uncertainty and conflict. This is because they are unusually sensitive to the feelings of others, sometimes to the extent that they don't know where their feelings end and another person's begin. As a result, despite their clear potential and suitability to be winners or innovators in life, they often end up feeling confused, purposeless and directionless.

If they can find a way to balance their sensitivity toward others with their ambitious urge to realize their own life goals, their success is assured. If, however, the balance tilts in either direction they can lose a sense of direction; the indecisiveness that results can stunt their psychological growth, blocking their chances of professional and personal success.

Until the age of thirty-three there is an emphasis in their lives on issues relating to freedom, adventure and expansion. They may want to study, travel or experiment with their choice of career in these years. After the age of thirty-four there is an important turning point when they are likely to become more responsible, precise and practical in their approach to life, seeking structure and order. Whatever age they are, however, they need to use their sharp and probing mind to investigate their own power and potential. This is because with greater self-awareness and greater belief in their star potential—and a lot of dedication and hard work—these vivacious individuals can achieve almost anything they set their mind to.

On the dark side

Needy, moody, confused

At your best

Innovative, entertaining, vivacious

19 November

the birthday of
the crusader

Your greatest challenge is

to think before you act

The way forward is ...

to understand that sometimes the best way to resolve a situation is by biding your time. Let some time pass and it may maximize your chances of success.

People born on November 19 tend to focus their energies outward onto their progressive goals. Born reformers, they are at their happiest and best when they can take on the role of crusader or of the representative of a revolutionary cause that aims to replace the old and the outdated with the new and innovative.

These people may have felt from an early age that they were destined to make a significant contribution to the world, and there is something about them which makes people stop and stare. Whatever life path they choose, their ultimate purpose is to play a part in changing the lives of others for the better. They will often do this by directing or organizing other people according to principles which they believe will benefit the greater good.

The confidence and crusading sense of purpose with which they are blessed will often propel them into the limelight as natural leaders; people tend to look to them for motivation and guidance. Their confidence, however, can also work against them because their self-belief can be so powerful at times that they close their ears and minds to alternative viewpoints, as well as to common sense. It is important for them to resist the urge to act on impulse. They should weigh up the pros and cons and listen to the advice of others before making decisions because, although they come close, they are not and never will be superhuman.

Until the age of thirty-two they may want to extend their mental horizons through study and travel, but after the age of thirty-three there is a turning point when they are likely to become more responsible, precise and hardworking in their approach to life. Whatever age they are, once they learn to pace themselves, take on board the advice of others and never allow pride to get in the way of progress, they will not only realize their dream of making a significant contribution to the world, they will play a vital part in changing it for the better.

On the dark side

Blinkered, over-confident, proud

At your best

Progressive, energetic, ambitious

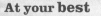

20 November

the birthday of
the wrestler

Your greatest challenge is

not to take yourself too seriously

The way forward is ...

to understand that a lighthearted, subtle approach can often have just as much impact and power as a forceful, direct one.

Struggle is a major theme for people born on November 20. This can express itself in a struggle for recognition in the outside world or an inner conflict where the impulsive and impatient aspects of their personality wrestle for dominance with the more self-controlled and disciplined urges.

From an early age, these people will never have been afraid of standing up for what is right, even if that means standing alone. They are capable of incredible fixity of purpose and energy; more often than not they will blaze a pioneering trail through life, inspiring many others along the way to follow their lead. If a cause or an authority figure does not have their respect, however, they will strongly and openly criticize or reject it, sometimes making enemies they don't need along the way. This impulsive response, although honest and direct, is not surprising given that they have an emotional response to life. In fact, much of their life is ruled by their never-changing emotions; one moment they are optimistic and enthusiastic, the next they are bitterly disillusioned and in the depths of despair. Although their intensity and seriousness of purpose will attract considerable success and respect, they would feel far happier and more fulfilled if they could find it within their hearts to take themselves just a little less seriously.

Before the age of thirty-one they are most likely to move forward with their lives in a spirit of optimism; these are the years when they are most likely to take risks. After the age of thirty-two, however, there is a turning point when they are likely gradually and over a period of years to become more practical, ambitious and realistic in their approach to life, desiring order and structure.

The key to their success—whatever their age and stage in life—will be their ability to acknowledge and accept their emotions, in particular their anger, successfully. This will give them the mental advantage they need to triumph over almost any obstacle, challenge or opponent that stands in their way.

On the dark side

Tactless, volatile, overly serious

At your best

Courageous, idealistic, energetic

452

21 November

the birthday of

finesse

Your greatest challenge is

intimacy

The way forward is ...

to understand that opening yourself up to someone else is not a sign of weakness, but a sign that you are human.

People born on November 21 love freedom and live by their own rules, but they also have a strong sense of justice, their mission being nothing less than to change the world. Regal and refined by nature, they are natural leaders who have no trouble working with the best, and more often than not being the best.

Those born on this day bring a quality touch to everything they do, and a major theme in their lives is refinement, and an insistence on creating and surrounding themselves with excellence. This finesse can manifest itself in their bewitchingly stylish appearance or approach, and it can manifest itself internally in the fine-tuning of their ideas. However it manifests itself over the years, they will be constantly improving and refining themselves in some way and, in the process, attracting considerable success and respect from others. This will not just be for their ability to learn from their mistakes, but also for their ability to make the impossible seem possible. The only downside with this careful, detailed approach is that it can make them a little too self-reliant, smooth and serious; they run the risk of losing their sense of humor and spontaneity along the way.

Until the age of thirty these people may find that they want to experiment and broaden their horizons; these are the years when they are most likely to make mistakes professionally or choose professions to which they are unsuited. After the age of thirty, however, there is a turning point when they are likely to take a more disciplined, determined and serious approach to life, ensuring that they make fewer and fewer mistakes professionally.

They need to beware of making the biggest mistake of all: denying themselves the happiness and fulfillment of close relationships with their fellow human beings. But once they have got in touch with their own feelings and the feelings of others, they have the ability to rise above any difficult situation and solve problems—perhaps even change the world for the better—with their inspired thinking.

On the dark side

Workaholic, closed off, depressive

At your best

Disciplined, elegant, influential

SAGITTARIUS

THE ARCHER
(NOVEMBER 22 – DECEMBER 21)

* **Element:** Fire
* **Ruling planet:** Jupiter, the philosopher
* **Symbol:** The Archer
* **Tarot card:** Temperance (moderation)
* **Number:** 3
* **Favorable colors:** Blue, purple, white
* **Key phrase:** I want to be challenged

Those born under the sign of Sagittarius are always hungry for knowledge and they thrive on challenges, both physical and mental. They view the future with hope, optimism and excitement. Sometimes in their restless hurry to speed onto the next challenge they don't see their current projects carefully through to the end, but even when they make mistakes their natural enthusiasm and zest for life is contagious.

Personality potential

Sagittarians are the restless seekers of the zodiac whose thirst for knowledge is insatiable. They always want to be learning something new. Freedom loving, they can't bear to be confined or pinned down by conformity or routine, and their need for personal space is very strong. Like the other two fire signs—Aries and Leo—they are risk takers who radiate warmth and optimism; but because they are the last fire sign, their passion tends to be more controlled.

Dependable, friendly, honest and lively, people born under the sun sign Sagittarius are ruled by the planet Jupiter, the planet of hope and expansion. This means that they naturally bring energy, optimism, hope and excitement to any situation or relationship they are in. They are also incredibly open-minded and flexible in their thinking; this gives them great versatility, which makes them multitalented and capable of mastering almost any task if they set their mind to it. This sign is also blessed with a philosopher's mind and their breadth of vision can be quite astonishing.

Bright, chatty, cheerful and enthusiastic Sagittarians have a reputation for being rather charming. They like to be stimulated by new faces and new places, and are almost always on the move—even if they settle in one place they are likely to travel extensively or to have dozens of activities and interests. They rarely book or plan ahead, however, for their adventures and approach to life are very much spontaneous and last minute.

Highly creative and imaginative with a love of adventure, Sagittarians bring enormous creativity to any project in which they are involved. They are generally well liked and personable individuals who enjoy significant personal power, both socially and personally, simply through being themselves. Although they do tend to exaggerate the truth or put a positive spin on everything, for the most part they are honest personalities and mind games are impossible for them to countenance or comprehend. With their optimism and enthusiasm always leading the way, it's hardly surprising that Sagittarians often have a definite knack for being in the right place at the right time and for attracting good fortune through their undeniable capacity for hard work.

> "Sagittarians often have a definite knack for being in the right place at the right time."

On the dark side

Subtlety isn't a strong point for people born under this sign. Don't ask a Sagittarian their opinion unless you want a brutally honest answer. Although you can count on them for being right most of the time, they will often say the right thing at completely the wrong time or the right thing in totally the wrong way; this can cause problems for them. In addition, their optimism about new projects, ventures or relationships can easily become over-optimism and an inability to face difficult truths. They may, for example, continue blindly in a situation for years, not wanting to deal with problems that are unpleasant or painful. Some may think of this approach to life as brave but for others might regard it as deluded. There's nothing sadder than seeing a Sagittarian's wonderful energy and intellect burned out and their opportunities wasted by battling on for years in a relationship or career to which they aren't suited.

Freedom and personal space are important issues for Sagittarians and this can make them come across as fickle, irresponsible, restless and sometimes emotionally cold in relationships that are important to them. They can often be reluctant to commit to long-term plans and are prone to bouts of illogical panic; this means that instead of staying and facing their panic, they may simply respond by packing their bags and moving to somewhere new to start again. And, finally, although their risk taking and love of danger make them exciting and opportunistic individuals, they can also be reckless and can live to regret their hasty decisions and actions.

Symbol

The symbol of Sagittarius is an archer with their bow poised to shoot. The arrow destined to fly through the air symbolizes the endless quest for knowledge that drives this sign, as well as their love of projecting their thoughts and energy to a future destination or target. Often the archer is represented in the shape of a centaur; this is a mythical creature that is half man and half beast, suggesting the dual nature of this sign that fuses instinct with intellect.

Darkest secret

Sagittarians hate rules and regulations more than any other sign of the zodiac, but deep down it's not really rules and regulations that they fear but the fact that rules and regulations are sometimes necessary. Without these, life would descend into chaos and injustice and, although Sagittarians believe in the power of optimism, they find it incredibly painful to admit to themselves that sometimes optimism and smiling your way through adversity isn't enough to change people's lives or a situation for the better.

Love

It may seem surprising, given that the Sagittarian is typically such a jovial, fun-loving and sociable individual, but people born under this sun sign are often more capable of living happily alone than any other sign of the zodiac. This is because they can often find being in committed relationships restrictive and they love the idea of being able to leave at a moment's notice—which, of course, they can't do so easily if they have a partner or a family to consider. However, if they do settle into a relationship they are generous, interested and helpful partners, and will work far harder than any other sign to make that relationship work, even if it's in deep trouble.

As a rule, Sagittarians have extremely high moral and personal standards, and they expect the same high standards from the people with whom they spend their time. This upstanding aspect of their personality can make them very unforgiving, not just of themselves but of others. These people don't forgive or forget easily if someone close to them transgresses the bounds of decency and civilized behavior. They may even decide to completely sever all ties with that person. In addition to sharing the same standards of decency and morality, the ideal partner for a Sagittarian would be someone who is supportive, intelligent, fun-loving, a great listener and willing to share but not dominate the limelight.

Love matches:
Aries, Leo and Libra

The Sagittarian man

Typically there will be a crowd of people surrounding a Sagittarian man and he won't be easy to pin down. His idealistic energy, exuberance and curiosity are endearing and infectious and, although his innocent energy can sometimes get out of hand with reckless and careless behavior, his boundless optimism will never fail to draw others to him. Although you may have to push your way through a lot of people to get to a Sagittarian man, the effort is certainly worth it. His soaring imagination, optimism and creativity can quite literally move mountains and there will never be a dull moment. There may, however, be a number of tense or difficult situations when his brutal honesty is nothing less than hurtful in its bluntness. So, as well as being optimistic, energetic and adventurous, potential partners of a Sagittarian man need to develop a thick skin. However, when it comes to affairs of the heart this man's frankness and openness is very refreshing. There are no mind games or falsehoods, and when he tells you he loves you and wants to spend the rest of his life with you, you can be sure that he means it.

Once in a relationship, freedom is essential for a Sagittarian man—freedom to explore and freedom to dream. A possessive, suspicious or jealous partner will not last long; the independent spirit of a Sagittarian man won't tolerate any restriction. Many of the dreams and plans a Sagittarian man has won't be as wise or as well thought out as they could be; this is because he doesn't just think with his mind, he also thinks with his heart. But somehow this doesn't matter because the love of a Sagittarian man is a truly special gift—the gift of love that is honest, genuine and pure.

The Sagittarian woman

Sagittarian women are the most blisteringly frank women of the entire zodiac. They see the world exactly as it is and will never lie to you. Fortunately, they often do this in such a charming, intelligent and optimistic manner that it's impossible to be upset. Extremely independent in their thinking, these women are most likely to live alone, sometimes even when they are in a relationship. They may marry later than expected or be fairly aloof—uninterested even—when there is talk of commitment and family ties. The reason is not that they don't ever want to get married but that marriage is something they always think about as something they will do in the future.

Right now there is so much they want to learn, see and do, and so many places to which they want to go.

The Sagittarian woman tends to have a lot of friends, but also tends to mistake friendship for love and love for friendship. Her affectionate social nature and breezy, unconventional approach to relationships can cause a lot of misunderstandings and hurt feelings. At times she may appear over-casual in her approach to relationships, but this isn't an accurate assessment. When she eventually meets someone who can challenge her intellectually and who matches her optimism, she is capable of incredible commitment and emotional involvement. As long as she doesn't feel tied down and is allowed to make her own decisions, a relationship with a Sagittarian woman can be unequalled when it comes to loyalty, trust, affection and honesty; there'll also be plenty of excitement and enough idealism to last a lifetime.

Family

The Sagittarian child is a bundle of enthusiasm and generous to a fault. Sometimes exuberance can turn into boisterousness, so it's important for parents of Sagittarian children to find a channel for their child's incredible energy. They should be encouraged, for example, to have as many hobbies and interests as possible and, if school work isn't sufficiently challenging, parents should ask their teachers to set them additional tasks. Parents of Sagittarian children had better get used to plenty of those "why" questions and honesty is the best policy when attempting to answer them; young Sagittarians can quickly spot bluffing or dishonesty. In the playground they are remarkably independent and can be counted on to make any newcomer to the group feel welcome. There is huge potential here for success both in and out of the classroom, but the secret is to ensure that potential is properly guided. The more a Sagittarian child achieves and everyone takes note of progress made, the more they will progress. In other words, these children should not be left to progress at their own rate. Having said that, Sagittarian children do struggle with rules and regulations so it's important that their parents, teachers and mentors offer them guidance rather than inflexible regulations; this is because they aren't blind to reason and will naturally choose the sensible option if it's presented to them in a way they can understand.

Sagittarian parents are often adored by their children for their lively, sometimes eccentric approach to life. They will often encourage their children to develop their interests and will take an active part in seeing that these interests are progressing well. There may be times when Sagittarian parents feel restricted by their role as parent and it's therefore important, especially for Sagittarian mothers, that they don't allow their own interests to fall by the wayside when children arrive on the scene. These women should definitely try to set aside time for themselves, because as rewarding as motherhood is, the conversations and activities involved in bringing up a child are not engrossing enough for them to feel truly fulfilled. New projects should be started as soon after the birth of a child as possible.

Career

With their love of freedom, travel and intellectual stimulation, Sagittarians will never be happy in careers that don't offer them these qualities. Jobs that may suit this sign include travel guiding, teaching, law, lecturing, piloting, interpreting, writing, publishing and therapy. The world of entertainment may also have strong appeal, as these people

66 Their spirit of adventure needs work that takes them out into the world... 99

simply love being in the limelight. Sagittarians with sporting ability may enjoy working in the field of health and fitness or personal training. More adventurous types may do well as stuntmen or explorers.

Whatever career they choose, the most important thing for a Sagittarian is challenge; repetitive work should be avoided, as should work that has a 9 to 5 routine. They also don't tend to thrive in stuffy, crowded offices. Their spirit of adventure needs work that takes them out into the world around them to meet people. Although they often do well in their careers, Sagittarians are not overly ambitious as far as money or status are concerned—what matters more to them is that they are being challenged, learning and experiencing something new and, above all, making their own decisions.

Health and leisure

Their abundant energy means that it's hardly surprising that many Sagittarians also have a hearty appetite, and they can consume vast amounts of food and drink. In many cases they are so active in their daily lives that they burn off the calories right away, but they do need to be careful that don't put on too much weight, especially around the bottom and hips. They are often tempted by fast food but should try as much as possible to avoid convenience food that has had all the goodness refined and processed out of it. One of the reasons Sagittarians tend to eat so much fast food is that when they are hungry they want something immediately to boost their energy; because of this they need to ensure they carry plenty of healthy snacks, such as fruits, nuts, seeds and raisins around them for when temptation strikes.

As far as exercise goes most people born under this sign will already be extremely active but they do need to be careful that they don't overdo it, and that their daredevil nature doesn't cause them to suffer injuries. It's also important for them to remember that they need to modify the way they exercise as

they get older—what worked in their twenties for example, may not work in their fifties.

When it comes to leisure interests, many Sagittarians enjoy the challenge of outdoor activities such as hiking, horse riding and camping, as well as team sports such as basketball. Archery is also a popular pastime, and they may find satisfaction and mental challenge in learning a language, reading, writing and the study of philosophy. Retirement offers them exciting opportunities for physical and intellectual travel, and many Sagittarians think of this time as the most rewarding in their life because they have the freedom they have always longed for to stretch both their mind and their body. There is a tendency for Sagittarians to overdo things, so they would also benefit from regular yoga and relaxation. A mantra they should repeat to themselves every day is "moderation in all things." Wearing or meditating on the color blue will encourage them to be more consistent, moderate and disciplined in their approach to life.

Born between November 22 and December 1

People born between these dates are perhaps the most positive of the entire zodiac. They see the possibilities life offers as endless and never take no for an answer. Their cup is always half full, not half empty, and—with their strong desire to travel and seek out new experiences—adventure is their second name.

Born between December 2 and December 10

These Sagittarians need plenty of stimulation and variety. They also love freedom, and this applies to relationships, family and work. They hate being tied down and, like Peter Pan, seem bright, exuberant, adventurous and free whatever their age.

Born between December 11 and December 21

Bold and dramatic, these people are often life's gamblers. Even when they lose, which they do from time to time, they always seem to land on their feet.

Life lessons

As long as they feel free and unrestricted, Sagittarians are wonderful people to have around because they are so optimistic and energetic. They never tire of learning something new but if restrictions, responsibilities and expectations start to pile up, as they often tend to do in life, Sagittarians may lose some of their spark. They have the mistaken idea that commitment somehow reduces their freedom so it's extremely important for them to learn that, although responsibility and freedom are two separate things, they are not necessarily mutually exclusive.

There is no doubt that the mind of a Sagittarian is astute but they also have a tendency to be incredibly blunt in the expression of what they perceive to be the truth. They need to learn to be more tactful in their approach to others and to understand that sometimes it's better to be more cautious when speaking their mind because other people may not be ready to hear the truth. Sagittarians also tend to be risk takers but, like their tendency to be too blunt or their tendency to argue for argument's sake, their risk taking may be only for its own sake, rather than for any actual benefit or particular outcome. The only things that Sagittarians need to do for their own sake are love and kindness. In addition, taking risks can cause disastrous outcomes and it will benefit Sagittarians enormously if they learn to look before they leap.

Other signs of the zodiac have much to teach Sagittarians. For example, they can learn caution, self-restraint and careful analysis to determine a course of action from Virgos. Cancerians can help them to be more compassionate and empathetic. Although Sagittarians are great listeners, they don't necessarily make great comforters because they listen to learn more rather than to help others or make them feel better. Finally, Geminis can teach Sagittarians to be lighter and more carefree in their pursuit of knowledge.

22 November

the birthday of
provocative aspiration

Your greatest challenge is

reminding yourself that you are not indispensable

The way forward is ...

to constantly remind yourself that, as important as you are, the world will continue to spin without you.

Even as a child, people born on November 22 will often have felt that they thought differently from other people. They are always slightly ahead, with a desire to free themselves from authority or conventional thinking.

These people like to make their own rules and they aren't that bothered about what other people think of them. Although these liberated people are like a breath of fresh air when it comes to challenging restrictive or unimaginative thinking, wherever they encounter it, their rebellious, provocative nature can get them into a lot of trouble. It is important for their psychological growth and professional success that they learn to be more tactful, reading their audience better for clues as to the appropriate level of intensity. If they don't, they will be branded as troublemakers.

Not surprisingly, given their free-thinking nature, these people work best independently in situations that give them lots of room for creative choice. In the right kind of environment they can be a powerful force for good, coming up with creative and innovative solutions to improve the welfare of those around them. In the wrong kind of environment—and this tends to be one that is structured or unchallenging—their provocative approach can, however, create tension and unrest.

Until they reach the age of twenty-nine they will want to expand their horizons and seek out opportunities through new ventures, study or travel. After the age of thirty, however, there is a turning point when they are likely to become more practical and realistic; these are the years when they are most likely to realize their professional goals. Ironically, because they love challenge so much, they may find in the thirties and beyond that despite achieving great success they pine for the time when anything in life seemed possible. The key to their success will be their ability to set themselves new goals and dream up new ideas to challenge and reinvent themselves. If they can do this, they will unlock the outstanding potential for personal fulfillment and happiness associated with this birthday.

On the dark side

Rebellious, provocative, frustrated

At your best

Exciting, liberated, innovative

466

23 November

Your greatest challenge is

stepping away from confrontation

The way forward is ...

to understand that by stepping back from situations you can develop the objectivity you need to deal more effectively with them.

People born on November 23 know how to think on their feet and their wit and grace make them much sought after, both at home and at work. They have a way with words and seem to know exactly the right thing to say at exactly the right time, whether they are comforting a friend, presenting at work or talking sweetly to their lover. When their communication skills are combined with their intelligence and originality, these people have the ability to make a significant and benevolent contribution to society.

There is a side to them, however, that seems to draw them irresistibly to confrontational people or situations. This often happens when their inspirational aims are challenged in any way; they may even go so far as to provoke unnecessary arguments to make their position clear. If they are not careful tension can become a constant theme in their lives, starting early in their childhood—they may have been in conflict with parents or teachers—and continuing right through their lives with colleagues, partners, friends and loved ones. This can be an extremely negative and difficult pattern to break, especially as they aren't that good at handling conflict despite their attraction to it. They can suffer greatly when others launch a counterattack on them and target their hidden insecurities.

Until the age of twenty-eight they are likely to be concerned with issues of freedom and expanding their horizons through education, study or travel, but after the age of twenty-nine they are likely to develop a more pragmatic, orderly and structured approach to life, with a powerful emphasis on achieving their professional goals.

If they want to avoid road blocks to their success, and spending a great deal of time alone, it is crucial for them to learn to avoid engaging in conflict for the sake of it. This is because once they have learned to choose their battles wisely, they can save their energy for what really matters: developing their outstanding potential for becoming authoritative, innovative, expressive and above all, truly motivational role models.

On the dark side

Argumentative, isolated, critical

At your best

Innovative, free-spirited, discerning

24 November

the birthday of

intrigue

Your greatest challenge is

overcoming the feeling that you don't fit in

The way forward is ...

to understand that everyone feels out of place at times; they just learn to hide it. You can do the same.

People born on November 24 tend to be energetic, outgoing and spirited individuals with the ability to strongly influence the opinions of others. They will never avoid problems or challenges, and are at their happiest and best when debating issues or troubleshooting for a solution. People are irresistibly drawn to their courageous spirit and exciting ideas, and the air of mystery that hangs around them only adds to their attraction.

It doesn't matter how settled or secure the life of these people is, intrigue will never be far behind. Whether this manifests in situations or relationships that are complicated, or internal conflicts that are all-absorbing, there is always some kind of question mark in their lives and the outcome never appears certain. Although this means that their lives are never boring and are an endless topic of conversation for others, there will be times when they feel overwhelmed by feelings of uncertainty and confusion and unsure what their motivations are. They may aim for the top in their professional life only to find that the sacrifices they need to make are ones they are unwilling to make; or they may create an active social life, only to find that they long to be left alone.

Until the age of twenty-seven they are likely to be adventurous and will seek to expand their horizons through enterprising ventures, study and travel. After the age of twenty-eight they may start to settle down and become more practical, goal orientated and realistic in their approach. Another turning point occurs at the age of fifty-eight when they have a growing need for freedom, new ideas and expressing their individuality.

At every age and stage in their life there are opportunities for them to develop their original notions and big plans, but the key to their success —and indeed to solving the mystery of their lives—is to simply accept themselves for who and what they are: highly unusual, creative and courageous individuals who can never fit into the mold because their destiny is to break it.

On the dark side

Confused, escapist, unaware

At your best

Interesting, spirited, attractive

25 November

the birthday of
social responsibility

Your
greatest
challenge is

establishing your
independence

*The way
forward is ...*

to understand that
until you are able
to strike out on
your own, the
contribution you
make to a team will
not be as effective
or valuable.

People born on November 25 are rational, capable and quietly progressive individuals who are willing to take all the time needed to complete a project perfectly. Their motivation is a benevolent urge to achieve excellence and make a difference, rather than gain power and money, and this gives them the staying power to make things happen and the humility to be the essential means of support for a powerful individual or social group.

Social responsibility is an important theme in their lives. This isn't to say that they are not independently minded; indeed their desire for personal fulfillment is strong. It's just that they are ultimately concerned with inspiring, enlightening or otherwise acting on behalf of others or society as a whole. Their fixity of purpose, self-discipline and high expectations of themselves and others can, however, make them become overly fixated on their goals and too judgmental of others. Learning to establish an identity for themselves outside of their work or the social group with which they identify, and learning to accept and work with those who have alternative views, are essential requirements for their psychological growth and fulfillment.

Until the age of twenty-six they may find that they are concerned with issues of freedom, and they should take advantage of opportunities to expand their horizons through study or travel. After the age of twenty-seven there is a turning point that is likely to focus their minds on a more pragmatic, ordered and structured approach to life. There is another turning point at the age of fifty-seven when there is a growing need for original and progressive ideas and, at long last, independence. Whatever age or stage they are at, they should try to find the courage to strike out on their own, directing their creative intellect toward finding a path in life that combines their need for personal fulfillment with their socially orientated concerns. Having done this, they will gain an enriching dimension to their lives by unlocking their potential for making a real and important difference in the world around them.

On the dark side

Workaholic,
judgmental, inflexible

At your best

Steady, accomplished,
supportive

26 November

the birthday of
multi-talented uniqueness

Your greatest challenge is

forming close relationships with others

The way forward is ...

to understand that the more comfortable you are with yourself, the more comfortable you will be with other people.

The free-thinking individuals born on November 26 would appear to have the world at their feet. Not only are they charismatic and intelligent, they are also creative, multi-talented and capable of excelling in just about any profession they choose.

Despite their incredible versatility, they may have felt from an early age that they were somehow different or removed from their fellow human begins. Part of the problem is that because they have so many talents and such an inquisitive mind, too many paths are open to them so choosing one becomes a daunting task. They may also struggle to reconcile their practical, logical orientation with the part of them that is highly creative and imaginative. At various points in their life they will lurch between these two extremes, but happiness and fulfillment can only be found when they are able to balance the two.

As success-orientated people, when they are not working toward a goal they can feel restless and unsatisfied, so the sooner they decide on a path in life and set themselves targets to achieve the better. If they don't do this, indecision, anxiety and uncertainty will submerge their huge potential.

Up to the age of twenty-five there may be a lot of experimentation regarding their career, as they focus on adventure, creativity and opportunity; but after the age of twenty-six they start to become more practical, goal orientated and realistic in their aims. This is a positive development, as long as they make sure they don't lose touch with their imagination and creative fire. Another turning point occurs at the age of fifty-six when expressing their individuality takes center stage. Hopefully, however, they will have realized far earlier in life that the key to their success is to celebrate and make full use of their uniqueness rather than try to hide it. They have been right all along; there is and never will be anybody quite like them with their unique talents, original perspective, and courage and determination to prove everyone wrong by achieving their fantastic aims.

On the dark side

Confused, indecisive, undirected

At your best

Innovative, unique, multi-talented

27 November

the birthday of
the vortex

Your greatest challenge is

asking for help

The way forward is ...

to understand that asking for help is not a sign of weakness but a sign of self-knowledge, honesty and inner strength.

People born on November 27 are vortexes of energy, enthusiasm and excitement. Fiercely individualistic, they go where their imagination leads them, preferring to seek out knowledge and truth for themselves and then formulating their own opinions and plans. The only trouble with this wildly spontaneous approach is that they often have no idea in which direction they are heading, and their enthusiasm tends to overwhelm their common sense.

They are not afraid to listen to their instincts, and although this intuitive approach can bring them spectacular success it can also lead to disappointments and rejection. It is important for them to learn to distinguish between intuition and wishful thinking, and the only way to do that is to try to understand themselves better and to take a more realistic view of situations before they decide to throw themselves in at the deep end. Although they will encounter setbacks along the way, they are remarkably resilient, possessing a buoyant spirit in the face of adversity. However, their self-reliance can also work against them; they are extremely proud and don't like to ask for help. This significantly decreases their chances of success.

Until the age of twenty-four they will probably keep their career options open, preferring to experiment, travel or study to broaden their horizons. However, around the age of twenty-five there is a turning point when they are likely to become more pragmatic, focused and orderly in order to realize their goals. Another turning point occurs around the age of fifty-five when they may feel a growing urge to be more adventurous and independent.

Whatever age they are, however, the secret to unlocking their potential for success and happiness will be their ability to control the powerful energy within them and direct it to a worthy cause. Once they are able to do that—and to ask for help and advice along the way—they will still be vortexes of dynamic energy and originality but this time they will be vortexes who know where they are heading, and that is usually to the very top.

On the dark side

Restless, unfocused, hasty

At your best

Energetic, intuitive, buoyant

28 November

the birthday of
impulse

Your greatest challenge is

making realistic plans

The way forward is ...

to set short-term goals that you can reach, then set more. In this way you'll be able to move ahead.

Those born on November 28 are free spirits with a thirst for knowledge. They are natural philosophers and their aim is to broaden their vision and sense of possibility. They are the scientists who never leave the lab, the composers and writers who labor late into the night, and the workers who stay late at the office—and forget to clean up their mess when they leave.

Filled with natural curiosity and eagerness for the future, there is a tendency for these people to overextend themselves with too many activities. Not surprisingly, they can be flirtatious—with ideas as well as people—tending to show their enthusiasm at the start of new endeavors or relationships but then withdrawing it as the project progresses into details, or the relationship settles into a routine. They need to learn that commitment and freedom are two separate entities that don't have to be mutually exclusive.

Despite the sparkling wit and apparent flightiness of these people, they have a deeper and more complex side to them. As they tend to feel their way through life, their emotions can go up and down, so it is important for them to find a trusted friend who can gently warn them when they are heading off track. When hurt, they withdraw into a cloud of silence, eventually emerging from their reticence with sarcastic comments that can be blunt, insensitive and tactless. Too emotionally honest to hide their feelings, whether disillusionment, frustration or boredom, they can't help but "say it like it is."

Others may criticize them for their moodiness and messiness, but they don't hold grudges for long and it's always a creative and innovative mess. But if they want to achieve the success and recognition their talents deserve, they need to combine this with dedication and discipline. Fortunately after the age of twenty-four there is a powerful and significant turning point when there will be greater emphasis on responsibility and the work they need to do to achieve their imaginative and progressive goals.

On the dark side

Scattered, restless, self-destructive

At your best

Spontaneous, optimistic, charismatic

29 November

the birthday of

controversy

Your greatest challenge is

learning to listen

The way forward is ...

to think like a mirror. A mirror doesn't judge or give advice. It reflects back what the person is saying.

When November 29 people walk into a room the atmosphere instantly changes, and everyone feels a sense of excitement and possibility. This is because they are energetic and dynamic individuals who are stimulated by challenge and the desire to move forward with their personal goals, career goals and, if possible, the greater good.

Although they are innovative, exciting and optimistic and can encourage others to be more courageous in their thinking, these people have a habit of stirring up controversy because they like to think outside the box. Challenging the status quo, whether necessary or not, is a way of life for them, and they are hopeless at keeping their unconventional ideas to themselves. In fact they love to express their opinions, and it doesn't matter to them if they get a negative response—what they really want from others is a reaction, and a negative one is better than none. Sometimes, however, their provocative manner does step over the mark and they need to ensure that they don't highlight emotional vulnerabilities in others for no reason but to demonstrate their own power over them.

Up to the age of twenty-one they may want to expand their opportunities through enterprising ventures, study or travel, but after the age of twenty-three they start to become more realistic and goal-orientated in their approach to their achievements. During this period, there will be a need for more order and structure in their lives. Another turning point occurs around the age of fifty-three when expressing their individuality comes into the spotlight.

Whatever age they are they will always be a catalyst for change. If they can make sure that this is not change for the sake of excitement but positive change that can encourage progress—on their own behalf as well as those of others—these invigorating people have the potential to become inspired thinkers with a gift not just for keeping everyone on their toes but with a gift to offer the world through their work or creative expression.

On the dark side

Provocative, stressed, shocking

At your best

Invigorating, dramatic, daring

473

30 November

the birthday of
incisive thoroughness

Your greatest challenge is

being spontaneous

The way forward is ...

to understand that sometimes the best and only response to a situation is to trust your instincts and go with the flow.

People born on November 30 often feel that there simply aren't enough hours in their day or years in their life to accomplish all their ambitions. They have so many talents and abilities that it can be hard for them to know where to invest their energies. Once they settle on a chosen course, their strong sense of responsibility and incisive mind ensure that they give it their complete concentration.

They are extremely thorough in their approach and their attention to detail is second to none. As a result they are always well prepared for virtually any situation in which they might find themselves and, because they never leave anything to the last minute, they are always composed, calm and convincing. Others will usually be influenced by what they have to say, but on the odd occasion that their preparation fails to pay off they can find it hard to accept that anyone could say no to them or not be impressed by them. If anyone tries to criticize them, they can become extremely defensive and at times hurtful themselves. They should therefore learn to handle criticism with as much grace and control as they demonstrate in other areas of their lives.

After the age of twenty-two they are likely to feel a need to be pragmatic, orderly and structured in their approach to life. Given the fact that they already have a tendency to be highly controlled and lacking in spontaneity, it is vital during the next thirty years that they get in touch with their intuition, take themselves and others less seriously, and incorporate more fun and laugher into their lives. After the age of fifty-two there is a turning point which highlights issues regarding friendships and personal identity.

Whatever age they are, the sooner they can loosen up and trust their heart and powerful intuition as much as they trust their rational side, the sooner they can maximize their potential for success, making their unique and valuable contribution to the world.

On the dark side

Inflexible, reactive, touchy

At your best

Thorough, multi-talented, convincing

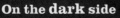

1 December

outrageous charm

Your greatest challenge is

knowing what you want

The way forward is ...

to appreciate that acquiring self-knowledge is not only the beginning of wisdom; it is also a lifelong task.

People born on December 1 are extremely energetic. Unhindered by convention, they express themselves freely and delight in surprising others with their outrageous wit and seducing them with their charm. Any attempts to restrict their freedom will simply have the effect of spurring them along their idiosyncratic path with renewed enthusiasm and determination.

Although these people will defend or promote their ideas fiercely, they are not necessarily combative or confrontational; they prefer to influence or win others over with the sheer force of their personalities. They may at times lack tact or diplomacy but they also radiate self-confidence, and this draws others to them. Underneath their entertaining, occasionally superficial but always eyebrow-raising mask, however, they are far more deep and complex than others realize. In fact sometimes they feel so complex that even they aren't sure what their motivations are; the vibrant, funny personality they present to the outside world is simply their way of coping with the confusion.

After a rebellious childhood, at around the age of twenty there is an important turning point for these people lasting about thirty years. During this period there are opportunities for them to become more pragmatic, orderly and structured in their approach to life. As long as they don't neglect friends and loved ones they should take advantage of these opportunities to focus on their career; the sooner they find a professional sense of direction and purpose the better, as work can be an important outlet for their energy and talents. After the age of fifty-one there is an another important turning point which highlights a growing need for independence and for sharing some of their progressive ideas with others.

Throughout their lives they should never forget that they are free spirits, but if they can learn to be a little more diplomatic, cautious and self-aware they will find that they will not only be able to bring pleasure, love and enlightenment to the lives of others; they will also be able to blaze their own, highly original, trail through life.

On the dark side

Confused, tactless, reckless

At your best

Energetic, generous, entertaining

2 December

the birthday of
the kaleidoscope

Your greatest challenge is

outgrowing your constant need for recognition

The way forward is ...

to realize that no matter how much recognition and applause others give you, it will never be enough until you can grow in self-esteem.

People born on December 2 are dynamic and colorful characters who tend to command attention wherever they go. They wear their heart on their sleeve and are so spontaneous that the whole kaleidoscope of their constantly changing emotions will be on display for all to see.

Their emotional honesty and energy can be refreshing, and their drive and determination make them excellent leaders and an inspiration to friends and co-workers. The effect they can have on others is dramatic, but it could be life changing for both themselves and others if they learned to balance their directness with a little tact, occasionally stepping back to examine what their emotions are telling them. With a little more self-understanding they might see that some kind of pattern is emerging.

Until the age of nineteen they may be something of a wild child, exploring and expanding their horizons in as many different directions as possible. After the age of twenty there is a turning point when there are opportunities for them to become more practical, goal-orientated and realistic in their approach to life. They should take advantage of these opportunities to establish order and structure in their life, because if they don't too many changes of direction can lead to confusion and uncertainty. After the age of fifty there is another turning point that highlights a growing need for more independence, but also a need to become more humanitarian in their approach.

Above all, these people are charismatic individuals, but they are also problem solvers looking for a deeper meaning or pattern to their life. Their inner sensitivity, however, may not always be visible from their colorful, confident front. Once they find a way to connect and work with it, not only will they be able to intuitively know the answer to other people's dilemmas; they will be able to take charge of their constantly changing and confusing emotions, find a cause in life that is worthy of their creative talents, and create the magical pattern of peace and happiness they so richly deserve.

On the dark side

Unaware, volatile, intimidating

At your best

Inspirational, creative, demonstrative

3 December

the birthday of
progressive expertise

Your greatest challenge is

finding an interest outside work

The way forward is ...

to understand that if you don't see to your own needs, not just your work but all aspects of your life will suffer as a result.

People born on December 3 are blessed with inquisitive and progressive minds and are at their happiest and best when formulating original strategies to bring about improvements. Although their ideas are highly original, unorthodox even, they are also thorough and rational types. When these qualities are added to their formidable organizational and technical skills, the result is a person with stunning expertise in their chosen field.

Not surprisingly, given their perfectionist nature, work plays a huge part in their lives and they will often dedicate themselves wholeheartedly to their career. They will also tend to seek out others with similar mind sets to their own and, while others respect their energy, ambition and focus and admire their well-deserved professional success, they can feel as if these individuals are hard to get to know. This is to some extent true, as they don't really have much time for socializing and often feel a need to simply be alone. This isn't for religious or spiritual reasons, but simply to help renew their focus and concentration, and fine-tune their skills. When they are ready they will emerge from their silence to astonish all those around them with their accomplishments.

The dedicated and ambitious aspects of their personality don't tend to emerge until they are at least in their twenties, but when they do they give them a focus and determination that is second to none. After the age of fifty, however, there is a significant turning point when there will be opportunities for them to focus on friendship and group awareness.

Whatever their age, they need to take advantage of any opportunity they can to participate more fully and freely with others because this will help them understand that their ambition is not only driven by a desire to achieve professional excellence but also by a desire to assist others and play an inspirational role in their lives. As long as they make sure their emotional needs do not take second place to their work, they have the innovative potential to become dynamic instruments of progress.

On the dark side

Withdrawn, workaholic, difficult

At your best

Innovative, meticulous, ambitious

4 December

the birthday of
the captain

Your
greatest
challenge is

coping with not
being listened to

*The way
forward is ...*

to understand that
authority is
something that
has to be earned;
balance your
leadership skills
with a concern for
the welfare of
others.

People born on December 4 are ambitious, hardworking and resilient individuals who can display remarkable self-control in both their professional and personal lives. They have the rare ability to take charge of their emotions without losing their creativity, and this gives them tremendous self-confidence, power over themselves and authority over others. They are like flamboyant and daring but highly skilled and well-prepared captains with a thirst for adventure and all the courage and ingenuity they need to successfully steer through uncharted waters to undiscovered lands.

Although they cherish their own individuality and are unwilling to submit themselves to the ideas or authority of others, they may feel compelled to impose their ideas on those around them, sometimes forcefully. Unaware of this contradiction between their directional urges and their own right to autonomy, they can come across as dictatorial or egotistical; but this is rarely the case. For the great majority of the time they are genuinely concerned for the greater good, rather than any selfish ambitions. Like a brave captain who will not leave their ship until everyone is safe, their natural sense of justice and honor will propel them toward activities that are intended to bring about a more enlightened or better-regulated society.

At the age of eighteen, people born on this day may start to manifest their natural leadership skills and over the next thirty years they will gradually become more practical, goal-orientated and realistic in their approach to achievement. They may also have a strong desire for order and structure in their lives. After the age of forty-eight there is another significant turning point which highlights a growing need for freedom, new ideas and expressing their individuality within a group setting.

Whatever age they are, if they can find a middle way between nobility and ambition, love and success, compassion and power, independence and the need to compromise, they will not only be capable of inspired leadership, they will also be capable of becoming the visionaries of their generation.

On the dark side

Authoritarian, hypocritical, inflexible

At your best

Powerful, ambitious, inspirational

5 December

the birthday of
the self-assured adventurer

Your greatest challenge is

taking the advice of others

The way forward is ...

to understand that other people always bring different perspectives; these are always worth listening to as you may have overlooked them.

People born on December 5 reach for the skies both personally and professionally and, although others may think they are overreaching themselves, somehow or other they manage to get to where they want—or at the very least, close to it.

From an early age they may have displayed unusual self-confidence and willingness to go it alone. If this isn't the case, life may have given them a series of knocks to dent their confidence; sooner or later their characteristic optimism will emerge. They truly believe that anything is possible, and throughout their lives they will be a shining example of what confidence and self-belief in the face of adversity can achieve. Sometimes they can be over-confident and unwilling to listen to the cautionary advice of others; although this may result in remarkable innovations, it can also lead to serious errors of judgment.

Around the age of seventeen they will start to think seriously about their life goals and the mark they want to leave on the world. Although they should never lose their idealism and optimism, it is important for them to make sure that the goals they set are realistic and achievable; otherwise they are setting themselves up for disappointment. Listening to the advice of others could be the key to unlocking their potential. After the age of forty-seven they may become even more progressive and original in their ideas and, if they have managed to learn from past experience and improve their judgment by taking a careful look at themselves and their situation, these are the years when they can really come into their own.

December 5 people are hard to ignore or dislike, and even though their ambitions may at times be over the top, colleagues and friends will often regard them with affection and tolerance. They have a real desire to make a positive contribution to society and, once they can direct their determination, focus and will-power to a worthy cause, they can and do find ways to benefit the greater good.

On the dark side

Over-confident, conceited, unaware

At your best

Self-assured, daring, energetic

479

6 December

the birthday of the developer

Your greatest challenge is

resisting the urge to interfere

The way forward is ...

to understand that sometimes people need to learn from their own mistakes.

Practical and clear sighted, people born on December 6 have a real talent for management. They will often be found organizing teams of people and trying to improve or develop situations or ideas so that they produce better results. They are the people to whom everyone turns first when things aren't working, and others value them for their consistently rational and perceptive way of looking at the world, as well as the tactful way they present their conclusions so that others feel motivated to make positive changes rather than feeling vulnerable and disappointed.

Lacking any hidden agenda, these people are direct, honest and to the point in both their professional and personal life. They can see immediately the weaknesses or flaws in a situation, and how these can be replaced, removed or improved so that the best possible result can be achieved. Although friends and co-workers are often extremely grateful for their sage advice, occasionally their desire to interfere and control can come across as meddling. As illogical as it may seem to them, they need to respect the fact that some people are stuck in their ways and don't actually want someone wading in with advice on how their situation can change or improve.

Until the age of forty-five they will feel a growing need for order and structure in their lives, and there is a big emphasis on practical issues. During these years, evaluating concepts and systems, and devising strategies to improve them, are likely to be top of their agenda. After the age of forty-six there is a turning point that highlights a growing need for more independence but also for group awareness. They will feel more experimental, but these are also the years when they are likely to enlist the support of others and be the spearhead for highly motivated and smoothly operating teams.

Although creativity isn't the strong point for these people, their highly developed qualities of clear thinking, objectivity and progressiveness make them natural leaders with the potential to achieve results that enhance their own lives and everyone else's they come into contact with.

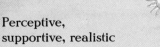

On the dark side

Interfering, controlling, unimaginative

At your best

Perceptive, supportive, realistic

7 December

the birthday of

the dreamer

Your greatest challenge is

finding the right career

The way forward is ...

to keep experimenting and gather as much information and advice as possible. Try also to develop outside interests; one of those may develop into a career.

People born on December 7 often feel as if there is a special purpose to their life. They dare to be different, and as highly original and creative thinkers they do indeed stand apart from the crowd. Although they have a thirst for adventure, they are first and foremost dreamers and their minds are capable of taking them to places others simply haven't the imagination to go.

They are often trendsetters who make up their own rules as they go along and their free-thinking, pioneering style will often startle others. Tending to be loners, they also know how to blend in when they want to, and their conversation is always colorful and interesting. The big problem, however, is that they tend to talk more than they act; if there is no follow-through people may dismiss them as dreamers not doers. To a certain extent this is true, as they are so creative and original they tend to get lost in their ideas.

Until the age of forty-four they will often feel a need to be more practical and realistic in their approach to their goals. They should pay attention to this because their tendency to flit from job to job or to stick with a job to which they are clearly unsuited can cause them great unhappiness. After the age of forty-five there is a turning point when their desire to express their individuality will be stronger than ever. If they haven't found their vocation by then, they are strongly advised to seek advice from experts about retraining for a new career. Alternatively, they may decide to seek satisfaction and fulfillment outside of work; if this is the case they need to make sure that they do not compromise too much of their spirit for the sake of financial security.

Conformity will never be for them, but these people need to find what makes their heart sing. It would truly be a tragedy if the world did not benefit from their unique but truly magical creativity.

On the dark side

Detached, stressed, muddled

At your best

Creative, individual, original

8 December

the birthday of passion

Your greatest challenge is

being responsible

The way forward is ...

to understand that being responsible and passionate are not mutually exclusive, and working together they can put you on the winning team.

People born on December 8 tend to sparkle with energy and enthusiasm and their lively personality will attract attention wherever they go. Their passionate approach to life is their defining feature, and they display intense emotional and sensual responses. When an opportunity presents itself in either their personal or professional life, they rarely hesitate and jump in head first.

Whether it is committing to an individual, a team, a project, or an idea, they can't see the point of being half-hearted; their nature is to give one hundred per cent. True idealists, people born on this day are constantly engaged in a quest to find fulfillment, emotional, intellectual or spiritual, and their infectious optimism may inspire others to seek their own personal nirvana. The trouble is that the perfect fulfillment they seek is unobtainable, and this can cause them to become manic or confused in their search for stimulation. Relaxing their expectations of perfection and understanding that imperfection is the natural human state is essential for their psychological growth.

Until the age of forty-three there is an emphasis in their lives on the need for order or structure; they should take advantage of opportunities presented to them to be more practical in their approach. This is because they don't always tend to direct their energy well, and their lack of good judgment can cause them to get involved in relationships or situations that are destructive or obsessive. After the age of forty-four there is another turning point, and this time they may feel a growing need to develop their individuality.

Whatever age they are, the key to their potential for happiness and success is to be more cautious and aware in their approach to people and situations so that their passionate intensity does not overpower their common sense. With a little more realism added to their stunning repertoire of creativity and idealism, they will find the fulfilling passion they have been searching for all their lives, in the process bringing great happiness to others.

On the dark side

Obsessive, addictive, irresponsible

At your best

Energetic, charismatic, passionate

9 December

the birthday of
the dashing hero

Your greatest challenge is

patience

The way forward is ...

to understand that sometimes you can't force progress; the **best** approach is to simply bide your time.

People born on December 9 are blessed with a fertile imagination. From childhood they will have cast themselves in the role of the dashing hero or heroine swooping in to save the day and astonishing everyone with acts of daring and courage. In adulthood they often become highly energetic individuals who love to be the center of attention.

They have a powerful urge to make important and inspirational contributions to the world and, with their imaginative mind, fixity of purpose and adventurous spirit they do possess outstanding pioneering potential. Born leaders, their biggest challenge is patience. Their patience can easily snap when things aren't going exactly the way they want them to or when people aren't listening to their suggestions. They need to learn when to promote their progressive ideals and when to step back and let things unfold. Calming their emotional intensity in response to any challenge they meet is crucial for their psychological growth, as well as for their chances of both professional and personal success.

Although they may have been shy as children, by the time they reach their twenties they will start to come out of their shells; if they can't manage this, developing their self-confidence is crucial because these people were born to be in the limelight. Until the age of forty-two there will be opportunities for them to find realistic ways to achieve their goals in life. They need to take advantage of these; if they don't, their dreams of progress and adventure will never move beyond the planning stage. After the age of forty-three there is a turning point when they may feel a desire to be more independent and to express their individuality.

At whatever age or stage in life they are, they have an all-encompassing, albeit occasionally self-centered urge to play a leading role in the lives of those around them. If they can implement their original and progressive visions it will give them the potential to make not just an imaginative but a real and significant contribution to the world.

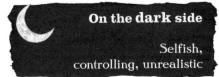

On the dark side

Selfish, controlling, unrealistic

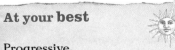

At your best

Progressive, romantic, dynamic

10 December

the birthday of
calm intensity

Your greatest challenge is

coping with rejection

The way forward is ...

to remind yourself that everyone gets knocked back at some point in their lives. The difference between success and failure is whether or not they get back up and try again.

A defining characteristic of people born on December 10 is their remarkable strength of spirit and steady determination to achieve their goals. Deep and intense thinkers, they are often driven by an urge to further human knowledge or instigate reform. Blessed with an inner calm that can help them stand back and make decisions objectively, their organizational skills are outstanding.

These people have leadership potential and, when they find a cause they believe in, they will wholly devote themselves to it. The key word here is "belief," because if they don't believe in what they are doing they simply won't be able to go through the motions. As a result their choice of career will often have a vocational element; they need to feel they are serving some kind of higher cause, be it in education or in spiritual matters. They will devote a great deal of time to examining the meaning of not just their own life, but the lives of everyone and even the universe. For this reason they can sometimes come across as slightly removed from the world they live in. This isn't to say they aren't sociable; they are. It's just that the sensitive part of them always seems to live in a world where injustice and suffering do not exist; not the real world, then.

Until the age of forty-one they will be presented with opportunities to be more practical and to put more order and structure into their lives. They should take advantage of these opportunities to develop a thicker skin and be more resilient in the face of adversity, as they don't tend to cope well during times of stress and conflict. After the age of forty-two there is a turning point that highlights a growing need for independence.

Whatever age they are, when they do finally find an ideal or cause about which they are passionate they will discover within themselves all the self-discipline, responsibility and passion they need to live up to their exceptional potential to become gifted, inspired and progressive leaders.

On the dark side

Elusive, isolated, overly sensitive

At your best

Determined, spiritual, devoted

11 December

the birthday of
intense purpose

Your greatest challenge is

having fun

The way forward is ...

to understand that the ability to take things less seriously is one of the most powerful and influential ways to influence people or get your point across.

People born on December 11 may have felt from an early age that there was a serious purpose to their lives. Whatever profession they choose, they are notable for the driving energy and determination they bring to their causes and visions.

As perfectionists they will demand as high a level of commitment and dedication from others as they demand from themselves. This will mean that they often excel professionally, but it can also work against them and exhaust everyone involved, including themselves. As far as their personal and social life is concerned, there is no let-up in their intensity; they are influential and persuasive individuals with the ability to win over—or in some cases wear down—others with their charming persistence. In fact, when it comes to advancing their cause or agenda, one of their favorite approaches is to cultivate influential contacts, because they know that with powerful backing almost anything is possible.

Until the age of forty a running theme will be the need for a more practical and realistic approach to achieving their goals in life. During these years they are likely to assume positions of responsibility or authority but they should ensure that the single-minded pursuit of their goals does not make them manipulative or overly materialistic. It is particularly important that their networking strategy does not slump into ambitious social climbing. After the age of forty-one there is a turning point, highlighting a desire to express their individuality and independence. They may become more involved with social issues and establishing a life outside work.

It would benefit these people always to consider the way others perceive them or the image they present to the world. Once they discover the lighter side of life, together with the spiritual ideals to balance their materialistic inclinations, they will find that their serious purpose is to become an outstanding human being capable of improving the lives of all around them—and in some cases humanity as a whole.

On the dark side

Materialistic, manipulative, selfish

At your best

Energetic, purposeful, charming

12 December

the birthday of
the outspoken teacher

Your greatest challenge is

overcoming the feeling of being boxed in

The way forward is ...

to understand that until you can generate a sense of freedom and excitement from within, no matter how many times you change your circumstances you will sooner or later feel trapped.

People born on December 12 often feel that they have an important message to deliver to the world—one that they believe will help others progress and learn. They also long to broaden their mind through study and travel, and as well as being mentally agile they also tend to be physically agile, enjoying traveling about from place to place or experience to experience.

These people's insatiable appetite for knowledge and experience is heavily influenced by their powerful desire to make a tangible, beneficial and enlightening contribution to the lives of others. Colleagues and friends will often admire their mental dexterity and their ability to identify areas in need of improvement and communicate their remedial visions to those around them in ways that are truly memorable.

Until the age of thirty-nine there is an emphasis in their lives on the need for order and structure. These are the years when they are most likely to feel boxed in or tied down, and the struggle between their desire to establish themselves and their thirst for adventure can be complicating and confusing for them. After the age of forty there is an important turning point when they are likely to become even more experimental in their approach to life and when the drive toward freedom will be particularly strong. The term mid-life crisis would not be inappropriate here, and these people may suddenly feel the need to make dramatic changes in their personal and professional life.

These people must never forget that they possess a tremendous amount of willpower and, when they finally devote themselves to a worthy career and set themselves clear goals and objectives, they have all the ambition and talent they need to be a success. When it comes to their personal life, if they can channel some of their energy inward to develop their intuition and spirituality, they will be able to draw on their extensive knowledge and life experience to realize their ambition of delivering an empowering message of hope, love and positive expectation to the world.

On the dark side

Scattered, unaware, materialistic

At your best

Informative, interesting, dramatic

13 December

erratic precision

Your greatest challenge is

letting go

The way forward is ...

to understand that sometimes things run their course and no amount of craftsmanship can make them run properly again.

People born on December 13 bring confidence, resourcefulness and tenacity to everything they do, plus a precise and occasionally painstaking attention to the smallest detail. Although their potential for professional and personal success in the long term is great, their careful and time-consuming approach can become over-cautious and hesitant. This, unfortunately, can lead to disillusionment.

These people with an eye for detail can be incredibly observant and perceptive when it comes to their fellow human beings. Regrettably, when it comes to themselves they can lack awareness and may not realize that they have erratic habits that not only irritate others, but also stop them working as efficiently as they might like. For example, they don't seem to know when to back off when an argument is going nowhere or when their point has been made, and will unnecessarily and hurtfully restate their case over and over again. In addition, they may have a habit of procrastinating when something important needs to be done, making life much harder for themselves than it need be.

Until the age of thirty-eight these people may feel a need for a practical and realistic approach to achieving their goals; these are the years when they need to be especially careful not to focus so much on the details that they lose sight of the bigger picture. After the age of thirty-nine there is a turning point and they are likely to want to express their individuality more. This can be an incredibly liberating time for them; they can start to put their personal mark on the success they have already built up for themselves.

Regardless of their age and stage in life, these people need to guard against becoming too exacting and finicky. This is because when they are able to step back and look at the impressive picture they are painting with their lives they will realize that they have both a lot to be grateful for and a lot to look forward to.

On the dark side

Fussy, exacting, procrastinating

At your best

Thorough, insightful, inquisitive

14 December

the birthday of
the flamboyant philosopher

Your greatest challenge is

getting your priorities right

The way forward is ...

to take the time for introspection, because until you get your priorities right, life will feel confusing and overwhelming.

People born on December 14 rarely merge into the crowd. This doesn't mean they are attention seekers. Quite the opposite; they can be deeply private individuals. It's just that their flamboyant tastes and unique ideas set them apart as much as their controlled energy, capability and efficiency. As natural philosophers, finding their own truth rather than conforming to the rules of others will always be important to them.

Although their provocative nature can outrage, it can also surprise and stimulate others, encouraging them to think outside the box. Nothing gives them greater satisfaction than the knowledge that they have fired someone's creativity or imagination. This is because activity and progress are their driving forces, and they cannot bear complacency when there are issues to explore and progress to be made. Blessed with strong organizational skills as well as considerable energy, they approach everything they do with enthusiasm, determination and insatiable curiosity.

These people are sociable and generous to others but in many respects they are also extremely self-contained and self-reliant. Their potential for fulfillment lies in the quest for discovery and progress, and although they will never turn away those who come to them for guidance, a part of them longs to shut out all outside distraction so they can pursue their personal goals undisturbed. They prefer to step into the limelight only when the time is right for them to reveal the fruits of their labor.

Until the age of thirty-eight there is an emphasis on practical order and structure in their lives, making them more goal-orientated and responsible; but after the age of thirty-nine there is a turning point when they will become more concerned with expressing their individuality and making contribution to the world. The keys to their success will be their ability to find a work–life balance and their willingness to develop their diplomatic skills so that they motivate others to follow their example and become potent, productive and truth-seeking forces for positive change and progress.

On the dark side

Withdrawn, workaholic, lonely

At your best

Dramatic, original, bold

15 December

the birthday of the optimist

Your greatest challenge is

accepting your limitations

The way forward is ...

to understand that an overly optimistic evaluation of a situation is just as unhelpful as one that is overly pessimistic. Strike a balance between the two.

People born on December 15 are among the most upbeat individuals of the year. Once they set their sights on something, however unattainable, they truly believe that they can attain it. This positive, can-do and can-have attitude tends to attract most, if not all, of the professional and personal success their many talents deserve.

As well as being expansive and optimistic in their outlook, they are also blessed with an insatiable curiosity. They delight in discovering new information and in sharing what they have learned with colleagues and friends. Although their curiosity is infectious and their optimism energizing, it is important for people born on this day to consider whether or not the information they are revealing and the sense of possibility they are encouraging are in the best interests of themselves and others. This is because they see the world through the eyes of an optimist, and an optimist doesn't take into account or protect themselves against the negative potential of a situation. In other words, their plans can sometimes be unrealistic or—worse still—foolish, and their influence on others can be condescending or irresponsible.

Until the age of thirty-five people born on this day will have many opportunities to develop a more practical and realistic approach to life and they need to take advantage of these because optimism can only take them so far. After the age of thirty-six, however, there is a turning point which highlights a growing need for independence, progressive ideas and expressing their individuality. During these years it is vital for them to learn to listen to the advice of others, weighing up the pros and cons of a situation before jumping in over their heads.

Throughout their lives the key to their success will be their ability to recognize and leave behind situations that are unproductive, so that they can invest their outstanding potential in doing what they do best: moving in the direction of progress, while motivating and inspiring others with their invigorating enthusiasm, stunning creativity and can-do attitude.

On the dark side

Uncontrolled, manipulative, foolish

At your best

Energizing, inspirational, popular

16 December

the birthday of
the creative anthropologist

Your greatest challenge is

resisting the impulse to criticize

The way forward is ...

to understand that sometimes the best approach to a situation is to focus on the solution not the problem.

People born on December 16 are blessed with a soaring imagination but their logical and objective approach to situations and people ensures that they never succumb to flights of fancy. In fact they have the ability to view everyone and everything in their life with the inquisitive detachment of an anthropologist.

Nothing escapes the scrutiny of these intelligent and sharp-witted people, and when their analytical, logical and determined mind is combined with their imaginative intellectual qualities, they have the potential to engineer far-reaching innovations. Once they have settled on their objectives, they will pursue them with remarkable determination, and although this dramatically enhances their potential for professional success—they often rise to management level or the very top of their careers—their single-minded focus on their career goals can isolate them emotionally from others.

Until the age of thirty-five they will lean toward a more practical and realistic approach to their goals, and these are the years when they are most likely to lose themselves in their career. During these years establishing a work–life balance and becoming more sensitive to the feelings of others are important. After the age of thirty-six, however, there is a significant turning point which highlights a need to be free from responsibilities, to be more independent and to express their individuality. They may become involved with humanitarian ideals or issues of universal spirituality. At first this shift in focus may feel confusing and disorientating for them, but as the years go by they start to understand themselves better and experience life less as a research lab and more on a deeper, intuitive level where certain things are simply to be experienced rather than examined.

They also begin to realize that the key to unlocking their potential for outstanding achievement is to keep their lives as real and as grounded as possible, so that they are relaxed and receptive enough to tune into their powerful intuition and make the right choices for themselves and others.

On the dark side

Impractical, isolated, unaware

At your best

Innovative, thorough, visionary

17 December

the birthday of
the practical realist

Your greatest challenge is

seeing the funny side

The way forward is ...

to understand that one of the quickest ways to improve life satisfaction is to take everything and everyone, including yourself, a little less seriously.

People born on December 17 tend to say exactly what they mean, and they expect others to do the same. Success to them is something that can be measured in concrete terms and, as a practical realist, they garner a good deal of responsibility and a reputation for honesty and hard work.

With the courage and vitality to achieve almost any goal they set for themselves, these people are doers rather than thinkers. What interests them is facts, results and actions, not dreams, debates or theories. Everything is focused on what can be achieved or produced right now; this ability to concentrate only on what is before their eyes means they can achieve spectacular results.

Although the friends and family of these people value their sincerity and steady temperament, social involvement with others can be an area of confusion and difficulty for them. Their organizational skills mean that they are excellent at keeping in touch with old friends, but somehow true intimacy may prove elusive. This is largely because they simply don't understand how important small talk and a sense of humor are for breaking down barriers between people. It's important for them to learn to be a little less serious and to recognize that emotions sometimes can't be explained or categorized.

Until the age of thirty-four there is an emphasis on practical issues, and a need for order and structure in their lives. Since they already have a tendency to be pragmatic and realistic, it is important during these years that they don't become too materialistic. After the age of thirty-five there is a turning point when they may want freedom or to be more experimental in their approach to life. Although this is disorientating at first, they will ultimately find this change of emphasis liberating. Above all the key to their success and happiness will be their ability to introduce a spiritual dimension into their lives, because this will give them the sense of certainty, truth, order and wonder that they have always been seeking.

On the dark side

Prosaic, tactless, uninvolved

At your best

Honest, structured, steady

18 December

the birthday of
possibility

Your greatest challenge is

silence

The way forward is ...

to understand that stillness and aloneness are powerful forces for enlightenment, change and progress.

People born on December 18 are blessed with a soaring imagination and a sense of possibility that those who are less imaginative would dismiss or even ridicule. Their determination to translate their dreams into reality is, however, so powerful that they can withstand almost any criticism.

From an early age people born on this day are likely to have been quick learners, soaking up information and mastering skills long before others; when all this knowledge is added to their incredible creativity, anything is quite literally possible. They may develop a game plan for life in their teens or twenties that includes far-reaching plans and then, as the years pass, they will devote themselves fully to achieving their goals and realizing their dreams. These people think in the long term and not in the short term, and although progress may appear slow to others, they are slowly, carefully and steadily climbing their way to the very top.

Until the age of thirty-three they may find that life offers them opportunities to develop a more practical and realistic approach to achieving their goals. They should take advantage of these opportunities by accepting assistance when it is offered, involving others in their plans, and simplifying their workload and their long-term goals. They run a real danger otherwise of becoming exhausted, disappointed and alienated. After the age of thirty-four there is a turning point when they may wish to become more independent and to express their individuality.

These years are filled with potential for people born on this day, but whatever age they are the key to their success is their ability to set themselves realistic goals and their willingness to slow down the pace of their lives so they can get in touch with their intuition or the silence within. Connecting with their feelings will help them see that the sense of wonder, discovery and possibility they long to—and are destined to—create in the world around them already exists within them; all they need to do is find it.

On the dark side

Unrealistic, preoccupied, unfocused

At your best

Imaginative, energetic, determined

492

19 December

the birthday of
revealing honesty

Your greatest challenge is

turning your back on self-pity

The way forward is ...

to understand that feeling sorry for yourself will bring absolutely nothing positive into your life, just the pity of those whose admiration you seek.

People born on December 19 come across as sensitive individuals, but this conceals their remarkable hidden strength and courage. They are not afraid to express themselves freely, and when people cross or upset them they are honest enough to reveal their true feelings. Others may mistake their sensitivity and outspokenness as weaknesses, but releasing their emotions in this way actually makes them feel stronger.

They are uncompromisingly individualistic in their approach and are unlikely to thrive in environments where they need to conform. They have a strong need to challenge convention, question norms and generate original alternatives. Although their revealing honesty can work against them, others tend to respect them for their integrity and individuality. Their greatest desires are to educate or enlighten others and to further human progress.

When faced with challenges or setbacks they will reveal their fighting spirit and steady determination to succeed. This gives them endless potential for professional success, but unfortunately they sometimes seem unable to show a similar resilience in their personal life. In fact they are prone to bouts of negativity and self-pity that can manifest in flashes of anger or outrageous behavior, perplexing and confusing themselves and others. If they can learn to get a grip on their negativity by turning inward the same spirit of daring and courage that they display in the outside world, there are no mountains too high for them to climb.

Until the age of thirty-two they are likely to focus on practical issues and there will be a need for order and focus in their lives. A turning point occurs around the age of thirty-three where there is a growing desire for more personal freedom and experimentation. If they can learn to think before they act and to positively redirect their thoughts when they start to spiral into negativity, these are the years when they can really come into their own, finally revealing to the world just how committed they are to making a valuable contribution to the greater good.

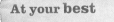

On the dark side

Negative, depressed, perplexing

At your best

Courageous, honest, expressive

20 December

the birthday of
the producer

Your greatest challenge is

learning from mistakes

The way forward is ...

to look at mistakes as opportunities to learn about what does or does not work in your life, so that you can constantly fine-tune and improve your performance.

People born on December 20 are energetic and gifted problem solvers and decision makers with a marked talent for motivating and organizing others. Born leaders, they are motivated by a desire to help society progress and are at their happiest and best when generating ideas and initiating projects. Once a project has got off the ground, however, they prefer to move on to the next project and put others at the helm, content in their self-appointed role of producer and creator.

There simply aren't enough hours in the day for people born on December 20. Their impulse to keep moving forward is strong, and because they are also efficient their output and achievements are often remarkable. Their instinct is always to understand the bigger picture, and when they are heading toward their goals criticism will not deter them. Hardworking and committed, they can, however, make the mistake of assuming that others are as tireless and determined as they are, becoming frustrated and impatient with those who simply can't keep up or match their output. Despite their vital concern for the welfare of others and their intense desire to make the world a better place, their interpersonal skills often need attention.

Until they reach the age of thirty-one they are likely to be more practical and realistic in their approach to achieving their goals, and their results-orientated approach will draw as much praise as it does criticism from those who feel that they are too superficial or paying insufficient attention to details. After the age of thirty-two there is a turning point when they will start to feel the need to be more independent and put their individual stamp on things. These are the years when both professional and personal success is most likely.

Whatever age they are, however, developing their latent imaginative and creative powers and rediscovering their joyful childlike spirit will give them the ability not only to generate innovative ideas—and to motivate and inspire others to develop them—but to lift people's spirits and really enjoy life.

On the dark side

Superficial, hasty, stubborn

At your best

Productive, energetic, fast

21 December

the birthday of the secret

Your greatest challenge is

trusting and sharing with others

The way forward is ...

to understand that everything in life, including relationships, involves a certain amount of risk-taking. Sometimes you just have to take a leap of faith.

Although they are energetic and strong willed, it's very hard to know what people born on December 21 are really thinking and feeling as they are by nature secretive. They prefer to express themselves with actions rather than words, and their powerful, silent presence can be inscrutable even to those closest to them.

Even though they might be a mystery to others, this does not mean they are reserved or passive. Quite the opposite; they are determined to achieve their goals and get their point across. It is just that instead of an exchange of opinions they usually prefer to push ahead regardless of what others are saying or thinking. If this means there will be battles along the way, so be it. In fact, their presence can be intimidating not just because others never know what to expect from them but because when they do lash out their few carefully chosen words can be harsh and cutting. Others may therefore feel that they can never relax around them because they are like a dormant volcano, quiet on the outside but with a burning intensity on the inside.

Despite sometimes appearing menacing or brooding, they are surprisingly insecure, although they would never allow others to know this. It's this insecurity, however, which forces them to be defensive, to nurture hidden resentments against those that cross them and, above all, to crave the admiration and respect of others. They should understand that they already have the admiration of others, but what they really need is their affection; this can only be earned when they learn to trust and share their feelings.

Around the age of thirty-two there will be a turning point when there are opportunities for them to focus less on proving themselves and more on finding their place within society. If they can take advantage of these opportunities and learn to open their minds to alternative viewpoints and their hearts to the magical potential within them and others, they will not only discover the secret of their happiness but the secret of everyone else's too.

On the dark side

Domineering, inflexible, self-involved

At your best

Strong-willed, authoritative, intriguing

CAPRICORN

THE GOAT (DECEMBER 22 – JANUARY 19)

❋ **Element:** Earth

❋ **Ruling planet:** Saturn, the teacher

❋ **Symbol:** The Goat

❋ **Tarot card:** The Devil (materialism)

❋ **Number:** 8

❋ **Favorable colors:** Green, brown, black

❋ **Key phrase:** I am ambitious, but responsible

Whether they are shy and retiring or outgoing and comfortable in the limelight, there is one thing that all Capricorns have in common and that is their ambition. Capricorn is the most disciplined and ambitious sign of the zodiac. Taking themselves very seriously, they are respectable and dependable people, although their dogmatic and black-and-white approach to life can sometimes make them seem overly serious and didactic.

Personality potential

Capricorns are ruled by the planet Saturn, which is the planet of responsibility, discipline and education, and Capricorn is perhaps the most ambitious, enduring and dependable signs of the entire zodiac. As the final earth sign—after Taurus and Virgo—it represents the richness and fertility of the earth. Associated with this sign are the many rewards and benefits of hard work.

Although Capricorns are ambitious, the secret of their success is that they are also highly responsible; when in positions of power, they will never abuse it. They are extremely disciplined, and with that discipline come patience, wisdom and the practicality to keep their feet firmly on the ground. With their dogged persistence they are likely to rise to the top of their field or profession, and they are more than capable of handling the loneliness and responsibility of power. They can also be very helpful and generous to those starting out or in need of their help and advice. Capricorns do take life seriously and have a cautious and steady approach, but this isn't to say they don't know how to laugh. At first glance they may appear to be serious, but those who know them better will often discover a wicked and unexpected sense of humor.

Of all the signs, Capricorns have the strongest sense of justice. They find it impossible to stand back and observe any kind of unfairness, and will do their best to correct unjust situations. They aren't hypocrites either, and apply the same strict sense of what is right and what is wrong to their own motives and behavior; in fact they are often far harder on themselves than on anyone else. Above all, determination and a will to progress are hallmarks of this sign. They are never afraid of hard work and their natural ability to be industrious means that the path of steady advancement is their preferred route in life. They also have the courage to pour their awe-inspiring will to achieve into any challenge that is worthy of them; it's not surprising, therefore, that all this diligence and focus tends to bring plenty of good fortune and success their way.

> **" They find it impossible to stand back and observe any kind of unfairness... "**

On the dark side

Warning words for Capricorns include narrow-mindedness, pessimism, rigidity and mean-spiritedness. They can also lack confidence in themselves and this inner dissatisfaction creates a driving need for success in the outside world. Low self-esteem means that they not only judge people according to their position or what they can do to help them climb the ladder of success; it can also stop them from taking risks. Their tendency to always err on the side of caution can make them over-cautious and hesitant when action is required, leading to frequent missed opportunities. In addition, their lack of confidence in their own attractiveness can lead to behavior that is "people pleasing," and this can stop them forming deep and lasting connections with others.

The ambitious streak in every Capricorn can lead them to run the risk of becoming workaholics. They need to be constantly reminded of the importance of a work–life balance. Being a determined sign but one that lacks self-confidence, they also need to avoid falling into the trap of always being the second in command or the power behind the throne.

Capricorns are sometimes prone to bouts of gloom and pessimism. Their presence can be an incredibly heavy one and when they are in one of their moods they are often guilty of putting the dampers on everyone else's enthusiasm. Another weakness is that they can be control freaks, and their controlling personality often views the world in narrow-minded terms, imposing rules and endless "shoulds" on themselves and others.

Symbol

The symbol for Capricorn is the goat and just like the mountain goat, Capricorns will persevere until they have climbed the mountain of success and reach the very top. As well as being dogged and determined, mountain goats are also loners and Capricorns often have a sense of reserve and detachment about them. In addition, the symbol of the goat suggests stability and conformity as embodied by the mythical sea goat that rose to bring civilization to the world.

Darkest secret

Capricorns are incredibly insightful and see the world as it really is, but they aren't really as cool and detached as they appear. Their clear perception of what's going on around them can often cause them a lot of pain and distress. In addition, inside every Capricorn is a secret desire to let themselves go from time to time and join in the fun with everyone else, but fear of looking foolish almost always holds them back.

Love

Good hearted, dependable and honest, Capricorns make very attractive friends and lovers. When they are content in a relationship they make loving, affectionate, faithful and protective partners that can be depended on. In fact the right relationship is often an essential ingredient for a Capricorn's success in life because it gives them the respite and strength they need when life seems to be getting too much. They should try to seek partners who are receptive to change and more willing to take risks than they are, because such partners will help balance out their over-cautious streak. They also need to seek partners who are not intimidated by their strong self-discipline.

Although a solid relationship is a key ingredient for their fulfillment, many Capricorns may postpone committing themselves to someone else until they feel they have established their career or financial security. This is a sensible approach but it isn't always the best thing to do and, later in life, Capricorns may regret that they didn't act sooner to follow their heart. Their ambition may also drive them to marry for money or social status; this is a disastrous approach. Alternatively, and equally disastrously, they may marry for love and then devote all their time and their energy to their career.

Love matches:
Taurus, Virgo and Pisces

The Capricorn man

The Capricorn man tends to come across as the silent-but-strong type but it's a mistake to think that he prefers to be alone, because he doesn't. He may not be the life and the soul of the party but deep down the Capricorn man craves attention and admiration. He also craves the spontaneity of romance but the practical, stern and disciplined part of his personality simply won't allow it. Sometimes, though, his yearnings will break through and you'll get flashes of humor and the unexpected from him.

Capricorns pretend they can live without romance, compliments and attention, but the way to the heart of this strong, dependable, trustworthy, modest but ambitious and successful man is to pay him compliments; then, when the relationship gets more intimate, give him plenty of affection. He needs to be encouraged to venture out of his silent prison and to see what a really wonderful man he is.

More often than not a Capricorn man will grow younger with age. He'll be incredibly serious in his teens and twenties but then, as he approaches mid life and beyond, he may start to relax and have more fun. He's unlikely to be unfaithful, though, as his strict moral sense and desire to do the right thing rarely relaxes. When he's busy building his career, or at the height of it, there may be a tendency for him to become routine in his scheduling, even when it comes to lovemaking. He may also seem constantly preoccupied with work; this lack of spontaneity can take its toll on any relationship. Fortunately, the older he gets, the less likely this is to be the case.

Although he may not be the most romantic of lovers, throughout his life the Capricorn man will always be that strong man with a gentle heart. And once he has given someone his heart, he will protect and provide for them and stand by them through the years, whether times are good or bad.

The Capricorn woman

It's virtually impossible to describe a typical Capricorn woman because she can appear in any number of guises, but whatever guise she appears in there will always be one thing in common—she'll be ruled by the disciplined and determined planet Saturn. A great many Capricorn women devote themselves to a high-flying career but when they marry their focus

does shift as long as their need for security and respect are met by their partner. If they aren't met or if the Capricorn woman feels unfulfilled in the role of wife and mother, gloom and despondency may sink in, so maintaining their own interests outside the family are essential.

The Capricorn woman often appears calm and collected, but she is less even-tempered and emotionally steady than she appears. In fact, she is prone to really black moods and is capable of brooding for a very long time. Her gloom may be triggered by disappointments or setbacks, but it's often far more deep rooted than that and tied up with her feelings of inadequacy. Deep down she never feels quite good enough and her mood swings will only disappear when she starts to truly believe in herself and her not inconsiderable talents.

Rest and relaxation don't come easy to a Capricorn woman because she always needs to feel that she is working or climbing the ladder to success; if she isn't working for herself or her family, she'll work for causes or a charity. She needs a partner who can patiently help her get over her lack of self-confidence. In return she'll give a love that is deep, lasting and capable of not just climbing but actually moving mountains.

Family

If ever the expression "old head on young shoulders" were true, then it can be no truer then when applied to the Capricorn child. Highly conventional and with a need for a secure, disciplined upbringing, these children are often wise beyond their years and will frequently surprise their parents with the insight they show about the world in which they live. As sensible and grown up as they appear, however, these children are in real need of reassurance and encouragement so that the Capricorn weakness of low self-confidence does not become a habit from early in life. A child is still a child even when that child is a Capricorn child, and parents should remember that children are still prey to irrational fears and need unconditional love and constant encouragement. Their sense of fun and spontaneity also should be encouraged if they are to avoid becoming too serious and old before their time. At school, they are unlikely to be the most popular child in the class but they will tend to have a select few friends—friends that they often keep for a lifetime. Their progress with schoolwork will be slow and steady rather than remarkable, but their quiet ambition will ensure that their final grades are highly respectable. They also often excel at getting prizes, awards and certificates.

Capricorn parents are likely to encourage their children to be hard workers, just like they themselves are. Discipline will be strong, especially moral discipline, but it's important for them to ensure they don't get too heavy handed and strict. They should also make sure they give their child or children plenty of love and affection and, just as important, plenty of time. Capricorn parents can be so ambitious and so fixated on giving their children financial security and the best education that they miss out on actually spending time with their kids. Boarding schools will probably be discussed but, unless this is absolutely necessary, a Capricorn parent may want to consider what they have to lose as well as what they may gain from sending their child away for long periods of time.

Career

Capricorns are ambitious and, whatever career they choose, the ladder of success is sure to be climbed. They can excel in many professions but are closely associated with jobs related to education, bureaucracy and government; employment as a civil servant, government employee, teacher, bank manager,

"They really do enjoy being the one everybody comes to for advice..."

chief executive officer, government employee and planner may suit them well They may also be drawn to medical careers and—with this sign's link to the skeleton—may also work as chiropractors, osteopaths and dentists. Many Capricorns can be found working as architects and builders, and their loving of structure may also reflect in career choices that include mathematics, engineering and science. Finally, they are well suited to all careers in the legal profession.

Other signs may find the responsibilities and loneliness of being at the top of the tree at work daunting, but Capricorns thrive on it. They really do enjoy being the one everybody comes to for advice and in most cases the advice they give is sound. Although they are destined to climb the ladder of success, they will do it slowly and carefully. However wealthy or successful they become, their attitude to money will be responsible and they rarely lack the finances to retire in comfort.

Health and leisure

Self-discipline is strong for people born under this sun sign, so Capricorns are likely to be sensible about both their diet and their lifestyle. They understand the importance of eating nutritious food and overindulgence is simply not in their nature, although they may be prone to comfort eating during bouts of low self-esteem. The best thing they can do for their health and well-being is to exercise, but unfortunately this is usually the one thing on which they tend to compromise. They often spend a lot of time at their desk or at work in a job that is fairly sedentary, and this can not only lead to weight gain but it can also lead to joint pain and bouts of depression. Regular, moderate exercise for at least 30 minutes a day will help them manage their weight and boost their mood, keep their joints and their mind flexible and their heart healthy.

Bones, teeth and skin are areas of special concern for Capricorns. They should make sure they wear sunscreen when there's strong sunlight and in addition to regular aerobic

exercise, such as brisk walking or jogging, they should also do some toning and weight training to keep their bones strong. Regular flossing and brushing is also essential for healthy teeth, as are regular visits to the dentist however busy things get at work.

As far as leisure interests are concerned, Capricorns are often drawn to the world of music in which they may display remarkable talent. They should make sure they get plenty of fresh air and daylight, especially if their jobs keep them indoors for most of the day. Hill walking and rambling are excellent pursuits for Capricorns. The sooner people born under this sun sign learn to play as hard as they work the better their lives will get, because unwinding and having fun can give them the balance and perspective they need to find the sense of fulfillment and security for which they long. Wearing, meditating on and surrounding themselves with the color orange will encourage them to be more open and fun loving.

Born between December 22 and January 1

People born between these dates are wonderfully stoical and resilient with an incredible capacity to withstand the blows of life. Their resilience and dedication are second to none and like the steel under the blacksmith's hammer, they get stronger and more powerful with every blow.

Born between January 2 and January 10

These Capricorns are more than capable of reaching the heights of any mountain. Their success is likely to occur later in life but, when it does come, they share what they have with others.

Born between January 11 and January 19

They may come across as modest and unassuming, but these people are excellent communicators with a knack for building success. If they accept a responsibility they give it their full commitment. Dependable and strong, they demand the same level of integrity from everyone they deal with both in the workplace and at home.

Life lessons

There is a tendency for people born under the sun sign Capricorn to become narrow-minded or blinkered in their approach to life, so it's essential for them to learn to see life from the point of view of others. They also need to find their own inner voice as, especially in their twenties and thirties, they tend to get their opinions from those in authority over them rather than from what they think is right. Another challenge is for them to let the spiritual into their life. With all their energy being expended on their career and on material gain, they often lose sight of the deeper, more meaningful and fulfilling aspects of life. Although this sign is the most ambitious and self-disciplined of the zodiac, they often neglect the importance of things money can't buy—such as love, relaxation, fun and laugher. In addition, their journey to the top may sometimes be quite a meaningless one because they often want to get to the top for the status and recognition it can bring. But status and recognition are not good enough reasons to want to do anything, and Capricorns could benefit from contributing more to the greater good rather than to the good of their career.

Perfectionist by nature, Capricorns are often terrified of making mistakes and when this is combined with their stern self-discipline it can make them overly tense and serious. Capricorns must learn to lighten up and not see one tiny mistake as a catastrophe. If they are in a position of authority they must not let their perfectionist mindset make them an over-controlling, interfering slave driver obsessed with the details. It's absolutely vital for Capricorns to give themselves and others room for error. They must also stop being so obsessive about what others think when they make a mistake, because in most cases others are understanding or simply don't even notice. If Capricorns can be less rigid, paranoid and perfectionist in their thinking, they have the potential to produce inspired work and to be inspired managers of others.

Other signs can offer Capricorns help and inspiration with their life lessons. Arians can teach them to move on quickly from disappointment and to do things to the best of their ability, rather than perfectly. Cancerians can help them value their friends, family and loved ones more than their career. Sagittarians can teach them to be more adventurous and inquisitive in their approach to life and Librans can show them how to take a more balanced view when they make mistakes, as well as being more subtle and kind when it comes to getting their point of view across.

22 December

the birthday of

enduring poise

Your greatest challenge is

broadening your outlook

The way forward is ...

to understand that there is a difference between being focused and being one-track in your approach to achieving success. The former is called determination, the latter is called stupidity.

People born on December 22 may have formulated a long-term plan for their lives as early as childhood. At various stages in their lives they will review their goals, setting themselves new ones to achieve in the next five or ten years ahead. These people know what they want out of life and how they are going to go about achieving it; this augurs well for both professional and personal success.

Understanding the importance of preparation, they are willing to bide their time and work steadily toward their goals in a self-assured and dignified way. Their remarkable poise is the result of an absolute belief that winning in the end is their absolute birthright; because they are so comfortable in their self-belief they can be a great role model for others. The danger, however, is that they can sometimes become a little too complacent, remaining for years in a position that doesn't challenge them. When a difficult challenge finally does emerge, they may fail to live up to their own and everybody's high expectations. The secret of their success is to keep learning, fine-tuning their skills and testing themselves; that way they can live up to the hype that they have created.

Until the age of twenty-nine they are likely to be goal-orientated and to have a practical approach to their achievements. But at the age of thirty they reach a turning point that highlights a growing need for freedom, new ideas and expressing their creativity. After the age of sixty there is another turning point when there is likely to be more emphasis on their emotional receptivity, imagination and intuitive awareness.

Whatever their age or stage in life, they need to find a balance between self-belief and humility, between long-term planning and spontaneity, and between seriousness and having more fun. As soon as they do strike this balance they will maintain it with their characteristic poise, finding themselves at last in exactly the right position to develop the unusual potential for happiness, success and fulfillment associated with this birthday.

On the dark side

Narrow-minded, controlling, workaholic

At your best

Prepared, self-confident, dignified

23 December

the **birthday of**
the **cautious revolutionary**

Your greatest challenge is

coping with sudden change

The way forward is ...

to understand that sometimes it is impossible to control the outcome of events; you simply have to bend in the direction that life is taking you.

People born on December 23 are hardworking, quietly ambitious individuals who are at their happiest and their best when they can identify areas of improvement and then formulate original, sometimes radical but always practical solutions. Gifted organizers, they prefer to plan and work toward and then carefully prepare for improvement.

Those born on this day distrust sudden change and feel uncomfortable when it is thrust upon them as it upsets their steady and determined plans for progressive change and progress. In fact, when they assume positions of power—which more often than not they do, given their authoritative presence and excellent communication skills—they can be resistant to change. They can also become controlling and authoritarian when challenged, and when alternative viewpoints to their own are given they can become hostile and defensive. It is therefore extremely important for their psychological growth and their professional success that they learn to be more flexible and open-minded in their approach to people and situations.

Before the age of twenty-eight, they may have shown a responsibility beyond their years, perhaps getting their foot on the property ladder long before their peers, taking on the responsibilities of a partner and family, or firmly establishing themselves in their career. After the age of twenty-nine, however, there is a gradual shift of emphasis which highlights a growing need to be more carefree and independent and to express their individuality. Another turning point occurs when they are sixty: they are likely to become more sensitive and responsive to their creative urges.

Whatever their age or stage in life, they need to resist the urge to withdraw into stubbornness, inflexibility and complacency. This is because when they start to be more spontaneous and to share their compassion, generosity, creativity and curiosity with others, they will discover that they have the ability to lead and inspire others to follow them along the optimum path to progress, in whatever direction, or directions, it takes everyone.

On the dark side

Complacent, authoritarian, inflexible

At your best

Responsible, innovative, steady

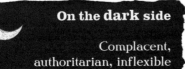

24 December

the birthday of
complicated far sight

Your greatest challenge is

learning from your mistakes

The way forward is ...

to understand that if an approach doesn't work the first time around, unless changes are made it won't work the second time either.

People born on December 24 seem destined to live complicated, uncertain but exciting and fast-moving lives. Life is never straightforward or stress-free for them, but they have a knack of rising above challenges and achieving great success.

There are many reasons why life can appear unnecessarily stressful for people born on this day. They can find it hard to react with tact and diplomacy to people and situations, and they aren't very good at learning from their mistakes. They also have a gift for seeing into the future, or for knowing which methods will or won't work. In this respect they could be described as visionary, but unfortunately for them it takes a while for others—and themselves—to recognize and appreciate their gift of far-sightedness. Until that recognition is forthcoming others will wonder why they insist on making life so difficult, and they themselves will wonder why life always feels so complicated.

Until the age of twenty-seven they tend to place practical considerations and a desire for order and security first, but after the age of twenty-eight things start to change and they will often feel a growing need for independence and a desire to express their individuality. After the age of fifty-eight there is more emphasis on emotional receptivity, and these are the years when their intuitive potential may develop into psychic ability. Whatever their age or stage in life, the key to their success will be their ability to learn from their mistakes and be more sensitive and tactful with others, especially those who recognize their potential and want to help them. If a dose of self-confidence is thrown into the mix, not only will they will start to understand themselves and the people around them better, but life will start to feel and become much easier and more rewarding for them. When all this comes together, they will finally be able to see their potential clearly and to attract considerable success and happiness into their lives.

On the dark side

Confusing, tactless, stubborn

At your best

Innovative, visionary, exciting

25 December

the birthday of
the peak experience

being realistic

*The way
forward is ...*

to understand that
setting yourself
goals or ideals that
are unattainable
isn't uplifting, it is
the path to
disillusionment
and unhappiness.

People born on December 25 can struggle with the more mundane aspects of life, and the main theme in their lives is their search for a state of heightened awareness where they can transcend the everyday. Others may dismiss them as unrealistic dreamers but may secretly admire the sense of awe and wonder they bring to everything they say and do.

In both their professional and their personal lives, they bring energy, strength of purpose and a gift for organization. Above all, they bring a willingness to push things just that little bit further than others would dare in search of the peak experience they long to experience. One of the reasons people born on this day may feel the need to make their experience of life extraordinary is because they generally receive less attention on their birthday than anyone else in the year. They may therefore feel they are missing out on life in some way. These feelings persist throughout their lives, giving them the drive and the determination to stand out and achieve their ambitious aspirations.

Before the age of twenty-six they are likely to have a goal-orientated, straightforward approach to their achievements, but after the age of twenty-seven and for the next thirty years they are likely to feel a growing need to experiment with different concepts and express their individuality. Another turning point comes at the age of fifty-seven when they are likely to place more emphasis on their already enhanced sensitivity and feelings.

Whatever their age or stage in life, however, they will always place spiritual aspirations above material ones; this doesn't just set them apart, it puts them way ahead of the rest. As long as these goals are not used as a means of escaping from the complications of life, and as long as they can find ways to increase their chances of success by injecting realism into their idealistic visions, these people are capable not only of great happiness and fulfillment, but of making lasting contributions to the greater good.

On the dark side

Escapist, restless,
sensation seeking

At your best

Visionary,
courageous, spiritual

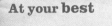

511

26 December

the birthday of
the vantage point

Your greatest challenge is

admitting you made mistakes

The way forward is ...

to understand that until you acknowledge that you may have been wrong you will not be able to learn or move away from your mistakes.

People born on December 26 are never afraid to push themselves and their ideas forward, and with their non-stop energy and determination it is not surprising that they often achieve what they strive for in life. Once they reach the top, however, they often refuse to move anywhere else and their energy is no longer devoted to moving forward but to sustaining their vantage point.

They are therefore a curious mixture of ambition, single-minded perseverance and a desire for security and stability. The danger with this combination, even though it does attract considerable professional success their way, is that they run the risk of becoming too mechanical or unfeeling, not just toward themselves but toward others. It is vital for their psychological growth that they get in touch with their feelings and those of others, as they can come across at times as intense, serious and "hard" individuals.

Until the age of twenty-five they will often feel a need for order and structure in their lives, and practical considerations are important. During these years—and indeed at any stage in their lives—the key to their success will be to practice the art of compromise, remembering that the feelings of other people should always be taken into consideration. After the age of twenty-six there is a significant turning point, giving them opportunities to express their individuality. After the age of fifty-six there is likely to be an increased emphasis on emotional receptivity, imagination, or psychic and spiritual awareness, and these are the years when they are likely to feel at their most content and fulfilled.

Whatever stage or age they are at, they must avoid the tendency to cling to what they know, or to become complacent or overly security conscious. Once they understand that often the greatest forward progress requires taking risks, giving up some ground, and exploring unfamiliar territory, they have the potential not only to make things happen on a grand scale, but also to inspire others.

On the dark side

Defensive, rigid, unfeeling

At your best

Energetic, methodical, inspirational

27 December

the birthday of
the golden heart

Your greatest challenge is

saying "no"

The way forward is ...

to understand that saying "no" when you are not in a position to give is saying "yes" to yourself.

People born on December 27 may give the impression of being sturdy and strong on the outside, but on the inside they have a heart of pure gold. Although they can be stubborn at times, they are life's givers, not takers. They also have a heroic side to them and will be the first to rush to offer their support or help when someone is in trouble.

These people set incredibly noble standards for themselves and are giving to the point of self-sacrifice. They pride themselves on being kind, thoughtful and compassionate human beings who will always do the right thing or offer their support if it is needed. However, because their goodwill makes it hard for them to refuse any request, they may become overburdened with problems that aren't their own. Their generosity and good-natured charm may win them many admirers, but underneath they can often be plagued by self-doubts and silent frustration. Part of the reason for their insecurity is that they can feel torn between their strong feelings of personal responsibility and the need for time and space to pursue their own interests.

Until the age of twenty-four they will often have a very goal-orientated, practical approach to life; but after the age of twenty-five there is a shift in emphasis, and opportunities will be presented to them to develop their individuality. It is important that they take advantage of these because only when they are able to reconcile their desire to help others with their desire to find personal fulfillment can they unlock their remarkable potential.

At first those who live and work with these people may find it unsettling to see them becoming more independent, but it is absolutely crucial that they don't allow this to unsettle them. They only have to make the effort to strike out on their own and pay attention to what they want to achieve in life to perform miracles, rise to the top of their career, and achieve long-lasting success while maintaining the respect and affection of those around them.

On the dark side

Self-sacrificing, insecure, frustrated

At your best

Generous, charming, noble

513

28 December

the birthday of
the shining example

Your greatest challenge is

coping with disappointment

The way forward is ...

to remember that everyone, however successful, makes mistakes and you are no exception. Start to view setbacks not as failures but as stepping stones on the road to success.

People born on December 28 tend to impress others greatly with their energy and clear sense of direction. They are a shining example of calmness, self-assurance and dependability to whom people often turn for support or advice during a crisis; and that support is typically given without hesitation.

The image that they tend to present to the world is one of capability and sophistication, but their competent exterior can often mask their intense search for a deeper and more fulfilling meaning to their lives. Their charismatic presence can have both a positive and a negative effect for them: positive, in that they gain enormous satisfaction from helping or motivating others; negative, in that their concern for the well-being of others may often cause them to neglect their own needs. Their careers, or having a family, will often give them a way of uniting these external and internal orientations with outstanding results, so they don't constantly feel torn between the two.

As self-assured individuals, they have the ability to inspire confidence and even awe in those around them by means of their incredible perception, compassion and real desire to help others progress. They would be almost perfect if it were not for the fact that they find it incredibly hard to deal with rejection and, instead of fighting back, will often slump into depression, bouts of uncertainty or confusion. They can also give the impression that they have all the answers, which is of course not the case. This over-confidence can alienate even those who previously championed them.

After the age of twenty-four there are opportunities for them to become less concerned about the image they are presenting to the world and more concerned about expressing their individuality. They should take advantage of these opportunities because, once they have recognized that personal fulfillment and being of service to others are not incompatible but highly compatible human needs, they can unlock their potential to be shining and inspirational examples to others.

On the dark side

Over-confident, fragile, serious

At your best

Inspiring, sophisticated, confident

29 December

the birthday of
the laid-back commander

Your greatest challenge is

living up to your potential

The way forward is ...

to direct your energy inward and discover the courage you need to step out of your comfort zone and put yourself on the line.

People born on December 29 are often in great demand because they are extremely confident, responsible and adaptable, and also because they relish opportunities to assist or enlighten others. They are not overly ambitious, but because they have a great sense of timing they will often find themselves in positions of responsibility.

Although people born on this day can be quite laid back, they are willing to work hard for what they want. They are also willing to work hard to help others get what they want, and while this may endear them to others they need to be careful not to take on too much. Their greatest strength is their facility for commanding or controlling people and situations without appearing domineering. Part of the reason they can do this so successfully is that they have excellent communication skills.

They can come across as serious or deadpan at times, but the more time people spend with them, the more they begin to appreciate their wonderful sense of irony and dry humor. Given the chance they can hypnotize audiences with their intelligent choice of words and wickedly perceptive observations, realizing that humor can get their message across strongly and effectively without others feeling offended or criticized.

After the age of twenty-three they become less influenced by rules and traditions and more willing to develop their own unique perspective. Another turning point arrives at the age of fifty-three when there is an emphasis on their emotional life, reflected in dreams and an intuitive understanding of others. Whatever age they are, the key to their success is to stop living in the past and stop doubting themselves, because they are bursting with creativity and have all the talent they need to make pioneering innovations that can advance knowledge or prosperity in some way. In short, they have the potential; all they need to do is to step into their own shoes, shake off any pessimism and negativity, and become the great leader or pioneer they are destined to be.

On the dark side

Unfulfilled, negative, unrealistic

At your best

Supportive, entertaining, commanding

30 December

the birthday of
the choreographer

Your greatest challenge is

expressing yourself

The way forward is ...

to understand that explaining yourself or your methods to others builds bridges of understanding.

People born on December 30 are at their happiest and their best when they are bringing order to confused situations. They are not only gifted in being able to identify what doesn't work or is in need of improvement; they also have the creativity and vision to make effective changes.

In many ways these people are like choreographers who can direct and coordinate the details with the bigger picture in mind. At times it may seem unclear what their intentions are, but in the end everything always seems to come together. Their ability to motivate and inspire those around them to perform at their best makes them successful leaders. They can occasionally be prone to a glass-half-empty approach to life but this doesn't mean they don't know how to have fun. Quite the opposite; they can appreciate humor and the lighter side of life, and love relaxing and having fun with friends. It is just that they are practical realists and will always consider worst-case scenarios in their game plan.

Their decisive tendency to take immediate charge of others to coordinate collective efforts can have excellent results, and they are often on the cutting edge when it comes to their professional life. One personality trait that can block their progress, however, is that they can at times come across to others as disinterested because they are a person of few words. When they do speak, however, others will often be stunned by their perceptiveness; but working on their communication skills will benefit them considerably in both their personal and their professional lives.

Before the age of twenty-one they are likely to have been cautious in their approach to life, but after the age of twenty-two there are opportunities for them to be more adventurous, more independent and less influenced by the opinions of others. They should take advantage of these opportunities to express their individuality because, once they come to realize how creative and capable they can be, their self-confidence will flower and they will attract all the success and happiness they deserve.

On the dark side

Misunderstood, negative, stressed

At your best

Perceptive, capable, authoritative

31 December

the birthday of
the connoisseur

Your greatest challenge is

accepting that you are not always right

The way forward is ...

to understand that what is right for you may not necessarily be right for someone else. We are all unique individuals and diversity makes life wonderful.

People born on 31 December pride themselves on their immaculate taste, and their confidence and charisma draw admirers to them wherever they go. They are esthetes and idealists at heart, aiming for perfection; but being realists they have the common sense to accept that there is a lot of ugliness in the world.

These people are on a mission to make the world a more beautiful place and they will try to add a touch of refinement or style to the environments they live and work in. They may also pay great attention to their own appearance, cultivating an attractive presence that is always well groomed and presented. They set high standards for themselves and others, but what makes them such gifted and fair leaders is that they will never expect more from others than they themselves can deliver.

The one big problem for them is that they are sometimes guilty of imposing their own standards of what is or is not beautiful or correct in a situation, the opinions or visions of others being dismissed out of hand. If this tendency isn't checked it can make them somewhat narrow-minded and intolerant of the opinions, taste and individuality of others. They need to remind themselves over and over again that beauty lies in the eye of the beholder.

Before the age of twenty they may come across as artistic but disciplined and sensible young adults, but after the age of twenty-one there is a dramatic turning point when they become less influenced by tradition and more independent. New opportunities to present their unique perspective will emerge and they will start to play a key role in making the world a more beautiful place. After the age of fifty-one there is another turning point which puts the emphasis on sensitivity and a strong inner life. But whatever age they are, getting in touch with their intuition will show them that beauty isn't just something that can be created in the outside world—first and foremost it must be created within.

On the dark side

Opinionated, materialistic, superficial

At your best

Tasteful, well groomed, charismatic

Birthday Power Thoughts

January 1
"When one door closes, another always opens for me"

January 2
"I deserve the best in life"

January 3
"The darkest hour is before the dawn and I will come shining through"

January 4
"Today, I will stick to my guns"

January 5
"It is OK to find out who I am and explore who other people are too"

January 6
"I help others by listening to them"

January 7
"I am good enough just the way I am"

January 8
"Recognizing the positive in others, I
recognize the positive in myself"

January 9
"I have a peaceful and calming heart and soul"

January 10
"Today, I will see something positive in
all situations"

January 11
"Today I will take it easy on myself and
everyone else"

January 12
"I can change my feelings by changing what
I do"

January 13
"I can and will reach my full potential"

January 14
"I can relax and think peacefully about my
goals"

January 15
"Today when I feel happy I will share it"

January 16
"Happiness is available to me now"

January 17
"It is my attitude that counts"

January 18
"I will finish what I started"

January 19
"I recognize my creativity and I honor it"

January 20
"I am good enough"

January 21
"My intuition works with me and for me"

January 22
"I choose balance, harmony and peace,
and I express it in my life"

January 23
"Today I will share my dreams with others"

January 24
"I joyously give to life and life joyously
gives to me"

January 25
"My goal is to love myself more today than
yesterday"

January 26
"Today I will be prepared to see life differently"

January 27
"I will learn to finish what I start"

January 28
"I am what I seek"

January 29
"My best relationship is the one I have with me"

January 30
"Today I will let go of expectations and let happiness in"

January 31
"I have a mission and I choose to accept it"

February 1
"The secret of my success is self-understanding"

February 2
"Today I will let my inner guide decide for me"

February 3
"Every day I will seek the quiet within me"

February 4
"I am pleased to be myself"

February 5
"Today I will smile and let others in on the secret"

February 6
"I also flourish with love and care"

February 7
"I can instruct but I can't enforce"

February 8
"The universe runs through me, giving me direction"

February 9
"I will always seek the possible, not the obligatory"

February 10
"Today I will notice what is going on around me as well as in me"

February 11
"I am aware that what I do not want to change is what I need to change"

February 12
"The equilibrium of my mind is mirrored in my life"

February 13
"Today is my bridge to greater self-knowledge and joy"

February 14
"Giving is its own reward"

February 15
"The harmony and balance in my mind is reflected in my life"

February 16
"Today I will seek to praise rather than criticize"

February 17
"Today I will look at life in a different way"

February 18
"Today I will find the stillness within me"

February 19
"Today I will let my happiness inspire me to listen and to give"

February 20
"I am in charge of all aspects of my life"

February 21
"Whatever I decide is right for me"

February 22
"I focus on people's good points and help them bring out their best qualities"

February 23
"My life is wonderful in every way"

February 24
"I am worthy of all life has to offer"

February 25
"Today I will seize the opportunities that come my way"

February 26
"Today I will try to laugh at everything, myself included"

February 27
"Today I will put love before all else"

February 28
"I celebrate what I have, and I meet new challenges with open arms"

February 29
"I am perfect just as I am"

March 1
"It is myself rather than my worry which will change things"

March 2
"I will always ask for the help that I need"

March 3
"My self-belief will inspire others to believe in me too"

March 4
"I can always learn something from others"

March 5
"I acknowledge my spirit at the start of each day"

March 6
"Today I will appreciate others for who they are and not as I want them to be"

March 7
"Today I will ask for what I desire"

March 8
"I will forgive instead of criticize"

March 9
"My intuition will always show me the best way forward"

March 10
"Every moment of my life fills me with joy"

March 11

"I can see the magic and beauty of the present moment"

March 12

"I want my life to be filled with direction and purpose"

March 13

"My positive thoughts create my positive world"

March 14

"Today I will stand up for myself"

March 15

"Today I will let others share in my success and happiness"

March 16

"I am constantly moving forward in the direction of my principles"

March 17

"Today I will confront my fears with boldness"

March 18

"Today I will seek out opportunities to be kind"

March 19
"I am ready to open up my world to something new"

March 20
"I extend my love and compassion to everyone, including myself"

March 21
"I can be a good example to others"

March 22
"Today I will say 'I want to' not 'I should'"

March 23
"The love in my heart refreshes and restores me"

March 24
"I am positive in my outlook and life brings me good things in response"

March 25
"I can only direct what is happening within me not around me"

March 26
"I love my life. It is wonderful to be alive"

March 27
"Every day is filled with chances to feel happier and more fulfilled"

March 28
"I am winning in the race of life"

March 29
"I deserve and expect only the very best"

March 30
"Tomorrow is another day"

March 31
"I radiate warmth and the love I project onto others is returned"

April 1
"I choose to be self-sufficient in loving, joyous ways"

April 2
"It is easy for me to adapt to the ebb and flow of my life"

April 3
"I have full faith in my inner resources"

April 4
"I can achieve anything if I truly want to"

April 5
"I take time to renew myself in silence"

April 6
"My life is a reflection of the positive choices I make"

April 7
"Today I will treat others as I want them to treat me"

April 8
"I am thankful for all that I am"

April 9
"I understand the principle of less is more and will incorporate it in my life"

April 10
"When I am kind without expecting something in return I feel truly alive"

April 11
"Today I will consider both sides of every argument"

April 12
"It is safe to believe in and trust myself"

April 13
"Today I will feel the fear and do it anyway"

April 14
"I step joyously from the past into my exciting future"

April 15
"Today my happiness will inspire my creativity"

April 16
"Today I will remember that I already am what I seek"

April 17
"Today I am prepared to look at myself and the world differently"

April 18
"I can change my life by changing how I think about it"

April 19
"Today I will not preach but listen"

April 20
"Today, and every day, I will make a point of getting curious about one thing"

April 21
"Today I bless and wish others well, and they do the same for me"

April 22
"Wonder and discovery are the keys to unlocking my spirit"

April 23
"I am always moving forward in the
direction of my goals"

April 24
"I am in charge of my life. I reclaim my
power"

April 25
"I am protected by the spirit that flows
through and inspires me"

April 26
"I am perfect in my imperfection and that is
the way it should be"

April 27
"Love is the thread that joins everyone
together"

April 28
"Today and every day I take time to find the
quiet and stillness within me"

April 29
"I listen attentively to the wise voice of
intuition"

April 30
"Today I will replace should with could"

May 1
"Today I will go further than usual"

May 2
"The more kind and gentle I am, the more positive energy I have"

May 3
"I now respect my body, my mind and my emotions. I feel wonderful"

May 4
"I am learning to love and take care of myself"

May 5
"I now notice when my intuition is speaking to me"

May 6
"I trust that every decision I make will enhance my life or the lives of others"

May 7
"Self-understanding is the beginning of my wisdom"

May 8
"Love and understanding can answer all my questions"

May 9
"I am ready to release myself from the habit of criticism"

May 10
"I am a soul with a body, rather than a body with a soul"

May 11
"I am respected by everyone because I respect myself"

May 12
"Today I will make compassion the heart of my life"

May 13
"I can choose how I will respond to every situation in my life"

May 14
"Today I live in the moment"

May 15
"I choose to love my life"

May 16
"Today I will be cool, calm and collected"

May 17
"I will always ask for whatever I need"

May 18
"I can easily adapt to all that life throws at me"

May 19
"I am grateful and happy to be alive"

May 20
"The answers I am seeking can only be found within me"

May 21
"To understand others I must understand myself first"

May 22
"I have control over my mind and the power to think wonderful things"

May 23
"What I desire from others I already possess"

May 24
"My intuition shows me the way forward"

May 25
"I am free to move on, unless I decide not to"

May 26
"I am willing to discover opportunities for me to change"

May 27
"Today I will replace old habits of judgment with new habits of flexibility"

May 28
"Today I will remember to stop and ask my intuition before acting"

May 29
"Everything that happens to me helps me learn and grow"

May 30
"I am powerful, balanced and here in the now"

May 31
"I am a still center in an ever-changing world"

June 1
"I relax and recognize my potential for greatness"

June 2
"Every day offers me an opportunity to learn something new about myself"

June 3
"I now choose to release every negative thought from my mind and my life"

June 4
"Today I am an open channel for original ideas"

June 5
"Today I let go of my worry and uncertainty"

June 6
"Every time I sit in silence my life energy is recharged"

June 7
"I can share and trust my feelings"

June 8
"Every day I will keep a clear focus on what is truly important"

June 9
"I draw strength from the still center within me"

June 10
"Everything I do is productive, fulfilling and successful"

June 11
"Every step forward in my life fills me with gratitude and respect"

June 12
"Any time I wish, the wisdom of my intuition is there for me to use"

June 13
"My intuition is waiting for me to simply
ask it for guidance"

June 14
"Today I will be kind to everyone I meet"

June 15
"I now choose to recognize the brilliance of
my being"

June 16
"Today I will act with speed, good judgment
and resolve"

June 17
"I don't need external force or validation to
feel at harmony with myself"

June 18
"Today I will reflect on all that I have to feel
grateful for"

June 19
"With practice my compassion deepens and
my life becomes richer"

June 20
"I don't need a crisis to feel alive"

June 21
"Every moment contains an opportunity for
me to feel inspired"

June 22
"I already have all the wisdom and power I will ever need"

June 23
"I think the best of others and spread nothing but the joy of life"

June 24
"Today I will use my manifold energy to work towards my dreams"

June 25
"Today I will look after body, mind, heart and soul. I feel great!"

June 26
"Everything in my life works better when I love and take care of myself"

June 27
"My understanding is clear, but my opinions are flexible"

June 28
"I am perfect, just as I am"

June 29
"I owe it to myself to develop my many talents and abilities"

June 30
"When I listen to my inner wisdom I find
the answers I need"

July 1
"The only constraints I have are the
constraints I decide to believe in"

July 2
"I am as fulfilled, successful and self-confident
as I decide to be"

July 3
"I am loving, warm and beautiful, and the
contribution I make is valuable"

July 4
"I bring good to others by discovering the
good in me"

July 5
"I am here, in the present, in the moment"

July 6
"I am always willing to experiment and
explore new possibilities"

July 7
"From now on I will look at every obstacle
as an opportunity"

July 8
"I am a human being, not a human doing"

July 9
"Every obstacle in my life is an opportunity for me to learn and grow"

July 10
"I express my feelings in joyous, positive ways"

July 11
"I follow my inner light. I am a shining example of love and clarity"

July 12
"I am relaxed, self-confident and serene"

July 13
"I am now free from self-doubt"

July 14
"I only desire that which is for my highest good"

July 15
"My spirit or soul is the real measure of my humanity"

July 16
"I am a good listener, to my intuition and to those with whom I live and work"

July 17
"I trust life to be wonderful. There are
wonderful things ahead of me"

July 18
"Today I will notice everything around me,
as well as in me"

July 19
"Today I will see my own beauty and believe
in my own power"

July 20
"The most exciting journey of all is the
journey within"

July 21
"Focus and concentration are the keys to
my success"

July 22
"I draw strength, wisdom and inspiration
from the stillness within me"

July 23
"I commit myself to the practice of
reflecting in silence"

July 24
"Nurturing inner peace positively affects
my life and the lives of others"

July 25
"I love who I am and reward myself daily with positive thoughts"

July 26
"Compassion brings me deeper into life"

July 27
"I am willing to face up to my feelings"

July 28
"My compassion produces positive energy in the world around me"

July 29
"I take my power back. My destiny is up to me"

July 30
"Taking time to relax is my gift to myself and to my spirit"

July 31
"My beautiful, loving thoughts create my beautiful, loving world"

August 1
"Other people are meant to be joyful, and so am I"

August 2
"I try to make the best of each new day"

August 3
"Perhaps the person most in need of rescuing is me"

August 4
"I choose harmony and loving communication wherever I find myself"

August 5
"My heart is open. I strive to be more aware of my feelings"

August 6
"I can see eternity in a grain of sand"

August 7
"I happily give to life and life lovingly gives back to me"

August 8
"True inspiration arises from the still silence within me"

August 9
"I release my need to control to the universe. I feel at peace with the world"

August 10
"My harmonious and creative thoughts create my harmonious and creative life"

August 11
"I can pause and reflect before I speak"

August 12
"I close my eyes and feel the happiness of being alive this moment"

August 13
"My intuition is always readily available. I just need to listen"

August 14
"When I connect with my inner wisdom, solutions come quickly to me"

August 15
"Being compassionate connects me to my higher self which is my true nobility"

August 16
"I honor the innocence, compassion and beauty in others and myself"

August 17
"My inner peace positively affects every aspect of my life"

August 18
"Obstacles are opportunities, and my life is more a dance than a battle"

August 19
"I do not need to be perfect, just human"

August 20
"When I focus on the here and now my life
is more magical and rewarding"

August 21
"I am special, wonderful and free and happy
to be myself"

August 22
"I am strong and creative and here in the
now"

August 23
"Today my happiness will inspire me to give"

August 24
"I enjoy discovering and working with my
intuition"

August 25
"I know that I am good enough"

August 26
"I give myself permission to take the lead"

August 27
"I keep my thoughts positive. My future is
glorious"

August 28
"I open the doors to the wonder and discovery of my spirit"

August 29
"The more I trust and let go, the greater my possibilities"

August 30
"Life shows me miracles every day"

August 31
"I trust and listen with love to my inner voice"

September 1
"To be happy I need to work smarter, not harder"

September 2
"I am not the person I was yesterday but a more enlightened being"

September 3
"I am now willing to see my own creativity, originality and magnificence"

September 4
"I remind myself that there will never be another day like this one"

September 5
"I take full responsibility for my life"

September 6
"I always have a choice"

September 7
"As I send out loving calmness, all those around me are inspired"

September 8
"One of the top priorities in my life is to be a source of love"

September 9
"I know what I want and where I am going"

September 10
"Whatever my mind can conceive it can achieve"

September 11
"Using and trusting my intuition leads to clarity"

September 12
"I simply enjoy helping others and being me"

September 13
"Today I will ask my heart to contribute to any decisions that I make"

September 14
"I look beyond the behavior of others to find the light within"

September 15
"I understand the difference between pleasure and happiness"

September 16
"Before I jump into my day, I will stop and connect with my spirit"

September 17
"I am a being of color, light and creativity"

September 18
"Today I will face my fears, think and act boldly, and feel amazing"

September 19
"I look inside myself and see limitless love, joy, beauty and light"

September 20
"As long as I learn from my setbacks I cannot fail"

September 21
"I know who I am and where I am going"

September 22
"I act appropriately on my intuition"

September 23
"I am now willing to see my own beauty and brilliance"

September 24
"There is nothing I cannot do when inspired by self-discipline and integrity"

September 25
"I improve the quality of my life and world with every positive word"

September 26
"Whenever I stop and sit in silence, my intuition is nourished and energized"

September 27
"It is safe for me to look within"

September 28
"I am powerful and inspired and enjoy getting my life in order"

September 29
"I appreciate and place the highest value on all that I am"

September 30
"I feel tolerance and consideration for everyone, myself included"

October 1
"It's fun being me"

October 2

"I listen with love to the messages my body and my heart send me"

October 3

"The treasure I am seeking is already within me"

October 4

"I am a soul with a body, not a body with a soul"

October 5

"World peace begins inside me"

October 6

"Every conflict is an opportunity for me to become more of who I am"

October 7

"What I don't want to change is probably what I need to change the most"

October 8

"Every time I look within, I move closer to who I really am"

October 9

"I see myself as talented and unique. I am proud of me"

October 10
"I open the doors to the wonder and
discovery of my imagination"

October 11
"Every struggle is an opportunity for me to
find myself"

October 12
"I choose to show that I care, rather than
just saying I care"

October 13
"I measure progress by how much I love,
not how much I can achieve"

October 14
"I am excited about my future and the next
step in my self-development"

October 15
"The greatest gift I give myself is the joy of
giving to others"

October 16
"I choose to be supportive rather than
critical"

October 17
"The truth isn't out there, it's within me"

October 18

"I am talented and creative; the only approval I really need is my own"

October 19

"I do not need a crisis to feel alive"

October 20

"I am capable of more than I can possibly dream"

October 21

"I express my creativity in ways that fulfill me and inspire others"

October 22

"My grateful heart is a constant source of joy to me and others"

October 23

"I only desire that which is for my highest good"

October 24

"I constantly find new ways to love the world around me"

October 25

"I am open to the light and wonder of the universe"

October 26
"Trusting my intuition is like taking in a deep cleansing breath of clarity"

October 27
"No matter what anyone thinks, I will listen to my gut feelings"

October 28
"I am a human being not a human doing"

October 29
"I am amazing and I have nothing to hide"

October 30
"It is what I *actually* do, not what I mean to do, that matters"

October 31
"I am now ready to stand up and be counted"

November 1
"I can be responsible, and when I relax my inner wisdom is clear and available"

November 2
"I am in a good place at a good time. It is safe to stay here"

November 3
"I release all feelings of failure. My wonderful future is in my hands"

November 4
"The greatest excitement and adventure is found within"

November 5
"I am at the center of my world. What I think and feel matters"

November 6
"I am filled with energy and enthusiasm to make positive changes in my life"

November 7
"Every day I can see my glorious future more clearly"

November 8
"I am now willing to move towards the light and my greater good"

November 9
"The path I choose is one of wisdom, light and joy"

November 10
"My life and friends reflect the positive and inspiring thoughts of my heart"

November 11
"I am a rich treasure ready to be found"

November 12
"Every moment I spend in stillness brings my true self closer"

November 13
"An open mind is an enlightened mind"

November 14
"To truly help others I must first help myself"

November 15
"I am open and receptive to all that is good in the universe"

November 16
"Today sincere warmth glows in my heart, bringing me closer to others"

November 17
"Today I will express my creativity in ways that fulfill me"

November 18
"I believe in myself. Anything is possible"

November 19
"My choices are based on thoughtfulness, humility, love and compassion"

November 20
"I am calm and in control"

November 21
"My progress as a loving and spontaneous person is my gift to the world"

November 22
"I constantly find new goals to set myself"

November 23
"I can only control what happens within me"

November 24
"A new attitude can change a stifling situation into one of joy"

November 25
"The happier I am, the more I can inspire others to find joy"

November 26
"The sense of direction, harmony and fulfillment I seek already lie within me"

November 27
"I am in charge of the way I feel"

November 28
"All is well in my world and I share my feelings of happiness with others"

November 29
"The adventure I seek is already within me"

November 30
"My intuition allows me to blend and connect with everyone and everything"

December 1
"Balancing my priorities helps me rediscover my happiness"

December 2
"Peace and understanding begin within me"

December 3
"I work to live, I don't live to work"

December 4
"In my world everyone is a winner"

December 5
"Every day my capacity for understanding myself and others grows"

December 6
"Today I change my beliefs about what is impossible"

December 7
"Today I will be part of the solution not the problem"

December 8
"I am the creative and responsible power in my world"

December 9
"My positive and patient thoughts keep me in harmony with the universe"

December 10
"My life is a celebration to be shared with everyone I know"

December 11
"Today I will invite happiness, laughter and love into my life"

December 12
"My intuition is the source of my knowledge and power"

December 13
"Every day I am more and more at ease with myself and with life"

December 14
"My positive energy attracts only good things into my life"

December 15
"I appreciate my life in this moment, just as it is"

December 16
"The universe flows through me and my intuition continually guides me"

December 17
"Life for me is a joyful dance"

December 18
"Using and trusting my intuition leads to clarity"

December 19
"When I focus on positive things it helps me and also the world"

December 20
"I am grateful for the precious breath of life"

December 21
"Whatever the question, I know that love is the answer"

December 22
"Problems are unique opportunities for me to learn and to grow"

December 23
"There is no greater power for me than the power of the present moment"

December 24
"I will grow wiser and stronger emotionally every day"

December 25

"I already have all of the joy I need to feel fulfilled and truly alive"

December 26

"My loving heart knows no bounds and my flexible mind knows no boundaries"

December 27

"If I put my mind and heart into it, there's nothing I cannot do"

December 28

"Keeping my thinking positive means I can overcome any problems"

December 29

"My possibilities are endless"

December 30

"I am rich in inner wisdom and can express my inspirations clearly and eloquently"

December 31

"Every day there are beautiful things happening in my life"